The Civil Rights Movement in Mississippi

The Civil Rights Movement in Mississippi

Edited by Ted Ownby

University Press of Mississippi   Jackson

www.upress.state.ms.us

The University Press of Mississippi is a member
of the Association of American University Presses.

First printing 2013

Library of Congress Cataloging-in-Publication Data

The civil rights movement in Mississippi / edited by Ted Ownby.
    pages cm. — (Chancellor Porter L. Fortune symposium in southern history series)
    Summary: "Based on new research and combining multiple scholarly approaches, these twelve
essays tell new stories about the civil rights movement in the state most resistant to change.
Wesley Hogan, Françoise N. Hamlin, and Michael Vinson Williams raise questions about how
civil rights organizing took place. Three pairs of essays address African Americans' and whites'
stories on education, religion, and the issues of violence. Jelani Favors and Robert Luckett analyze civil rights issues on the campuses of Jackson State University and the University of Mississippi. Carter Dalton Lyon and Joseph T. Reiff study people who confronted the question of
how their religion related to their possible involvement in civil rights activism. By studying the
Ku Klux Klan and the Deacons for Defense in Mississippi, David Cunningham and Akinyele
Umoja ask who chose to use violence or to raise its possibility. The final three chapters describe
some of the consequences and continuing questions raised by the civil rights movement. Byron
D'Andra Orey analyzes the degree to which voting rights translated into political power for
African American legislators. Chris Myers Asch studies a Freedom School that started in re-
cent years in the Mississippi Delta. Emilye Crosby details the conflicting memories of Claiborne
County residents and the parts of the civil rights movement they recall or ignore. As a group,
the essays introduce numerous new characters and conundrums into civil rights scholarship,
advance efforts to study African Americans and whites as interactive agents in the complex
stories, and encourage historians to pull civil rights scholarship closer toward the present"—
Provided by publisher.
    Includes bibliographical references and index.
    ISBN 978-1-61703-933-1 (hardback) — ISBN 978-1-61703-934-8 (ebook) 1. Civil rights move-
ments—Mississippi—History—20th century. 2. African Americans—Civil rights—Mississippi—History—20th century. 3. African American civil rights workers—Mississippi—Biography.
4. Race discrimination—Mississippi—History—20th century. 5. Mississippi—Race relations—
History—20th century. I. Ownby, Ted, editor of compilation.
    E185.9.M6C58 2013
    323.1196'0730762—dc23   2013016386
                British Library Cataloging-in-Publication Data available

Contents

Introduction

Ted Ownby

Beginning as part of the Porter Fortune, Jr. History Symposium at the University of Mississippi, this collection of essays attempts to raise some new questions and tell some new stories about the history of the civil rights movement in Mississippi.

For years the history of the civil rights movement in Mississippi seemed relatively clear. Activism, or so it seemed, started slowly due to the kind of powerful oppression sustained by the sharecropping system, disfranchisement, and segregation, and dramatized by the assassinations of Emmett Till in 1955 and Medgar Evers in 1963. Then, according to the old story, Mississippi briefly became central to the national movement in 1964 with the Freedom Summer movement, the rise of the Mississippi Freedom Democratic Party, and the demands by African Americans to be seated at the Democratic National Convention. For some time, civil rights scholarship focused especially on the National Association for the Advancement of Colored People (NAACP) and the *Brown v. Board of Education* decision, Martin Luther King Jr. and the Southern Christian Leadership Conference (SCLC), the Student Nonviolent Coordinating Committee (SNCC), and 1960s landmarks such as the Civil Rights Act and the Voting Rights Act. Before the mid-1990s, Mississippi appeared in civil rights literature especially for the excitement, the internal conflicts, and also the violence of Freedom Summer. Then the Mississippi civil rights movement splintered into numerous other movements, some of which, such as Head Start, the language of Black Power, and the large number of African Americans running for office, had lasting consequences, and others that perhaps did not. For years the history of the civil rights movement in the state seemed, to oversimplify, fairly brief and extraordinarily dramatic.

Scholarship of the past two decades has worked to push that story back in time, to expand the cast of characters, and to recognize both the dramatic moments and movements as well as the everyday and less dramatic struggles that made them possible. From being a relatively understudied state, Mississippi in the years of the civil rights movement and massive resistance has become one of the most studied states.

This collection of essays builds on at least four scholarly movements prominent in the past twenty years. The first is best embodied by the title of John Dittmer's 1994 volume, *Local People: The Struggle for Civil Rights in Mississippi*. Dittmer argued that scholars of the civil rights movement should pay less attention to court decisions, national organizations, and national leaders, and should instead concentrate more on people working in individual communities at the everyday and person-to-person level. Dittmer stressed the importance of black institutions and the rise of organized political activism in the 1940s. Supporting that approach was Charles Payne's 1995 *I've Got the Light of Freedom: The Organizing Tradition and the Mississippi Freedom Struggle*, which amplified the value of looking to traditions of protest, especially evident in some labor activism associated with Amzie Moore, within African American communities.[1] Since then, a number of important historians, several of them contributors to this volume, have produced studies of movements and individuals in particular Mississippi locations such as Clarksdale, Port Gibson, Sunflower County, and Jackson. Since the volumes by Dittmer and Payne, Mississippi may actually lead the way in the popularity of local studies.[2] Part of the movement toward local studies has come from the goal of getting inside the intricacies of particular situations and especially the goal of seeing how numerous issues intersect with politics and the law. A recent collection edited by symposium participant Emilye Crosby highlights the accomplishments and continuing potential of the local studies approach.[3] There is a clear political dimension to this approach as well, as some scholars use their stories in part to encourage people to recognize that activism is (or can be) part of everyday life, not just a monumental and televised moment of triumph or tragedy.

A second movement has rephrased activism as part of a "long civil rights movement," a concept first named by historian Jacquelyn Dowd Hall to challenge the concentration on the civil rights movement as something that happened between the mid-1950s and the late 1960s.[4] The concept has encouraged scholars to move back in time, perhaps to the 1930s and 1940s, perhaps substantially earlier, to understand activism as part of a continuum with a longer history. Using this perspective, scholars have studied efforts as early as the late 1800s by labor activists, women's organizations, individual churches and denominational organizations, teachers, lawyers, farmers working in cooperatives, and other groups in the American South, other parts of the

United States, and beyond. The organizing of African American businesses in Mound Bayou and other places, the formation of Rosenwald schools in Mississippi, and the important personal and institutional connections between Mississippi and Chicago all were crucial in showing the long history of African American activism and institution building. From this perspective, the civil rights movement may have changed in the 1950s and 1960s, but it was not new. In Mississippi, Charles Payne's study and Charles Bolton's history of segregation and desegregation in education are among the works that take the long approach.[5] The concept also encourages the study of activism and responses in the 1970s and beyond to make the important point that local organizing and activism have had consequences long after they were part of the national news.

A third direction—perhaps not properly called a movement—of scholarship in the past generation has been an ever-growing definition of "the political." In contrast to some previous scholarly efforts to take different approaches to politics, the law, society, and cultural life, scholars of the past generation have argued that understandings of gender, race, and other concepts are crucial and in fact absolutely central to definitions of political history.[6] Scholars such as Elizabeth Brooks Higginbotham helped argue that issues of manners and respectability—performing them, claiming them, and dismissing insults about them—have been a big part of, or at least a major question within, African American activism.[7] More recently, the study of memory has shown that understandings and uses of the past are also part of a broad definition of politics.[8] Thus the politics of the civil rights movement looks quite different to contemporary scholars who are studying the shifting strategies and issues of multiple groups, their claims to legitimate and respectable authority, the language they use about gender and family, their approach to issues of race and diversity, their understandings and uses of the past, and their changing responses to each other. This volume draws on these broadened definitions of politics in several ways by discussing organizing as a concept, by analyzing both African Americans and whites as part of interacting stories, by discussing self-defense and carrying weapons as part of politics, and by discussing memory and calls for legitimacy.

A fourth direction of scholarship has analyzed the interactions between civil rights activists and white southerners whose responses ranged from resistance to support to inaction. One of the more vivid examples of the expansion of the topics covered in civil rights scholarship is a series of books on white elites and their various forms of resistance, whether or not it was "massive resistance," to civil rights activism.[9] Some of the best scholarship in recent years analyzes shifting strategies and allegiances among white south-erners, with journalists, educators, businesspeople, and other groups be-coming more visible as part of the story, along with politicians, lawyers, and law enforcement personnel. This approach helps produce a fuller civil rights history because it recognizes a multiplicity of groups, with many of them responding to the efforts of the others, and it carries forward the expanding definition of politics by asking when and how some forms of white privilege became acceptable and respectable, when and how national or international forces made certain expressions of white supremacy unacceptable, and how various groups of African American activists were part of those definitions.

Essays in this volume display all four of these approaches, studying local activists at the community level, expanding the time period of study, broad-ening the definitions of political activity, and doing more to study African Americans and whites as part of the same story. The collection includes stud-ies of specific communities—church visits and college professors in Jackson, multiple strategies of activism in Clarksdale, the potential for armed self-defense in several south Mississippi communities, and conflicting memories in Port Gibson. In each case, studying things at a community level illustrates local people, often with connections that reached far beyond Mississippi, making decisions and shifting strategies for specific reasons. Expanding the time period allows greater understanding of the roots of very different activ-ists such as Medgar Evers, Margaret Walker Alexander, and James Silver. Us-ing a broad definition of political action encourages more discussion of basic questions. What is organizing? What should be the relationship between church life and issues of race? What are educational institutions supposed to teach? How do people remember and teach about the civil rights movement? And the fourth point—studying African Americans and white Mississippi-ans as part of the same story—may be an especially notable point about this volume, which pairs articles studying whites and African Americans first on the topic of education, then religion, then on the issue of violence.

While essays in this volume draw on and exemplify recent movements in scholarship, it is also important to note that several essays address some questions that many scholars have asked in the past. Where did the impetus for activism come from? How did different groups of activists work with each other, and did their different approaches limit or strengthen them? How and why were schools and churches so important to both supporters and op-ponents of desegregation, and were there possibilities for universities and church organizations to serve as locations for open thinking about potential for change? How, when, and why did groups arm themselves and threaten or use violence? Should we see the civil rights movement as a success, as less than a success, or as an ongoing process? And, along with asking new questions and some older questions, part of the accomplishment of this volume comes simply from new research, which produces some stories historians have not told before. There is plenty here about Medgar Evers and Aaron Henry, for example, but there are also stories about Jackson State University professor Jane McAllister, churchgoers' efforts to send racially integrated groups into all-white churches in Jackson, white Methodists calling for desegregation, the Deacons for Defense in Mississippi, the various klans in the state, the challenges faced by Mississippi's first African American legislators, and recent efforts to remember and teach about the Mississippi movement.

The volume begins with three articles on organizing, then proceeds with pairs of essays on higher education, religion, and self-defense and the use of weapons, and ends with three essays on politics and memory. Wesley Hogan's chapter begins the volume with a fundamental question of the meaning of organizing. Calling for more attention to the history of organizing as a concept, she uses the distinctive efforts of SNCC in Mississippi to describe organizing as something far different from the large-scale efforts to organize money and attract voters common in electoral politics. She describes the uniqueness of the Mississippi Freedom Democratic Party and discusses how a range of topics—Freedom Schools, efforts to house activists, self-defense, legal challenges, the arts, and efforts to gain sustained access to federal programs—exemplified particular forms of organizing. Françoise Hamlin takes up Hogan's challenge to study how people organized. Concentrating on Clarksdale from the 1950s through the 1990s, Hamlin analyzes how activists in different groups (and some, like Aaron Henry, who were in multiple groups) made pragmatic use of the differences among those groups. Instead of viewing different approaches as a problem, she sees them as an ongoing opportunity for new strategies, and, like Hogan, she finds that the special challenges activists faced in Mississippi led to a great deal of creativity. Michael Vinson Williams takes a detailed, biographical approach to the early years of the activism of Medgar Evers, whose life dramatized many of the issues Hogan and Hamlin raised in their essays. What are the roots of activism? How did individual action turn into group organizing, and how did different groups work together? By taking a biographical approach, Williams can dramatize topics such as the roots of activism before the mid-1950s, the vital role college students played for African American leaders, the importance of World War II in providing new opportunities and encouraging new demands, the continuing threat of violence, and the challenge of multiple organizations and multiple strategies.

Two essays on higher education, one about Jackson State University and the other about the University of Mississippi, highlight the possibilities and also the limitations of universities as places for civil rights leadership or organizing. Like many essays in this volume, Jelani Favors starts in the post–World War II period. Favors studies the "second curriculum," a broad term involving leadership, uplift, and the possibility of protest, and the pressures Jane McAllister and Margaret Walker Alexander faced in teaching it at Jackson State University. Favors examines the distinctiveness of the two professors, who encouraged their students to consider education and its possible uses as a form of political action, while they also encountered resistance from university president Jacob L. Reddix and his bosses in the state educational system, all of whom wished to distance Jackson State from the sort of overt activism common across town at Tougaloo College. To return to Wesley Hogan's essay, faculty and students at Jackson State faced great difficulties in organizing, so except for some protests in the 1960s, much of the work of people like McAllister and Alexander took place somewhat quietly through discussions of ideas and examples. Robert Luckett studies the pressures University of Mississippi historian James Silver faced after he published *Mississippi: The Closed Society*. Silver, like Margaret Walker Alexander and Jane McAllister, faced the difficulty of teaching and doing scholarship that challenged orthodoxy, but unlike them, white supremacists called for his firing when he criticized white Mississippians for being intolerant of new thinking on issues of race. Luckett emphasizes that part of the response to Silver was quiet, with state education leaders finding a way to encourage and allow him to leave the state without inspiring national condemnation. Both essays ultimately deal with issues of respectability, with university presidents trying to keep down rebellion from their faculty and students without seeming dictatorial, unprofessional, and unfair.

If the potential for higher education to address Mississippi's racial hierarchy always faced significant challenges, what of religion? Many scholars have discussed churches as sites of possibility for African American organizing and as places where inspired people might call for major social changes.[10] In a close study of organizing in 1963 and 1964, Carter Dalton Lyon examines the church visits campaign in Jackson, a movement that joined African American Tougaloo College students and whites, mostly ministers and other religious figures from outside the South, in efforts to attend and thus desegregate all-white churches. Lyon argues that the participants considered the church visits campaign part of their "witness," an effort to join Christian belief with personal action. Joseph Reiff analyzes the theologies of supporters and opponents of the "Born of Conviction" statement, in which twenty-eight white Mississippi ministers declared their opposition to segregation. Concentrating on responses to the "Born of Conviction" statement, he finds a wide variety, which ranged from enthusiastic support to quiet attempts to change the subject to angry condemnation. Both essays describe people confronting basic questions of the meanings and responsibilities of Christian belief and church practices.

In chapters on the Ku Klux Klan and the Deacons for Defense, David Cunningham and Akinyele Umoja analyze groups that offered the potential of violence or armed self-defense as part of how to address issues of race and politics in the mid-1960s. Cunningham rejects assumptions that the Ku Klux Klan was a constant presence or unified organization. Instead, his essay shows that there were multiple klans in Mississippi, that they were located primarily in parts of southern Mississippi, and that beginning in 1963, they organized and grew quickly. The klans diverged somewhat on tactics, membership, and rituals, with some being more or less open about violence, and some being more secretive and hierarchical than others. Part of Cunningham's contribution is to show that at least some of the klans knew they were suffering from reputations as terrorists, so some aspired to a degree of respectability by claiming they were officially nonviolent and that they distanced themselves from bombing churches. Cunningham's essay helps illustrate the setting of Akinyele Umoja's analysis of the Deacons for Defense in Mississippi. Umoja describes how the Deacons represented one option for African Americans troubled by the lack of local or federal government protection for protest efforts. Beginning in 1965, the paramilitary group from Louisiana responded to invitations to discuss their work in Jackson and several Mississippi counties, especially in the south Mississippi areas where the Ku Klux Klan was growing quickly. Several Deacons groups started then and had important roles in Natchez in 1965 and Claiborne County in 1966, and the group gained new public significance in Mississippi during the "March against Fear" in 1966. Umoja's essay returns to the issues of organizing and multiple strategies in the chapters by Hogan and Hamlin, showing the significance that Mississippi's Deacons were local people working with local issues, and detailing the differences among various groups over public acceptance of the need for self-defense.

Byron D'Andra Orey addresses a different meaning of Black Power in the essay that begins the volume's final section. The last three essays analyze three forms of politics in government, education, and memory. Orey, a political scientist, asks about which issues that African Americans who were elected to the Mississippi legislature since 1967 have been able to address, whether through influence or new laws. He shows that African American legislators went from Robert Clark's initial inability to gain recognition on the floor, much less have a bill considered, to a situation by the late 1980s in which African American legislators were head of five committees and helped determine who was Speaker of the House. Orey shows that most African Americans' legislative efforts have addressed issues of education, suffrage, and health care, and he emphasizes that African American legislators often responded to either inattention or racial prejudice with political pragmatism. In a more personal essay, Chris Myers Asch describes the educational organization he helped originate and lead in Sunflower County. His story of the principal who did not want him to show *Eyes on the Prize* episodes perhaps recalls other stories of other educational leaders in this volume who hoped to avoid conflict, and his discussion of limited funds for African American schools recalls Orey's discussion of a history of opposition to improved educational funding in the Mississippi legislature. Above all, Asch's essay offers a direct connection to the creative organizing Wesley Hogan discusses in this volume's first chapter, because the Sunflower County Freedom Project was intended to train people for the kind of ongoing, creative, participatory citizenship Hogan analyzed. In the volume's concluding essay, Emilye Crosby, author of a respected study of the civil rights movement in Claiborne County, turns to issues of memory and the civil rights movement. Analyzing how African Americans and whites remember the Claiborne County movement, and what they choose to discuss and omit, Crosby shows that memories are not just a result of different political perspectives—they are part of politics. Agreeing with Asch's point about local memory, Crosby shows that groups use memories in strategic ways, either to encourage more change or to distance the present from the past and discourage new challenges. And in discussions of education, a sustained consumer boycott, and a revealing public forum in 1994, Crosby analyzes issues of respectability and language as having power and challenging that power.

As a group, the scholars in this volume seem committed to studying the civil rights movement at the local level, to extending the time period under discussion, to understanding the perspectives of multiple groups of African Americans and whites, and to using concepts such as respectability and memory along with race, class, and gender as part of the language of analysis. They seem committed to expanding the range of people who need to be studied and to questioning the ongoing meaning of the movement, and they seem dedicated to studying the past to raise questions about social justice, how to define it, and how to pursue it.

• • •

For the University of Mississippi conference where these essays were presented as papers, the Porter Fortune, Jr. History Symposium partnered with the Future of the South Conference, sponsored by the Center for the Study of Southern Culture. John Dittmer concluded the conference with responses to the various papers and the issues they raised. And in the spirit of connecting history, memory, and the potential for activism, the two-day conference about history was followed by a third day of discussion about how to teach history. Panels about teaching the civil rights movement involved Rita Bender and Bill Bender, who were teaching a class at the University of Mississippi's William Winter Institute for Racial Reconciliation; Curtis Austin of the University of Southern Mississippi; Chauncey Spears of the Mississippi Department of Education; Geoff Ward from the University of California–Irvine; Penn State University's Nan Woodruff; and Diana Freelon Foster of the *Southern Echo*. The conference received assistance from graduate students in the History and the Southern Studies program, Cathryn Stout, Katrina Sims, Will Hustwit, Anna Kaplan, Daphne Chamberlain, and Patrick Weems. The conference benefited from support from History Department chair Joe Ward and the William Winter Institute and its director, Susan Glisson, and this volume received considerable editorial and technological assistance from the work of Carter Dalton Lyon, Becca Walton, Sally Lyon, Melanie Young, and LaTonya Pittman.

NOTES

1. John Dittmer, *Local People: The Struggle for Civil Rights in Mississippi* (Urbana: University of Illinois Press, 1994); Charles M. Payne, *I've Got the Light of Freedom: The Organizing Tradition and the Mississippi Freedom Struggle* (Berkeley: University of California Press, 1995).

2. Some examples of local studies and biographical studies on Mississippi movement topics include Emilye Crosby, *A Little Taste of Freedom: The Black Freedom Struggle in Claiborne County, Mississippi* (Chapel Hill: University of North Carolina Press, 2005); Chana Kai Lee, *For Freedom's Sake: The Life of Fannie Lou Hamer* (Urbana: University of Illinois Press, 2004); J. Todd Moye, *Let the People Decide: Black Freedom and White Resistance Movements in Sunflower County, Mississippi, 1945–1986* (Chapel Hill: University of North Carolina Press, 2004); Chris Myers-Asch, *The Senator and the Sharecropper: The Freedom Struggles of James O. Eastland and Fannie Lou Hamer* (Chapel Hill: University of North Carolina Press, 2008); Françoise N.

Hamlin, *Crossroads at Clarksdale: The Black Freedom Struggle in the Mississippi Delta after World War II* (Chapel Hill: University of North Carolina Press, 2012); Charles Eagles, *The Price of Defiance: James Meredith and the Integration of Ole Miss* (Chapel Hill: University of North Carolina Press, 2009); Charles Marsh, *God's Long Summer: Stories of Faith and Civil Rights* (Princeton, N.J.: Princeton University Press, 1997); Carter Dalton Lyon, "Lifting the Color Bar from the House of God: The 1963–1964 Church Visit Campaign to Challenge Segregated Sanctuaries in Jackson, Mississippi" (Ph.D. diss., University of Mississippi, 2010); Daphne Rochelle Chamberlain, "'And a Child Shall Lead the Way': Children's Participation in the Jackson, Mississippi Black Freedom Struggle, 1946–1970" (Ph.D. diss., University of Mississippi, 2009).

3. Emilye Crosby, ed., *Civil Rights History from the Ground Up: Local Struggles, A National Movement* (Athens: University of Georgia Press, 2011).

4. Jacquelyn Dowd Hall, "The Long Civil Rights Movement and the Political Uses of the Past," *Journal of American History* 91 (March 2005): 1233–1263.

5. Payne, *I've Got the Light of Freedom*; Charles C. Bolton, *The Hardest Deal of All: The Battle over School Integration in Mississippi* (Jackson: University Press of Mississippi, 2005).

6. Particularly clear examples of gendered definitions of politics in southern history appear in Jane Dailey, Glenda Gilmore, and Bryant Simon, eds., *Jumpin' Jim Crow: Southern Politics from Civil War to Civil Rights* (Princeton, N.J.: Princeton University Press, 2000); Nancy Bercaw, ed., *Gender and the Southern Body Politics: Essays and Comments* (Jackson: University Press of Mississippi, 2000).

7. Evelyn Brooks Higginbotham, *Righteous Discontent: The Women's Movement in the Black Baptist Church, 1880–1920* (Cambridge, Mass.: Harvard University Press, 1994).

8. For example, Renee Romano and Leigh Raiford, eds., *The Civil Rights Movement and American Memory* (Athens: University of Georgia Press, 2006); Owen J. Dwyer and Derek H. Alderman, *Civil Rights Memorials and the Geography of Memory* (Chicago: Center for American Places, 2008); David Blight, *American Oracle: The Civil War in the Civil Rights Era* (Cambridge, Mass.: Belknap Press of Harvard University Press, 2011).

9. Examples include Joseph Crespino, *In Search of Another Country: Mississippi and the Conservative Counterrevolution* (Princeton, N.J.: Princeton University Press, 2007); Jason Ward, *Defending White Democracy: The Making of a Segregationist Movement and the Remaking of Racial Politics, 1936–1965* (Chapel Hill: University of North Carolina Press, 2011); Matthew Lassiter, *The Silent Majority: Suburban Politics in the Sunbelt South* (Princeton, N.J.: Princeton University Press, 2006); Kevin M. Kruse, *White Flight: Atlanta and the Making of Modern Conservatism* (Princeton, N.J.: Princeton University Press, 2005).

10. Among the readings on religion and civil rights that are specific to Mississippi, see Marsh, *God's Long* Summer; Mark Newman, *Divine Agitators: The Delta Ministry and Civil Rights in Mississippi* (Athens: University of Georgia Press, 2004).

The Civil Rights Movement in Mississippi

Grassroots Organizing in Mississippi That Changed National Politics

Wesley Hogan

The top people in this country operate in thousands of organizations simultaneously; but the poor have no voice, nor organization. SNCC field workers can
help people set up their *own* organizations—*not* set up affiliates of SNCC in all
the counties.
—Bob Parris [Moses]

There are three ways of organizing any government: around organized
money, organized military, or organized people. Our libraries and classrooms are filled with books about societies that have created governments
based on organized money or organized militaries. The scholarship is shock-
ingly thin on governments based on organized people. Such books, indeed,
would hardly fill a room, much less a library. And the reason why is quite
straightforward.

People do not ordinarily have "organizing" as a category in their heads.
It's missing from most political history courses and books. It's missing from
popular culture. Somehow, those who have really felt the power and exhilara-
tion of *how* democratic organizing works have had a hard time sharing that
knowledge with others. Fannie Lou Hamer was an exception to this rule.
Speaking to a group in Cleveland, Ohio, in 1965, she used concrete metaphors to explain what most of America missed:

> One fellow brought a big round sign and said "Go back to Africa." So I said,
> "Well, I don't know who you are but I'll always tell you before I go, so if
> you're there it can reach you. After you send the Jews back to Jerusalem, the
> Chinese back to China, you'll give the Indians their land back, you get on
> the mainland from which you came. It looks as if all of us is on borrowed

land and we plan to enjoy some of it too. That's why I think it's important for people in every city to have the Freedom Democratic Party set up. You just don't know how much grass roots people can do. You see, *whether you know it or not, you're excluded from politics too.*"[1]

Like the man holding the "Go back to Africa" sign, most of us do not realize the extent to which we are excluded from political life. Worse still, even those of us who *do* have an inkling are routinely clueless as to how to respond. More often than not, our activities are limited to what civil rights activists called "speechifying." Some who feel excluded spend an inordinate amount of time with their own versions of "Go Back to Africa" signs. In our own time, these signs might read "No Death Panels!" or "Where's the Birth Certificate?" Student Nonviolent Coordinating Committee (SNCC) organizer Courtland Cox's summary insight from 1965 still rings true in our own time: "People know how things are, but they don't know what to do about it."[2]

As a problem, this is not new. Indeed, history is littered with famous, infamous, and little-known moments of people *not* able to figure out what to do (the most famous, perhaps: Lenin trying to answer this question in "What Is To Be Done," and in the process turning egalitarianism completely on its head). Nor is this a problem restricted to people who lack power, as anyone who observed Clinton's, and then Obama's, efforts to pass comprehensive health care reform can attest. But unlike people at the levers of decision making, people outside the corridors of power usually have only one way to get their voices heard: organizing. Today, one of the best places we can go to learn about organizing is the Mississippi movement of the 1960s. While as a culture we are still blind to several of the key dynamics of organizing, once these aspects of the Mississippi movement become visible, it is evident that Mississippi still has many things to teach about the history of democracy in the United States.

What Is Organizing?

Throughout U.S. history, this has been true for workers, women, students, and African Americans: little if anything happened without organizing. And yet what is meant by "organizing" is still far from clear. Is it "organizing" to get people to listen to a speech, achieve electoral victory, or get people to sign a petition? Or, for that matter, is it a sign of "lack of organizing" to lose an election, fail to have people show up for the speech, or sign the petition?

More often than not, political commentators only talk about organized money—they just don't talk about organized people. And even when they do, real people, and real people's past efforts to organize, are often curiously absent from their reflections. Organizing becomes an abstraction, devoid of real meaning and specificity. "SNCC organized a successful voter-registration campaign" has as much meaning as "life happened and then he was elected chairman." What replaces a serious analysis of organizing in such statements are a series of commonplace, but deeply erroneous, assumptions, chief among them: things happen because someone had a good idea; *or* things don't happen because people are apathetic. But the house doesn't get built just because there is a nice blueprint—someone with training and skills has to do the actual constructing. Without tools, however, people—however willing they may be—cannot construct (and in turn may be seen, from up high, to be "apathetic").

How, specifically, to get from point A to point B is the problem, especially if one does not want B to get completely compromised in the process. It is a hugely complicated process: so complicated, in fact, that it rarely happens. People need to find a reason to come together; they need to find ways to talk and listen; they need to find things to do (that make sense to everyone). But even that merely marks the beginning. Without access to money that can grease wheels, buy votes, or provide ready entry to the halls of power, making something happen through the organized collective activities of people is the only way to move things—political processes, cultural values, habits, laws.

It matters a great deal, in short, that we live in a culture in which "organizing" merely occupies the terrain of an afterthought, frequently not important enough to be seriously researched and discussed. Organizing is the most important tool for people without power. Ignore, dismiss, or simply cloud the tool in abstractions, and the effect is inevitably debilitating. The mere abstract reference to the hammer cannot drive the nail into the lumber. To learn about organizing is to learn from *people who organized*, not from people who just thought about organizing, or who already assumed someone had done the organizing.

Some important scholarship has begun to change this. John Dittmer and Charles Payne initiated a vital focus on local leaders and local struggles. But less remarked upon by scholars is their innovative emphasis on how everyday people used inventive, courageous activities to leverage real change. James Scott, an anthropologist, began to draw increasing attention in the 1980s and 1990s to the ways everyday people resist oppressive circumstances, itself a form of organizing. Todd Moye, Emilye Crosby, Hasan Jeffries, and I (among others) have followed in the wake of these path-breaking scholars, clarifying how "outside" organizers and "local people" came together in different areas of Georgia, Alabama, and Mississippi, looking at the specific mechanics of organizing. Recently, Black Power scholar and Stokely Carmichael biographer Peniel Joseph has claimed that "the best of the new black power scholarship is already forcing scholars to reassess conventional wisdom by focusing on the impact of community organizing."[3]

But this is not to say that those of us who focus on the nitty-gritty of grassroots organizing are somehow dominating the scholarship, or the scholarly trends. One need only look at the recent 700-page tome by widely regarded scholar Thomas Sugrue on civil rights in the North, *Sweet Land of Liberty*. In many ways a magnificent work, synthesizing years of his own and others' scholarship, Sugrue situates a huge swath of northern activism within the domestic politics, intellectual trends, economic settings, and international events of the day. Despite this, the reader has very little sense of how and why people come together, or how they work together to challenge the racial status quo, or how they form networks. It is extremely difficult—if not impossible—to understand social movements without this piece of the story. To put it boldly: in the face of the extraordinary power of intrepid cultural tradition, habit, and often well-organized money, only "organized" people can succeed. How did they get organized? Sugrue simply doesn't tell us. As was the case in the South, the central task for activists, and particularly for civil rights activists, was to recruit and organize. They needed people coming together, and for a time staying together. Without it, there was no movement. Nothing changes. Sugrue, despite his gigantic story and massive footnotes, never tells us how people come together, or how they organized. It is safe to say that "organizing" is simply not a category on his conceptual radar screen, or perhaps not one he takes seriously.[4]

Still, since the 2008 presidential campaign, unlike any time in the last forty years, there's been a lot of talk in popular and academic discourse about "grassroots organizing"—Barack Obama publicly celebrated his early work as a community organizer, contrasting his choice to those of his law school peer group who went to work in corporate law. He backed up that rhetoric in 2008 when he sent thousands of paid staffers to "organize for change," putting millions of dollars into organizing as well as the usual inordinate sums spent by all candidates on television and other advertising.[5] Community organizing as a visible public job received an inadvertent assist when Sarah Palin mocked Obama's past as a community organizer. This in turn spurred network news to actually ask, and at least superficially explore, "what is a community organizer?"[6]

But despite all this recent attention, in the academy as well as the media, it is unclear whether we as a culture understand organizing any better than we did before 2008. Today there is no better place to learn about organizing, successful and effective organizing, organizing of the community, but also organizing that changed the dominant culture and dominant cultural institutions, than Mississippi in the 1960s. You may ask: "Why Mississippi?" Couldn't we just as easily look at organizing in Alabama, or Georgia, or Louisiana, or California—all places where significant "grassroots organizing" occurred in the 1960s? The answer is "yes" and "no." Many of SNCC's organizing accomplishments were not restricted to Mississippi.[7] But I think there are at least three good reasons for focusing on Mississippi: activists in Mississippi ran the largest and most successful experiment in popular politics in the twentieth century; they did so in a state, and at a time, that was the most difficult state for blacks to vote in; and more than in any other place, the Mississippi movement managed to dislodge old power structures and, in the process, generate viable and inclusive alternatives of democratic governance.[8] Put differently: they've been the most successful, and they've been the most successful under the most difficult conditions. Organizers in Mississippi (most natives of the state, some from outside) upended Jim Crow in American politics in a single decade.[9] More recently, U.S. historians have been forced to examine the long-term changes generated by the work of the Mississippi Freedom Democratic Party (MFDP). "The outcome did not just affect Mississippi," SNCC organizer Charlie Cobb remarked in 2009. "The job we did resulted in changing forever the rules of the national Democratic Party, and was the groundwork that prepared the way for the Obama presidency. In fighting for the right to vote—and winning—the door was opened to the possibility of winning any elected office, even the highest in the land."[10]

Despite these accomplishments, however, Mississippi's organizing experience is not widely understood. It certainly hasn't penetrated to the popular culture the way, for instance, that students in the third and fourth grades learn about the "committees of correspondence" during the Revolution or even the way high schoolers learn about the Constitutional Convention debates of the 1780s. And yet the MFDP was and is just as important a development for U.S. democratic practice as either of these foundational struggles.[11] Twenty-five years before the former Soviet bloc countries transitioned to representative government, and thirty years before South Africans created their landmark egalitarian constitution, African Americans forced first the state of Mississippi, then the Democratic Party, and subsequently the nation as a whole to live out its *uncashed* promise of "one man, one vote." Their success became an *icon* for similar subsequent freedom struggles in Czechoslovakia, China, South Africa, and Iran, and launched a series of freedom movements in the United States as well: the women's movement, Brown Power movement, American Indian Movement, Gay Liberation movement, and prison justice movement, to name just a few. Therefore, it is critical to examine: in the Mississippi movement between 1961 and 1965, the peak of Council of Federated Organizations (COFO)/MFDP organizing in Mississippi, what exactly were organizers doing? What did *they* call "grassroots organizing"?

At the risk of stating the obvious, there was quite a bit of variation in tactics in the Mississippi movement, both because it was made up of very eclectic individuals and because different local circumstances required different approaches. Still, all of the organizing that took place under the COFO banner in Mississippi generally used a similar approach. When SNCC moved into McComb in 1961, and then began to work under COFO's umbrella starting in early 1962, followed by the MFDP umbrella in the spring of 1964, people shared an understanding about organizing that then spread throughout all projects that joined the MFDP. To illuminate and explain SNCC's rich organizing tradition in Mississippi, one needs to show the following:

• Why and how organizing is an alien and difficult concept in a culture dominated by top-down, organized-money models of politics.

• The ways in which Mississippi's organizing experience fits into, and is similar to, SNCC organizing in other parts of the South, but also how Mississippi organizers crafted organizing strategies that were unique to Mississippi.

• How the Mississippi civil rights struggle, perhaps better than any other, serves as a historical model for organizing that can be used to understand other grassroots people's movements.

Some Basic Thoughts On Organizing

Moving people from idea to action is a lot harder than most of us think. Indeed, for those of us who have never tried to get five people to come to an organizing meeting, or ten people to show up for a sit-in, or 100 people to show up at a school board meeting, or 100,000 to show up for a demonstration on the Mall in Washington, D.C., we get kind of bored to hear others tell the tale. It seems very ho-hum until you care passionately about an issue, and want to get enough people there to make an impact on policy.

A typical story illustrates the problem. Last year I was asked to give a workshop on teaching the civil rights movement. The workshop participants would consist of current college students training to be history teachers, some movement veterans, and current teachers interested in getting their students more information about the freedom struggle. The workshop was to last four hours, and I had total freedom to structure both format and content. Past failures to convey the experiential reality of the movement to those who are then charged with teaching it had led me to the understanding that we teachers need to understand the core of the civil rights movement to teach it.

I've seen people teach about the civil rights movement using strikingly different methods. But what all successful attempts have in common is that they vividly convey that at its core, the movement taught people to act on their own deepest democratic impulses. Another way to put that is to say that it is virtually impossible to successfully convey a concept or process if the person you are teaching has no experience with it, no context for it. For those who have never been asked to trust themselves, to make a decision completely on their own, learning about people who made decisions that could threaten their own lives is usually beyond reach. So I decided to run a role-play simulation with the participants similar to the one I run with my own students, to allow them to experience, even if only fleetingly, the complex choices faced by nonviolent protestors in the early 1960s. My goal was to have them experience some of the dilemma of deciding on what course of action—for having to make the decision, and then having to live with its consequences, is a lot harder than standing on the sidelines commenting on it.

The first eighty minutes of the four-hour workshop were spent running two role-plays, and then unpacking them, walking around them, exploring the dynamics of what happened and how that knowledge could help us explore/explain the civil rights movement with our students in the classroom. It seemed, at the time, to go very well. A lot of good observations and questions came forward from many people. We went on with the rest of the workshop, and at the end I handed out evaluations. Later that night, looking through the evolutions of the workshop, I read: "Wayyyyyyyyy too much time spent on the role play," from a disgruntled participant. "I wanted more lesson plans, you spent so much time on just the sit-in that I didn't learn about Selma or Birmingham or Freedom Summer." There were four similar feedback sheets, all clearly from the table of preservice teachers that I had, in the corner of my mind, perceived as reticent, not alienated. Everyone else seemed engaged. And those others, of course (movement veterans and veteran teachers), did write glowingly about learning how to teach using a role-play. But it was the preservice teachers who really were mad. They came to the workshop thinking it was going to be "hard," "cold" content. They didn't like the experiential material; it was too loose, too much like "winging it." It didn't feel like "school." I failed to convince them that teaching people to act on their own deepest democratic impulses was a thousand times more intellectually important than knowing the civil rights movement timeline, or breaking down photos of Birmingham's dogs, or knowing how many people crossed the Edmund Pettis Bridge in Selma. I failed to get these young people to see that moving from idea to action is the hardest and the most important political act in civic life. So, of course, they by definition can't pass this on to their own students. For them, it was just another tedious in-service, a definite waste of their time. So that's one key impediment: people don't even know what they don't know.

A second impediment, though, appears even for the people who want to act, who know how important it is to act, and just have trouble overcoming the second greatest hurdle: fear. A brilliant young Howard student, Muriel Tillinghast, captured this preaction mentality perfectly, recalling her first weeks trying to move herself from idea ("end Jim Crow") to action ("register Mississippi voters"): "I spent my first two weeks in the upstairs office of the Greenville Project. I was petrified. How was I going to survive Mississippi? It dawned on me that I would never get anybody to register to vote staying in the office, so s-l-o-w-l-y I started coming downstairs and cautiously going out into the town. I walked like a shadow on the wall, edgy, just getting used to walking in the streets."[12]

This kind of activity—participating in a sit-in, or encouraging others to register in Greenville in 1964—changes the way participants think about politics. Let me emphasize this point. What changes is not what we might call "passive perception"—changing one's views or perceptions about a politician, or a party, or a community, or an idea. No. What changes is one's understanding of oneself in the community, an "active perception" of what I can do as an active participant, not as a passive bystander. There can be nothing more important to political science, democratic theory, or understanding movements. Participants in the movement no longer saw politics as what you talk about (much less who you took money from or made deals with). They began to experience politics as part of their lives, seeing themselves as having to make active choices, figuring out how to live "as if" without getting crushed. It is perhaps the most empowering, but also the most sobering, experience. Either way, it is essential to organizing.

It is difficult to have a meaningful conversation about organizing when so many people don't understand why it matters. Before going further, let us turn to specifics. Based on the example of Mississippi, what can we say organizing is, and what is it not?

Grassroots Organizing: What It Was in Mississippi

Many state that they are grassroots organizers, or that they are studying a grassroots campaign. It is, to say the least, a widely misused term. For it to be grassroots, as John Dittmer pointed out, local people—not the organizers—had to be at the center of the activity.[13] Recently, a group of women in SNCC put together a collective memoir. They reflected that theirs had been "an unusually democratic movement, one linking college students and sharecroppers, a movement that respected and admired the wisdom and courage of everyday people, and an organizational model which opposed authoritarian and centralized decision-making." This focus, on developing the program ideas of local people, and doing so in a horizontal decision-making structure, is key to grassroots organizing. But it runs counter to much of what we learn ordinary "politics" (that is, organized money) is.[14]

SNCC organizers very early developed a clear understanding that their model of organizing differed from virtually everyone else—from traditional Democrats, the National Association for the Advancement of Colored People (NAACP), the leadership of the Southern Christian Leadership Conference (SCLC). SNCC first opposed and then dismissed the basic contention of such groups that direct democracy (one person, one vote) somehow wouldn't work because there were too many people out there. Even more important, SNCC activists from the beginning rejected the condescending arrogance of established organizations that implied that everyday people were presumably too uneducated and/or dense to understand issues. The way established organizations like the Democratic Party (or the SCLC, or the NAACP) operated seemed to always be based on the assumption, in the mocking words of Frank Smith, that what was really needed "was a few sober-headed, intelligent, educated people to sit down and make decisions" for all. A SNCC organizer in Mississippi, Smith drew this in vivid imagery: "SNCC has a picture of a Negro farmer who is sitting on a stool. He is an elderly man with brogan shoes, old overalls, and a beat-up hat. His mouth is bare and his hands are very rough from many, many years of hard labor on the farm," Smith wrote. "He more than likely lives in an old, worn-out house with a wash pot in the backyard and an outdoor toilet. He has never been to school." Should this man have the right to vote? "Does 'one man—one vote' include the sharecropper who has never been to school?" he asked. "Do we really believe what the white man tells us, that the Negro is really too stupid to vote?" It was such a deeply conditioned belief that there were even "some Negroes in SNCC who believe that."[15] Smith adopted, and as an organizer lived by, the idea behind "one man, one vote." Everybody contributed, and "leaders" didn't decide for the less educated or less articulate. This is grassroots organizing.

What exactly was SNCC's role in bringing grassroots organizing to the Mississippi movement? As numerous scholars and movement participants alike have pointed out, plenty of challenges to Jim Crow happened in Mississippi prior to SNCC's arrival. Not only had many individuals been active for decades, but significant civil rights activity had been "softening the ground" for SNCC before it came, as Joyce Ladner noted.[16] During the fall of 1961, Bob Moses worked with elder movement veterans such as C. C. Bryant, Webb Owens, and Amzie Moore, and simultaneously developed a staff of young people who were willing to risk everything, including death—"plain and simple, this was what you had to risk if you were going to work in the state." They all worked to try to get people in different communities to go down to the courthouse to register. Amzie Moore had seen the sit-in student energy, and decided it might be effective: "He admired what the students were doing, but was not interested in organizing sit-ins in his town," recalled Charlie Cobb. "He wanted a voter registration campaign. *He* put that idea on our political plate, challenging our idea that 'direct action' only meant sit-ins and picket lines of protest. Moore wanted to see the emergence of black power in the Delta. Black people in enough numbers were there; the registered black voters were not." So what SNCC brought was this new way to move, a grassroots organizing approach. But just to be clear, SNCC was not the first to move in the state.[17]

And some adults moved toward SNCC's model, from the role of community "leader" to grassroots organizer, when SNCC arrived, such as Fannie Lou Hamer, Aaron Henry, and Victoria Gray Adams. Adams, for instance, responded with vigor when her pastor denied SNCC church space to organize. "No, he doesn't control the church that I go to; SNCC people are welcome there. I'm quite sure that if we meet with my pastor, everything will be okay." The Reverend Leonard P. Ponder quickly arranged to open his church to SNCC meetings. As Mendy Samstein recalled, "At that time for any community person to become a leader, in a sense, was also to become a target and that's what happened in Liberty when Herb Lee and a couple other people really became . . . organizers. There's one thing to leave your home and go to the courthouse, it's another thing to become an active force in the community so that whites sense that you're a key person and once they sense that you're a target—Herbert Lee was killed because he was becoming a focal person."[18]

Here it might be useful to elucidate the terms "leader" and "organizer." A leader is someone whom others in a given community look up to and respond to. In other words, a leader has a following, and can deliver that following (show up at a meeting, sign this petition, picket this supermarket). An organizer's role is different. He or she seeks to find and develop leaders, to bring them into public relationships toward a common goal. To make this perhaps a little clearer, the difference between being a politician and an organizer is that a politician says what you want to hear (and may or may not act on his or her statement), and the organizer teaches you how to hold people publicly accountable for their actions, *within the context of a civic relationship.*[19]

How did these SNCC organizers or local leaders-turned-organizers get people up and moving? Bob Moses recalled that people often labeled "apathetic" by outsiders simply hadn't found a key to civic participation yet. He gave an example: the mother of movement activist June Johnson came with a busload of movement people from Greenwood to Greenville to stand witness at a movement person's trial in early 1963. "It transformed her," said Moses. "Just getting out and going those sixty miles and working in Greenville. I remember her saying that 'you would have never gotten me out in the streets in Greenwood to talk with people to register to vote.'" Movement organizers "were always looking for the key to that kind of personal transformation," Moses remembered. He and the others were always asking: "What is the key to getting people to move? That was an important event—seeing that if you took people and just transferred them a few miles out of their local situation then some energy was released." As Lawrence Guyot noted, "all of us learned what can be done in a community in Greenwood which we then used everywhere else." Jean Wheeler Smith Young recalled a similar experience while running her first MFDP precinct meeting in Hattiesburg in 1964, explaining not just how it released energy for the newly activated participants but also for her as an organizer. She laid out the reasons behind the MFDP, and then stopped to see if people were following. "Not only were they listening; but they were also rocking and nodding their heads, and shouting, 'Amen, sister,' the sweetest sound I'd ever heard—Amen! to me, with me! I felt wonderful. Thirty minutes before I had been tongue-tied and helpless. Now here I was connected to all these people; I was them and they were me. We were sharing a great vision." And then they began to do the single most important thing a grassroots organizer cares about: they began to move: "One by one, those who felt prepared to take the next risk for freedom rose from their chairs and carefully approached the long table to pick up a ballot and vote. Those who didn't feel ready to go that far sat quietly and waited. At the table I explained the ballots and gave help if a person couldn't read and write. I felt a thrill of excitement each time a man or woman who had never voted in their lives stuffed a carefully folded freedom ballot into the homemade ballot box." At day's end, she had "certified about fifty ballots and by three o'clock, I was on my way to carry them to the state capital in Jackson, Mississippi, for the statewide MFDP vote count."[20] She had built a context for each person in the room to have a civic presence: the ballots she collected taught people one way to hold Mississippi Democrats publicly accountable for their refusal to count ballots cast by blacks in the Democratic primary.

Another key role of an organizer was to find new people to move into civic action. Once moving, new recruits often brought forward others, as Muriel Tillinghast explained: "We worked, family by family, person by person. Once a person had a sense of the Movement and of us, they would introduce us to the next contact." In an environment where the local police, the White Citizens' Council, and the Mississippi State Sovereignty Commission all paid informants large sums of money and threatened them with beatings in order to extract information about the movement, "black Mississippians were risking economic reprisals, the loss of their jobs, or worse" to house and feed organizers from COFO. "We stayed with people who were just barely getting by themselves, yet they were willing to risk all to allow us to bring the message of their rights and the Movement to them."[21]

For Jean Wheeler, accepting the job of organizer meant picking a "righteous goal" from those she heard local leaders supporting, and then "organizers must face fear and model that for others." They had to "maintain trusting and dependable relationships with the local people and with each other, no matter what else is going on in their lives. Finally, whenever possible, organizers should use music and art to communicate." She found that "to the extent I was successful as an organizer it was because I maintained close and open relations, of mutual dependence, with the people I was trying to organize and with my coworkers in SNCC. Even though the language may come from women's psychology, I'm sure this was not just a female thing. I believe that the men in SNCC valued this relationality as much as the women." Indeed, regardless of gender, time and again the most successful organizers in SNCC were those who focused on building relationships with local people, and then challenging them to act within the context of those relationships. This was "relational power" as opposed to the hierarchical power traditionally mobilized by politicians, parties, and established organizations alike.[22]

Such important first steps of organizing—recruiting, listening, building relationships, and accompanying people to register—occupied SNCC/

COFO work throughout 1961–1962. Now the key question among movement organizers became: how could they *translate* straightforward "voter registration" into real political power?[23] Again, it was a question with significance far beyond the Mississippi movement. A series of acts of civil disobedience (like the sit-ins) does not immediately lead to the 1964 Civil Rights Act, changing policy for the entire nation. There was no obvious path from voter registration to the 1965 Voting Rights Act. What, in fact, *could be* the steps between "registering voters" and giving black Mississippians seats at the political table commensurate with their numbers in the population at large? No one in 1963 knew the answer.[24]

People within COFO put several ideas on the table. They considered a "general strike at the height of the cotton-picking season in the Delta," and then dismissed it because they didn't think they could move it effectively *from idea to action*: they couldn't guarantee they could keep people from starving, or recruit enough people to make the strike successful, or prevent a tidal wave of white violence, or prevent planters from mechanizing their plantations. They got 733 black Mississippians to vote in the August 6, 1963, primary for the governor's race, but that did not force open the Mississippi state Democratic Party. Finally, in the relative safety of their own black churches and businesses, 27,000 blacks turned out to post protest ballots in the Democratic primary runoff. Now organizers began to see that large numbers of people could move from idea to action, and (this was essential) live to see another day. "The movement in Mississippi took a political turn in that time," recalled Bob Moses.[25]

In the fall of 1963 SNCC/COFO organizers thus moved forward with a new tactic, "Freedom Days." As Mendy Samstein explained, "rather than bring down a trickle of people steadily who would just get turned down and doing that just became repetitive, it tried to create, to build up the community and on a given day you brought down a large number of people to vote. It sharpened the confrontation of the issue that when people in large numbers could be seen blocked at the courthouse. I mean they just [couldn't] get in there to vote." In a COFO meeting, people decided to force white Mississippi politicians to be accountable for the exclusion of black voters: if they wouldn't let blacks vote, blacks would run their own candidate, Aaron Henry, for governor. There was a convention held on October 6, and SNCC's organizing through relationships was strong enough that people came out. They moved. "People came from all over the state, from the north, south, east, west, all over the state to Jackson; about 200 people," said Samstein.[26]

Again denied entry at the polling places in November 1963, 83,000 Mississippians, most of them African Americans, voted for Aaron Henry for governor. "We were using the [Aaron Henry] campaign to register people as a tool for organizing people," said Moses. The campaign unified black Mississippians around the quest for the vote. Since voting was officially a federally protected activity, Moses recalled, "they were eligible for some kind of support from the Justice Department, even if it was minimal." Subsequent COFO conventions followed in December, then again in February and March 1964. The Democratic Party represented the entirety of political power in the state. There was no Republican Party. Democrats had doled out jobs, benefits, and subsidies for 100 years. The MFDP challenged Democrats to include its members, while simultaneously building a parallel structure. Thus, after years of trying to gain entry to the state's Democratic Party, movement people launched the MFDP on April 26, 1964. That year, 50,000 more people registered in the MFDP. During the weeks of July 19 and 26, 1964, the MFDP held county conventions in thirty-five counties and elected 282 delegates.[27]

The movement had created a statewide organization to move people politically. No longer were people just bringing folks to the courthouse to register. They were "going beyond just registering to focus attention on the actual political process," said Moses. As Ella Baker had suggested at the state convention in early August, Mississippians in the MFDP treated the process as a giant civic classroom—they learned not only how power worked at the local, state, and federal levels, but they learned how to lobby, how to protest, and how to build their own organizations where they could no longer be ignored. And so empowered, they sent forty-four delegates and twenty-two alternates to the Democratic National Convention in Atlantic City, New Jersey.[28]

Here is where the MFDP story begins to diverge from the other voter registration campaigns in the Deep South at this time, notably those in Alabama, Georgia, and Louisiana. The *most important* thing that made it different from these other crucial campaigns is that the MFDP figured out how to "break the back of apartheid" within the southern Democratic Party at this convention, though the MFDP didn't realize it at the time.[29] There would never be another all-white delegation to the Democrats' national convention.

Hundreds of thousands of words have been written about the MFDP's quest to replace the "regular," or lily-white, state Democrats at the Democratic National Convention at Atlantic City in 1964, and their second campaign to unseat the congressmen voted in by the all-white state party in 1965. For the purpose of uncovering the mechanics of grassroots organizing for political power, let us further explore just two aspects of the broader MFDP challenge to the regular Democrats.

First, why did the MFDP reject the "compromise" offered by the Democratic National Committee leaders? At the time, many political pundits and Democratic Party leaders could simply not believe that the MFDP rejected the "compromise."[30] They thought it naive and idealistic. This is akin to the British calling the Declaration of Independence and the resulting War for Independence an "ill-conceived political misread." As Victoria Gray Adams stated: "I never saw the 1964 exploration as a lost cause although many other people did. I believe if we had accepted those two seats in 1964, then 1968 would have been the lost cause. Because if we had accepted less than we went for, that's what we would have gotten and it wouldn't have gotten any better. Also, in between the two conventions, there was the Congressional Challenge. The Congressional Challenge really frightened the powers that be." And indeed, if the MFDP had "settled" for the two-seat "compromise," the Democratic Party would have felt entitled to its own version of "all deliberate speed," a glacially slow change. Instead, as Charlie Cobb noted recently: "After turning its back on the MFDP because of the power wielded by southern white Democrats—power they owed to their exclusion of blacks from the political process—the national Democratic Party, to ameliorate its betrayal, promised future changes that would expand the participation of women and minorities." First, in 1968, the MFDP mounted a partial (albeit compromised and controversial) challenge to the Mississippi delegation, and then with much broader reverberations in 1972, when "these changes were formalized into what are now called the McGovern Rules, outlawing explicitly racist local party affiliates and increasing the number of women and minorities in party leadership roles," Cobb stated. "The candidacy of Barack Obama—and Hillary Clinton for that matter—would not have been possible without the 1964 MFDP challenge that generated the pressure for these new rules; that in fact was the trigger for changes in the process."[31]

Thus there were two major lessons for political power coming out of the MFDP interaction with the national Democrats: it is more important to stay accountable to your constituents than take home crumbs from the political table; and the power black Mississippians were able to marshal as a result of staying true to their constituents eventually resulted in transformations that triggered *both* a sea change within the national Democratic Party *and* a party realignment. By 1968 Republicans launched their now infamous "Southern Strategy" to recruit whites disaffected by Democrats support for civil rights, and by 1980 most southern whites were in the Republican Party. The Democratic Party had opened to all, wedged open by the MFDP.

Grassroots Organizing: What Supported It in Mississippi?

It is helpful at this point to be clear as to which political activities are "organizing for political power at the grassroots" and which activities are *not* grassroots political organizing. It's important because if and when television or newspaper pundits, political scientists, and political theorists do think of "grassroots organizing," they think of a whole range of activities. Many of these activities may help organizing, and in some cases they are necessary accompaniments, but they are not, themselves, organizing for creating political power at the base, or at the grassroots.

It is important to note that the list of activities that follows is a partial, not a comprehensive one. It is also a sketch, not a full portrait, of the activities that supported organizing.

Freedom Schools

During the early 1960s, as high schoolers in Mississippi were expelled for their movement work, SNCC began to open "Freedom Schools" for them, which later spread across the state during the 1964 Summer Project. These schools, taught by COFO staffers and volunteers, "encouraged political thinking by asking students to define their needs and pose solutions." As Muriel Tillinghast recalled: "Out of natural curiosity schoolchildren wanted to know, 'Why can't we vote?' To answer this, there was a need to put voting and our current registration efforts into an historical context. As we talked about the history of black people in this country, a change took place in our listeners, young and old. Before they had not challenged what they were taught in school, but with our presence they found the courage and the personal strength to speak up, to challenge certain information, and to bring 'other' information into the classroom." She noticed that the change happened slowly, but "every day one or another of these freedom schoolers was sent home from the local school and told, 'Don't come back!' Before long we had a class of fifteen to twenty children every day."[32] As Emmie Schrader Adams called it, these children had developed a key democratic habit: "Freedom Thinking."[33] It bolstered the MFDP's work, as Gwendolyn Zohorah Simmons recalled: "The Laurel Project established a freedom school, with a satellite freedom day care center, held successful mock voter registration campaigns in which we registered hundreds of black residents, and had a good turn-out for the mock elections. We built a strong Laurel Chapter of the MFDP and selected the delegates for the state convention."[34] The townspeople were so inspired by their own expanding knowledge they eventually organized a 1,500-volume library with the help of COFO workers. Boycotting the schools in the Deep South eventually caught on as a tactic in the North and West. In January 1964 SNCC supported a multicity boycott of public schools in Chester and Philadelphia, Pennsylvania; Cambridge, Maryland; Boston; Chicago; New York; Cleveland, Ohio; Gary and Indianapolis, Indiana; and St. Louis. In Chicago, the boycott was organized by Larry Landrick, head of SNCC's Chicago office.[35] Freedom Schools were essential to developing citizens who could act, but in themselves, they could not leverage political power.

Housing

Another key activity that supported organizing was the job of cooking for and housing civil rights activists, and then donating money under the table to support the organizers. Sandy Leigh remembered: "We as SNCC people weren't getting too much money at the time. We couldn't afford to pay rent and so we would stay with a family. So that this family wouldn't be put out too much by our having stayed there and eaten their food, they formed another committee of concerned mothers from the various areas from about five distinct Negro areas there in Hattiesburg and they would be responsible for donating food and coming over to the office and cooking the food and laying it out for the people to eat. Then we kind of rotated from house to house to house so that we wouldn't importune one family too long."[36] Leigh noted that this system worked so well, it was replicated throughout the state's other MFDP projects.

Self-Defense

Another mostly male job was self-defense, both to protect the organizers and to protect the movement meetings. Both the level of organization and the degree to which self-defense was "public" and visible, or mostly behind-the-scenes, varied a great deal by locale. Victoria Gray Adams recalled that in Hattiesburg, due to the centuries of white public violence against any black male who stepped up to support his community, "the men were involved in less public ways. I knew some of the men in my community who appeared totally uninterested and uninvolved, but when night fell, they set up guards at every entry route that could be taken to my house. I remember seeing them sitting there—they sat up on the nearby icehouse, watching. Besides, the men had to be willing for us to be active. Otherwise, you know, as wives and mothers and sisters and sweethearts, we couldn't have done it." Self-defense could take less-explicit forms: Jean Wheeler went back to set up a project in Philadelphia, Mississippi, after the murder of James Chaney, Michael Schwerner, and Andrew Goodman: "SNCC field secretary Ralph Featherstone decided that, even though we were nonviolent, we should do something to protect ourselves. So we strung barbed wire across the stairs to at least make it hard for the Klan to surprise us." Simmons recalled that self-defense was not merely a male domain: "Mrs. Spinks had begun sitting up all night with her shotgun at the ready in case there was an attack upon her and/or Mrs. Clayton who lived across the street." Simmons heard her laugh, then say: "'They might get me but I'm going to get one or two of them first.' She was so wonderful, she would tell me, 'Sleep soundly honey, Mrs. Spinks ain't going to let no one harm you. They'll get to you over my dead body!'" For Simmons, this was a lifeline allowing her to continue to organize: Spinks "and so many others in Laurel and across that state were willing to give their lives for us and this Movement." In an environment where organizers lived nearly every minute filled with the threat of beating, bombing, or worse, realizing that local people were willing to defend them at this level provided the necessary space for them to rest and recuperate to organize another day.[37]

Legal Challenges

The legal challenges brought first by the NAACP, and later by the MFDP, also supported the movement's organizers. The legal challenges not only resulted in support for organizing but also could provide something for people to organize around, like equal distribution of federal subsidies. As Muriel Tillinghast stated, "By the fall of 1964, we began to look at other things aside from general voting. For example, how the local power structure obtained its cash flow. There were white gentlemen farmers who planted nothing, but made an awful lot of money. Then there were black people who were planting cotton and if they owned it, they were barely able to get it ginned." Legal challenges to the cotton allotment system set up under the U.S. Department of Agriculture, which determined federal subsidies to farmers, eventually resulted in more open elections in some counties. "When we ran candidates for local cotton allotment boards, that hit the economic bell which, in turn, brought out the Klan," said Tillinghast.[38]

Music, Photography, Theater

Art, photography, music, and theater also provided key psychological, ideological, and expressive support to help organizers reframe their activity in the state. Reframing what they were doing was absolutely key: throughout their time in the state, SNCC/COFO/MFDP workers were branded as troublemakers, agitators, Communists, incendiary rioters, and underhanded dirty-dealers by the white powers-that-be, but sometimes also by blacks who had established a small toehold in this most inhospitable of climates. SNCC workers often had to start off by reassuring people that they did not, as whites advertised, have horns and tails. To do this reframing quickly and efficiently, they came up with a straightforward tactic: before and during meetings, SNCC workers started with a hymn or spiritual. By rooting their appeals in lyrics and structural forms of the black freedom church, organizers comforted people while simultaneously encouraging them to move differently. Songs not only allowed movement people to name the oppressor—"Ain't gonna let Ross Barnett turn me 'round"—they also strengthened people's collective resolve: it was simply too hard to stop the sound of the full group. Even when lawmen tried to break up mass meetings, often the singing continued right through arrest and jailing.[39]

Theater provided another context for understanding what was happening all around them. When the Free Southern Theater performed Martin Duberman's *In White America* throughout the MFDP projects during the summer of 1964, "We had discussions after all the performances, so people had an opportunity to voice what they got from the experience of the play and how it and we connected to their lives and how we connected to the political changes that were going on in the South," recalled Denise Nichols. "The theater, like literature, can be a tool of community, of illumination of the human condition."[40] People talked back to the actors, and then among themselves about what they'd seen. This, too, released them from previous ways of thinking, and encouraged them to move in new ways, like down to the courthouse.

Adult Education

By the fall of 1963 Bob Moses had recruited Doris Derby and Casey Hayden to set up an adult education program to support the many local people who joined the movement and wanted to further their own education. Maria Varela, who joined the project in 1964, later reported that adults were very clear about what they would support and what they would not: "If educational programming does not meet people's felt needs, the program does not sustain itself and on-going self education after the program does not continue. (In most cases, people even forget the reading skills they did learn)." The programs that *did* work were "programs which either moved with the people's own movement for socio-economic change or programs which brought almost immediate gratification of needs by transmitting information instrumental in bettering one's living conditions." She noted that "the movement here in the South is involved with people moving and speaking for themselves around their basic needs." People were "going about the job of confronting institutions and structures—local, state and federal—which persist in segregating out from decision-making those considered 'unqualified' by color, educational or economic status."[41] Of course, the more people learned about the way government was supposed to work, the better able they were to challenge government when it did not work as promised. This empowerment through education amplified local leaders' confidence and skills, allowing them to challenge an ever-widening circle of lines that used to limit them in the civic arena.

Federal Programs

Charles McLaurin and Charlie Cobb reported as early as November 1962 that as a result of voter registration efforts in Sunflower County, white county officials were going to deny black citizens access to the federal commodities program, and "commodities are the only way many Negroes make it from cotton season to cotton season. If this is taken from them, they have nothing at all, and our voter registration program depends on the protection we can offer the individual while he is waiting for his one small vote to become a part of a strong Negro vote."[42] Such struggles to maintain federal program benefits to movement participants continued over the next two years, through the MFDP challenge. Simply put, if they could not help people meet their basic needs, they could not continue to work with them as civic participants, the struggle for survival would be too intense. Basic necessities were a prerequisite for moving people to public action. "Visits to federal agencies weren't part of the MFDP's original plans," recalled northern volunteer Elaine Delott Baker of her work to make federal programs more responsive to MFDP participants. "But the MFDP recognized their value and gave me the approval to begin setting up meetings at Washington agencies, like Health Education and Welfare, Veterans Affairs, the Department of Agriculture, and others." She and other movement veterans traveled to Washington in January 1965, and "filed into the offices of highly placed federal officials. With the national conscience sensitized by the violence of Freedom Summer, it had not been difficult for me to arrange these visits. Once inside these offices, people stood up and told their stories—a veteran's pension denied, an application for old-age assistance ignored, aid to the blind cut after an individual was seen participating in a demonstration. With each story, I felt the fear that was woven into the fabric of segregation begin to unravel." Such work had two useful impacts on organizing: it had the potential to provide more material sustenance for movement people, and the process itself allowed people to learn how to lobby within federal agencies and operate efficiently within the large federal bureaucracies.[43] This was lobbying that grew out of an organizing base.

Of course, outsiders sending money to sustain the projects were critical. Friends of SNCC networks in the North and West provided the vast majority of funding to support organizing in the Magnolia State. Scholars are still unclear to what degree funding sources impacted the strategic choices of SNCC/COFO/MFDP. Certainly, to attract (mostly middle-class) northern donors, SNCC omitted all tactics except nonviolence from its promotional material, even when its staff's daily practices included a wide range of methods to support organizing, including self-defense.[44] It was an insanely difficult balancing act: organizers faced daily white terrorism in the South, which required self-defense since the police at best refused to protect them and at worst were their persecutors. One the other hand, white northerners only pledged money to organizations committed to nonviolent methods of social change. As white activist Anne Braden remarked to a SNCC worker, "Don't get me wrong. I don't think anybody sitting in a safe comfortable apartment in New York has any right to tell you not to arm yourself . . . but frankly some people react this way." It's a key dynamic between the southern movement and its northern allies, and the recent work by Simon Wendt brings it more squarely to movement scholars' attention.[45]

All of these activities—Freedom Schools and libraries; providing housing, food, and self-defense; adult education; federal programs; and the Friends of SNCC networks—supported the political organizing in Mississippi. They were not, however, directly geared toward asserting political power.

Grassroots Organizing: What It Wasn't in Mississippi

In Mississippi after 1965, movement outsiders began to use movement structures and resources, and tried to take them over. This was the contentious, complex, difficult, and ultimately successful takeover by organized money, otherwise known as "politics as usual." It's a story culturally familiar to all of us, one where politicians became accountable not to their constituents but to their own egos, pocketbooks, or powerful interests who bankrolled their campaigns.[46] This was not a Mississippi-only problem. Indeed, it was a crisis confronted by SNCC, Students for a Democratic Society (SDS), and other movements for democracy in the 1960s, and continues to devastate politics today.[47]

There were also people who tried to organize, and called themselves organizers, but searched fruitlessly for a base. Phil Hutchins spoke in poignant detail on Pacifica radio in 1969 about SNCC's attempts to find people to move: "SNCC's trying to do a lot of organizing in four different types of things," he noted. While they had relied on youth in the past, now "we're trying to expand the base, to three different classes of black people": black workers, black soldiers, and black student unions. Repression by all levels of law enforcement personnel had forced unity among "all the black power leaders, [who are] now going to base of organizations to get [informants] off the street."[48] Somewhere along the way, SNCC had stopped supporting organizers who could bring together local people, build leadership, and create new organizations by and for the people, like the MFDP. What was left were organizers without a constituency, lacking basic civic relationships with a wide enough range of community people to build an organization. As a result, few of their ideas moved to action.

Why Most People Don't Think About Organizing

Most journalists, academics, and politicians missed the boat on grassroots organizing then, and miss it now, as a category of analysis. For them, it's a fairly dumb question to ask where political power is and how to get it: only the naive refuse to see the straightforward nature of what is routinely called Realpolitik, or what everyone from right to left calls "hardball." Power equals money, and with it, the power to control others through leveraging media or buying politicians.

The MFDP represented power of a different nature. It was a bottom-up political organization, supported by everyday people, and accountable to those same people. Most don't understand it, because we don't have an image or framework in our heads for quite literally seeing it, or understanding it. The MFDP delegates simply could not be bought by monied interests or manipulated by other established power representatives because they were accountable to everyday people.[49] But once people *could* see this kind of power, they were permanently changed. Margaret Herring realized in 1964, after attending the Democratic National Convention as secretary to nationally known columnist Drew Pearson, that "Mrs. Hamer moved me deeply. I decided that I wanted my life and my energy to be spent with her and people like her, rather than with my boss and my liberal friends in Washington. I saw in the people from Mississippi a different, more honorable and authentic power than what my boss and his friends in Washington, DC, practiced."[50] MFDP delegate Victoria Gray Adams possessed a clarity and insight about the Democratic Party that most political commentators still lack. As she recalled after seeing how the Democrats operated: "I said, 'We are here representing people in Mississippi who have everything on the line. And they're looking to us to bring back something that's going to make a difference. Two seats at-large aren't going to make any difference. So I'm not going back to the people and lie. We came here with nothing, so let's go on back with nothing. Quite frankly, if what I've seen since we've been here is what it's like, I'm not sure I even want to be a part of it.'" The most powerful liberals in the Democratic Party were shocked. They called the MFDP representatives "naive," but in reality it was they who did not understand the kind of grassroots political power represented by the MFDP. As Milton Viorst recalled: "The liberals of the Democratic Party couldn't quite understand why this magnificent compromise, which they felt achieved so many of the ends of the MFDP, was looked upon with such contempt."[51] But the MFDP didn't want to integrate into a system that wasn't small-d democratic. As Fannie Lou Hamer said to women organizing for welfare rights in Cleveland in 1965: "If we can get people to organize ourselves together and work together as human beings for dignity. I'm not going to say equal rights because somehow I feel I don't want it. I'm working for something better than just equal rights because if we requested equal rights, what would we be, to be equal with some of the people that's in town now. To get equal rights that means that the power structure that *we have is doing same thing to other people that they are doing to us.*"[52]

As Dona Richards Moses (Marimba Ani) said in 1965, "the importance of [the] [M]FDP is that [it] creates [a] context in which people have control of their representatives once they get into office. If we don't create this context, will have same thing as in North once we get Negroes in office."[53] In the absence of such an alternative, the buy-a-politician model dominated.

Where to Go from Here

Where do we go from here? What can we learn from this Mississippi experience? First, we must find an agreed-upon usage—"organizing" or "grassroots organizing"—and use it as a category of political analysis to assess the grassroots strength (for the people, by the people) of a given political campaign, particularly compared to its organized-money strength. It is important for historians as well as other political analysts to figure out where the people-power is in a given political movement, and ask organizers: What activities are allowing you to recruit, educate recruits, build political power, maintain recruits/grow, and, most important, use the power you have? Will you try to integrate into the major parties, or create a third party? Which changes are you going to try to force at the state and national levels that really positively impact your people's lives, and respond to their deepest needs?

Today, as in the 1960s, pundits and journalists during each election cycle focus on the large percentage of the population who do not vote. They routinely use words like "apathetic" and "uninformed" to explain why so many adults choose not to cast a ballot. The MFDP experience reveals this understanding to be totally hollow and inaccurate. Black Mississippians, who were constantly called "apathetic," in reality simply could not find a way to vote. Once the COFO machinery was set up, 83,000 voted in the fall of 1963. As Bob Moses recalled, "what the people were saying and somehow believing in their own minds was that they were not qualified. So we had to come to grips with this notion. Who can legitimize people? How do a people get legitimate?" The Freedom vote of 1964 "was an effort to reach for legitimacy, and to overcome the argument in the press that what basically was the problem was that people were apathetic."[54]

Legitimate questions have been raised about what the MFDP decided to do with its power after 1964. Indeed, those questions had been raised inside the movement since its earliest days: Should the focus be on economics or politics? A third party or integration into the Democratic Party?[55] SNCC's organizing in other areas, particularly in Georgia and Alabama, but also in Arkansas, Virginia, Maryland, and South Carolina, was never able to leverage enough power to shatter apartheid in the Democratic Party. Alabama's organizing effort would focus in fact on creating a third party to challenge the Democrats. But given the 2008 election cycle, one must note that it was the 1964 MFDP challenge that forced the eventual changes that came with the 1972 "McGovern Rules," opening the Democratic Party and thus institutional political power to African Americans and indeed all people of color, and to women in numbers proportional to their state population. It is not yet clear whether this was just an aesthetic change or one that will find more deep and sustaining roots in a fundamental alteration of power relations in the nation.

The MFDP struggle for grassroots power inspires at least as much as it sobers. Without necessarily setting out to do so from the start, those in the MFDP accomplished an enormous amount. They changed the rules of the national Democratic Party. They opened up the Mississippi Democratic Party to African Americans. They taught everyday people that they could act on their own behalf in a public democratic forum, and sometimes win.

Above all, they taught people what can be summarized in the lived wisdom of one of the Mississippi movement's most astute organizers, Victoria Gray Adams: "To young people today, I would say, 'Get to know everyday people. Make sure you acquire, to the degree possible, the wisdom and knowledge of these people. Everybody has something to say and something to offer. There should be an opportunity for that to happen. Make the information available, and all of the sources accessible. Then hear what the people have to say. If you do, you will find, to borrow a phrase from Miss Ella Baker, "Strong people don't need strong leaders."''[56] This may be the most important pathway to teach people how to generate power from the bottom-up.

NOTES

1. Fannie Lou Hamer, transcript of Cleveland [Ohio] Community Conference, 1965, Box 24, Students for a Democratic Society (SDS) Papers, State Historical Society of Wisconsin (SHSW), Madison (emphasis added).

2. Courtland Cox, Minutes for SNCC meeting April 25, 1965, [Alabama], Mary King Papers, SHSW.

3. John Dittmer, *Local People: The Struggle for Civil Rights in Mississippi* (Urbana: University of Illinois Press, 1994); Charles Payne, *I've Got the Light of Freedom: The Organizing Tradition and the Mississippi Freedom Struggle* (Berkeley: University California Press, 1995); J. Todd Moye, *Let the People Decide: Black Freedom and White Resistance Movements in Sunflower County Mississippi, 1945–1986* (Chapel Hill: University North Carolina Press, 2004); Emilye Crosby, *A Little Taste of Freedom: The Black Freedom Struggle in Claiborne County, Mississippi* (Chapel Hill: University of North Carolina Press, 2005); Wesley Hogan, *Many Minds, One Heart: SNCC and the Dream for a New America* (Chapel Hill: University North Carolina Press, 2007); Hasan Jeffries, *Bloody Lowndes: Civil Rights and Black Power in Alabama's Black Belt* (New York: New York University Press, 2009); Peniel Joseph, "The Black Power Movement: A State of the Field," *Journal of American History* 96, no. 3 (December 2009): 751–776. Glenn Eskew looks at the impact of local movements, but not through the lens of organizing. See Glenn Eskew, *But for Birmingham: The Local and National Movements in the Civil Rights Struggle* (Chapel Hill: University North Carolina Press, 1997). For a recent collection, see Emilye Crosby, ed., *Civil Rights History from the Ground Up: Local Struggles, A National Movement* (Athens: University of Georgia Press, 2011).

4. Thomas Sugrue, *Sweet Land of Liberty: The Forgotten Struggle for Civil Rights in the North* (New York: Random House, 2008).

5. Marshall Ganz, "Organizing America: Obama 2008," March 28, 2007, paper in author's possession.

6. This coverage peaked in early September 2008 when, after the Republican National Convention, both Sarah Palin and Rudy Guiliani mocked Obama's prior work as a community organizer. For an exception to this superficial coverage, see Bill Moyers's interview with James Thindwa, *The Journal with Bill Moyers*, PBS, airdate March 27, 2009, http://www.pbs.org/moyers/journal/03272009/profile2.html. For examples of superficial coverage, see Teddy Davis and Imtiyaz Delawala, "Palin to Zing Obama's 'Community Organizer' Days," ABC News, September 3, 2008; and Byron York, "What Did Obama Really Do as a Community Organizer?" *National Review Online*, reprinted on CBS.com, September 3, 2008, http://www.cbsnews.com/stories/2008/09/08/opinion/main4426965.shtml?tag=contentMain;contentBody.

7. For work that examines SNCC organizing in other states, see Jeffries, *Bloody Lowndes*; and Hogan, *Many Minds, One Heart*, chapter 3. The SNCC papers on microfilm remain an essential source for SNCC's organizing in Arkansas, Virginia, North Carolina, South Carolina, Georgia, and Alabama. See also SNCC volunteer Marshall Ganz's book, *Why David Sometimes Wins: Leadership, Organization and Strategy in the California Farm Worker Movement* (New York: Oxford University Press, 2009).

8. Wiley Branton, interview by James Mosby Jr., January 16, 1969, and October 20, 1969, Civil Rights Documentation Project, Moorland-Spingarn Research Center, Howard University, Washington, D.C. Dittmer, *Local People*, 424–425, explores the reasons behind the character of the Mississippi movement. In addition to the local people, the SNCC/CORE full-time organizers, and the violent repression, they stumbled upon the MFDP statewide model. It did not happen elsewhere. In the thin documentation we have on this question, it is unclear whether this is Moses's idea (as almost everyone in the movement thinks), or whether it is an organic development out of the Aaron Henry campaign (Moses's theory).

9. This seemed to take far too long at the time for participants who suffered beatings, economic reprisals, and the murder of their organizers, but appears astonishing to those familiar with the long struggle for equality over the course of U.S. history. It also, of course, depends on one's definition of success. For example, the Lowndes County Freedom Organization did not win national elections or even sustain itself beyond a few election cycles. Yet it fundamentally altered the rhythms of Alabama politics and provided an essential training ground for two generations of people in "freedom politics." See Jeffries, *Bloody Lowndes*, 249–252. I would like to thank Ross Brand for his excellent questions that provide important food for thought for all political historians: What measures the success of organized people? Is it meeting the goals that are determined at the initial mobilization of people, or some other measure? More specifically, if you argue that the MFDP was successful, how would you define that success (and the success of organizations in general)? Ross Brand, e-mail to author, February 25, 2010.

10. Charlie Cobb, "From the Mississippi Freedom Democratic Party to Barack Obama," lecture, February 2009, 5, paper in author's possession. The "McGovern Rules" ensured that as of the 1972 presidential election cycle, the national Democratic Party would only accept state delegations if those delegations reflected the racial and gender distribution of the Democratic Party in the state itself. For example, if Mississippi Democrats were half female, then the delegation had to be half female. If Alabama's Democrats were 60 percent African American, at least 60 percent of the Alabama delegates had to be black. For more on this change, see William Cavala, "Changing the Rules Changes the Game: Party Reform and the 1972 California Delegation to the Democratic National Convention," *American Political Science Review* 68, no. 1 (1974): 27–42; James Lengle and Byron Shafer, "Primary Rules, Political Power, and Social Change," *American Political Science Review* 70, no. 1 (March 1976): 25–40; and Thomas H. Hammond, "Another Look at the Role of 'Rules' in the 1972 Democratic Presidential Primaries," *Political Research Quarterly* 33, no. 1 (1980): 50–72.

11. There are, of course, other examples of essential democratic experiments that are not incorporated into the popular culture and schoolroom history class: the abolitionists, the Populist movement of the 1870s and 1880s, and the labor movement of the 1930s leap to mind, as well as even less well known examples like the Whiskey Rebellion and the Detroit Revolutionary Workers Movement. See Lawrence Goodwyn, *The Populist Moment: A Short History of the Agrarian Revolution* (New York: Oxford University Press, 1978); Terry Bouton, *Taming Democracy: "The People," the Founders, and the Troubled Ending of the American Revolution* (New York: Oxford University Press, 2007); Dan Georgakas and Marvin Surkin, *Detroit I Do Mind Dying: A Study in Urban Revolution* (Boston: Beacon Press, 1999); and Marina Sitrin, ed., *Horizontalism: Voices of Popular Power in Argentina* (Fayetteville: University of Arkansas Press, 2006).

12. Muriel Tillinghast, "Depending on Ourselves," in *Hands on the Freedom Plow: Personal Accounts by Women in SNCC*, ed. Faith S. Holsaert, Martha Prescod Norman Noonan, Judy Richardson, Betty Garman Robinson, Jean Smith Young, and Dorothy M. Zellner (Urbana: University of Illinois Press, 2010), 250–256.

13. Dittmer, *Local People*, 128. See also Payne, *I've Got the Light of Freedom*; Ganz, *Why David Sometimes Wins*; and Robert Moses and Charles E. Cobb Jr., *Radical Equations: Math Literacy and Civil Rights* (Boston: Beacon Press, 2001).

14. Dittmer, *Local People*, chapters 6–9; Faith S. Holsaert, Martha Prescod Norman Noonan, Judy Richardson, Betty Garman Robinson, Jean Smith Young, and Dorothy M. Zellner, "Introduction," in Holsaert et al., *Hands on the Freedom Plow*, 1–6.

15. Frank Smith, "Position Paper #1," [November 1964], Walter Tillow Papers, SHSW. Bob Moses noted in his testimony before the U.S. Senate Judiciary Committee in 2007 that SNCC was indeed publicly asked this question by Federal District Judge

Clayton: "Why are you taking illiterates down to register to vote?" Robert Moses, "Constitutional People," September 4, 2007, testimony before the U.S. Senate Judiciary Committee, http://judiciary.senate.gov/hearings/testimony.cfm?renderforprint =1&id=2885&wit_id=6635.

16. Joyce Ladner, "Standing Up for Our Beliefs," in Holsaert et al., *Hands on the Freedom Plow*, 217–222; Dittmer, *Local People*, chapters 1–4; Payne, *I've Got the Light of Freedom*, chapters 1–3, 7; J. Todd Moye, *Let the People Decide*, chapters 2–3; Crosby, *Taste of Freedom*, chapters 1–4.

17. Cobb, "From the Mississippi Freedom Democratic Party to Barack Obama"; see also Charlie Cobb, *On the Road to Freedom: A Guided Tour of the Civil Rights Trail* (Chapel Hill, N.C.: Algonquin Books, 2008), 262–263. Fannie Lou Hamer explained how important working with the SNCC youth was for her: it was "the first time I ever been treated like a human being, whether the kids was white or black. This is what's been there all the time and we had a chance to get it off our chests and nobody else had ever give us that chance. That's why today, that b/c my life I can never forsake those kids that . . . every hope in the state of Mississippi." Fannie Lou Hamer, interview by Anne Romaine and Howard Romaine, 1966, transcript, Anne Romaine Papers, SHSW.

18. Victoria Gray Adams, "They Didn't Know the Power of Women," in Holsaert et al., *Hands on the Freedom Plow*, 230–239; Dittmer, *Local People*, 99–103; Payne, *I've Got the Light*, 106, 111–115; Mendy Samstein, interview by Anne Romaine, transcript, Anne Romaine Papers, SHSW.

19. For more on organizing, see Mary Beth Rogers, *Cold Anger: A Story of Faith and Power Politics* (Denton: University of North Texas Press, 1990).

20. Bob Moses, interview by Joseph Sinsheimer, John Hope Franklin Research Center, Duke University Library, Durham, N.C.; Lawrence Guyot, interview by Anne Romaine and Howard Romaine, 1966, transcript, Anne Romaine Papers, SHSW; Jean Smith Young, "Do Whatever You Are Big Enough to Do," in Holsaert et al., *Hands on the Freedom Plow*, 240–249.

21. Tillinghast, "Depending on Ourselves."

22. Charles McLaurin, "On Organizing," frame 53, reel 40, SNCC Papers, microfilm. For recent work on organizing in the United States, see SNCC worker Mike Miller's *Community Organizer's Tale: People and Power in San Francisco* (Berkeley, Calif.: Heydey Books, 2009). See also Jim Rooney, *Organizing the South Bronx* (Albany: State University of New York Press, 1995); Mark Warren, *Dry Bones Rattling: Community Building to Revitalize American Democracy* (Princeton, N.J.: Princeton University Press, 2001); Michael Gacan, *Going Public: The Inside Story of Disrupting Politics as Usual* (Boston: Beacon Press, 2002); and Quilen Blackwell, *Holding Corporate America's Feet to the Fire: The Industrial Areas Foundation's Collision Course with Kodak* (Saarbrucken, Germany: Lambert Academic Publishing, 2010).

23. Different movement people framed this understanding in various ways. Not everyone understood the movement as a pure push for political power. To see the debates among the staff concerning the purpose of the movement, see especially reels 11 and 14 of the SNCC microfilm.

24. Joseph Sinsheimer, "The Freedom Vote of 1963: New Strategies of Racial Protest in Mississippi," *Journal of Southern History* 55 (May 1989): 220–221.

25. Ibid., 219; Dittmer, *Local People*, 200–201.

26. Mendy Samstein, interview by Anne Romaine, [1966?], Highlander Center, transcript, Mendy Samstein Papers, SHSW.

27. Moses interview; Samstein interview; "Brief Submitted by the MFDP for the Consideration of the Credentials Subcommittee of the DNC, the DNC Committee, Credentials Cmte of the DNC, prepared by Joseph Rauh, Eleanor K. Homes, H. Miles Jaffe," Box 86, Joseph Rauh Papers, Manuscripts Division, Library of Congress, Washington, D.C. Samstein thought that it was in fact the concrete activity of very active and successful building precinct organizations for the MFDP that led to James Chaney and Michael Schwerner being targeted and murdered by whites in Neshoba County. When these precincts started holding workshops, some in the movement believed that was the tipping point pushing whites to react with murder.

28. Hogan, *Many Minds*, 192.

29. Cobb, "From the MFDP to Barack Obama."

30. "Compromise" is put into quotations for a specific reason. As SNCC volunteer and later lawyer Lisa Todd Anderson noted, "compromise to me means a mutual agreement in which both sides give up something and go away unhappy after an offer and counter offer or a proposal and counter proposal which are the subjects of negotiations. The Johnson-Reuther final terms were dictated, take it or leave it." The decision was reached without ever consulting the MFDP delegation. Such a situation cannot accurately be deemed a compromise, though in the scholarly and primary source literature, it has been. Lisa Todd Anderson, e-mail to author, April 30, 2010.

31. It wasn't just their constituents who wanted the MFDP to reject the "compromise" at the time. As Aaron Henry noted, "Of the 1067 messages, letters telegraphs received by the MFDP in Atlantic City, 1011 support the MFDP in rejecting the Compromise worked out by the National leadership of the National Democracy [*sic*] party while 56 thought the MFDP should have accepted the compromise." Aaron Henry, "Position Paper," August 29, 1964, Box 86, Joseph Rauh Papers. See Dittmer, *Local People*, 422–423, on the contested nature of the 1968 delegation; Cobb, "From MFDP to Barack Obama."

32. Tillinghast, "Depending On Ourselves," 253.

33. Emmie Schrader Adams, "An Interracial Alliance of the Poor: An Illusive Populist Fantasy"? in Holsaert et al., *Hands on the Freedom Plow*, 418.

34. Gwendolyn Zohorah Simmons, "From Little Memphis Girl to Mississippi Amazon," in Holsaert et al., *Hands on the Freedom Plow*, 12.

35. "SNCC Backs Boycott," *Student Voice*, January 20, 1964; Ivanhoe Donaldson, interview by Anne Romaine, March 23, 1967, transcript, Anne Romaine Papers, SHSW. A flyer for a Freedom School in Canton read: "THEY SAY THAT *FREEDOM IS A CONSTANT STRUGGLE*, A CONSTANT *TRYING*, A CONSTANT *LEARNING*. No one should be ashamed to admit that he doesn't know. Anyone should be ashamed if he doesn't try to find out. The Canton Community Center is a place where we find out together how to *read* and *write* and *express* our *feelings* and make them *felt understand* the world we live in build a *more beautiful world*. FREEDOM SCHOOL BEGINS TUES NIGHT, SEPT. 29. FREEDOM SCHOOL is for *adults and young people* who would like to build up their reading and writing skills. FREEDOM SCHOOL is for *anybody* who wants to learn about such subjects as Negro History. FREEDOM SCHOOL is for *everybody* who wants a FREEDOM that will grow and last." See Box 1, Jo Ann Ooiman Robinson Papers, SHSW.

36. Sandy Leigh, interview by Anne Romaine, November 8, [1966?], MFDP Office, Washington, D.C., transcript, Anne Romaine Papers, SHSW. See also Adams, "They Didn't Know the Power of Women," 230–239. Akinyele Umoja was the first to point this dynamic out in "1964: The Beginning of the End of Nonviolence in the Mississippi Freedom Movement," *Radical History Review* 85 (2003): 201–226.

37. Simmons, "From Little Memphis Girl to Mississippi Amazon," 9–32. Michael Thelwell's excellent piece on organizing and self-defense is helpful here. See Zohorah Thelwell, "The Organizer," in *Duties, Pleasures, and Conflicts* (Amherst: University of Massachusetts Press, 1987).

38. Tillinghast, "Depending on Ourselves"; Dittmer, *Local People*, 334–335; Hogan, *Many Minds*, 168, 272, 353; Jeffries, *Bloody Lowndes*, chapter 4.

39. Bernice Johnson Reagon, "The Lined Hymn as a Song of Freedom," *Black Music Research Bulletin* 12, no. 1 (Spring 1990): 4–7; Bernice Johnson Reagan "Nobody Knows the Trouble I See," *Journal of American History* 78, no. 1 (June 1991): 111–119; Jean Smith Young, "Do Whatever You Are Big Enough to Do," 240–249; and Hogan, *Many Minds*, 40, 259–260, 307–308.

40. Denise Nicholas, "A Great Romantic Notion"" in Holsaert et al., *Hands on the Freedom Plow*, 257–265.

41. Maria Varela to Mrs. Deborah Cole, n.d. [1965?], 1–5, Maria Varela Papers, SHSW.

42. Charles Cobb and Charles McLaurin, "RE: Preliminary Survey on the condition of Negro farmers in Ruleville," November 19, 1962, frames 424–426, reel 38, SNCC Papers, microfilm. See Payne, *I've Got the Light*, chapter 5; Moye, *Let the People Decide*, chapter 4.

43. Elaine DeLott Baker, "The Freedom Struggle Was the Flame," in Holsaert et al., *Hands on the Freedom Plow*, 409–416. See also Constance Curry et al., *Deep in Our Hearts: Nine White Women in the Freedom Movement* (Athens: University of Georgia Press, 2000).

44. Wendt, *Spirit and the Shotgun*, 68, 130, 145.

45. Ibid., 106; Payne, *I've Got the Light of Freedom*; Hogan, *Many Minds*, 225, 376, n.17. Wendt's budget-source analysis is crucial, and needs to be juxtaposed with Akinyele Umoja's contention that the movement people were committed to nonviolence to keep the federal government and liberal allies on board.

46. Dittmer, *Local People*, chapters 16, 18; Crosby, *Taste of Freedom*, chapters 13, 14, 16.

47. Peter Countryman, Tape 8, SDS Tapes 517A, Side 1, SHSW. Peter Countryman, addressing the SDS convention in December 1962, explained pretty clearly how difficult it was to explain what people like Charles Sherrod and Bob Moses were doing as organizers. "In the North," he said, "we really haven't been able to communicate to ourselves or to our people this kind of a vision that Moses and Sherrod have of justice and democracy as a whole, not just integration. We've drawn in people through tutorial programs etc. w/very little political sophistication, don't' see relation of technical work to basic problems of alienation, and economic and political institutions which reinforce this alienation-student social work rather than student social change." He urged SDS to "go into that community, and talk the language of the people and be sensitive to their problems, and not be compromised by outside people, and to be limited by these people's mandate, to have faith in these people, to be lead by them.

48. Phil Hutchins, interview by Kay Lindsay on KPFA, "SDS and SNCC Currents and Cross Currents," March 7, 1969, transcript and tape available in Freedom Archives, 522 Valencia St., San Francisco.

49. Bob Moses later noted that even the most contentious of the decisions, to bring in 800–1,000 mostly northern college students, was done in response to local people. Moses brought his support to this because Louis Allen was killed, and no one was held accountable. Moses (correctly in hindsight) believed that white kids from middle-class northern homes coming into the state and being terrorized, beaten, and killed would not be ignored by the federal government. See Robert Moses, interview by Joseph Sinsheimer, November 19, 1983, Cambridge, Mass., transcript, Duke University Special Collections, Durham, N.C.; Samstein interview.

50. Margaret Herring, "A Simple Question," in Holsaert et al., *Hands on the Freedom Plow*, 399–402. Compare this understanding to the "moral" one set out by Rauh: "And so, ladies and gentlemen, the case comes down to some pretty fundamental things. Will the DP stand for the oppressors or for the oppressed? . . . The DP cannot fight the white backlash by surrendering to it. The seating of the Freedom delegation

is legally and equitably right. . . . The DP has won over the years when it stood fast for principle. It cannot win this time by hauling down the flag [of principle]. . . . Your choice comes down to whether you vote for the power structure of Mississippi that is responsible for the death of those three boys, or whether you vote for the people for whom those three boys gave their lives."

51. Milton Viorst, remarks, Jackson, Miss. [1979], Folder 2, "Mississippi Freedom Summer Revisited," SHSW. Harry McPherson's autobiography is a perfect example of the mainstream Democrats' befuddlement. See Harry McPherson, *A Political Education* (Boston: Little, Brown, 1975).

52. Fannie Lou Hamer, transcript of Cleveland Community Conference, 1965, Box 24, SDS Papers, SHSW.

53. Dona [Moses], "Alabama Staff Workshop, April 21–23, 1965," notes, Mary King Papers, SHSW.

54. Moses interview. Moses states that reporters interviewing him were "always reaching for that word ['apathy']." He remembers "coming to the point of rejecting that concept completely on the grounds that what was being done was not so much defining an objective state of the people, a condition of the people, but what was being done was defining a way of acting, a way of action, because if you said that the basic problem was the apathy of the people you were also channeling your actions in a certain way. In terms of what you would focus on to do about the apathy of the people. If you rejected that completely, if you didn't even for a second let it cross your mind that the problem was apathy on the part of black people but lay elsewhere, then you would focus your attention elsewhere."

55. See Reels 39 and 40 from SNCC Papers, microfilm, for debates in 1962–1964 over the strategic value of voter registration in Mississippi. John Dittmer raised a series of important questions at the end of his monumental book on the Mississippi movement: "Could different strategies have produced more substantial and permanent gains for the majority of Mississippi blacks? Was the decision to focus on voter registration the correct one? Should fundamental economic questions have been raised earlier and more forcefully? Did MFDP err in pursuing an independent course after the 1964 Atlantic City convention? Was the move to disband COFO a mistake?" See Dittmer, *Local People*, 428–429. As Charlie Cobb discusses: "maids, sharecroppers, day workers, cooks, janitors, farmers, factory workers, housewives, students, as I said, *ordinary* people who were usually spoken for or of—*these* voices began to be heard, or at least could no longer be ignored in the mid 20th century. And, in raising their voices, changed a way of life." "Charlie Cobb Discusses the Freedom Movement, February 2009," www.crmvet.org/disc/0902moad.htm.

56. Adams, "They Didn't Know the Power of Women," 239.

Collision and Collusion

Local Activism, Local Agency, and Flexible Alliances

Françoise N. Hamlin

As a scholar and teacher of the black freedom struggle in the United States, I am often asked why there is not another civil rights movement. Why did direct action and activism work so well then, and where is it now? I teach primarily in the Northeast to those with little experience of the South and its unique social quirks and traits, and to those less experienced in the national racial realities. Therefore explaining the complexity of these questions (and answers) and prodding students to hone their critical thinking skills have become almost as important as uncovering the new, valuable local stories of courage and mass movement.

Admittedly, the questions about activism and agency require book-length considerations, but in a short essay I can point to specific moments when local African American activism (the kind of activism that occurs within, among, and between communities and groups in a county or a region) worked best, or at least to moments when the effects proved more enduring. Through these examples, it is easier to explain how and why strategies worked in the past. The case study revolves around Clarksdale, Mississippi—a Delta city in Coahoma County approximately eighty miles south of Memphis on Highway 61. These moments open up further discussion about long-term strategies for activism, and how the tensions in the mass movement years were as troublesome then for activists as they are between activists now.[1]

Rather than a "mass movement," one might accurately call the high point of civil rights protests "a mass of movements"—a pluralized concept of multiple spheres of activity occurring on multiple scales in multiple spaces. This more precise terminology expands definitions of the mass of movements to move beyond the sole leadership of Rev. Martin Luther King Jr., the pure pursuit of civil rights, or the dominance of one organization over another in particular areas. It allows for a wider understanding of the role and importance of local movements that existed sometimes in isolation, and sometimes in collusion with larger demonstrations and protests across the region, nation, and globe. In doing so, we are able to embrace local school desegregation and economic justice campaigns more easily into our definitions of mass black activism during this period as they become layers of movement activity that interface with the civil rights marches, petitions, sit-ins, freedom rides, and more public or better documented protest fronts. This construction situates local movements within the national spectrum. It also permits local activists to retain ownership of the struggles and outcomes they endured, and the victories won. What becomes most evident under this plurality of activities is that negotiations and collisions occurred daily in pursuit of larger shared goals of black freedom, citizenship, and justice, but did so in a way that coalesced these movements together, albeit haphazardly. This conceptualization shatters prevailing public beliefs that people worked within the confines of one organization or another, and it better explains activism at its core.

My study of this nexus of movements in Clarksdale spans five decades, from 1951 to 1999.[2] During those years there are plenty of examples of what I call "flexible alliances," where seemingly opposed individuals and/or groups united, sometimes for short periods, for a specific purpose or goal. Here I will use the terms "flexible loyalties" and "flexible collaborations" interchangeably, both of which refer to building coalitions of various sorts, with varying life expectancies, for multiple reasons at the grassroots level. I also focus concretely on local people and leaders and their relationship to the national New York–based offices of the National Association for the Advancement of Colored People (NAACP). There are many more examples available, however, as Clarksdale's activists worked with and through many organizations, including the "big four" (the NAACP, the Student Nonviolent Coordinating Committee [SNCC], the Southern Christian Leadership Conference [SCLC], and the Congress of Racial Equality [CORE]), and the concept of flexible alliance is applicable to a host of other communities and circumstances beyond the Delta and African Americans. In this way, imagine a dimensional picture of movement itself, the fluidity of the movements, of groups and individuals forming coalitions or alliances then separating in different formations at different times.

A local study is an ideal way to view this strategy at work. Local black civil rights groups worked to improve their members' life choices in the everyday. They lived in the community, and, through their work, sought their own improved opportunities too. Many activists passed through Clarksdale with their respective affiliations, each with their own story. Organizations rose and fell in visibility and levels of activity in locales, and memberships shifted depending on the ebb and flow of strengths and weaknesses between coalitions. Flexible loyalties to and collaborations among organizations helped local people adapt to their current crises and pool resources as quickly as possible. Their allegiance to certain national organizations remained fluid, and they could move between groups as circumstances demanded. Whether they organized under other names to disguise group identification from white supremacist targeting or maintained memberships in multiple organizations, activists found ways to safely strategize, harnessing resources from several competing groups at the same time, thus rising above the fray to fulfill their specific needs. Leaders had to adapt to constituents' needs and procure resources at the grassroots as they negotiated their loyalties and alliances among larger organizations. Flexibility helped the people survive. This concept of flexibility provides a bridge between protest movements on the margins and social/political movements more firmly situated as mainstream, allowing for easier passage between the two and a commingling of ideas, supporters, and resources.[3]

In this way, local people exercised a political consciousness that enabled them to utilize multiple and different ways to achieve their goals more quickly. Like mainstream politicians—whose loyalty bends with the assailing winds, in the direction of the prized electorate—black people without access to formal political power formed effective coalitions during the years of mass movements. The evolution of Mississippi's mass of movements in the 1950s and early 1960s clearly demonstrates the effectiveness of adopting flexible alliances and loyalties. My description differs from formal electoral political maneuverings in that those outside of the electoral system have more freedom of choice in their collaborations. What is achieved in the mass movements is due, in part, to flexibility. Formal systems have too many restrictions upon them and therefore reduce politicians' accessibility to a myriad of alternative resources. This is, of course, a double-edged sword, as flexible loyalty, although a bridge to formal politics, keeps most actors off the "official" political stage and therefore farther from the political capital available through electoral visibility.[4]

As a strategy, activists who could maintain flexible alliances proved effective in Mississippi. A "closed society" for most outsiders, due to the hostile environment for change created by the staunch enforcement of Jim Crow and Old South traditions, by diversifying the groups, people, and resources on the ground, many civil rights activists dispersed multiple targets for detractors to shoot at, rather than concentrating operations from one source.[5] They did not put their eggs, oftentimes their lives, in one basket. Each organization on its own had its own strengths and weaknesses depending on its structure, leadership, and focus, so cherry-picking allowed activists to tap the strength of each and minimize the weaknesses that made them vulnerable.

What this long-term work on Clarksdale made crystal clear is that alliances were necessary and but always shaky. The "kumbayah" image of the civil rights movement—with people arm-in-arm singing freedom songs constantly in the face of clubs and attack dogs—was exactly that, an image. Although I place enormous value on the use of song and fellowship as tools to empower and embolden activists before and after (and sometimes during) campaigns, enemies of the changes and the media have distorted and misused these images to represent activism fueled by emotion, youthfulness, and spontaneity rather than acknowledging the complex planning, training, and strategizing that took place. Behind-the-scenes collisions over authority, strategy, leadership, and resources occurred daily. I half-joke to students that it is a miracle that anything was achieved given the extent of the shifting strife between individuals and groups. Dissension is normal within movements. It is more useful, then, to learn the lessons of collaboration and flexibility from those who survived, making sure to understand the stakes and not to repeat the mistakes.

I am inspired here by the work of Robin Kelley and his essay on infrapolitics among the black working classes in the first half of the twentieth century when they labored under the thumb of Jim Crow.[6] Kelley challenged scholars to look outside the mainstream political box for a more widespread black political consciousness—not one necessarily able or willing to mount a visible or vocal protest, particularly in the era of state-sanctioned lynching for lesser "infractions." Rather, Kelley encouraged us to look beneath the register of organization and electoral politics for activities surreptitiously conducted out of the limelight, sometimes in concert with others, often alone, to elicit a result that might produce some modicum of satisfaction for even the slightest protest. These acts suggest a political consciousness beyond traditional definitions in the realm of "high politics," he argued. Indeed, African Americans, even during their enslavement, have long employed infrapolitics in their quotidian existences, finding spaces, however small and insignificant to others, to act out defiance and claim their humanity. Here I build on Kelley's idea of broader demonstrations of political consciousness later on the temporal continuum of the black freedom struggle in a different political context, where protest was more visible and more abundant, yet just as dangerous for activists. In this way, the analysis allows for a clearer understanding of the strengths of black activism despite the odds, and in spite of how we might assess the successes.

Using flexible loyalties as a means for understanding black activism and agency helps historians highlight a broader political consciousness among African Americans in particular. Starting with local activist and World War II veteran Amzie Moore's disillusionment with the NAACP that turned his attention to the work of SNCC, I move to a more in-depth look at another veteran, Aaron Henry, and his conscious juggling of institutional roles to maximize resources for people in the state at whatever cost. Moore's relationship to the national NAACP highlighted the group's unwillingness to be malleable during the mass of movements years, an inflexibility that subsequently minimized the national NAACP's dominance at Mississippi's grassroots.

The NAACP struggled to find footholds in Mississippi's "closed society" in the 1950s. It had its hands full in other arenas—funneling resources to the momentous legal battles in the Supreme Court and lower courts across the country and fending off attacks from conservatives happily throwing the mud of Red-baiting on all organizations they disliked. Their hope, regarding the NAACP, was to sap the organization's valuable resources as it fought to defend and preserve itself from charges of engaging in "un-American activities." As a result, the NAACP could boast only a few branches of any real standing in Mississippi, usually in the more populated areas and with a nervous, mostly anonymous membership.[7] Their strictly enforced hierarchical system exacerbated the limitations accompanying the branches' meager numbers. Attempting to control their image, the national office kept tight reins on their few field employees and monitored branches closely. In places with a more concentrated and larger black population, such as urban branches, the group's top-down orientation was more viable. In rural areas, however, where events could turn on a dime and communication to New York was more precarious, branches struggled much more with the organizational rigidity than did their urban counterparts.

In Clarksdale, Coahoma County's seat, the local branch organized formally in 1953 as a direct result of local protests over the rape of two black young women in 1951. Their white attacker walked free from all charges; indeed, it was more surprising that he had been indicted in the first place—and only after much pressure. As the dust settled, local black leaders recognized that in order to pull more weight in town to ensure justice, they needed the

NAACP and its resources. In that way, the branch evolved from the founders' explicit motivation of using the might and skills of the national organization to change the local situation. The branch in the 1950s settled into a leadership structure headed by pharmacist Aaron Henry.[8]

The slaying of Emmett Till in 1955 and a string of killings that year and those following sustained considerable amounts of fear in all but a few brave souls, thereby ensuring that the NAACP got very little accomplished in Mississippi during the 1950s. Citizens' Councils, established across the state in response to the 1954 decision in *Brown v. Board of Education*, immediately set to work to snuff out activism, drawing allies and members from most police departments, local judiciaries, and city or town council chambers statewide, later bolstered by resources and personnel from the Mississippi State Sovereignty Commission (created in 1957). Despite efforts by the state NAACP and the newly appointed national field secretary, Medgar Evers, to create branches and encourage communities to sue local school boards in the name of enforcing *Brown*, membership ebbed. The NAACP's membership fell to the point where even the national office considered reducing its resources to, and therefore its investment in, the state organization. In fact, historians have argued that the "national office of the NAACP considered Mississippi a lost cause," and it responded "by dropping Mississippi like a hot potato."[9]

The national office's lack of attention in many ways forced local NAACP leaders to develop homegrown, adaptable strategies and alliances—to be flexible—to accept or invite willing individuals or groups to assist. This did not mean that they abandoned the NAACP; indeed, that organization helped give local black leaders a platform in Mississippi from which to work. Dire circumstances left beleaguered state and local NAACP officers looking for alternative and additional strategies and assistance. One of those searching for a new approach was Amzie Moore. He had joined the NAACP while in the service with segregation snapping at his heels from his Delta home, around the United States, and all the way to Calcutta, India, Burma, and Japan. "Here I'm being shipped overseas, and I been segregated from this man whom I might have to save or he save my life. I didn't fail to tell it."[10] He continued his membership activities with gusto when he returned to Mississippi.

Nevertheless, his commitment and loyalty had been severely tested as he struggled to lead the Cleveland (Bolivar County, Mississippi) branch of the NAACP in the face of repercussions from the Citizens' Council. As early as December 1954 Moore complained to the national NAACP office that a Citizens' Council economic pressure campaign had targeted his newly opened service station, café, and beauty shop (run by wife, Ruth) located on Highway 61 in Cleveland due to his refusal to post "All Colored" or "Colored Only" signs as segregation laws demanded. Earlier, his rejection of Jim Crow signage had earned him a visit from two local policemen, who suggested that compliance might stave off violent retaliations. Moore's continued refusal prompted the Citizens' Council to pressure his white customers, and his local bank refused him a loan to cover the costs incurred from the resulting drop in business.[11] In spite of the cushioning Moore's relative wealth provided him, the extent of the intimidation and years of stress he suffered spurred him to appeal to the NAACP for help, financial and legal. To save his businesses, he petitioned several banks and organizations, including the NAACP, for loans—mostly to no avail. This lack of acknowledgment or assistance from the NAACP national office caused Moore to harbor bitterness toward the organization he had promoted in Mississippi, the one organization in which he had put all his trust and faith to deliver. He severely criticized the group's national bureaucracy that rendered them unable to react quickly in times of crises.

Allies better suited to meet Moore's needs emerged in 1957 when he contacted Bayard Rustin and Ella Baker in the New York–based organization In Friendship for clothing donations to the Delta. This fund-raising organization was created in New York, by Baker and others, as a clearinghouse for those donating resources to activists sustaining the Montgomery Bus Boycott of 1955 and 1956 in Alabama. Baker knew the Moores from earlier NAACP-sponsored visits to Mississippi.[12] In response to Moore's request, the American Friends Service Committee agreed to send a shipment of children's clothes.[13] That round of correspondence initiated a relationship that resulted in an exchange between Moore and Robert Moses in 1960. Ella Baker, by then adviser to the young SNCC, had asked Moses to recruit young people from the Deep South to attend SNCC's second conference, and had put him in touch with Moore, who subsequently attended the conference and made the case for SNCC's presence in Mississippi for voter registration.[14] If the NAACP could not help materially or be a viable presence in the state, local activists like Moore forged ties with other organizations willing to help.

Resentful of and frustrated by what he considered the NAACP's lack of response to his sacrifices for the cause, Amzie Moore believed meeting Bob Moses served as a turning point in his life as an activist. Speaking later to journalist Howell Raines about the NAACP, he said, "Nobody dared move a peg without some lawyer advisin' him," and because the base of operation resided in Jackson with Medgar Evers, the organization in Mississippi remained fettered, not functioning at its full potential.[15] To Moore, SNCC embodied the antithesis to the legalistic NAACP. SNCC was about "business, live or die, sink or swim, survive or perish. They were moving, and nobody seemed to worry about whether he was gonna live or die."[16] Moore is best remembered as a teacher and elder who taught younger activists in SNCC how to cultivate local leadership, activities, and campaigns in Mississippi. Ironically, he honed these skills and gathered his contacts in the NAACP, the organization that had set him on his political feet in the first place.[17]

Another opportunity for alliance and collaboration arose for besieged local and state NAACP leaders when the SCLC organized in 1957 as a new force in the region, testing anew the flexibility and malleability of organizational boundaries. The SCLC's leadership was eager to extend their influence and penetrate Mississippi's "closed society." Likewise, Aaron Henry and Medgar Evers, just elected to the SCLC board, were especially eager to engage with the ministers from Alabama, given black Alabamans' successful, against-all-odds boycott of segregationist busing in Montgomery. Writing directly to Martin Luther King Jr. in August 1957, Henry asked the SCLC to hold a meeting in Mississippi, "the state where it is perhaps needed most."[18] Evers, the new assistant secretary, however, received curt instructions from the NAACP's executive secretary Roy Wilkins to resign from the SCLC due to what Wilkins deemed a conflict of interest. Since Wilkins was his boss, Evers had little choice but to comply, but he made clear to Wilkins that he was "sincere in trying to do what I possibly could to bring first-class citizenship to our section of the country as hurriedly as possible."[19]

Evers tried hard to get national officers to understand the urgency of the situation in Mississippi and to persuade them to give him the latitude to organize creatively, letting the ends justify the means. Evers knew that only through collaboration could movements be successful in Mississippi. Despite his pleas to his bosses, he continued to do their work. The SCLC's opening southern campaign, the "Crusade for Citizenship," began on February 12, 1958, organized by Ella Baker, who had joined the SCLC staff to kick off this first program—organizing meetings throughout the South in 1958 in commemoration of Abraham Lincoln's birthday. By January Clarksdale had already claimed its spot on the itinerary, the only Mississippi city on the roster. With a program of education and action, the crusade sought to double the number of qualified black voters in the South.[20] Four days after King opened the campaign, however, Evers had managed to thwart efforts to establish an SCLC operation in Jackson. Evers wrote to the NAACP regional secretary, Ruby Hurley, "It will be our design through the NAACP and the Progressive Voters League, of which our leaders are in key positions, to control the present state of affairs."[21] Evers's life revolved around his work with the NAACP, but it was not always easy for him to agree on the tactical specifics. Interoffice correspondence reveals that he swallowed the bitter pill of hierarchical subordination, especially when orders and delays from the New York office kept him from reacting promptly to incidents on the ground.[22] Evers weathered accusations from Moore and other activists who expressed their disappointment with Evers's more conservative approaches to swift and crushing reprisals. He was caught between a rock and a hard place—the hierarchical national office that had little control over the nuance and textures of local branches but could clip Evers's wings as his employer, and the constant threat of white violence and reaction that required decisive response and leadership. Nevertheless, as a result of his labors, the Crusade for Citizenship had only a minor presence in Mississippi, and the SCLC was unable to establish major programming in the state.

Aaron Henry, on the other hand, accepted the SCLC's offer. He served as an SCLC representative for Mississippi, along with Evers's replacement, R. L. Drew. In 1968, over a decade later, Henry was still on the SCLC board and quipped that he was the only man in America to serve on the national boards of both the NAACP and the SCLC: "I have responsibilities of keeping each group honest to the other. . . . It's a great tribute in terms of the respect and the trust that I enjoy from both organizations and I work tremendously hard to try to put over the programs of both."[23] Henry remembered, "The SCLC program and philosophy advocated nonviolence and appealing to the moral conscience of the community to do right for the sake of doing right. They wanted to 'love the hell out of Mississippi.'"[24] Through his involvement, he sought to maximize access to the alternative organizing that SCLC offered, strategies based on Christian morality that might complement the NAACP's legalistic approaches and fortify communities for daring to register voters or file suits against segregationist school boards. These links, forged early, allowed the SCLC, through Henry, some access to operate in Mississippi.

For most of his activist career, Aaron Henry held the presidency in the local and state NAACP, yet adeptly manipulated the competition between civil rights organizations to pool resources in the state. As he himself claimed in a 1968 interview, "I've been very ecumenical in terms of total civil rights struggle because I identify across the board."[25] His loyalty to the SCLC allowed him to request King's presence during certain critical campaigns, knowing that the media would follow King into the Delta. To the chagrin of the national NAACP, Henry was pivotal in introducing the SCLC to Mississippi activists, and later increasing SNCC's presence on Mississippi's civil rights landscape. Regardless, he remained an NAACP man, noting, "I find really more projects in the NAACP because I feel comfortable with about identifying with them than I do any of the other groups. But this does not exclude my participation with any other group and I would say next to NAACP would be SCLC, because of long years of affinity with the national cadre of SCLC."[26] He was a self-appointed power broker between various groups in Mississippi.

Aaron Henry's ecumenical attitude rested on his acknowledgment that the national NAACP did not intend to invest all its attention and resources in Mississippi, given the organization's perception of better chances for success elsewhere. Very few Mississippians wanted Henry's unsalaried and dangerous position, and Henry himself understood his place in the NAACP as tantamount to being a sitting target for any trigger-happy segregationist. However, he drew a measure of strength from his volunteer status. He stated that his volunteerism "gives me a kind of freedom . . . to do what I want to do and can't nobody buy me cause ain't nobody hired me."[27] He also knew the state needed the NAACP. He worked closely, therefore, with his friend and colleague Evers (who, through Henry, probably had vicarious contact with many other organizations as well). In this way, Henry let Evers straddle the state and national offices, while he steered the state conference toward coalition building and resource sharing, approaches that, jointly, promised to increase the likelihood for success. The creation of the Coahoma County Council of Federated Organizations (CCCFO) is a case in point.

The forerunner to the Council of Federated Organizations (COFO), the CCCFO was established in early 1961. By this time, the national NAACP office, particularly the NAACP's director of branches, Gloster Current, fretted constantly about the number of groups in the area, all vying for membership and prominence. Aaron Henry wrote to Current: "just between me and you [it] is a paper organization which the NAACP controls but it offers an opportunity of expression for the Teachers without them having the fear of participating in an NAACP-only sponsored affair. Technically represented on the council is the president or chairman of all the organizations and Churches in the area which can aid cooperation in any project we desire."[28] Reassuring Current that the NAACP remained in control in Clarksdale, the CCCFO became an organizing screen for those unable to work under the auspices of the NAACP.[29] It was a way to compromise and work with each other under an umbrella for specific campaigns, without necessarily compromising their respective institutional loyalty.

The idea had percolated when Henry and Evers traveled to Louisiana in 1960 and visited a building that housed several Jewish organizations involved in social activism. Henry recognized, "Usually there was a casual overlapping of the membership of the organizations with the goal of equal rights as the common bond."[30] It was no different in black communities. The CCCFO therefore expanded to include all black leaders in the state. Indeed, the founding of these federations affirms wide recognition among Mississippi's grassroots activists of the necessity of coalitions and flexible alliances and loyalties. Individual attempts like Henry's to maximize the strengths of sometimes competing organizations, and indeed, the tensions within organizations themselves, prompted black activists to establish new organization structures like the statewide COFO to harness coalition building in the face of crippling opposition.

COFO (coordinating efforts of the "big four" civil rights organizations) came into being in the summer of 1961 in the same way as the CCCFO, to be a strategic alias to meet with Governor Barnett, who refused to negotiate with the NAACP. Although the meeting with Barnett proved fruitless, COFO now existed, albeit in name only at that point. Henry noted, "We were convinced that COFO would increase our effectiveness in civil rights work all over the state, and at last the federal government had its eyes on Mississippi."[31] Henry wrote a telegram to the White House on August 29, 1962, as COFO's president, introducing the organization as "a state wide civil rights leadership organization representing at least the forty-three percent of the Mississippi population that is Negro."[32] In January 1962 Bob Moses, Henry, and Evers met to expand COFO beyond the previous year's letterhead existence and to join forces for a broader attack. Henry reasoned, "The united efforts of the four major civil rights groups would mean greater efficiency and we would have the advantage of working with the head personnel of four main groups to develop new ideas and approaches based on the pool of experience and knowledge."[33]

The national office of the NAACP continued to worry about its influence in COFO as SNCC enthusiastically embraced the organization, playing the largest role from the beginning. The Mississippi state conference of the NAACP participated in COFO (as did many local branches), but the national office remained aloof. Evers's presence and support underscored his personal preference to ally with other groups despite the constant rebuffs from the national office. Henry, always with his eye on the end, stated, "one of the healthiest things about COFO was that petty political disagreements never stood in the way of our major objectives."[34] He reiterated how his volunteerism freed him from organizational tethers: "as a volunteer I've got as much rights to work for who I want as I want to when I want to. And certainly the man that has his freedom and I find that there are projects that they produce that I can work with, find a project that SCLC produces that I can work with—that CORE produces that I can work with—NAACP produces that I can work with."[35] COFO was on the ground, working and organizing under one banner. Some campaigns organized under COFO and others under member organizations (at times the sources of paperwork or sponsorship becomes unclear), but activists always held multiple memberships and wore different hats. This is part of the flexibility necessary for progress. Despite Henry's attempts to pacify and reassure Current and the national NAACP, activists in Mississippi, the majority of whom came from SNCC and CORE, carried the lion's share of COFO's direct action work statewide.

In Coahoma County, where the local NAACP had reigned supreme and had the most influence, national leaders funded and instigated the latest voter registration drive in 1962. Sensing the NAACP's sustained hesitation and the fear of losing control in the county, Henry approached Roy Wilkins, this time with resolve. He asked the national office for more legal assistance, stressing that without financial contributions, funds allotted for the program would only cover legal fees, fines, and bonds. To appease Wilkins, Henry pledged to clear all projects with the headquarters. In 1962 the Mississippi State NAACP had a growing membership. The Coahoma County Branch became the second largest in the state after Jackson, with 374 new members since January 1 (106 were Youth Council members).[36] The national office, pleased with the growth, knew it had little control of the state conference activity with Henry at the helm. Indeed, Henry dangled local loyalty and the organizing successes in front of Wilkins, urging him to be flexible, hinting that other organizations hovered to catch dropped memberships. Yet rather than throw support behind alliances that would strengthen the fight, the NAACP national office continued to fret over the increased presence of other groups in Mississippi and worried about CORE as a parallel group competing for members. Concerned about organizational turf, national NAACP leaders also worried over the powerful images from Birmingham, Alabama, as the NAACP ban continued there.[37] Given the growing support of the organization by local African Americans, and the other organizations prominently stepping onto the stage, could New York afford not to answer Henry's call?

By 1964 Myrlie Evers had laid her husband to rest, and massive resistance to change in the state reached new heights. Yet that war barely concealed simmering organizational tensions between leaders within and between the movements. For most local Mississippians and SNCC staff and Freedom Summer volunteers on the frontlines, this conflict mattered little as they bonded and bled together under COFO. The national NAACP office continued to tussle with state leaders, especially Henry and Charles Evers, who took over his slain brother's position. Charles Evers, as historian Emily Crosbye beautifully described, was no Medgar Evers, but a consummate politician who understood how to play his loyalties.[38] He actually did cross the bridge into electoral politics, becoming in 1969 the mayor of Fayette, and the first black mayor of an integrated town in Mississippi since Reconstruction.[39] In an increasingly hostile environment that more than ever favored flexible alliances and loyalties, national NAACP executives once again wanted Henry and Evers to ensure that SNCC and COFO would not undermine the NAACP's presence and efficacy in Mississippi. It was an uphill battle, however, as SNCC and other COFO workers poured into Coahoma County and the state with Henry's open arms. Four years later Henry recalled, "Well really my loyalties right now are closer to Mississippi than to the national office. And I think that this is where I have to be in order to help interpret the program."[40] His allegiance to the national office took a backseat to his fervent desire to harness the enthusiasm and organizational energy of SNCC in the heady and always dangerous days leading up to Freedom Summer.

Despite Henry's success in drawing the spotlight onto Clarksdale and the rest of the state and amassing considerable allies, contacts, and resources, clearly the NAACP director of branches, Gloster Current, never shared Henry's strategy of flexible group activism and membership. The tensions between Henry's agenda and the New York office's desire for political dominance over black activism always existed, flaring up at meetings or in correspondence. The irony, of course, is that these different groups ultimately shared the same goal and foe(s). All the same, by the end of July 1964, during Freedom Summer, the state NAACP was seriously considering withdrawing from COFO, the project's sponsor. Current even asked the national board for permission to research a way for the state conference to pull out diplomatically. The national office could not forsake its long-standing investments in state branches and staff, but abhorred the current situation and criticized Aaron Henry's views of organizational management on record.[41] Although most local and state NAACP members supported continued involvement in COFO, not everyone did, and the national office sought their support to win the vote to withdraw. Aaron Henry's branch colleague Vera Pigee, the secretary and Youth Council adviser, felt no love for COFO during or after Freedom Summer.[42] The beautician had worked since the mid-1950s (a dangerous time when most black Mississippians shied from open protest or membership) to build the Youth Councils in Clarksdale and across the state and felt protective over what she considered her territory. Although Pigee had supported the founding of COFO and welcomed SNCC staff and volunteers who helped with local projects and brought aid and resources from outside of the state, the hundreds of students who poured into Mississippi in 1964 were too much for her.

While SNCC's overall philosophy aimed to support local leadership who would ultimately direct projects, moments of cultural clashes and miscommunication occurred that merely angered Pigee. As the local coordinator and the one who made local arrangements (given Henry's persistent absence from Clarksdale while he attended to statewide duties), she wielded considerable influence. Her way of curtailing what she termed the "SNCC kid catch," which effectively (albeit unintentionally) decimated the NAACP Youth Councils, was at one point to call her friends who hosted volunteers to ask them to turn them out.[43] She said defiantly, "I didn't like their program, and I didn't have to put up with it."[44] Informal conversations with her daughter, Mary Jane, and Zoya Zeman (a Freedom Summer volunteer in Clarksdale from Nebraska) reveal that cultural differences and what Pigee may have deemed disrespectful behavior fueled her indignation, particularly toward those staying in her home. The mores of liberal northern college youthfulness would have rubbed against her more conservative southern "home-training," and with the demise of her beloved Youth Councils the sting of both realities precipitated a wholesale rejection of COFO during Freedom Summer. Nonetheless, her heavy-handedness made her few friends in SNCC, and she never received her earned praise for her contributions to the local and state movements in the many years prior to Freedom Summer.[45]

The national NAACP office faced tough choices as COFO workers in Mississippi held Aaron Henry in high regard. His open attitude and lack of concern for organizational purity or loyalty (unlike Pigee) won their trust. Student activist Ivanhoe Donaldson recalled, "Despite the general contempt in SNCC ranks for NAACP 'conservatives,' Aaron Henry enjoyed a personal respect like that accorded to Amzie Moore."[46] SNCC staff recognized his commitment and offered their services to effect change and help local people achieve their own freedom.[47] Henry's personal influence in managing the Mississippi movement through his state NAACP presidency and his leadership of COFO rendered his Fourth Street Drugstore in Clarksdale an "important SNCC way station in the Delta." The national NAACP knew that the organization risked losing its momentum in Mississippi altogether if Henry completely redirected his energies. It had already lost Amzie Moore's un-wavering dedication that way. In the end, the national NAACP ordered the state conference (and constituent local branches) to withdraw from COFO, waiting until the winter after the Freedom Summer project. From then on, activities in Mississippi continued, but on much smaller local scales and under the official jurisdiction of one group or another.

After Freedom Summer in 1964, COFO dissolved, in large part due to the NAACP's national office pressuring the state conference to withdraw. This marks a turning point in the chronology of the mass of movements in Mississippi—indeed the political story becomes a lot more complicated. The failure of the Mississippi Freedom Democratic Party (MFDP) to unseat the lily-white Mississippi delegation at the Democratic National Convention in Atlantic City, New Jersey, in August 1964 widened the number of cracks in SNCC and accelerated the end of COFO. Many black members became increasingly radicalized after President Johnson played his political hand and offered the MFDP only two at-large seats, handpicking their delegates. Henry, always a political moderate, wanted to accept the offer, reasoning that two seats were better than none, but most MFDP delegates present flatly refused in protest.[48] Henry's apparent willingness to settle for less than the desired and rightful demands did not win him many friends on Mississippi's radical left. More than simply the generational disconnect between younger and older activists was perhaps at work. We see here the moral downside of flexibility and some of the limitations inherent in Aaron Henry's leadership style, particularly his readiness at times to compromise radicalism and principle for smaller concrete gains.

Henry threw his support behind efforts to reorganize the dormant chapter of the Young Democrats of Mississippi in early 1965, led by moderate whites, particularly Hodding Carter III (editor of the *Greenville Delta-Democrat Times*). In the struggle between this interracial coalition and the MFDP to obtain the coveted charter, the national Young Democrats sided with the moderates, summoning yet another blow to the MFDP. Strengthened by this victory, the moderate coalition effectively controlled the Loyal Democrats of Mississippi, often known as the Loyalists, in the challenge for seating at the 1968 convention. Indeed, historian Charles Payne called the Loyalists "an organizational clone" of the Young Democrats, and stated that the participation of black leaders like Aaron Henry provided "substantial legitimacy" in the successful bid to overthrow the regular state delegation. As the more mainstream organizations replicated many of the MFDP's revolutionary demands, the radical group lost its radical potency and raison d'être.[49]

Another case in point was the eventual demise of the Child Development Group of Mississippi (CDGM), an organization created in 1964 and funded by War on Poverty funds through the Office of Economic Opportunity (OEO). As did most Head Start programs, the organization focused on early education, but also continued the holistic work done in movement Freedom Schools by centering on black culture and politics along with nutrition and health care in the curriculum. Staffed by women and men with direct movement ties, the CDGM fell squarely in the sights of Mississippi's white state politicians and bureaucrats, who from the group's inception relentlessly sought to undermine the organization and find some way to halt the flow of federal money into the hands of African Americans, in general, and known agitators, in particular. White officials dug until they found minor financial inaccuracies in the accounts, and then used the group's accounting errors to push for an end to the organization's federal funding. At the height of operations, the CDGM had successfully served a huge number of black children in over eighty Head Start centers in the state. The downfall of this agency spelled potential disaster for these youngsters, who desperately needed the help.

The OEO, eager to keep programs running but tired of the unyielding pressure from U.S. senator John Stennis (the ardent segregationist Democrat from Kemper County), worked to create a new organization to transition the children out of the beleaguered CDGM. OEO director Sargent Shriver called Aaron Henry and Hodding Carter III to Washington for urgent talks in August 1966. Charles Payne identified the collaboration as a "recycling of the Loyal Democrats."[50] Out of these talks, Mississippi Action for Progress, Inc. (MAP) was created in less than a month. Uniting against the young radicals of SNCC, Henry (appointed onto the original MAP governing board) and the Mississippi State Sovereignty Commission ironically worked together, causing Erle Johnston, onetime commission director, to note, "With the known militancy of some of the groups that had invaded Mississippi, I began to wonder if the NAACP—once the ugliest letters in the language of Mississippi whites—seemed to be the best agency for communication at the national level and could work better with local leadership in providing a smoother path into the future."[51] It is unclear, and it is probably unlikely, that Henry wore his NAACP hat during these negotiations. Clearly he had many hats, but he remained the state NAACP president, and the commission always tagged him that way. Nevertheless, Johnston's assessment was right in many ways—the NAACP continues to survive (not without its own internal difficulties) when most of these other groups failed to thrive long term (or only exist as mere shadows of their former selves).

Henry employed his tried and tested technique of flexible alliances and loyalty temporarily with the senator and other segregationists, enabling them to be in cahoots to minimize militant activity and harness a little more control. Henry reasoned that the alternative organization would continue to serve the needed population and not abandon them. Without state sanction, no organization of this kind would be allowed to function without interference.[52] He continued his pragmatic approach of focusing on the end product, utilizing the national gains and connections he had in light (and despite) of the MFDP debacle. Again, the strategy of compromise over principle ensured that the children had a program, albeit compromised and moderate.

Not all felt the same way. Radical activists attacked Henry mercilessly for what they called selling out once again. Fannie Lou Hamer pulled no punches, calling the black members (or conspirators) on MAP, "Uncle Tom's [*sic*] who couldn't care less."[53] Bayard Rustin had foreseen this scenario in his 1965 article, "From Protest to Politics," when he stated, "the difference between expediency and morality in politics is the difference between selling out a principle and making smaller concessions to win larger ones. The leader who shrinks from this task reveals not his purity but his lack of political sense."[54] In this article, Rustin had sided with Aaron Henry in the Atlantic City controversy, saying that the "FDP made a tactical error in spurning the compromise."[55] Henry respected Rustin, and both recognized the limits of holding to a principle when the rubber hit the road, and the lack of flexibility in holding the moral line prevented CDGM leaders from serving *any* children and hastened their own demise.

Clarksdale's own economic rights story, which ran in parallel to the CDGM, involved extensive coalition building, but Aaron Henry's input did not produce statewide controversies. The successful establishment of Coahoma Opportunities Incorporated (COI) in 1965, the antipoverty agency flagged by the OEO as a prototype for rural agencies, can be boiled down to the tried and tested skills of negotiation and compromise that local leaders had used for at least a decade in the quest for broader equality and desegregation. The local NAACP branch, which played a central role in the movement chronicles in Clarksdale, did not adopt a prominent position in this economic dimension of the struggle, which concentrated more on policy and distribution of federal funds.

Henry, willing to negotiate and compromise in order to make some gains, did not deviate on his flexibility. From his role as state NAACP president to his splash on the national political scene at the 1964 Democratic National Convention in Atlantic City, the federal government knew him better than most African Americans in Mississippi. He also had a local strong cohort around and beside him in Coahoma County. Recognizing the sustained leadership in the African American community in Clarksdale, a leadership that had withstood over a decade of public and organizational struggles, the OEO picked the county as the site for a rural demonstration project and invested millions into the resulting private agency. Coahoma County, for many observers, became one of the "show-place programs in the Nation."[56] Local politics and resistance from white city officials meant that Henry took a backseat role in the actual management of the COI. Even though he had other projects statewide and still held the state NAACP presidency, Henry's influence flowed from his longtime approach to building strategic alliances. Had it not been for his malleability and subsequent visibility, which, despite the controversy and criticism, exposed Henry to larger numbers of people and potential allies, Clarksdale may not have benefited from the economic boost that the COI brought to the county.

Aaron Henry did have political aspirations and served from 1982 to 1996 as a state legislator. He focused on the cumulative effect of all of his actions rather than on the logistics and the mixed messages that his strange bedfellows elicited. Indeed, in a 1968 interview he said, "You don't get into the political mainstream of an organization or you don't get your project funded or you don't get your bridge built or you don't get your road graveled . . . when your every word is cussing the administration that's in Washington. That's not political. So once, however, the Young Democrats were chartered by the National party then this [led to the] development of a bridge between the National Party in Mississippi that we were all willing to travel over."[57] Through his many years as a coalition builder, he managed to amass enough formal political capital from the smaller caches and accomplishments to cross the bridge, like Charles Evers, into electoral politics. It is not surprising that there are many activists, those who did not cross over and remained loyal to their ideals, who saw Henry's journey to electoral politics as evidence of self-motivated action, and not altruistic service to "his" people or "the cause."[58]

What emerges from these stories is not a romantic view of a harmonious and cohesive movement bathed in sisterly and brotherly solidarity. Instead, the battles against segregation in Clarksdale and across the state in the first half of the 1960s—years immortalized in civil rights iconography—reveal a grittier reality. The campaigns of these years combined fractious organizational infighting (collisions) with determined mass action (collusions). The national NAACP took great exception to SNCC's and COFO's influence on the ground as the latter two organizations entered communities in large organized numbers, oftentimes bringing the attention of the national press to the state. Despite some successes, the fundamentally united position against segregationists, and the heart-wrenching losses of lives and campaigns, discord in and between groups came to a head during these years. We also see how flexibility presented more problems when individuals, in this case Aaron Henry, chose pragmatism over moral principle and at times mirrored conventional rather than transformative politics. These conflicts may not have done irreparable damage to civil rights activism in Mississippi, because activists managed to leave their collective marks on the national and international political landscape, but clashes did affect sustained pressure against Jim Crow and may have revealed too many cracks to sustain more long-term momentum.

These stories demonstrate how issues and tensions were negotiated locally, acknowledging the shakiness of coalitions and the shifting sands on which each side stood over time. Aaron Henry was only one activist working in Clarksdale and in Mississippi. On a wider plane, in Washington, the focus of national politics in the latter half of the 1960s moved to Vietnam and away from the southern (mine)fields to the urban battlefields. Increasing conservatism quickly and quietly smudged the ink on not-quite-dry civil rights legislation and court orders, guaranteeing the accelerated crumbling enforcement of civil rights well documented during and since Nixon's presidency. These national stories took decades to play out in Clarksdale and in many parts of the state as issues and crises developed and as the political winds changed direction. Nevertheless, the local stories reveal continued activism that adapted (or not) to the assailing winds. Henry evolved as his life advanced; his loyalties and alliances remained flexible and ready to divert when required and as the cast evolved constantly. The organizations in which the cast belonged and still belongs also evolved as leadership and agenda shifted. As a bridge between activism and electoral politics, seeing how flexible alliances and collaborations worked over time encourages us to think about present-day activism as part of locales and national campaigns. Seeing the strategy played out in a local arena over time forces us to acknowledge and expect conflict and discord and yet embrace coalition building, while all the time keeping our eyes on the prize. It is in this way that the black freedom struggle must continue.

NOTES

1. The author would like to thank Andrea Becksvoort, Charles E. Cobb, Nathan Connolly, Delphain Demosthenes, John Dittmer, Christopher Geissler, Leigh Raiford,

and Naoko Shibusawa for their comments and suggestions that improved the initial lecture delivered at the University of Mississippi and this final essay.

2. Françoise N. Hamlin, *Crossroads at Clarksdale: The Black Freedom Struggle in the Mississippi Delta after World War II* (Chapel Hill: University of North Carolina Press, 2012).

3. Bayard Rustin articulated a version of this bridge argument in his 1965 article, "From Protest to Politics: The Future of the Civil Rights Movement," *Commentary* (February 1965), 25–31.

4. Theorist Audre Lorde's words profoundly influence my thoughts about the political activism of the oppressed. She said, "For the master's tools will never dismantle the master's house. They may allow us temporarily to beat him at his own game, but they will never enable us to bring about genuine change." Audre Lorde, *Sister Outsider* (Berkeley, Calif.: Crossing Press, 1984), 112.

5. James W. Silver, *Mississippi: The Closed Society* (New York: Harcourt, Brace & World, 1964). This remains a seminal text that outlined the insularity of the state, particularly during the Jim Crow years.

6. Robin D. G. Kelley, "We Are Not What We Seem: Rethinking Black Working-Class Opposition in the Jim Crow South," *Journal of American History* 80, no. 1 (June 1993): 75–112.

7. The membership numbers are hard to pin down from branch to branch, in part because many members kept their names off the logs for fear of recrimination. In the Clarksdale/Coahoma County branch, for example, local figures showed a membership of 104 in 1953, but the official numbers in the national office only totaled 59. For the 1953 branch report, see NAACP Microfilm, Part 25, Reel 19, Series A, II C270; for the national office table, see "Funds received from branches as of Nov. 30, 1953," NAACP Microfilm, Part 25, Reel 5, Series A, II C224.

8. Annie Wright to national office, August 22, 1953, and branch department to Annie Wright, August 24, 1953, both in NAACP Papers II C96, Coahoma County File 1953–4; Memorandum, September 14, 1953, NAACP Papers II C325, Committee on Branches Memoranda 1953. The NAACP Papers are archived at the Library of Congress, Washington, D.C. Aaron Henry, like Medgar Evers, utilized the GI Bill to attend Xavier University and become a pharmacist, and therefore was somewhat insulated from the plantation economy. Evers worked as an insurance salesman before his job with the NAACP.

9. First quote from Adam Nossiter, *Of Long Memory: Mississippi and the Murder of Medgar Evers* (Reading, Mass.: Addison-Wesley, 1994), 39. Second quote from John Dittmer, *Local People: The Struggle for Civil Rights in Mississippi* (Urbana: University of Illinois Press, 1994), 52. Medgar Evers assumed his role in 1954. The entire region saw losses to its membership; see Gloster Current, Report and Recommendations on membership and staff, 1958, NAACP Papers II C279, Membership campaign losses

1957. Immediately after the Till killing, enrollment spiked briefly as anger against such unpunished atrocities prompted many to hand over their dues. The differences in the type of white terrorism made a difference. The Citizens' Councils' obstructionist strategies forced greater flexibility in activists, as Red-baiting and laws that required state workers (including teachers) to disclose their organizational memberships rendered them more vulnerable to any association with the NAACP. It did not help that the NAACP used the Till murder to organize nationally—publicly and loudly denouncing Mississippi, and sending Till's grieving mother on a speaking tour to fund-raise and galvanize memberships. These various scales of contestation require historians to track the fluid nature of both protest and white reactions.

10. Howell Raines, *My Soul Is Rested: Movement Days in the Deep South Remembered* (New York: G. P. Putnam's Sons, 1977), 233.

11. Affidavit from Amzie Moore, December 29, 1954, NAACP Microfilm, Part 18, Reel 12, Series C. See also Barbara Ransby, *Ella Baker and the Black Freedom Movement: A Radical Democratic Vision* (Chapel Hill: University of North Carolina Press, 2003), 301–302.

12. Ransby, *Ella Baker*, 161–168.

13. Russell Johnson, Peace Education Secretary of the American Friends Service Committee, to Amzie Moore, February 12, 1957, Amzie Moore Papers, Box 1, Folder 3, Wisconsin Historical Society, Madison. See also correspondence from Ella Baker to Ruth Moore, February 25, 1957, and F. E. Hutchens in the AFSC Southwest Regional office to Amzie Moore, February 28, 1957, both in Amzie Moore Papers, Box 1, Folder 3; and Aaron Henry Papers, Box 74, VIA Folder 1411, RCNL meeting minutes, Mississippi Department of Archives and History, Jackson.

14. Thanks to writer and former SNCC worker Charles Cobb for this information; see also Ransby, *Ella Baker*, 302.

15. Raines, *My Soul Is Rested*, 234.

16. Ibid., 236.

17. Amzie Moore, whose marriage crumbled in the mid-1960s, never rose in prominence as a leader like Aaron Henry, and no one has yet published a work about his influence outside of Bolivar County and SNCC.

18. Aaron Henry to MLK, August 28, 1957, Martin Luther King, Jr., Papers, Box 71A, Folder 9A, Howard Gotlieb Archival Research Center, Boston University.

19. Dittmer, *Local People*, 78; Evers to Wilkins, March 11, 1957, NAACP Papers III C244.

20. Martin Luther King Jr. to membership, January 20, 1958, Amzie Moore Papers, Box 7, Folder 7.

21. Medgar Evers to Ruby Hurley, January 24, 1958, NAACP Papers III C244, Evers 1958.

22. For examples, in 1956 Gloster Current reprimanded Evers for his "quality of our

correspondence to NAACP standards." Current to Evers, March 20, 1956, NAACP Papers III C243. That same year, Roy Wilkins questioned Evers's irregular billing for the use of his car on NAACP business. Evers traveled thousands of miles in his own car throughout Mississippi that year, visiting those hit by economic repression, collecting affidavits for the national office. Wilkins to Evers, December 18, 1956, January 2, 1957, NAACP Papers III C243 and C244. This incident is also mentioned in Nossiter, *Of Long Memory*, 49.

23. Aaron Henry, interview by Robert Wright, September 25, 1968, Clarksdale, Mississippi, Ralph Bunche Collection, Moorland-Spingarn Research Center Oral History Collection, Howard University Archives, Washington, D.C.; Aaron Henry, interview by T. H. Baker, Clarksdale, Miss., September 12, 1970, tape 1, 9, Lyndon Baines Johnson Library, Austin, Texas.

24. Aaron Henry, with Constance Curry, *Aaron Henry: The Fire Ever Burning* (Jackson: University Press of Mississippi, 2000), 101. See also Denton L. Watson, "Assessing the Role of the NAACP in the Civil Rights Movement," *Historian* 55, no. 3 (1993): 453.

25. Henry interview, 20.

26. Ibid., 71.

27. Ibid., 70.

28. Henry to Current, November 25, 1961, NAACP Papers III A229, Mississippi Pressure Clarksdale, 1956–1963. The organization rotated its chairmanships monthly to maintain the aura of partnership with, and not merely an extension of, the NAACP. For instance, in a letter dated February 20, 1962, signed by Rev. Rayford, the subtext was "Chairman, Month of February." Coahoma County Folder File, Sovereignty Commission Papers, Mississippi Department of Archives and History, Jackson.

29. Indeed, by this time, the local NAACP branch enjoyed strong numbers. In 1961 the branch had 200 paid members and fifty youth. NAACP Papers III C190, Annual Reports Mississippi 1956–65.

30. Henry, *Fire*, 107.

31. Ibid., 109.

32. White House Central Files, Box 1192, John F. Kennedy Library, Boston.

33. Henry, *Fire*, 115.

34. Ibid.

35. Henry interview, 70.

36. Report to Mississippi State Conference memberships and FFF Contributions Received to Date, October 29, 1962, NAACP Papers III C75, Mississippi State and Conference Statement, Amzie Moore Papers, Box 6, Folder 1.

37. NAACP Papers III A199, CORE and NAACP Papers III A212, SCLC 1963–65.

38. Emilye Crosbye, *A Little Taste of Freedom: The Black Freedom Struggle in Clai-*

borne County, Mississippi (Chapel Hill: University of North Carolina Press, 2005), 86–90.

39. Charles Evers ran unsuccessfully for the gubernatorial seat in 1971 and for James O. Eastland's U.S. Senate seat in 1978.

40. Henry interview, 34.

41. NAACP Papers III A200, COFO 1964–65.

42. For more information on Vera Pigee, see Françoise N. Hamilin, "Vera Mae Pigee (1925–): Mothering the Movement," in *Mississippi Women: Their Histories, Their Lives,* ed. Martha H. Swain, Elizabeth A. Payne, and Marjorie J. Spruill (Athens: University of Georgia Press, 2003), 281–298; Hamlin, *The Story Isn't Finished*; and Vera Pigee's two-part autobiography, *Struggle of Struggles* (Detroit: Harlo Press, 1975).

43. Pigee, *Struggles: Part One,* 35.

44. Vera Pigee, interview by author, 2001.

45. Author's conversations with Mary Jane Pigee Davis from July 2005 to December 2009; author's conversations with Zoya Zeman from October 2009 to May 2010. Vera Pigee died in 2007 in Detroit.

46. Ivanhoe Donaldson quoted in Raines, *My Soul Is Rested,* 257.

47. Author's conversation with Charlie Cobb, February and April 2010.

48. The MFDP's push was revolutionary. Despite their failure to get seated on the delegation floor in Atlantic City, MFDP members' presence and vocal protest resulted in major changes in the democratic process, particularly in 1968 with the Committee on Party Structure and Delegation Selection, otherwise known as the McGovern-Fraser Commission. For more details on the MFDP challenge, see Charles M Payne, *I've Got the Light of Freedom: The Organizing Tradition and the Mississippi Freedom Struggle* (Berkeley: University of California Press, 1995), 340; and Dittmer, *Local People,* 272–302.

49. Dittmer, *Local People,* 346–349, 419–423; Payne, *I've Got the Light of Freedom,* 341; Jere Nash and Andy Taggart, *Mississippi Politics: The Struggle for Power, 1976–2000* (Jackson: University Press of Mississippi, 2006), 28–30. Again, although the MFDP failed to thrive, it succeeded in moving the Democratic Party agenda in a more progressive direction.

50. Payne, *I've Got the Light of Freedom,* 343.

51. Erle Johnston, *Mississippi's Defiant Years—1953–1973* (Forest, Miss.: Lake Harbor Publishers, 1990), 291.

52. For an overview of the messy history of the CDGM and MAP, see Dittmer, *Local People,* 369–388; and Payne, *I've Got the Light of Freedom,* 342–345.

53. Hamer quoted in Dittmer, *Local People,* 378.

54. Rustin, "From Protest to Politics," 29.

55. Ibid., 31.

56. Donald C. Mosley and D. C. Williams Jr., "An Analysis and Evaluation of a Community Action Anti-Poverty Program in the Mississippi Delta," July 1967, RG 381, OEO Community Services Administration Office of Operations, Migrant Division, Box 50, Grant Files 1966–1971, National Archives, College Park, Md., i. For more details on the COI, see Hamlin, *Story Isn't Finished.*

57. Henry interview, 56.

58. Here I think primarily of the critiques from Fannie Lou Hamer (disgusted by the MFDP debacle in Atlantic City and the destruction of the CDGM) and Vera Pigee (lifelong member of the NAACP and secretary of the Clarksdale branch, working with Aaron Henry for nearly two decades). Although both women organized in different organizations, both criticized Henry. Henry died in 1997.

The Struggle for Black Citizenship

Medgar Wiley Evers and the Fight for Civil Rights
in Mississippi

Michael Vinson Williams

This essay briefly examines the history and activism of Medgar Wiley Evers and his participation in the African American struggle for full citizenship rights.[1] Here I examine some of the social, political, and cultural firestorms that raged throughout the mid-1950s and early 1960s and their impact upon Mississippi's combative race relations. As a consequence, this discussion is about the human element of and meaning behind the civil rights struggle, the impact of that struggle on violent oppression in the state, and the influence of violent resistance upon the African American personality.

The long and intense struggle African Americans waged for full citizenship recognition has been, and continues to be, marked by key historic battles for freedom and defense of the democratic principle. African Americans declared their involvement in the American Revolution, the War of 1812, the Civil War, and both world wars as proof of their desires for and worthiness of full citizenship, and each endeavor helped define and strengthen the formation of resistance movements. The famed orator and activist Frederick Douglass expressed this belief as early as 1863: "Once let the black man get upon his person the brass letters, U.S.," Douglass remarked, "let him get an eagle on his button, and a musket on his shoulder and bullets in his pocket, and there is not power on earth which can deny that he had earned the rights to citizenship in the United States."[2] Although the question of the true meaning of citizenship lay at the heart of civil rights activism, that struggle has constantly been shaped and reshaped by questions regarding the extent to which state and national agencies were responsible for protecting the rights and privileges of their entire population. Yet how do you fight against a system determined to limit certain segments of the population's access to the core essentials of Americanism? This proved a vital question for civil rights activists in Mississippi. The African American struggle for full citizenship proved a struggle for the rights, privileges, and protection guaranteed to those who made up the country and thus were protected by the Constitution that defined it.

For Medgar Evers, that struggle began during his childhood in Decatur, Mississippi. Medgar Wiley Evers was born on July 2, 1925, to James and Jessie Evers. In addition to Medgar, the Everses had six other children between them and lived in a quiet area of Newton County. Both parents touted the importance of personal responsibility, self-worth, and racial pride, but the actions of the father proved crucial to Medgar's ideas regarding the meaning of manhood, familial responsibility, and citizenship. The respect James Evers commanded from whites, combined with his refusal to cower in their presence, inspired Medgar to challenge the legitimacy of Jim Crow segregation. Strong family backgrounds were often the catalyst behind civil rights activism. Noted activists such as James Meredith, Marcus Garvey, Martin Luther King Jr., Malcolm X, and Theodore Roosevelt Mason Howard had strong, opinionated fathers whose forceful actions and personalities proved to be important factors in developing activist-oriented ideologies in their children.[3]

James Evers believed in hard work and led by example. He stood over six feet tall and weighed 200 pounds, and many described him as a hardworking man who could, at times, be stern, abrasive, and "mean." James refused to cower in the face of white intimidation and challenged any attempt to cheat him or to intimidate his family.[4] As children, Medgar and his older brother Charles witnessed an incident involving their father that forever changed their notion of what it meant to be a man. In this instance, both boys accompanied their father to the local commissary to pay the balance of the family's bill. Discussions with white commissary manager, Jimmy Boware, resulted in a heated argument that ended with James breaking a Coca Cola bottle. With the broken piece firmly grasped in his hand, he threatened to kill Boware if he advanced toward him or the area of the store where everybody knew he kept a gun. The confrontation resulted from Boware's attempts to force James to pay more on his bill than he actually owed. James refused and, bottle in hand, backed out of the store to what must have been a shocked and somewhat befuddled white audience.[5] Although money was the immediate root of the confrontation, the real source of the altercation spoke not so much to the inflated dollar amount as to the attempt by one individual to restrict the rights of another and the latter's willingness to die in defense of those rights.

In this light, the altercation reflected the essential elements of the civil rights struggle in Mississippi—a struggle built upon wits, individual and group will, and a desire to define the meaning of citizenship and political participation. For Medgar Evers, constant examples of manhood and accountability were seared into his psyche and helped mold an independent character.[6]

After his confrontation with Boware, James and his sons "walked home down along the railroad tracks," Charles recalled, with "Medgar on one side of Daddy, me on the other. We put our arms around Daddy's waist, he put his hands on our heads. We were so happy." Both Medgar and Charles would remember their father's counsel, "Don't ever let *anybody* beat you." "Anyone ever kicks you," James advised, "you kick the hell out of him."[7]

The devout dedication to equality and justice demonstrated by James and Jessie Evers was an important factor in Medgar's growing awareness of the wrongs of segregation. Love of the individual self, combined with personal confidence and devotion to the community, remain a powerful tool of racial uplift. These were lessons Medgar Evers received in abundance, and they shaped his belief that equality belonged to all groups. Jessie Evers further enhanced that ideal by instilling in her children the knowledge that "White Folk are no better than you are."[8] Medgar Evers, like so many others, would also use America's involvement in the Second World War as a catalyst for creating social, political, and institutional change.

In 1943 Evers joined the more than 85,000 black Mississippians who would enlist in the military during the 1940s. He left high school and joined the U.S. Army, where he served from October 7 of that year to April 16, 1946.[9] For Evers, the military provided respite from the dehumanizing actions that whites practiced against blacks in Decatur. Prior to enlisting, he had wondered just how long he could take living in Mississippi under a system of segregation and degradation. As a black male, he admitted that it pained him "to watch the Saturday night sport of white men trying to run down a Negro with their car, or white gangs coming through town to beat up a Negro."[10]

Evers and his unit were sent to the European theater of operations and were stationed in both England and France. He served in the 325th Port Company, a segregated unit commanded by white officers, which followed the Normandy invasion into France. Port battalions entered an area shortly after an assault began and delivered needed supplies to assault troops engaged in battle. Evers reported that he also served on the famed "Red Ball Express [while] in France and Germany."[11] As an organized system of supply trucks often driven by black soldiers, the Red Ball Express transported provisions to American troops.[12] In an interview with military specialist David

Colley, John Shevlin, an assistant tank driver, admitted that had it not been "for the Red Ball we couldn't have moved. They all were black drivers and they delivered in the heat of combat. We'd be in our tanks praying for them to come up."[13] Sentiments such as these attesting to the effectiveness of and dependency on the service of black soldiers underscored their intolerance for any system of inequality upon returning stateside.

World War II had a profound effect upon African Americans' notions of manhood and citizenship. War magnified these two ideals through the success black soldiers achieved in meeting the challenges associated with military service. Historians such as Jennifer Brooks maintain that fulfilling military duties enhanced African American veterans' sense "of who they were and where they fit into postwar political life. In putting a premium on the role of men as citizens—as soldiers performing the highest of civic duties—the war tended to strengthen the historic connection between male identity and political rights."[14] Thus, for African American men, citizenship, military service, and manhood were all intertwined with the need to protect both the physical community and the psychological viability of the family. Medgar's wife, Myrlie, who in this instance spoke the often unspoken expectations of community women, remarked that the "willingness—the ability—of a man to protect his family is probably the basic element in our concept of manhood."[15] Civil rights activists applied that same ideal of protection to the fight for citizenship rights.

Medgar Evers returned to Mississippi in 1946 with two combat stars, the Good Conduct medal, and a record of notable military service.[16] He also returned much less tolerant of the liberties whites took in denying African Americans the right to vote in Decatur or anyplace else. On July 2, 1946, Medgar, his brother Charles, and four other friends went to the courthouse determined to vote. When they arrived, the band of brothers met a white mob just as determined to deny them the opportunity to cast their ballots. Evers discussed the courthouse incident in an interview with *Ebony* correspondent Francis H. Mitchell:

> The six of us gathered at my house and we walked to the polls. I'll never forget it. Not a Negro was on the streets, and when we got to the courthouse, the clerk said he wanted to talk with us. When we got into his office, some 15 or 20 armed white men surged in behind us, men I had grown up with, had played with. We split up and went home. Around town, Negroes said we had been whipped, beaten up and run out of town. Well, in a way we were whipped, I guess, but I made up my mind then that it would not be like that again—at least not for me.[17]

Although denied the opportunity to vote, the stand Evers took that day fueled his desire for social equality. The political statement the Evers brothers made that July 2 proved not to be a unique occurrence. All over the South, conservative whites witnessed these political challenges with startling results. In 1946 and 1947 alone, historian Glenda Gilmore notes, "black World War II veterans formed impromptu regiments to assault the polls of southern cities."[18] In fact, the same year Evers flouted voting restrictions in Decatur, 100 black veterans marched on the courthouse in Birmingham, Alabama, demanding the right to the ballot. These political demonstrations brought the issue of black citizenship to the forefront of state politics throughout the South, heightened white fears, and forced the federal government to reevaluate the country's global image and reputation.[19] In 1947 President Harry S. Truman's Committee on Civil Rights acknowledged that the country could no longer "escape the fact that our civil rights record has been an issue in world politics. The world's Press and radio are full of it." The committee reminded the country, *"the final triumph of the democratic ideal is not so inevitable that we can ignore what the world thinks of us or our record."*[20]

For many white Mississippians, returning veterans represented the ultimate threat to white control and authority at the local level. Men such as Evers were trained soldiers with military experience in combat zones where *white men* had been identified as enemies of democracy and freedom and where nations had banded together in a global war to prevent their success. The fear many white southerners showed toward returning black veterans proved not to be completely unwarranted. Evers had briefly flirted with the idea of implementing a violent plan of resistance to white hegemony. He later admitted that it "didn't take much reading of the Bible, though, to convince me that two wrongs would not make the situation any different, and that I couldn't hate the white man and at the same time hope to convert him."[21]

In the fall of 1946 Evers enrolled in the high school program of Alcorn A&M College (now Alcorn State University) located on its campus in Lorman, Mississippi. He completed the requirements for the high school diploma and enrolled as a freshman majoring in business administration during the 1948 fall term; he graduated with a business administration degree in 1952. Two years later Evers joined the staff of the National Association for the Advancement of Colored People (NAACP) as the association's first full-time field secretary for the state of Mississippi. He held this position until his assassination in 1963 at the hands of white supremacist Byron De La Beckwith.

His work in Mound Bayou proved a defining period in helping to construct his civil rights ideology.[22] In 1952 Dr. Theodore Roosevelt Mason Howard, an active member of the NAACP, offered Evers a job as an insurance salesman for Magnolia Mutual Life Insurance Company. Started by Howard and a group of African American businessmen who were also from the Delta area, Magnolia Mutual proved a new business venture with unlimited potential. Fresh out of college, Evers could not have known just how strong an impact his insurance work in the Delta would have upon his work in the area of civil rights.[23]

The Delta region represented the epicenter of Mississippi's economic power, and it had a reputation as one of the most oppressive areas for African Americans in the state.[24] The sharecropping system, through economic exploitation and physical violence, victimized and shackled African Americans to the land in ways that resembled chattel slavery. Sharecroppers often found themselves at the complete mercy of white Delta landowners who exploited their labor for cotton production without remorse.[25] Evers found that the violent methods whites employed in the Delta to ensure control over black labor made grassroots organizing difficult at best. As a consequence, Evers took advantage of every opportunity to help sharecroppers escape their repression as well as those who witnessed white violence and feared for their safety. He provided financial assistance when possible and subterfuge tactics when necessary to help individuals escape repression. "I remember one very distinct case," Myrlie Evers recalled, "where he used a casket, put a person in a casket in conjunction with a mortuary, and got the person out of the state, across the border to Tennessee."[26] Medgar Evers understood, however, that escapism—whether physical or mental—would not solve the overall problem of racial inequality. Only through organized resistance did he believe the oppressed could ever hope to replace the tenets of racism with equality and sociopolitical progress.

The economic boycott organized against white gas station owners in 1952 proved one of Evers's earliest structured undertakings in the fight for social equality. Although white businessmen in Mound Bayou gladly accepted dollars from black customers, gas station owners refused those customers the use of their restrooms.[27] Established in 1951, the Regional Council of Negro Leadership (RCNL) had influential members who were capable of fighting against racism and violence and addressing the economic and social concerns of African Americans in the Delta. As an organization, the RCNL strengthened resistance measures in Mound Bayou by providing Evers and other local leaders with resources, economic support for maneuverability, and community collaboration within a hostile environment of white economic and physical repression. The RCNL also provided Evers with a blueprint for understanding the importance and significance of organizational support in the fight for true citizenship rights. The boycott proved an effective strategy as most "white stations began to install extra restrooms," historians David Beito and Linda Beito note. "They acted both because of the decline in customers and pressure from national suppliers and chains."[28] By participating in the boycott, African Americans demonstrated that when properly motivated, they were quite willing to put their lives on the line to achieve common goals, regardless of the consequences. Myrlie Evers maintained that the Mound Bayou boycott represented the first of many boycott campaigns that her husband would initiate, oversee, and participate in.[29]

By 1953 Medgar Evers proved more determined to challenge Mississippi's practice of denying Negroes the right to attend the state's white colleges and universities. His decision to focus upon the University of Mississippi helped propel him to the forefront of the civil rights struggle in the state and brought him to the full attention of the NAACP leadership. On January 11, 1954, Evers sent a formal request for Alcorn to "forward to the Registrar of the University of Mississippi School of Law, the collegiate transcript of one, Medgar W. Evers, as soon as possible."[30] His announcement made headlines across the state in papers like the *Jackson Advocate*, a black newspaper, and its white counterpart, the *Jackson Daily News*.[31] If university officials were unaware of his racial background at the beginning of the application process, they were surely tipped off when the *Jackson Advocate* reported that "Thurgood Marshall . . . [would] act as [Medgar's] attorney in any and all matters pertaining to the admission of the applicant to the University of Mississippi."[32] Regardless of the moment in which university officials attached the term "Negro" to the name Medgar Evers, the Mississippi Board of Higher Learning rejected his application on a technicality. For Medgar Evers, however, applying to the University of Mississippi represented the proverbial crack in the dam of Mississippi oppression.[33]

Despite Evers's failure to integrate the University of Mississippi, his efforts brought him to the attention of the national officers of the NAACP who, in light of the *Brown* decision, were looking to establish a stronghold in the state. The job of field secretary would also help Evers overcome the conflicting issues between thought and deed regarding his selling insurance to the poor while advocating sociopolitical struggle. His promotion to field secretary in December 1954 ended these internal conflicts and strengthened his resolve to bring about real social, political, and cultural change in Mississippi.[34] Civil rights activists operating in the twentieth state of the Union already knew that challenging the status quo would not be an easy endeavor.

On April 7, 1957, Martin Luther King Jr. warned blacks that they had "better get ready" for violent responses to civil rights work. Mississippi activists in 1955, however, were all too familiar with those violent responses. Although the violence black Mississippians witnessed in 1955 produced fear and anger, it also solidified resistance efforts, and it proved a turning point for Medgar Evers.[35] Three high-profile lynchings in 1955 exposed white Mississippians' commitment to keeping their African American counterparts intimidated and controlled, demonstrating both the difficult challenges ahead for civil rights activists and the nature of oppression in Mississippi. Two of those murdered, the Reverend George Lee of Belzoni and Lamar Smith of Brookhaven, were people Evers respected for their dedication to sociopolitical change. Ultimately, the murders were not only significant to the civil rights movement in Mississippi but also to the ideological growth of Medgar Evers and the expansion and intensity of the civil rights struggle in the South.

Rev. George W. Lee was an independent businessman, minister, and active member of the NAACP in Belzoni, Mississippi. Owning a grocery store and printing shop, he was less vulnerable to the economic pressures that whites inflicted upon the less financially stable. Unlike most ministers during his time, Lee openly advocated voting rights for African Americans and demanded that Negroes stand against white oppression and unequal treatment. This brand of liberation theology permeated his sermons. He preached with an unyielding consistency that black people had to fight for *all* of their rights in the here and now and not be content to wait upon death to obtain equality. He touted this message to the four Baptist congregations for which he rode circuit: two in Jackson, one in Lexington, and one in Tchula, Mississippi.[36]

His independence served him well as he labored to open the voting polls to African Americans in Mississippi on an equal basis with that of whites. On a personal level, Lee had accomplished a remarkable amount in terms of gaining access to the political process. George Lee, Medgar Evers noted in his 1955 annual report to the NAACP, "was the only Negro who had qualified himself in both County and City elections, in a county where Negroes have not voted since Reconstruction and where Negroes outnumber whites at the rate of more than two to one."[37] Lee had tried for years to vote but could not because of the sheriff's refusal to accept his poll tax payments. In 1953 Lee and "a small group of other Negroes," Myrlie Evers remarked, complained to federal authorities, and only the threat of federal prosecution forced Sheriff Ike Shelton to agree to accept future payments.[38] Despite constant warnings from whites to cease stirring up trouble, the many death threats he received, and the knowledge that his name appeared upon a death list, Lee continued to encourage African Americans to register and vote. In response, whites

warned Lee that they would kill him if he continued along this path of resistance. True to form, the minister ignored the warnings and continued organizing African Americans to resist intimidation and to demand the rights
entitled them as citizens of the United States. Lee's militant messages and
personal bravado did not come without a cost. On May 7, 1955, several white
men in a convertible pulled along side Rev. Lee's car and fired two gun blasts
into his automobile, one of which tore away his lower jaw.[39] He died shortly
afterward.

Although disgusted by the Lee murder, Evers did not seem surprised that
it had occurred. He deduced that in light of the minister's economic independence and determination to obtain voting rights for African Americans
in Mississippi, the only alternative that organizations such as the Citizens'
Council had for stopping Lee "was to kill him."[40] One of the most public murders of 1955 occurred in the small town of Brookhaven, Mississippi. Lamar
Smith, a sixty-three-year-old farmer, had encouraged African Americans to
utilize the absentee ballot as a means of ousting political incumbents. As
a result of this type of continued agitation, whites gunned Smith down in
broad daylight on the courthouse lawn.[41]

As a registered voter, Lamar Smith believed that voting equaled citizenship. He upheld this belief when he cast his ballot in the primary election
days prior to his murder. Thus his political participation stood as an example
to the many black men and women he had convinced of the importance of
fighting for their right to participate in the political process.[42] Within hours
of Smith's murder, Evers arrived in Brookhaven to find out what had trans-
pired and what mechanisms were in place to apprehend the killer or killers.
He discovered that Smith had "kept an unknown political appointment" that
day and had been shot in broad daylight around 10:00 on the busy Court
House Square with no apparent witnesses.[43] District Attorney E. C. Barlow
later announced that the murder of Smith was "politically inspired . . . because he was campaigning against the incumbent supervisor, J. Hugh James,
whose office was up for grabs in Brookhaven's 'Democratic primary.'"[44] News
reports from the *Jackson Daily News* and the *State Times* (Jackson) identified Noah Smith, a white farmer, as the shooter. Sheriff Robert Case refused
to arrest Smith, even though he supposedly saw him run to his truck with
blood-spattered clothing after the shooting. His refusal prompted District
Attorney Barlow to issue a warrant for Smith's arrest.[45]

Although Evers acknowledged that "Mr. Smith's assailants were apprehended, [and] placed under a $20,000 bond each[,] . . . [they] were not
brought to trial because the grand jury had no witnesses and did not indict

them." Here, when speaking of "assailants," Evers was referring to the report of several men who accosted Smith on the courthouse lawn before he was killed. *Jet* magazine reported that Noah Smith, Mack Smith, and Charles Falvey were involved in the attack on Lamar Smith.[46] These two murders bolstered Evers's growing belief that only through the use of more intensified resistance tactics would the civil rights movement record any measurable progress.

No act of violence assaulted the sensibilities of Evers, African Americans, and progressive whites in Mississippi and the rest of the nation than the August lynching of fourteen-year-old Emmett Louis Till. African Americans' spirits sank to a low point when it came to light that half-brothers Roy Bryant and J. W. Milam had kidnapped, tortured, brutalized, and eventually shot to death the fourteen-year-old in August before dumping his body in the Tallahatchie River. That low point deepened considerably when the legal system run by white Mississippians absolved the brothers of any responsibility for the horrible crime. In response to the lynching, people across the nation erupted with disgust and vented their frustrations through tears and massive demonstrations. The NAACP reported that on October 11, 1955, 20,000 individuals joined a "midday street rally in New York City" to protest the lynching.[47] The murder of Till also had a psychological impact on African American youth in the state that produced psychological dissonance in abundance.

Anne Moody, a civil rights activist and Mississippi native, believed that the Till lynching added a deeper and more insidious component to the fear blacks harbored in Mississippi. "Before Emmett Till's murder," Moody recalled, "I had known the fear of hunger, hell, and the Devil. But now there was a new fear known to me—the fear of being killed just because I was black. This was the worse of my fears." Till's murder created psychological tensions in African American youth that were almost impossible to counter or prepare for the way one would approach more tangible concerns. Both the brutality and random nature of the Till lynching caused many African Americans to weigh their fears against their anger, and, in many instances, anger won out. Although the murder of Emmett Till increased civil rights activism and involvement, it also intensified antagonism between African Americans and whites that had been boiling since the *Brown* decision.

White Mississippians considered the *Brown* decision an all-out attack upon their way of life. In response to the court's ruling, "white Mississippians," Dittmer remarked, "had developed a siege mentality so pervasive it encompassed virtually every citizen and institution." Thus conservative southern leaders began to see the fight for equality as an entity that had grown much larger than the local black population.[48] The proper counterattack, many whites believed, demanded that they retake control over their communities by instilling fear in a black population that seemed to be advancing at the sociopolitical expense and welfare of white Mississippians. Thus by 1955, understanding that they had no power over the actions of national civil rights organizations and leaders outside of the state, white Mississippians intensified attempts to control interactions between blacks and whites on the local level, and oftentimes extreme violence proved to be their method of choice.

Edwin King, a white chaplain at Tougaloo College, pointed to the Till lynching as an indicator of the growing level of intense violence conservative whites were willing to use to maintain the status quo in race relations. King believed that had the Till incident happened "earlier that Emmett Till would not have been murdered for whistling at a white woman, he would have been whipped." After the *Brown* decision, as indicative of the Till lynching, interracial interactions of any degree produced greater scrutiny, particularly when "outsiders" were the so-called offending party. Mississippi officials organized to effectively counter any attack upon the status quo that *Brown* invited. "The interracial meetings between schools like Tougaloo and Millsaps or even Ole Miss," King remarked, "and Mississippi State through the YMCA, the YWCA, interracial meetings between church women . . . those kinds of things all collapsed by 1955, 56." Dittmer stretches the social ramifications of *Brown* even farther. "From 1954 to the early 1960s," he exclaimed, "the Mississippi State Legislature enacted a series of statutes aimed at the enemies of white supremacy, a category so broad it encompassed literally every attempt to modify the status quo in race relations."[49] The Till murder brought Mississippi national attention as people within and outside of the state watched to see what would happen.

The open and very public murders of Lee, Smith, and Till took a toll on civil rights leaders. Many thought that the murders required vindication, and Evers believed that only by remaining vigilant in the fight for social equality could these senseless deaths translate into something positive.[50] As a consequence, Evers traveled to Washington, D.C., as a part of an NAACP delegation to discuss the "three lynchings" with Assistant U.S. Attorney General Warren Olney III.[51] After the meeting Evers and other NAACP representatives "made it clear to the Department of Justice official of the need for Federal intervention into the State of Mississippi for the assurance that the Civil Rights of Negroes of that state would not be abridged," Evers reported. The group received a promise "that 'appropriate' actions" would be forthcoming from the Justice Department.[52] Evers had hoped that the Justice Department would get involved in the Till case. Olney, however, later informed Roy Wilkins that there was "no evidence of a violation of the Federal Kidnapping Statute in this case. Therefore, we [the Justice Department] are without jurisdiction to proceed in this matter."[53] Despite the D.C. meeting, 1955 continued to produce atrocities for African Americans. One such act of violence included the December 13 shotgun murder of gas station attendant Clinton Melton in Glendora, Mississippi. The murder occurred when white patron Elmer Kimbell denied requesting the amount of gasoline Melton had pumped and later killed him in a fit of rage.[54] These types of events led civil rights activists closer to the question of whether Mississippi would or could change without a full-scale race war, something Medgar Evers and his wife discussed and made preparations for.[55]

The struggle for civil rights also lay in the economic sphere as black Mississippians suffered under financial oppression. Whites often placed a great deal of economic pressure on African Americans in order to stifle civil rights activism, and this proved to be one of the biggest hurdles for activists to overcome. The tactics of economic repression hit African American farmers and businessmen harder than others because of their dependency upon loans for seeds, supplies, or start-up funds for business ventures. Both represented the socioeconomic group that Evers relied upon the most to carry out NAACP programs. The NAACP sought to deflate this type of economic tactic by working with the African American–owned and –controlled Tri-State Bank of Memphis, Tennessee. Thus the civil rights push in Mississippi proved also to be a push for economic liberation. The NAACP responded to the economic threats of the White Citizens' Council by establishing an economic relationship with Tri-State Bank. Gloster Current, NAACP director of branches, pointed out that the NAACP had "met the propaganda effects of their [White Citizens' Council] announcements, which was to scare Negroes, with a counter-propaganda by announcing a program to build up a financial institution in Memphis whereby a Negro institution would offer relief to those who constituted good credit risk."[56] As a result of this partnership, Tri-State Bank agreed to work with farmers who met its loan requirements and who also agreed to deposit money with the bank as a means of helping it to expand.[57]

The economic plight of farmers occupied much of Evers's attention and thus that of the NAACP. He had worked with sharecroppers most of his professional career with Magnolia Mutual and continued to do so as NAACP field secretary. Because of their need for credit and funds for equipment, African American farmers were the most vulnerable to economic pressures. Whites counted on this vulnerability to both frustrate and keep African Americans from participating in any struggle for sociopolitical equality. Many black farmers, however, were unable to meet the requirements to obtain a loan from Tri-State Bank and thus were overwhelmed by financial hardships. In 1956 the NAACP established the Committee on Emergency Aid to Farmers in Mississippi as a means of addressing their economic concerns.

The committee, although a separate entity, remained subordinate to the NAACP and subject to its authority. Organization reports described it as an entity designed to

> assist on [a] limited basis Mississippi landowners who because of activities or connection with the NAACP and/or the desegregation program and who were formerly considered good credit risk but at the present time unable to get loans they need at prevailing rates in their own communities from banks and other lending institutions and who are unable to qualify or secure loans from the Tri-State Bank in Memphis or other lending institutions.

Each farmer would receive no more than $1,500 in aid, and all loans were made through Tri-State Bank with donations and NAACP assurance that monies would be repaid.[58] The committee conducted strict background checks to determine eligibility and credit worthiness, and for this it depended upon the investigatory work of Medgar Evers and NAACP Field Secretary-at-large Mildred Bond.

The committee requested wide, sweeping investigations to identify victims of economic repression. Once identified, the committee worked to offset the economic pressure and intimidation to which whites subjected African Americans. By January 23, 1956, Evers and Bond had interviewed a total of seventy persons, logged 800 miles, obtained seven notarized affidavits, and filled out fourteen "detailed information sheets" on individuals willing to air their grievances in public. Throughout the process, they visited a total of ten counties and provided the percentages of the African American population within each.[59] Both Evers and Bond were seen by African Americans in various communities as figures of hope and representatives of change for those mired in poverty and despair.

Evers served, in a real sense, as a physical link between the realities of African Americans struggling in Mississippi and the NAACP leadership hundreds of miles away. Association leaders were often unaware of both the extent and severity of the problems black Mississippians faced when combat-

ing southern racism. Although Evers worked hard to eliminate problems motivated by racial discrimination, he also considered NAACP financial coffers
as legitimate mechanisms for protecting victims of Mississippi's oppressive
social and political regimes. He often petitioned the NAACP for funds to
support those victimized by white oppression due to their activist work. In
one such instance, Evers wrote to Roy Wilkins asking for $50,000 to help save
George Jefferson's housing development. Whites in the area were applying
economic pressure to run him out of business and thus undercut civil rights
activism in Vicksburg, Mississippi.[60]

Evers's constant reports about Mississippi's brutal nature helped force the
federal government to take notice of the political events in Mississippi concerning African Americans' struggles for equality. Every time an unpunished
murder, rape, or beating of a black person in Mississippi showed up in a national newspaper, it created national and international attention that produced a great deal of embarrassment for U.S. officials. For Evers, civil rights
struggle meant a national as well as an international fight for sociopolitical
parity, and his battle tactics reflected this belief. Despite knowing that he
was under constant surveillance, Evers increased his work and exposure in
Mississippi during the late 1950s and expended more of his time and energy
toward connecting the Mississippi struggle with the growing national movement for civil and political equality. Again, registering African Americans to
vote proved to be a crucial part of his daily work.

For Medgar Evers, the ballot represented one of the most visible and important symbols of citizenship. Without this basic right, he believed, African Americans could not defend their political interests or effectively select
those who would represent them. As a consequence, Evers worked with other
groups to keep the voting campaign center stage in the minds of Mississippi's
black citizenry. The more African Americans agitated for political equality
around the nation, the more Mississippi officials took seriously the Negro
push for voting rights in the state. As a consequence, Mississippi maintained
a culture of voter denial, and local leaders manufactured a series of obstacles
to refuse their black residents access to the polls.

Evers reminded Roy Wilkins of the varied obstacles in place to hinder the
black vote and thus the work he had in front of him to counter such attempts.
"Mississippi is one of the last 'Frontier' states," Evers remarked, "that is still
holding on to the poll tax system as a subterfuge to voting." As a means of
countering this "subterfuge," the NAACP, Progressive Voters Leagues, Elks,
and American Legion "launched a 'Pay Your Poll Tax Campaign' to get as
many persons to pay their poll tax as possible so as to take advantage of the

'present forces' in the office of the registrar." Here Evers meant Hinds County circuit clerk, Registrar H. T. Ashford, who appeared opposed to the implantation of voting obstacles. Ashford had made it quite clear that he was "going to register anyone that comes up here who can read and write," Evers noted. This proved to be important, as there were a total of 32,697 voters in Jackson as of November 6, 1956, of which 3,946 were Negro, Evers reported. However, there were "47,000 or more" Negroes in the city of Jackson whom Evers and the other groups sought to target in their voting campaign. In addition to using radio, television, telephones, and correspondence to reach the masses, they were also planning to use "Register Now" bumper stickers that would be placed "on some 5,000 or more automobiles in the city," Evers explained. This proved to be grueling work, but the atmosphere had changed for the better, and Evers believed that the NAACP had to strike while the iron was hot. He advised Wilkins that contrary "to the southern pet expression 'the time ain't ripe,' the time is ripe, for in this particular area we can get even our ultra-conservative Negroes to voice a positive reply when you ask them to pay their poll tax and register. Even our city teachers are getting into the act, generously without reservations."[61] Amid the positive swing activism seemed to be taking in the late 1950s, there were also important developments upon the continent of Africa that yielded a great deal of influence on the thought processes of African American activists across the country and on Evers in particular.

The 1950s and 1960s recorded a multitude of victories against colonialism, and African Americans witnessed the birth of independent African nations. The meaning of citizenship discussed and formulated abroad had a profound impact on the actions of civil rights activists in the United States. In March 1957 African American leaders such as Adam Clayton Powell, A. Philip Randolph, Congressman Charles Diggs, Ralph Bunche, and Martin Luther King Jr. attended the Ghanaian celebration marking the end of colonial rule in that country. The celebration spoke volumes to all present but to African American leaders in particular. King recalled the lessons Ghana offered to civil rights activists in America. "Ghana has something to say to us," he remarked. "It says to us first, that the oppressor never voluntarily gives freedom to the oppressed. You have to work for it. . . . Freedom is never given to anybody. For the oppressor has you in domination because he plans to keep you there, and he never voluntarily gives it up. And that is where the strong resistance comes. Privileged classes never give up their privileges without strong resistance."[62]

Medgar Evers's growing awareness of the ways Africans were challenging oppression abroad with positive results bolstered that connection between male identity, political rights, and citizenship. It also enhanced his belief in one's personal responsibility toward racial uplift. Evers also witnessed more rebellious activities from area youth, a development he monitored with a great deal of excitement and anticipation.

In March Alcorn students rebelled in response to a series of articles written by African American history professor Clennon King. King's first article, Evers reported, had "ridiculed and castigated the NAACP, Supreme Court justices, etc., which lead [sic] to a complete boycott of the school's facilities by its 570 students." The board of trustees demanded that the students end the boycott and return to their classes or face expulsion. The students refused "on the grounds that Professor King had not been dismissed," and on March 8 Ernest McEwen, president of the student body, "read a statement that the entire student body," Evers reported, "had approved agreeing unanimously to withdraw, rather than be expelled." The students packed their belongings, and many left for home. The students' revolt "shocked the very foundation that the white supremacists thought they had reinforced so very substantially," Evers proclaimed. "(Imagine Negro students defying an ultimatum issued by a Board of Trustees in the State of Mississippi who happened to be white!)." Although many of the students were allowed to return, the leaders of the boycott were "denied the privilege to reenter." With assistance from the NAACP national office, scholarships were provided for seven of the expelled students "for the remainder of the 1956–57 school term." The students attended Virginia Union University in Richmond, Virginia, and Central State University in Wilberforce, Ohio.[63] Evers had also met McEwen, by accident, while at a Trailways bus station and arranged a meeting between the two in Jackson.[64]

Evers took what had happened at Alcorn as an indication that the social climate was rapidly changing. In conjunction with the February testimonies of Rev. W. D. Ridgeway and Beatrice Young at the civil rights hearings before the U.S. Senate Sub-Committee on Civil Rights in Washington, D.C., and the ongoing investigation of abuse and prison conditions at the Hinds County jail, Evers noted that these occurrences served as indicators "that everything is not tranquil as the Governor and others would have the nation believe." He now considered Alcorn A&M College as a "smoldering inferno . . . that could possibly be repetitious of foregoing events." The only hindrance he saw to that process was "the fact that [Clennon] King will not permit himself to return to campus, which would undoubtedly activate any dormant feeling of tranquility."[65] With this type of encouragement, Evers worked harder to connect the Mississippi struggle for political and civil equality with the growing national movement.

During the latter part of the 1950s, Evers heightened his activist role in response to white communities' increasingly violent reactions to African Americans' demands for social change. In a personal statement Evers recounted the events of March 11, 1958, in which he purchased a "Trailway [*sic*] bus ticket from Meridian to Jackson." Evers sat behind the driver and refused to move when bus operator G. V. Shelton ordered him to the back of the bus. His refusal initiated the involvement of the police, who ordered Evers off the bus and questioned him at a nearby police station "for some ten minutes." Here the officers questioned Evers, wanting to make sure that he "realized the seriousness of his action." After the brief interrogation, they allowed him to reboard. Evers defiantly manned the front seat all the way back to Jackson, despite the actions of a cab driver who stopped the bus, boarded, and struck him repeatedly in the face.[66] It is important to note here that his defiance in the face of Jim Crow seating places Medgar Evers in the tradition of challenging transportation segregation in the same vein as civil rights activists Rosa Parks, Edgar Daniel (E. D.) Nixon, and Martin Luther King Jr.

In 1958 *Ebony* magazine published an interview with Medgar Evers titled "Why I Live in Mississippi." Evers spoke candidly with *Ebony* correspondent Francis H. Mitchell throughout the article concerning his love for the state of his birth. From his comments it is easy to understand his reasons for remaining in Mississippi; there was too much to lose by leaving. Evers envisioned a better Mississippi and understood that to leave it would be to turn his back upon what Mississippi *could* be, for an acceptance of what it *now* was: chaotic, merciless, and uncivilized. He maintained that Mississippi represents "home. [It] is a part of the United States. And whether the whites like it or not, I don't plan to live here as a parasite. The things that I don't like I will try to change."[67] During the final two months of his life, the things he did not like were more pronounced, as were his strategies for defeating them. During May and June 1963, Evers's fight for full citizenship rights intensified in conjunction with applied direct-action tactics by area youth. These flurries of intense activity brought Jackson, Mississippi, national attention and heightened the civil rights struggle and agitation throughout the state.

Jackson mayor Allen C. Thompson had, through the media and organized rallies, sought to stifle the effectiveness of the Jackson civil rights movement at every turn, a movement that by 1963 had been implementing effective economic boycotts of staple businesses in the downtown area. In response, Thompson attempted to use his political office as a brush break to weaken the momentum of civil rights activism. His heavy-handed tactics against boycott participants, combined with his media blitz touting the benefits of the status quo in race relations, assured southern conservatives of the city's commitment to maintaining current racial hierarchies and white-dominated control of the political process. Thompson exploited every opportunity to draw black support from the boycotts while pushing the conservative line that Negroes in Jackson were satisfied with the way things were and that the races worked together to solve any problem that developed. This notion proved to be extremely important to political officials in light of area boycotts, and they worked hard to sell this manufactured fantasy to the public. On May 13 Thompson presented his defense of race relations in Jackson on radio station WJDX and television station WLBT. This would prove to be a monumental turning point between Evers and white conservative leaders in the state of Mississippi.

Thompson argued throughout his speech that what made Jackson such a great city were its beautiful facilities, libraries, parks, and an absence of slums that were prevalent, he pointed out, in larger urban metropolises. He cautioned the "Nigra" citizens to realize the good they were afforded by living "in a city where you . . . are treated, no matter what anybody else tells you, with dignity, courtesy and respect." His optimism, however, failed to acknowledge the fact that African Americans suffered from extreme levels of violence, social inequality, and the intimidating tactics of the ever-present Mississippi State Sovereignty Commission. In defense of conservative ideas on race and political authority in Jackson, Thompson made it clear that there would be no change in policy, and neither he nor the city of Jackson would submit to the threats of racial agitators and subversives. He further warned that no outsiders from President Kennedy down could tell Jackson how to govern.[68]

The same day that Thompson delivered his speech, Evers and members of the NAACP branches released a statement acknowledging their plans to "end all state and government sponsored segregation in the parks, playgrounds, schools, libraries and other public facilities." "To accomplish this," the statement read, "we shall use all lawful means of protests—picketing, marches, mass meetings, litigation and whatever legal means we deem necessary."[69] The NAACP leadership, however, proved to be willing to include political officials in the decision making process. The *Jackson Daily News* carried portions of the released statement, and Thompson was, undoubtedly, aware of its existence and thus could not have missed the more aggressive stance of the local NAACP and its leadership.[70]

In the days after Thompson's speech, the struggle for sociopolitical parity in Jackson intensified. The mayor's refusal to acquiesce to NAACP requests for a biracial committee to address the racial problems plaguing the city only added to the animosity between city officials and NAACP members. Thompson announced that "he would meet with responsible local Negro leaders, but would not talk to representatives of the NAACP, CORE, or agitator groups." He also called for Negroes to "reject any bid for leadership by outside agitators" and to support the city's segregationist stance, which had resulted, according to Thompson, in successful race relations in Jackson. Because Thompson refused to meet with NAACP officials, Medgar Evers announced that "national representatives were [now here] to plan 'possible direct action in the City of Jackson provided conferences to negotiate with our city officials are not worked out.'"[71] By national leaders, Evers was referring to the arrival of NAACP executive secretary Roy Wilkins.

Medgar Evers and other leaders responded immediately to the conservative position of the mayor and city officials. The Citizens Committee for Human Rights of Jackson, headed by local black businessman I. S. Sanders, announced its rejection of "the position stated by Mayor Allen Thompson, who claims that Negro citizens of Jackson are satisfied with the status quo." Responding to Thompson's willingness to "meet with responsible local Negro leaders," Evers openly charged the mayor with attempting to meet with "Yes-men" who were assured of going along with his program. As a means of further rejecting the current political structure of Jackson, Evers warned all who were willing to collaborate with Jackson officials that "we consider Negroes who would sell out our program as being Uncle Tom's [sic] of the first order and we will deal with them economically as we are dealing with those [who are enabling inequality to continue] downtown."[72] Both the national media and civil rights activists across the nation paid close attention to events occurring in Jackson and to the militant stance of its outspoken field secretary. By 1963 both Evers and the NAACP stepped up the rhetoric in challenging inequality, so much so that Evers openly challenged and chastised the highest political officials in the state to make meaningful changes.

The backbone of Thompson's attack on the movement for equality rested on his rosy outlook on race relations and African Americans' inferior sociopolitical standing within the city. Evers insisted upon equal television time to respond to the claims presented by Thompson and made known his intentions to receive equal time. He announced that the NAACP was "going to insist upon having this time because we were attacked by Mayor Thompson." He further pointed out that the "ethics of the Federal Communications Commission will require it. Whether public service time or paid time, our interest is in getting time." WLBT finally capitulated and granted Evers airtime in which he would present a seventeen-minute televised response to Thompson.[73]

On May 20, 1963, Evers appeared on television sets across Jackson and warned Mississippi's conservative leadership of the futility of trying to keep their Negro residents from learning about events in the rest of the world. He pointed to the strength black Mississippians derived from knowing the story of others fighting for freedom. "Tonight, the Negro plantation worker in the Delta," Evers proclaimed, "knows from his radio and television what happened today all over the world. He knows what black people are doing and he knows what white people are doing. He can see on the 6:00 o'clock news screen the picture of a 3:00 o'clock bite by a police dog. . . . He knows about the new free nations in Africa and knows that a Congo native can be a locomotive engineer, but in Jackson he cannot even drive a garbage truck. He sees black prime ministers and ambassadors, financiers and technicians."[74]

Evers also warned conservative Mississippians that Negroes were beginning to look about their home state and compare their problems with those abroad. This proved to be a powerful awakening, Evers observed, for it intensified personal and group introspection. After looking to see what types of struggles other groups were engaged in, Evers explained, the Negro then began to look "about his home community and what does he see, to quote our Mayor, in this 'progressive, beautiful, friendly, prosperous city with an exciting future?' He sees a city where Negro citizens are refused admittance to the City Auditorium and the Coliseum; his children refused a ticket to a good movie in a downtown theater; his wife and children refused service at a lunch counter in a downtown store where they trade; students refused the use of the main public libraries, parks, playgrounds and other tax-supported recreational facilities."[75] Evers's poignant response effectively placed Jackson within the overall movement for equality by linking Mississippi residents to the national and international struggle for citizenship and sociopolitical equality.

Evers's response to Thompson marked an all-out confrontation between civil rights activists and Mississippi's conservative white leadership. On May 21 Evers and other leaders such as A. D. Beittel, president of Tougaloo College, and Dean Charles A. Jones of Campbell College held a mass meeting at the Pearl Street AME Church to elect representatives who could meet with Thompson and effectively convey and defend the interests of the black community. The fourteen chosen representatives included Evers, I. S. Sanders, and John Salter Jr. As many expected, Thompson rejected a majority of the representatives chosen at the Pearl Street meeting. He objected to ten of the fourteen members elected but accepted Sanders, Revs. Leon Whitney and G. R. Haughton, and funeral director E. W. Banks. To these he added ten of his own choosing, including *Jackson Advocate* editor Percy Greene, Jackson State College president Jacob L. Reddix, and attorney Sydney Tharp. The others he chose consisted of individuals who either supported the Thompson administration or people he considered nonthreatening, such as Joseph Albright, the *Crisis* reported, "a public relations man who worked with the Mississippi State Sovereignty Commission." Evers acknowledged that the group could not guarantee acceptance of the mayor's selection. Of more importance, he maintained that the black community could not allow the mayor to "pick our leaders." The result, Evers argued, would be "'hit and-miss discussions with hand-picked colored citizens personally known and approved' by city officials." Although he admitted the readiness of the biracial group "to begin negotiations as in other progressive cities," he warned that blacks were not going to "wait a week or two weeks for . . . [Thompson] to make up his mind. Within the very near future we will begin to picket, to march and to sit-in." On May 24, in fact, black and white clergymen, "for the first time in Jackson," met to discuss the racial problems in the city and "agreed to devote their sermons the following Sunday . . . to this issue," the *Crisis* announced. After a few alterations, the group met with government officials on May 27 but could not agree, and talks stalled.[76] The following day, violence erupted at a local Woolworth's store in response to a sit-in protest conducted by local students and teachers from Tougaloo College. Due to the negative media coverage, Thompson agreed to a series of concessions, including a "declaration that all public facilities would be opened to all citizens on an equal basis." He later reneged on this agreement, claming "misrepresentation." After Thompson's claims of "misrepresentation" went public, the NAACP held another meeting at the Pearl Street AME church with an overflow audience of 2,000 attending. Evers informed the crowd of Mayor Thompson's recent act of treachery and demanded to know who in the audience stood ready to march. In response to his query, the 2,000 or so individuals rose as a single unit.[77]

The struggles raging in Jackson during May and June were bolstered by key U.S. Supreme Court decisions delivered during the spring of the year. The Supreme Court issued a number of crucial rulings addressing civil rights cases and the various protest tactics employed in the struggle for equality. Evers had reminded Jackson officials in his televised address that it was the

"American tradition to demonstrate, to assemble peacefully and to petition the government for a redress of grievances." "Such a petition," he noted, "may legitimately take the form of picketing, although, in Jackson, Negroes are immediately arrested when they attempt to exercise this constitutional right."[78] The constitutional right of peaceful assembly and protest of which Evers spoke received judicial support in *Peterson v. City of Greenville*. On May 20 the Supreme Court ruled that ten sit-in protestors in South Carolina were justified in their challenge of segregation through direct action. Evers notified Mayor Thompson by telegram that "Monday's sweeping decision by [the] Supreme Court gives additional support to our legal position and right to demonstrate peaceably and otherwise protest. We are fully prepared to do this, if necessary."[79] African Americans intensified their demands for the rights and privileges guaranteed them as citizens and looked to the courts for validation.

Thus in 1963 segregationists witnessed an emergence of renewed support for the African American struggle for social and political equality, support that enhanced open challenges to conservative political power in Mississippi. Seven days after *Peterson v. City of Greenville*, the Supreme Court ruled in *Watson et al. v. Memphis et al.* that the city of Memphis, Tennessee, could no longer wait to desegregate its parks and playgrounds.[80] Mississippi activists considered these rulings to be open forums on the question of citizenship rights, and Jackson students continued to protest, march, and resist police attempts to quell demonstrations.[81]

Throughout May and June black Mississippians physically challenged segregation while championing a new racial hierarchy based upon sociopolitical equality. In the process, they had refused to accept invisibility and had taken to the airways to speak out against racism and the rampant political inequities plaguing the city and state. African American men, women, and children had boycotted economic discrimination and filed affidavits challenging school segregation and voter discrimination at both the poll and registration levels, and Evers had been a fundamental part of these strategic challenges.

During the early morning hours of June 12, 1963, the issues of race, politics, and citizenship rights collided on a carport in a quiet middle-class black neighborhood. When the community awoke to screams of anguish, Medgar Wiley Evers lay drenched in blood with a bullet hole in his back surrounded by T-shirts with the words "Jim Crow Must Go" printed across each. These four powerful words served as his final commentary on racism, oppression, and second-class citizenship in Mississippi. Evers's contributions to the history of the civil rights movement in Mississippi continue to be a testament to the need for constant and sustained sociopolitical struggle against inequality. As a consequence, his life and death embody the true meaning of citizenship in America and the role we all must play in protecting its most essential elements for the benefit of those to come.[82]

NOTES

1. Throughout this essay, I use the term "Negro" without quotation marks when period appropriate and use the terms "African American" and "black" interchangeably.

2. Frederick Douglass quoted in Melvin Drimmer, ed., *Black History: A Reappraisal* (New York: Doubleday, 1968), 259.

3. For works dealing with the above-mentioned activists, see Charles Eagles, *The Price of Defiance: James Meredith and the Integration of Ole Miss* (Chapel Hill: University of North Carolina Press, 2009); Tony Martin, *Race First: The Ideological and Organizational Struggles of Marcus Garvey and the Universal Negro Improvement Association* (Dover, Del.: Majority Press, 1976); Harvard Sitkoff, *King: Pilgrimage to the Mountaintop* (New York: Hill and Wang, 2008); Malcolm X with Alex Haley, *The Autobiography of Malcolm X* (New York: Grove Press, 1965); and David T. Beito and Linda Royster Beito, *Black Maverick: T. R. M. Howard's Fight for Civil Rights and Economic Power* (Urbana: University of Illinois Press, 2009).

4. Myrlie Evers-Williams and Manning Marable, *The Autobiography of Medgar Evers: A Hero's Life and Legacy Revealed through His Writings, Letters, and Speeches* (New York: Basic Civitas Books, 2005), 4–5.

5. Charles Evers and Andrew Szanton, *Have No Fear: The Charles Evers Story* (New York: John Wiley and Sons, 1997), 1–2, 11; Myrlie Evers and William Peters, *For Us, the Living* (New York: Doubleday, 1967), 16.

6. Evers and Szanton, *Have No Fear*, 13–14.

7. Ibid., 1–2; Evers-Williams and Marable, *Autobiography of Medgar Evers*, 4–5; Evers and Peters, *For Us, the Living*, 16.

8. Evers and Szanton, *Have No Fear*, 13.

9. Information regarding Evers's enlistment in and discharge from the U.S. military acquired through the National Personnel Records Center, Military Personnel Records, St. Louis. For statistics regarding the number of African American–enlisted soldiers from Mississippi, see John Dittmer, *Local People: The Struggle for Civil Rights in Mississippi* (Urbana: University of Illinois Press, 1994), 17.

10. Jack Mendelsohn, *The Martyrs: Sixteen Who Gave Their Lives for Racial Justice* (New York: Harper & Row, 1966), 64–65.

11. Maryanne Vollers, *Ghosts of Mississippi: The Murder of Medgar Evers, the Trials of Byron De La Beckwith, and the Haunting of the New South* (Boston: Little, Brown, 1995), 31; John Hope Franklin and Alfred Moss Jr., *From Slavery to Freedom: A History of African Americans*, 8th ed. (Boston: McGraw-Hill, 2000), 483; Medgar Evers, "Why I Live in Mississippi," *Ebony*, November 1958, 66; Evers-Williams and Marable, *Autobiography of Medgar Evers*, 6; Evers and Szanton, *Have No Fear*, 47; Mendelsohn, *Martyrs*, 65.

12. David Colley, *The Road to Victory: The Untold Story of World War II's Red Ball Express* (Washington, D.C.: Brassey, 2000), 37, 43, 47. According to Colley, "Red Ball was a common railway term in the 1940s that had the same meaning as today's express mail." Ibid., 47.

13. John Shevlin quoted in ibid., 58.

14. Jennifer Brooks, *Defining the Peace: World War II Veterans, Race, and the Remaking of Southern Political Tradition* (Chapel Hill: University of North Carolina Press, 2004), 4. Historian Neil R. McMillen also speaks to the importance of World War II on civil rights activism in *Dark Journey: Black Mississippians in the Age of Jim Crow*, Illini Books edition (Urbana: University of Illinois Press, 1990), 286–287. See also Christopher S. Parker, *Fighting for Democracy: Black Veterans and the Struggle against White Supremacy in the Postwar South* (Princeton, N.J.: Princeton University Press, 2009).

15. Evers and Peters, *For Us, the Living*, 124.

16. George R. Metcalf, *Black Profiles* (New York: McGraw-Hill, 1968), 197; "Funeral March Finishes in White-Led Agitation," *Jackson Daily News*, June 16, 1963, 1A. The *Jackson Daily News* also reported that Evers served with both "bakery . . . and general quartermaster companies." *Jackson Daily News*, June 16, 1963, 14A.

17. Evers, "Why I Live in Mississippi," 66. See also Evers and Szanton, *Have No Fear*, 60–64; and Evers-Williams and Marable, *Autobiography of Medgar Evers*, 6–7.

18. Glenda Elizabeth Gilmore, *Defying Dixie: The Radical Roots of Civil Rights, 1919–1950* (New York: W. W. Norton, 2008), 414.

19. Charles M. Payne, *I've Got the Light of Freedom: The Organizing Tradition and the Mississippi Freedom Struggle* (Berkeley: University of California Press, 1995), 24–25; Dittmer, *Local People*, 13–19; McMillen, *Dark Journey*, 252–253. For further discussions on the impact of World War II on African Americans' sense of place in society outside of the state of Mississippi, see Adam Fairclough, *Race & Democracy: The Civil Rights Struggle in Louisiana, 1915–1972* (Athens: University of Georgia Press, 1999), 73–80.

20. President's Committee, *To Secure These Rights: The Report of the President's Committee on Civil Rights* (Washington, D.C.: Government Printing Office, 1947), 147–148. The committee ended by suggesting a series of recommendations. See "The Committee's Recommendations," in ibid., 151–173.

21. Evers, "Why I Live in Mississippi," 66; Evers and Szanton, *Have No Fear*, 76. Many returning black veterans were no longer willing to choose nonviolence as a strategy when confronted with racism or white aggression. Many joined organizations whose members fought for equality but were also willing to defend themselves when confronted with white-generated violence. For discussions on these types of organizations and their members, see Robert F. Williams, *Negroes with Guns* (Detroit: Wayne State University Press, 1998); Lance Hill, *The Deacons for Defense: Armed Resistance and the Civil Rights Movement* (Chapel Hill: University of North Carolina Press, 2004); and Simon Wendt, *The Spirit and the Shotgun: Armed Resistance and the Struggle for Civil Rights* (Gainesville: University Press of Florida, 2007).

22. Evers and Peters, *For Us, the Living*, 27, 32. See also the biographical description of the Everses in Evers (Medgar and Myrlie Beasley) Papers, Mississippi Department of Archives and History, Jackson, Archives & Library Division, Special Collections Section, Manuscript Collection, no. Z/2231.000/S.

23. Myrlie Evers interview with Nicholas Hordern for the *Delta Democrat-Times*, Evers (Medgar Wiley and Myrlie Beasley) Papers, Box 3, Folder 48. Myrlie Evers discusses the opportunities afforded African Americans by Magnolia Mutual, as well as the origins of the company, in Evers and Peters, *For Us, the Living*, 72.

24. James C. Cobb, *The Most Southern Place on Earth: The Mississippi Delta and the Roots of Regional Identity* (New York: Oxford University Press, 1992), 229, 231; Kim Lacy Rogers, *Life and Death in the Delta: African American Narratives of Violence, Resilience, and Social Change* (New York: Palgrave Macmillan, 2006), 5.

25. See Nan Elizabeth Woodruff, *American Congo: The African American Freedom Struggle in the Delta* (Cambridge, Mass.: Harvard University Press, 2003).

26. Myrlie Evers quoted in Henry Hampton and Steve Fayer, eds., *Voices of Freedom: An Oral History of the Civil Rights Movement from the 1950s through the 1980s* (New York: Bantam Books, 1990), 7.

27. Metcalf, *Black Profiles*, 199; Myrlie Evers-Williams and Melinda Blau, *Watch Me Fly: What I Learned on the Way to Becoming the Woman I Was Meant to Be* (Boston: Little, Brown, 1999), 62; Aaron Henry, with Constance Curry, *Aaron Henry: The Fire Ever Burning* (Jackson: University Press of Mississippi, 2000), 81; David Beito and Linda Royster Beito, "T. R. M. Howard: Pragmatism over Strict Integrationist Ideology in the Mississippi Delta, 1942–1954," in *Before Brown: Civil Rights and White Backlash in the Modern South*, ed. Glenn Feldman (Tuscaloosa: University of Alabama Press, 2004), 87.

28. Beito and Beito, *Black Maverick*, 81; Henry, *Aaron Henry*, 81.

29. Myrlie Evers, "He Said He Wouldn't Mind Dying—If . . . ," *Life*, June 28, 1963, 36.

30. Medgar Evers to Alcorn A&M Registrar, January 11, 1954, Evers (Medgar Wiley and Myrlie Beasley) Papers, Box 3, Folder 39.

31. "Negro Applies to Ole Miss," *Jackson Daily News*, January 22, 1954, newspaper

clipping, Evers (Medgar and Myrlie Beasley) Papers, Box 24, Folder 1; "Alcorn Graduate Applies for Admission to University of Mississippi Law School," *Jackson Advocate*, January 30, 1954, 1.

32. "Alcorn Graduate Applies for Admission," 1. The *Jackson Daily News*, the Associated Press, and the *Commercial Appeal* also reported that the NAACP would serve as Evers's representative in "Coleman to Decide Case of Negro Who Wants to Be Lawyer," January 22, 1954, "Mound Bayou Man Files Application at 'U' Law School," January 22, 1954, and "Negro Seeks to Enter Ole Miss Law School," January 23, 1954, respectively, newspaper clippings, Evers (Medgar and Myrlie Beasley) Papers, Box 24, Folder 1.

33. "Medgar Evers, Assistant Field Secretary, NAACP, Memorandum," in Evers-Williams and Marable, *Autobiography of Medgar Evers*, 17. The board members attributed their rejection of Evers's application to the fact that he had submitted recommendation letters from residents of Newton County instead of from his current residence in Bolivar County. The University of Mississippi later changed its admission requirements to include recommendation letters from five "Ole Miss" alumni. For a history of the University of Mississippi and discussions of Evers's attempt to integrate the law school and the university's response, see David G. Sansing, *The University of Mississippi: A Sesquicentennial History* (Jackson: University Press of Mississippi, 1999); and David G. Sansing, *Making Haste Slowly: The Troubled History of Higher Education in Mississippi* (Jackson: University Press of Mississippi, 1990).

34. Cleveland Donald Jr., "The Civil Rights Leader as Utopianist," in *Mississippi Heroes*, ed. Dean Faulkner Cole and Hunter Cole (Jackson: University Press of Mississippi, 1980), 220. Myrlie Evers also discusses her husband's internal battles with selling insurance to the impoverished. See Evers interview, 2.

35. Martin Luther King Jr., "The Birth of a New Nation," in *A Call to Conscience: The Landmark Speeches of Dr. Martin Luther King, Jr.*, ed. Clayborne Carson and Kris Shepard (New York: Warner Books, 2001), 33.

36. Mendelsohn, *Martyrs*, 2–3, 7; Medgar Evers, "1955 Annual Report," Evers (Medgar Wiley and Myrlie Beasley) Papers, Box 2, Folder 39, 5. For works addressing the history and concept of liberation theology, see James H. Cone, *Black Theology and Black Power* (New York: Seabury Press, 1969); Diana L. Hayes, *And Still We Rise: An Introduction to Black Liberation Theology* (New York: Paulist Press, 1996); and Dwight N. Hopkins, *Introducing Black Theology of Liberation* (Maryknoll, N.Y.: Orbis Books, 1999).

37. Evers, "1955 Annual Report," 5.

38. Evers and Peters, *For Us, the Living*, 154–155.

39. Ibid., 155–160; Pete Daniel, *Lost Revolutions: The South in the 1950s* (Chapel Hill: University of North Carolina Press, 2000), 222–224; Dittmer, *Local People*, 53–

54; Erle Johnston, *Mississippi's Defiant Years 1953–1973: An Interpretive Documentary with Personal Experiences* (Forest, Miss.: Lake Harbor Publishers, 1990), 34; Manfred Berg, *"The Ticket to Freedom": The NAACP and the Struggle for Black Integration* (Gainesville: University Press of Florida, 2005), 150–151; *NAACP Annual Report*, Forty-Seventh Year, "Progress and Reaction, 1955," 23. See also "M Is for Mississippi and Murder," NAACP Papers, LOC, Group II, Box A-423, Folder 1, 4.

40. Evers, "1955 Annual Report," 5.

41. *NAACP Annual Report*, Forty-Seventh Year, "Progress and Reaction, 1955," 9, 24–25; Dittmer, *Local People*, 54; Payne, *I've Got the Light of Freedom*, 39; Evers and Peters, *For Us, the Living*, 169–170; "White Farmer Faces Murder Charge after Lincoln Negro Killed," *Jackson Daily News*, August 15, 1955, 1; "DA Arrests Suspect in Political Killing," *State Times* (Jackson), August 15, 1955, 1A; Evers, "1955 Annual Report," 5–6.

42. Evers and Peters, *For Us, the Living*, 169–170.

43. Evers, "1955 Annual Report," 5.

44. "Pin Vote Slaying on Trio," n.d., newspaper clipping, NAACP Papers, LOC, Group II, Box A-422, Folder 1.

45. "White Farmer Faces Murder," 1; "DA Arrests Suspect," 1; and *NAACP Annual Report*, Forty-Seventh Year, "Progress and Reaction, 1955," 9, 24–25.

46. Evers, "1955 Annual Report," 5–6; "Who Slew Negro Leader in Trap," *Jet*, September 1, 1955, 5. Although Evers discussed the Smith murder in his 1955 report, he provided a little more clarity regarding the physical attack upon Smith and the lack of an indictment during an address before the Los Angeles branch of the NAACP on May 31, 1959. The address is cataloged under Medgar Evers, "Address to the Los Angeles, California Branch NAACP," Mississippi Department of Archives and History, Subject File, "Medgar Evers 1954–1973," 4.

47. *NAACP Annual Report*, Forty-Seventh Year, "Progress and Reaction, 1955," 25; Evers, "1955 Annual Report," 6; "Emmett Till's Bravado Led to Killing, It Is Disclosed," *Look*, January 9, 1956, 1–3; National Association for the Advancement of Colored People, Papers of the NAACP: Part 20, White Resistance and Reprisals, 1956–1965 (Bethesda, Md.: University Publications of America, 1995), Group III, Series A, Administrative File, General Office File, Box A-232, microfilm reel 2 (hereafter cited as Papers of the NAACP: Part 20), "M Is for Mississippi and Murder," 5–6; Gene Roberts and Hank Klibanoff, *The Race Beat: The Press, the Civil Rights Struggle, and the Awakening of a Nation* (New York: Alfred A. Knopf, 2006), 86–108. For a detailed examination of the Till murder and individuals' desire not to allow his death to be in vain, see the September 1, 1956, issue of the *Pittsburgh Courier*. A Sumner, Mississippi, jury acquitted Bryant and Milam of the murder of Emmett Till, and the brothers later agreed to an interview with journalist William Bradford Huie for *Look* magazine, for which they were paid a substantial amount of money. Bryant and Milam admitted

during the interview that they had indeed killed Till for his brashness and admissions that he had "had white women" before. For the interview with Bryant and Milam, see *Look*, January 24, 1956. For a closer examination of the impact of the Till lynching on the civil rights movement, see Clenora Hudson-Weems, *Emmett Till: The Sacrificial Lamb of the Civil Rights Movement* (Troy, Mich.: Bedford, 1994); and Stephen J. Whitfield, *A Death in the Delta: The Story of Emmett Till* (Baltimore: John Hopkins University Press, 1988). See also NAACP *Annual Report*, Forty-Seventh Year, "Progress and Reaction, 1955," 8. For visual analyses of the Till lynching and its significance to the civil rights movement, see *Eyes on the Prize: America's Civil Rights Movement, 1954–1985* (Blackside Productions, 1987); and *The Untold Story of Emmett Louis Till* (Velocity Home Entertainment, 2006, DVD).

48. Dittmer, *Local People*, 58.

49. Ed King, interview with Worth Long, August 23, 1991, Southern Regional Council: Will the Circle Be Unbroken? Program Files and Sound Recordings, 1956–1998, Box 8, Folder 17, Manuscript, Archives and Rare Book Library, Emory University, Atlanta, 8 (hereafter cited as SRC: Will the Circle Be Unbroken?); Dittmer, *Local People*, 59. Although King notes that Till whistled at Carolyn Bryant, which put the eventual tragedy in motion, there exists a variety of accounts detailing what happened in the store between Bryant and Till, with his whistling being one of the many. For further discussion of the Till case, in particular the night Milam and Bryant kidnapped the young child, see Juan Williams, *Eyes on the Prize: America's Civil Rights Years, 1954–1965*, 15th anniversary ed. (New York: Penguin Books, 2002), 39–57.

50. Evers and Peters, *For Us, the Living*, 158–159.

51. See "Eyes of Nation Focused on Monday Trial in Miss.," *Pittsburgh Courier*, September 17, 1955, 1. See also "The Picture Story of a Little Boy's Murder," *Pittsburgh Courier*, September 17, 1955, 9, second section; and Evers and Peters, *For Us, the Living*, 158–159.

52. Evers, "1955 Annual Report," 9–10. Evers noted that the other NAACP officials attending the meeting included Executive Secretary Roy Wilkins, attorney Thurgood Marshall, Southeast Regional Secretary Ruby Hurley, and the director of the Washington Bureau, Clarence Mitchell. For a group photograph of those attending the meeting, see "Will Mississippi 'Whitewash' the Emmett Till Slaying?" *Jet*, September 22, 1955, 7.

53. Assistant U.S. Attorney General Warren Olney III to Roy Wilkins, December 6, 1955, NAACP Papers, LOC, Group II, Box A-422, Folder 3.

54. Medgar Evers, "Report: Killing of Clinton Melton, Negro, by Elmer Kimbel, White," December 13, 1955, Evers (Medgar Wiley and Myrlie Beasley) Papers, Box 3, Folder 14, 1–3. Kimbell was also a supposedly good friend of J. W. Milam, one of

the killers of Emmett Till, and was reportedly driving Milam's car the day he killed Melton. See, Dittmer, *Local People*, 58; Beito and Beito, *Black Maverick*, 140.

55. Evers-Williams and Marable, *Autobiography of Medgar Evers*, 11–12.

56. Gloster Current to Medgar Evers, January 26, 1955, NAACP Papers, LOC, Group II, Box C-346, Folder 4, 4.

57. The Tri-State Bank of Memphis proved to be an effective economic brush break against the fires of financial intimidation in Mississippi. The brainchild of Joseph E. Walker and his son A. Maceo Walker, Tri-State Bank was founded in 1946 to provide the black community with financial opportunities that would transform communities for the better. Although a Memphis entity, Mississippi businessmen such as T. R. M. Howard and civil rights leaders such as Gloster Current and Roy Wilkins saw its potential for changing the Jim Crow landscape in Mississippi. For a brief historical outline of the Tri-State Bank of Memphis, see Tri-State Bank of Memphis's webpage at http://www.tristatebank.com/114673.html.

58. "Committee on Emergency Aid to Farmers in Mississippi," January 11, 1956, Papers of the NAACP: Part 20, Group III, Series A, Administrative File, General Office File, Box A-233, microfilm reel 3.

59. Medgar Evers and Mildred Bond, "Economic Needs of Farmers in Delta Area," report to Gloster Current, January 23, 1956, and "Committee on Emergency Aid to Farmers in Mississippi," both in Papers of the NAACP: Part 20, Group III, Series A, Administrative File, General Office File, Box A-233, microfilm reel 3.

60. Medgar Evers to Roy Wilkins, January 11, 1956, Papers of the NAACP: Part 20, Group III, Series A, Administrative File, General Office File, Box A-114, microfilm reel 14. To view the actual letter written by Jefferson, see George L. Jefferson to Roy Wilkins, January 10, 1955, NAACP Papers, LOC, Group II, Box A-422, Folder 2.

61. Medgar Evers to Roy Wilkins, February 1, 1957, NAACP Papers, LOC, Group II, Box A-270, Folder 9.

62. Martin Luther King Jr., "The Birth of a New Nation," in Carson and Shepard, *Call to Conscience*, 29–30.

63. Medgar Evers, "Monthly Report," March 25, 1957, NAACP Papers, LOC, Group III, Box C-244, Folder 1, 2–3; Henry Jay Kirksey, interview with Worth Long, n.d., SRC: Will the Circle Be Unbroken?, Box 8, Folder 18, 17.

64. Evers, "Monthly Report," 3.

65. Medgar Evers to Gloster Current, April 9, 1957, NAACP Papers, LOC, Group III, Box C-244, Folder 1.

66. See Medgar Evers, "Personal Statement," and "rec'd via phone from Medgar Evers," March 13, 1958, Papers of the NAACP: Part 20, Group III, Series A, Administrative File, General Office File, Box A-114, microfilm reel 14. His statement was

dictated but not signed. The incident was also reported in "Negro Says Civil Rights Violated in Bus Controversy," *Birmingham News, Facts on File*, 54/58, Microfilm Code No., J14 4736,; and "Attacked on Bus in Miss.: Beat NAACP Exec," *Pittsburgh Courier*, March 22, 1958, 3, newspaper clipping, Evers (Medgar and Myrlie Beasley) Papers, Box 24, Folder 5.

67. Evers, "Why I Live in Mississippi," 65.

68. Allen C. Thompson speech, Tougaloo College Archives and Special Collections, Lillian P. Benbow Room of Special Collections, Medgar Wiley Evers Collection, unprocessed, Folder 1, 1–5.

69. NAACP Release, Papers of the NAACP: Part 20, Group III, Series A, Administrative File, General Office File, Box A-232, microfilm reel 2.

70. "Mayor Plans Preventive Actions Here," *Jackson Daily News*, May 13, 1963, 1, 14.

71. "Jackson Leader Pledge No Deals with Demonstrators," *Jackson Daily News*, May 14, 1963, 1; "Officials Plan Talk with Negroes Here," *Jackson Daily News*, May 15, 1963, 14.

72. "NAACP Says Allen Seeking 'Yes-Men,'" *Jackson Daily News*, May 16, 1963, 1.

73. Evers-Williams and Marable, *Autobiography of Medgar Evers*, 260; Kay Mills, *Changing Channels: The Civil Rights Case That Transformed Television* (Jackson: University Press of Mississippi, 2004), 27; Stephen D. Classen, *Watching Jim Crow: The Struggles over Mississippi TV, 1955–1969* (Durham, N.C.: Duke University Press, 2004), 45. Evers's demands for equal televised response time were, in fact, supported by the Fairness Doctrine. According to journalist Kay Mills, the Fairness Doctrine required that "broadcasters had to provide 'a reasonable amount of time for the presentation . . . of programs devoted to the discussion and consideration of public issues' while also encouraging and enabling broadcast of all sides of controversial issues." See Mills, *Changing Channels*, 27.

74. Medgar Evers, "The Years of Change Are Upon Us," Tougaloo College Archives and Special Collections, Lillian P. Benbow Room of Special Collections, Medgar Wiley Evers Collection, unprocessed, Folder 1, 4.

75. Ibid.

76. NAACP, "Background Information on New Desegregation Drive in Jackson, Miss.," May 28, 1963, NAACP Papers, LOC, Group III, Box C-74, Folder 1, 5–6; John R. Salter Jr., *Jackson, Mississippi: An American Chronicle of Struggle and Schism* (Malabar, Fla.: Robert E. Krieger, 1987), 123–125, 130–131; *The Crisis: A Record of the Darker Races* 70, no. 6 (June–July 1963): 357–359. For newspaper accounts, see "Mix Drive Talked Up," *Jackson Daily News*, May 21, 1963; "Mayor Proposes Racial Meeting," *Jackson Daily News*, May 22, 1963; "Mayor Sets Parley Despite Conflicts," *Jackson Daily News*, May 23, 1963; "New Plea to Negro Group," *Jackson Daily News*, May 24, 1963; "Race Tension Here Eases Up Slightly," *Jackson Daily News*, May 26, 1963; and

"Negro Apologizes for Walking Out in 'Wrong Group,'" *Jackson Daily News*, May 28, 1963. See also "Mayor Lists Names for Racial Meeting," *Clarion-Ledger*, May 23, 1963; and "Thompson Vows 'No Surrender,'" *Clarion-Ledger*, May 24, 1963. Evers quotes taken from "Mix Drive Talked Up" and "Mayor Proposes Racial Meeting." See also "Ask Jackson Mayor for Bi-Racial Talks: Plan Protests Marches, Sit-ins, Picketing if Demands Not Met," *Mississippi Free Press*, May 25, 1963, in the *American Historical Newspapers* database. For discussions on the "Failing" of biracial committees, see "Bi-Racial Committees Failing in Many Racially-Torn Cities," *Clarion-Ledger*, May 22, 1963; for a counterargument, see "Bi-Racial Body Seeks Bi-Racial Group in City," *Clarion-Ledger*, May 22, 1963.

77. Moody, *Coming of Age in Mississippi*, 264–267; "Attacked by White at Lunch Counter," *Jackson Daily News*, May 28, 1963, 1; Richard Hofstadter and Michael Wallace, eds., *American Violence: A Documentary History* (New York: Alfred A. Knopf, 1970), 434; Elizabeth Jacoway and David R. Colburn, eds., *Southern Businessmen and Desegregation* (Baton Rouge: Louisiana State University Press, 1982), 240. For information regarding Thompson's concessions, broken promises, and Evers's response, see Evers and Peters, *For Us, the Living*, 271; Adam Nossiter, *Of Long Memory: Mississippi and the Murder of Medgar Evers* (New York: Addison-Wesley, 1994), 59; Salter, *Jackson, Mississippi*, 137–139; "Mayor Declares Made No 'Deals,'" *Jackson Daily News*, May 29, 1963, 1; NAACP News Release, "Jackson, Miss. Mayor Reneges on Promises, Negro Community Mobilizing Behind NAACP," May 30, 1963, Papers of the NAACP: Part 20, Group III, Series A, Administrative File, General Office File, Box A-233, microfilm reel 2; Mississippi State Sovereignty Commission Records online, SCR# 2-55-10-2-1-1-1, Mississippi Department of Archives and History; and NAACP 1963 *Annual Report*, "In Freedom's Vanguard, NAACP Report for 1963," 108.

78. Evers, "Years of Change Are Upon Us," 2.

79. *Peterson v. City of Greenville*, 373 U.S. 244 (1963). The *Peterson* (No. 71) case was one of five dealing with sit-ins heard by the court. The other four cases were comprised of *Lombard* (No. 58) in New Orleans, Louisiana; *Gober* (No. 66) in Birmingham, Alabama; *Avent* (No. 11) in Durham, North Carolina; and *Shuttlesworth* (No. 67) also in Birmingham, Alabama. Regarding Evers's comments, see "Telegram to the Mayor," *Crisis* 70, no. 6, (June–July 1963); and NAACP, "Background Information," 358.

80. *Watson et al. v. City of Memphis et al.*, 373 U.S. 526, (1963).

81. Vollers, *Ghosts of Mississippi*, 111–112; "Negroes Make Little Headway With Campaign," *Jackson Daily News*, May 31, 1963, 1, 12; Salter, *Jackson, Mississippi*, 148–150; "Jackson Police Jail 600 Negro Students," *New York Times*, June 1, 1963, 1, 8.

82. This essay is a part of a larger work, *Medgar Evers: Mississippi Martyr* (Fayetteville: University of Arkansas Press, 2011).

Trouble in My Way

Curriculum, Conflict, and Confrontation at Jackson State University, 1945–1963

Jelani Favors

In the larger town, few Negroes vote, but in the thickly settled rural areas, particularly in the counties in the delta, very few, if any Negroes vote. Why? Is it true that Negroes in Mississippi are satisfied with segregation, as Coleman and Eastland repeatedly tell the nation on TV programs? Why don't we challenge them? Why don't we speak out? Why are we so cowardly? No one wants to admit that we are living under a blanket of fear, with constant threats and undertones of violence. . . . What if we open our mouths? We are threatened with our jobs, our homes, our lives, we can not stay here and speak out. We must be silent or leave Mississippi. A revolution is surely taking place, will we win the peace or lose as always in the past to the reactionaries.

—Margaret Walker Alexander, August 12, 1957

George Swan returned to the campus of Jackson State University in the fall of 1947, eager to bear witness to what he had just experienced. That October Swan stood shoulder to shoulder with 1,000 other students from black colleges and secondary schools who gathered in Columbia, South Carolina, to declare war against the stranglehold of white supremacy. Their defiant stand in the heart of Dixie was not uncharacteristic of the growing discontent and brewing insurgency that was beginning to define black life in post–World War II America. "The Southern Youth met in solemn session," noted Swan. "Militant, courageous, Negro youth of the South. Youth—which must and will be served. Youth—dedicated to the struggle for freedom. Youth—determined to achieve that freedom in its lifetime."[1] Swan and Estemore A. Wolfe, another conference attendee, returned to campus to share these new declarations with their professors and peers as they recounted the conference proceedings in the student newspaper. They channeled their newfound energies into the creation of the Jackson State chapter of the Student Negro Youth Congress (SNYC), with Swan as its first president.[2] Although the viability of the SNYC quickly dissolved with its collapse after 1949, Swan held true to the pledge of the organization for the next three decades of his life, dedicating himself to the "struggle for freedom."

Swan married Henrene Wolfe, also a member of the Jackson State chapter of the SNYC, and they eventually moved to Detroit, where Henrene worked in the public school systems as a teacher. George's transition into the public workforce was more complicated. Upon graduation from Jackson State, he briefly sold life insurance for Universal Life Insurance in Mississippi, where, under the tutelage of attorney W. L. Mhoon, Swan worked his way into the homes of African Americans and sold more than policies; he also sold them on voter registration education and engaged them in discussions of freedom rights. Mhoon had used this tactic for years and additionally served as legal counsel for African Americans who had run-ins with local law enforcement. Indeed, by 1948, the year the Swans departed from Mississippi, George and Henrene shared concerns that the letters they wrote to each other while Henrene took graduate course at Atlanta University were being intercepted and that George's political activities were under surveillance.[3]

When he finally arrived in Detroit, George struggled to find work in the civil service, despite scoring well on the exams, holding a bachelor's degree, and having a veterans' preference. Nevertheless, he persevered, ultimately landing at the Chrysler Detroit Tank Arsenal, where he would work his way up to be manager of a quality control lab by 1960. As George and Henrene settled into the Detroit community, they never relinquished the activist roots they had embraced as young students at Jackson State. They became members of the National Negro Citizens Alliance and worshipped at Detroit's Hartford Baptist Church under the guidance of Rev. Charles Hill, an outspoken advocate for civil rights whose church was a hub for social activism. George played an integral role in bringing historian Lerone Bennett and activist Medgar Evers (both of whom were his former schoolmates in Mississippi) to the church, and as president of the local chapter of the Jackson State Alumni Association, George welcomed to Detroit a young man who was formerly enrolled at Jackson State but who now sought bravely to challenge the restraints of Jim Crow by registering at the University of Mississippi: James Meredith.

The narrative of George and Henrene Swan presents an intriguing twist to the widely adopted perception of Jackson State University as a bastion of conservatism. Scholars have neither recorded their names and deeds nor those of the scores of young students from their generation who have been dismissed as irrelevant to the continued struggle for black liberation. Indeed, youth altogether had been characterized as disengaged from any form of social or political insurgency during the Cold War era and were thought to be bound by their own selfish dreams or desires. In the fall of 1951, *Time* magazine's cover story, "The Younger Generation," declared, "Youth today is waiting for the hand of fate to fall on its shoulders, meanwhile working fairly hard and saying almost nothing. The most startling fact about the younger generation is its silence. . . . It does not issue manifestoes, make speeches or carry posters. It has been called the 'Silent Generation.'"[4]

Despite arguments that historically black colleges were ineffective in fostering radicalization and dissent among students during the nascent stages of the civil rights movement, strong evidence exists that draws important linkages between the culture of black colleges and the politicization and mobilization of scores of students from one generation to the next. The most overlooked of these generations, however, belongs to students such as George and Henrene Swan. Despite mounting troubles (both internal and external) that plagued administrators, faculty, and students working within the enclaves of historically black colleges and universities, the constructive and redemptive work of racial uplift continued. Moreover, a second curriculum existed that ensconced students in racial consciousness, gave them political motive, and presented black youth with a blueprint on how to tackle the hypocrisies embedded in American culture. Black college students, educated within the southern Black Belt during World War II and the Cold War, formed a critical nexus between the "New Negro" of the 1920s and 1930s and the college militant of the 1960s.

Training toward a Social End: Race Consciousness and the Second Curriculum

In September 1947 a young Marine sergeant stepped off a bus as it pulled into the terminal in Jackson, Mississippi. He was returning from the perils of war abroad, but as a young African American from Mississippi he was also reentering the harsh environment of the Magnolia State with newfound determination to stand tall against the forces of white supremacy. The sergeant's military experiences convinced him and countless other black veterans returning from World War II that things could never be the same again. Indeed, many changes did take place, especially for Sergeant John Peoples, who, twenty years later, would assume the presidency of Jackson State University. Raised in Starkville as the only son of working-class parents, Peoples, upon discharge, enrolled at Jackson State College, never once imagining the role he would later assume in the destiny and direction of his alma mater. The administration of John Peoples became the axis upon which change presented itself to the students, faculty, and staff of Jackson State in the late 1960s.

He was a man of his time, influenced by war, by his military training, and through the nurturing and leadership opportunities presented to him as a student of the very school he would later oversee.[5] He immediately demonstrated his commitment to justice by taking bold steps in claiming the democracy that he had fought for abroad. Peoples recalled:

> I decided when I came back to Mississippi that I was going to have a certain
> conduct. That I was not going to accept any old discrimination or racism.
> In the city of Jackson, there was no movement necessarily for civil rights,
> but we veterans took advantage of the fact that Mississippi had passed a law
> which said that veterans would be exempted from the poll tax. . . . So those
> of us went down to challenge that and we did register to vote. I registered to
> vote in 1948.[6]

Young men such as John Peoples and George Swan were not only receiving direction from external movements for justice, they were also being molded to carry on a broader fight for equality for all African Americans. Over the years, African American youth flocked to the friendly confines of black universities, thus escaping the corrosive messages of white America that sought to deny them a dignified purpose or a strong sense of self-worth. "People who experience a kind of holistic oppression find ways to develop an enclave," noted historian Manning Marable. "They find ways to develop values that nurture young children so that they are not given the message and internalize the message that we are nobody. And they are also given one other value; a sense of dignity and a sense of mission."[7] Manning could easily have been describing the role of educators who toiled in the structures that housed and trained generations of black youth.

The diverse faculty of black colleges worked diligently and often under great duress to enlighten and embolden black collegians to believe in their own potential to act as agents for the betterment of society.[8] This message was not always expressed explicitly, nor was it delivered by all faculty. Openly dispatching calls for black liberation (particularly in Mississippi) could be interpreted as a frontal attack against white supremacy, thus creating friction for the administrators of the institution and perhaps violent repercussions for the instructor.

What ensued was a delicate balancing act between self-preservation in a hostile environment and the dogged pursuit of equality and full citizenship. The latter of these goals called for consistent creativity for those faculty members and administrators willing to engage in such a cause. Other institutions important to the black community that had previously challenged the policies of Jim Crow suffered extreme reprisals, which included the firebombing of radical churches, the persecution of civil rights organizations, and the brazen execution of countless organizers and activists. Black colleges, therefore, became the most important and seemingly noncollapsible passageway for transferring idealism and agency to impressionable young minds. Scholar Joy Ann Williamson concluded her study on the role of these invaluable spaces and their importance to the freedom struggle in Mississippi by suggesting, "Their conversion into movement centers actively plotting against white supremacy was made possible by constituents determined to use any and all means for their cause."[9]

Numerous professors adopted techniques that resembled thinly veiled critiques of American society and encouraged their students to question the inherent contradictions of a country that professed democracy but sanctioned discrimination and violence against its own citizens. In an interview conducted in the waning stages of the civil rights movement, longtime Jackson State professor Margaret Walker Alexander illuminated the strategy that made her scholarship and her intimate contact with black collegians supremely significant. "I personally believe that black people need to preach in their work, but to preach so subtly that you don't think of it as preaching," noted Alexander. "The greatest art is the greatest propaganda. The greatest propaganda is not necessarily the greatest art."[10] Perspectives such as these shaped a second curriculum that subsequently encouraged students at Jackson State to form campus organizations that called for heightened discussion on the pernicious effects of the color line.

One of the most poorly explored sources among historians has been the student newspapers at historically black colleges. Although several scholars have cited student papers to chronicle the celebrated 1960s era of student activism, few have perused and documented what the collective voices of these papers have told us about radicalism and dissent during the Cold War era. The Jackson State student newspaper, *The Blue and White Flash*, touted to be "the true voice of Jackson College," was published on a monthly basis and contained stories and editorials that measured the pulse of student awareness. Race consciousness and an expanding worldview were prominently exhibited throughout its pages. Four years before George Swan started the SNYC chapter on campus, a student named Susie Baughns challenged her peers to defy the boundaries of the closed society and to unite in solidarity for freedom. Her article read:

> This is the time for plain speaking. The Negro's vital stake in victory, his unexcelled record of patriotism give him the right to be concerned about his civil liberties. In an hour of crisis, broad social problems come into sharp focus. . . . Here on campus we have an organization, the Youth Council, which uses psychological and constitutional procedures to help Negroes in their struggle for full emancipation and to secure this ideal. . . . Help solve the problem of segregation and racial discrimination.[11]

Baughns's call to arms resonated with her peers, who embraced the black press's campaign that challenged African Americans to achieve victory at home and abroad. In that same month, student representatives attended the National Association for the Advancement of Colored People's (NAACP) fourth annual student conference, which was held at Clark College in Atlanta. The conference's theme that year was "War and Post War Problems for Negro Youth."[12]

Unveiled protest surely would have stirred trouble on campus and perhaps may have even brought students into harm's way. Nevertheless, students took cues from the second curriculum and the budding social movements around them to pour out reflections of their hopes, dreams, and prayers for justice and equality. The development of campus organizations, students attending conferences, and articles written in the campus paper were all forms of dissent that could be shielded from the state in some reasonable way. The thin veneer the walls of the campus provided was just enough space to plant seeds of insurgency that would develop in due time. The white power structure ostensibly overlooked the safe spaces of black colleges. Historian Adam Fairclough noted, "They never succeeded in completely subordinating black schools to their political ends. Indeed, education remained one of the principal arenas of resistance to white supremacy."[13] What is undoubtedly clear is that students at Jackson State did not sit idly by as more radical and militant forms of protests were emerging. Furthermore, no one appeared to prevent them from joining in the struggle as it flowered in its early stages.

The violent barriers that confronted students in Mississippi proved to be all too real upon their graduation. No longer protected by the shelter of the black college environment, their vulnerability to the forces of white supremacy prompted many graduates to call upon their academic training to find ways to subvert oppression, especially through education. Jackson State's long tradition of being one of the leading producers of African American teachers allowed alums to apply the same second curriculum training that they received to young students caught in the web of a hostile world. Onezimae Clark was fully prepared for the challenge. She recorded her petition to God in *The Blue and White Flash* and dedicated it to her graduating class:

> Grant us O' God the ability as prospective teachers to inspire instead of discourage, to give light, where there is darkness. To help where it is needed, and to fight for justice for all. Unless O' God we are able to do these things there will be so few leaders and great men and women of tomorrow that the progress of our race will be impeded. Today we launch, O' God, teach us how to sail and where to anchor.[14]

Race consciousness was the most critical component of the second curriculum. Students attending black colleges were constantly reminded of their self-worth and their importance to the collective struggle for black liberation. Clark's prayer strongly suggests that students internalized these ideals in their own pedagogies as they assumed the holistic role of teachers in the segregated South. Moreover, her words should be interpreted not only as a display of liberation theology but also as a clear intent to become engaged in activism and dissent in the manner that was most accessible and pragmatic to her and countless others living underneath an encompassing blanket of fear.

The stories of black students taking on roles in the growing movement were not buried on the back pages of *The Blue and White Flash*. They were front-page material, often serving as the lead story. Reports chronicling the budding movement are of considerable significance, signaling that those responsible for editing or even censoring were not hindered in their support for highly politicized messages. In the 1940s and 1950s students consistently demonstrated that the instruction they received carried a requirement to pursue the full citizenship that had escaped previous generations of African Americans. "We are moving forward to serve humanity," wrote student Johnny Edwards,

> and we have been thoroughly oriented in how to solve our own problems;
> for our teacher training has been directed toward social ends, that is, toward

the perpetuation, progress and welfare of all men. . . . We realize that the educational objectives that we now possess should become consciously integrated with all social organization to the end that the educational objectives may determine the direction of social change, whereby all men would reap the benefits of our democratic society.[15]

In 1949, when Edwards wrote these words, the American political landscape was still years away from making a significant shift. Students attending black colleges throughout the South would ultimately prove to be one of the major catalysts toward that transformation. It is clear, however, that this evolution did not miraculously happen overnight. For students living in a society that constantly promoted ideas of citizenship and democracy for all, the black college environment proved to be the perfect laboratory for these ideals to be thoroughly scrutinized, questioned, and rejected as hollow and even fraudulent.

The collegians who raised these informed critiques were student leaders. They were editors of the newspapers; presidents of fraternities, sororities, and campus organizations; and officers in the student government association. The pendulum between hope and doubt swung freely in the 1950s. Black college students at Southern University, South Carolina State, Alcorn State, Florida A&M, Morgan State, and Alabama State would all play significant roles in local protests against Jim Crow policies. Students would become emboldened by achievements through the judicial branch and conversely shattered by the lynching of Emmett Till. The shared experiences and concerns of students bound them together as more difficult days rapidly approached. Fueling their slow march to justice was a sense of idealism and purpose, and the stinging hypocrisy of American society. Encouraging his fellow students to press on, Jackson State student Earl Gooden wrote:

To find self-contentment one must be satisfied with his or her responses to the forces encountered; the most successful way that this may be achieved is to set up a definite set of values and on these to stand at all times, not succumbing to doubt, peril, or any subduing forces. On these I stand: democracy, self realization, faith, and love of and respect for all mankind.[16]

Navigating their way through the conservative climate of Mississippi, students found supporters of such messages wherever they could. In January 1951 a valuable ally and student advocate arrived in the person of Jane McAllister.

Evil Will Triumph If the Good Do Nothing:
Constraint and Conflict at Jackson State

Born in 1899 in Vicksburg, Mississippi, Jane McAllister was a 1919 graduate of Talladega College, a small black liberal arts college in Alabama. McAllister received her graduate training at the University of Michigan, and in 1929 she became the first black woman to earn a Ph.D. in education at Columbia University. She returned to Mississippi in 1951 to serve first as a consultant and later as a full-time faculty member in the Department of Education at Jackson State. Her tour of duty as an educator had taken her to black colleges throughout the South, but she returned to Mississippi to be closer to her mother in Vicksburg. McAllister was well respected in her field and brought her sterling reputation with her to Jackson State. Her arrival on campus earned the lead story in the campus newspaper; students were excited to have someone with such credibility join the faculty. When asked about her feelings of arriving at Jackson State, McAllister displayed the sensitivity and compassion that made her well loved among her students:

> At present time Jackson College to me is young men and women who demand leadership training given not by a verbal theory-level type of performance but by direct experience in living and working with groups. It is a faculty with each individual aware of the tragedy of wasting the human resources of the college by not understanding (1) the cultural patterns of the students and (2) the rural scene from which they come.[17]

McAllister was an idealist. She loved promoting free thought and encouraged her students to engage in it often. Moreover, McAllister never hesitated to advocate freedom and equality to her students at Jackson State, regardless of the political or campus climate. McAllister stated, "In my own opinion, and I am a native Mississippian, and nothing can do more for the South than breaking down its isolation of ideas."[18] Her arrival at Jackson State coincided with the celebration of the college's seventy-fifth anniversary. The theme that year was "Education for a Free Nation." The use of the words "free" in describing America in the 1950s was a clear contradiction.

Black students, faculty, and even administrators clearly understood the hypocrisy behind the notion of American freedom and democracy, especially in Mississippi. Nevertheless, McAllister and others on the organizing committee focused on the continued preparation of their students as instruments of social and political change. The seventy-fifth anniversary celebration included lectures and symposiums, and McAllister hinted at the promotion of the second curriculum. She noted that the forums grew "out of the regular daily college curriculum experiences and return to enrich these experiences. Second, they point the regular college curriculum experiences more directly toward the goal of making students effective citizens in the free nation."[19]

Black educators impressed upon their students the ideas and responsibilities of full citizenship and constantly reminded them to be prepared for a transition that the older generation prayed they would see in their lifetime. While this argument for inclusion carried limited forethought about the flaws inherent in America's economic and political infrastructure, it did promote the concept of discipline and diligence among youth who were informed to be ever ready for the opportunity to prove themselves. Unlike the majority of black college faculty, McAllister had a reputation of not mincing her words when discussing Mississippi's state of affairs. Former student Rita Kinard recalled, "She spoke her mind about everything. She was not afraid, and she talked about the people here in Mississippi. About how they were so prejudiced and all."[20] Serving as a drill sergeant for justice, McAllister converted her classroom into a training ground and openly urged students to take bold strides against white supremacy. McAllister used to say, "Only evil will triumph if the good do nothing," recalled activist and former student Dorie Ladner. "She told us that we had to take a stand, and to sit and do nothing we wouldn't triumph."[21]

McAllister's political interests also played an important role in broadening the worldview of her students, thus connecting them with struggles for freedom that were beginning to unfold on an international stage. Independence for Africa became one of her most important concerns. In her work outside of Jackson State, McAllister served on several boards, most noticeably the board of trustees of her alma mater, Talladega College. McAllister was very influential in initiating the Teacher Training Program at Talladega, even proposing an exchange program between Ghana and Talladega in 1958. The purpose of this program was not to re-create the old missionary relationships that had characterized previous contact with Africa. McAllister and the board envisioned Talladega students becoming active builders in a new Ghana by serving as civil servants and teachers. In a letter to the president of Talladega, McAllister wrote, "I know you and Dean Simpson will laugh at the wildness of my dreams but it seems to me that Talladega is well fitted to take the lead in seizing this opportunity to help in African education."[22] Hardly a week had passed between Ghana declaring its independence and McAllister's petition for an exchange program with the new sovereign nation. Its independence was interpreted as an important step in a worldwide freedom movement for which McAllister continued to prepare her students.

The vision and idealism of Jane McAllister kept afloat the promise of dissent on Jackson State's campus in the 1950s. Amazingly, her constant acts of student advocacy and promotion of activism never brought her in harm's way of either the administration or the state. Her papers show she was well respected for her work on campus and in the larger academic community. Her courage, in spite of overwhelming odds and racism, made her an extraordinary instructor, role model, and mentor. Her outward support of political insurgency made her an anomaly among most professors at Jackson State. Many black faculty members at Jackson State either felt bridled in their desire to support student activism openly or were not inclined to support radical thought at all.

Most instructors at Jackson State College were native southerners and, like much of the black adult population of the South, were hesitant to cross that psychological river of fear that contributed to the longevity of Jim Crow policies. Economic reprisal and physical harm were still looming threats for those bold enough to voice publicly their displeasure with white society. Most of Jackson State's all-black faculty wrestled with the ideas of livelihood versus liberation. This internal struggle made them more than hesitant to endorse rebellious student behavior. No Jackson State professor represented the conflicted scholar more than the literary giant Margaret Walker Alexander.

Born in Birmingham, Alabama, in 1915 to a Jamaican-born Methodist minister and a mother who worked as a musician and teacher, Margaret Walker soon developed a love for the written word. At the age of ten, her family moved to New Orleans, where she honed her poetry skills. As a young woman, she moved to New York and took residence in Harlem, befriending fellow artists and scribes like Richard Wright, Arna Bontemps, Langston Hughes, and Elizabeth Catlett. In 1937 she published her most recognizable poem, "For My People." She became indoctrinated with Marxism and the militant tone of the New Negro movement, and the Harlem Renaissance intrigued and inspired her. She married Firnist Alexander in 1943 and accepted a teaching position at Jackson State in 1949.

Margaret Walker was a mystic and a self-professed God-fearing woman who felt compelled to make her religious beliefs an essential part of her teaching and writing. She wrote, "As a Negro woman, my religion is necessary to my integrity, to help me build a ground, moral and spiritualistic life, and I find it necessary often in order to maintain anything like emotional stability and equilibrium."[23] Her personal diaries reflect an individual who was unswervingly convicted in her spiritual beliefs. She frequently struggled with depression and suffered setbacks in her health. As an outlet, Walker often composed in her journals what can best be described as psalms of praise and contrition. She was fascinated with astrology and quite frequently practiced the art of prophesy. Yet despite her spiritual outlets, Margaret Walker was deeply conflicted. Her tenure in Mississippi added to her warring consciousness as she directed her anger toward the repressive climate of the state and her disappointment with the harsh and stringent work environment of Jackson State. It is an extreme and tragic irony that one of the greatest writers of the twentieth century felt voiceless and confined to the margins of her journals as the civil rights movement emerged before her eyes.

Like countless other African Americans in Mississippi, Alexander observed world events with a hopeful heart. If the struggle for black liberation continued to expand, then perhaps it would soon make its way to the state with the most notorious reputation for the marginalization of black freedom rights. In 1949 Walker foresaw future events that soon consumed the Magnolia State. She prophetically declared:

> Prejudice, segregation and Jim Crow are in for a death struggle and I hope they will die. Our schools will no longer be separated, neither our churches and acts of prejudice in the commercial place like stores and hotels, places of amusement, etc. will be punished as crimes against the people. I think it will take only a mere ten years for that change to take place.[24]

How frustrating it must have been for someone to possess the clairvoyant powers of Walker yet to be unable to swiftly bring such prophetic words into fruition. Although her writing served as an important outlet, she had limited space to practice the activism that had defined her life as a young women dabbling in Marxism and attending meetings with young radicals in the streets of New York. She continued to prophesize, however, that liberation was within reach. "Eisenhower will station troops in the south because of serious trouble and unrest over Jim Crow law in Dixie," she wrote in 1950, seven years before Little Rock. "All of this is due to happen while Uranus is in Cancer and it does not leave for good until 1956 . . . and a great new era for art and religion and all forms of culture will be ushered in."[25] Walker's visions, despite their general realization, did little to prepare her for the frustration she was about to endure as a professor at Jackson State.

A War of Nerves and Harassments:
Jackson State University and the Politics of Confrontation/

In 1955, after earning her graduate degree, Margaret Walker noted that ever since the *Brown v. Board* decision, "Mississippi has been in a worse state than the world had been over the atomic bomb. I came back to tension and fear which has steadily increased; incidents of violence, intimidation, reprisal, indignity and gross injustices fill a huge volume."[26] Cutting through the fear of reprisals was a herculean task for black Mississippians. This was not comparable to the Red Scare or McCarthyism, where individuals were unfairly targeted and persecuted for their beliefs. The consequences were much more dire, and the stakes were much higher. Black folks were now openly confronting the white power structure, and whites were more than prepared to enact terrorist tactics to defend their way of life. "The war of nerves and harassments have included real bullets to back up threats," wrote Walker. "We on our job at Jackson College have been told that if we make any frontal attack on segregation we will not get our checks. Very few of the faculty members dare belong to the NAACP."[27]

As a politically aware and racially conscious writer, Walker mulled over her options. Her poetry was still well celebrated, and obtaining a job outside of Mississippi was not a problem. Her husband and family wanted out of Mississippi, but that ultimate decision rested with her as the breadwinner for the household. She decided to stay in Mississippi; although she questioned her decision quite frequently in her writings, her reasoning was not unlike millions of other African Americans who felt a vested interest in the land of their mothers and fathers.[28] In Mississippi, flustered and temporarily neutralized on the sidelines of the war against Jim Crow, Walker captured the struggle that many African Americans across the country dealt with as they contended with their human frailties in the midst of a brewing confrontation for civil rights. "Why don't we challenge them? Why don't we speak out? Why are we so cowardly?" She openly pined:

> No one wants to admit that we are living under a blanket of fear, with constant threats and undertones of violence. . . . What if we open our mouths? We are threatened with our jobs, our homes, our lives, we cannot stay here and speak out. We must be silent or leave Mississippi. A revolution is surely taking place, will we win the peace or lose as always in the past to the reactionaries.[29]

Much like numerous other professors working on the frontlines of a growing black student revolt, Walker chose to confront her obstacles by dedicating herself to her students and her work. A young professor, she shared close relationships with her students. Walker used various teaching methods, and former students recalled that she was capable of entrancing her students with vivid images of slavery from the pages of her work. She worked continuously on what would become her signature work, *Jubilee*. Published in 1966, *Jubilee* was a novel that wove together the horrors of slavery and gave literary voice to slaves, their perspectives and experiences, rather than masters. "There were so many memories about her book *Jubilee* that she told in her class," recalled Gloria Douglas. "Her expressions and how she told the story were very inspirational."[30] Her classes often intertwined discussions of literature with innuendos about racial liberation, a clever way to alleviate fears of reprisal from the administration or the state. One class in particular, Bible as Literature, presented Alexander with the opportunity to combine her profound knowledge of the Bible with her understanding of black liberation theology, a staple of the black church. "She knew that Bible and she could just make it come alive; you would just sit there in awe," recalled former student Rita Kinard. "She would discuss the Bible as literature. . . . If she was really talking about the Bible she would somehow inject that [race] into her discussion of the Bible."[31]

Jackson State in the 1950s was becoming a less than ideal working environment for those who openly supported the spirit of rebellion that was sweeping across black America. Nevertheless, professors such as Margaret Walker Alexander, Jane McAllister, Lee Williams, and Willie Dobbs Blackburn touched the lives of their students in a very real and significant way. Former student Gloria Douglass noted, "I knew I wanted to be a teacher or a nurse. And then at Jackson State I learned that you could be a writer if you wanted to or do other things besides become a teacher or nurse. And I remember that Margaret [Walker] was a college professor and she was a writer."[32] A likely explanation of what occurred at Jackson State was that black professors represented what was possible for their students; conversely, students represented what was possible for the future of black America. Margaret Walker had one final prophetic vision before the close of the decade, foreshadowing what was to come. She wrote, "There are going to be cataclysmic changes in my job in the next three calendar years, 1959, 1960, 1961. Only God knows what those years will be bring. Change is inevitable and the greatest change obviously is going to take place in 1960."[33]

As the white power structure of Mississippi tried to come to grips with the sudden outbreak of black student activism, they increasingly pressured black college administrators. White legislators and authorities seldom sat in on classes or infiltrated the office hours of university instructors. Those environments were important sanctuaries for professors who engaged students in discussion of radical action against Jim Crow. Black college presidents, however, were called into the chambers of legislators frequently in the 1960s. As Adam Fairclough noted, "When college campuses became centers of civil rights militancy, white politicians expected the men who ran these institutions to prevent challenges to segregation."[34] While a few university presidents resisted efforts to enlist them as the chief subordinator of student protests, most complied, and some did so in grand fashion.

Few black college presidents represented the politics of confrontation as well as Jacob L. Reddix. A distinguished educator who served as president of Jackson State from 1940 to 1967, the longest tenure of any president there, Reddix was a native son of Mississippi, born in Jackson County. He left Mississippi to earn his college degree from the Illinois Institute of Technology and completed his graduate work at the University of Chicago. As a young man, Reddix's professional work reflected the words and sounds of black resistance and uplift that defined the 1920s and 1930s. Reddix was fascinated with the concepts of self-dependence and collective economics, the very doctrines that served as the ideological foundations for leaders such as Booker T. Washington and Marcus Garvey. Shortly after the completion of his graduate work, Reddix published numerous works on the merit and worth of cooperatives for African Americans. These publications were well received in devitalized communities seeking to pull together their limited economic resources and won Reddix numerous supporters, most noticeably W. E. B. Du Bois and John Hope II, past president of Morehouse College and former professor of economics at Atlanta University. DuBois touted Reddix's research on cooperatives in the renowned black newspaper the *Pittsburgh Courier,* causing Reddix to receive numerous written inquiries about his work.[35] Writing in 1939, Hope conveyed to Reddix that "the story of your courageous trail-blazing effort and that of others like you in pointing the way to economic and social betterment through mutual self-help needs to be told to our youth who will shortly step forward to be a liability or an asset to the group."[36]

Reddix's message of self-sufficiency and determination did not fail to resonate with many youth inspired by his work. Furthermore, a fifteen-year veteran of teaching in the public school systems of Birmingham, Alabama, and Gary, Indiana, Reddix had a passion for the instruction and guidance of youth. Those inspired by his research on cooperatives did not hesitate to reach out to the young educator, often writing to him for research advice. One student from Tougaloo College wrote, "I've read your pamphlet, 'The Negro Seeks Economic Freedom Through Cooperation,' and I am asking you to send me the latest statistics or reports of your cooperative store."[37] An inspired student from Hampton sought his help, noting, "I am interested in the Cooperative movement among the Negro, and have selected 'Cooperation, The Hope of the Negro' as a topic for a thesis which I am about to write. I am also preparing an address for Negro History Week on the same subject."[38] As Reddix's message of empowerment and economic resourcefulness spread, his opportunities for advancement increased. He was awarded the position of adviser on cooperatives with the Farm Security Administration, but stayed only briefly. Ninety days later, on July 22, 1940, he was selected to become the fifth president of Jackson State.[39]

It is difficult to imagine what thoughts entered into Reddix's mind as he returned south to begin his work. Surely he understood that he was treading into familiar territory, where southern whites were unsympathetic and unwilling to endure polemics on race. There was little room to continue research that might unsettle white supporters or deliberately embolden African Americans. An all-white board selected him with the understanding that his teachings and guidance of Jackson State would be consistent with Mississippi's long-standing traditions and culture, which had zero tolerance for educated blacks who sought to break stride with the expectations of local custom or law. To this end, Reddix embraced the conservative nature that defined Mississippi's black leadership. In his memoirs he wrote, "I have never personally participated in an organized protest. Undoubtedly, I have been criticized for not doing so. For more than fifty years, I have devoted my life to the education and enlightenment of young people. . . . I believe this contribution is as important as participating in organized protests."[40]

Reddix became the prototypical black college administrator during an era when the black Left boldly and increasingly critiqued the policies of Jim Crow. The influences of determined World War II veterans and the conservative yet steadfast efforts of organizations such as the NAACP and the Congress of Racial Equality (CORE) were not the agenda that most black college presidents were prepared to adopt. Facing the pressures of economic survival and political posturing to please state legislators or white benefactors, many black college presidents wielded a kind of vainglorious machismo on their campuses in efforts to ensure that faculty, staff, and students toed the line that the white power structure expected.

As prominent and respected leaders in the black community, college presidents represented the supreme custodians of college-bound black youth and
were often venerated as such. Yet many presidents struggled to connect the
idea of subservience to white "supporters" with the charge of uplift, a concept
that had driven black institutions and their students since their inception.
This personal and sociopolitical battle with the power structure took its toll
on Mississippi's black educators, who relinquished the challenge of openly
confronting white supremacy to the next generation. Peoples recalled one
confrontation that Reddix faced in 1965:

> He got a call from the governor's office, wanting him to check the roll of all
> his teachers and workers, and they wanted to know if there were any of them
> in that march [Selma Right to Vote March]. If they are not present, they
> want to know where they are. He covered and said they're all here . . . but
> he was so angry that they would do that you know. So I saw what he had to
> go through. I sat there by his desk and he was angry that they were going to
> call and tell him to check the roll of his teachers and make sure that nobody
> was in that march with Martin Luther King and if they were he wanted
> them fired right now. He didn't even check, but he said he did. He would
> say things like "things are going to change, and you're the young man who
> can probably do it." He said, "these people, they're all racists but it's going to
> change."[41]

This incident took place during the twilight of Reddix's administration.
During the twenty-five years that preceded it, Reddix guided Jackson State
with little or no compromise for those who were not on board with his agenda. But the actions and direction of the national student sit-in movement,
which in a domino effect across southern black colleges arrived in Mississippi on March 27, 1961, increasingly influenced Reddix's presidency. In early
spring of 1961, the flowering of activism that took generations to cultivate
burst forth in downtown Jackson when nine students from nearby Tougaloo College challenged public accommodation laws at the local library.[42] Any
boundaries that gave previous generations of Jackson State students space
to express radical opinions or create militant organizations on campus were
now erased. Reddix moved quickly to save what he believed was the university and perhaps himself from the spectacle that would surely be generated.
Jackson State students, however, were primed and ready to assume their
place in the insurgent movement becoming so powerful on black colleges.

Word of the Tougaloo Nine arrived on the campus of Jackson State College, and the news immediately invigorated students. An instrument of the state, Reddix was in no position to provide shelter to students openly engaged in a struggle to dismantle Jim Crow. The contempt white supremacists had for Tougaloo was exacerbated by the fact that they had no direct control over the institution's daily operations or the spirit of liberalism that ran throughout the campus. But Jackson State was a different story, and Reddix watched with great concern as the events of March 27 unfolded. It became quite clear that his students had no intentions of letting their fellow students from Tougaloo stand alone in their struggle.

Dorie and Joyce Ladner were enrolled as freshmen at Jackson State when the student movement first arrived in Mississippi. The two sisters shared a close relationship all of their lives. Growing up in the small community of Palmers Court located in Hattiesburg, both sisters were exposed to the ravaging effects of white supremacy. Hattiesburg activists Vernon Dahmer and Clyde Kennard mentored Dorie and Joyce during their formative years.[43] Commenting on their relationship with Kennard and Dahmer, Dorie Ladner remembered, "He [Kennard] also helped to develop the NAACP youth chapter, which we were members [of] and we were also exposed to Vernon Dahmer and his sister Ilene Beard. They would take us to NAACP meetings here in Jackson."[44]

The Ladner sisters arrived on Jackson State's campus in the fall of 1960. Like many other new college students arriving that fall, they were of the same generation as the movement's "sacrificial lamb," Emmett Till. As the civil rights movement expanded into Mississippi, very few failed to recall the bitter anger that brewed within them that fateful summer of 1955 when the brutalities of southern life were uncovered to the world. Hundreds of students, the Ladner sisters included, moved quickly to show their solidarity with their crosstown companions, and students bolted from their dormitories in an effort to seize the moment. Later that afternoon, throngs of students began to gather in front of the campus library, "where they sang hymns, prayed, and chanted, 'We Want Freedom.'"[45]

As Jacob Reddix concluded yet another day as president of the only state-controlled institution in the city of Jackson, he was abruptly disturbed when reports of student protests reached his on-campus home. Visions of harsh reprimands from state officials and perhaps even the possibility of closing the school must have entered into his mind. Reddix moved quickly to intercept the students. He later explained to the media, "I don't know what happened. This is more trouble than we have had here in 20 years."[46] Gripped with fear and rage, Reddix lashed out at students who jeopardized his status as president and the survival of the college. Dorie Ladner recalled, "Emmett Burns was President of the student government and he was attacked by the President. The President came running out from his home . . . like a wild man. He was just flailing his arms, and just trying to strike me out too. Because I guess he saw his whole world crumbling being a state employee."[47]

Reddix's fears were not without merit—the Jackson police department was already on the scene. Reddix linked forces with local authorities to order a cease and desist to the students' "illegal" rally. With the threat of expulsion initially doing its work, the crowd soon disbanded. But they still gathered in smaller groups along the edge of Lynch Street, the busy thoroughfare that ran through the middle of campus. Protesters could be heard proclaiming, "They haven't seen anything yet. This will go on until we have freedom."[48] It was later reported that Reddix had assaulted two students, striking one female in addition to pushing another student to the ground. Although they knew they were taking a gamble by challenging Reddix's authority, hundreds of Jackson State students decided to join the burgeoning student movement.

Jackson State students should not be understood as simply reacting to the Tougaloo protest. The Mississippi State Sovereignty Commission identified at least forty-five Jackson State students as possible threats to the status quo. In a written communication between Reddix and the director of the Sovereignty Commission, Albert Jones, the names, class ranks, and home addresses of the students "whose name appears on the propaganda list" were requested.[49] The list was generated on March 23, four days before the Tougaloo protest. The purpose of the Sovereignty Commission's propaganda list is not quite clear; however, it included the names of Dorie and Joyce Ladner. Both sisters were eventually expelled from Jackson State, and they then enrolled at Tougaloo. Dorie Ladner remembered, "We had been told we weren't going to be allowed to come back, plus we didn't want to come back."[50] Reddix did not fail to provide the information that was requested of him, relinquishing all names and home addresses in a move that could have brought harm to the students and their families.

On Jackson State's campus, the student body was buzzing with excitement. In dormitories across campus students discussed the events of March 27. Many had serious reservations about staging protests and standing up to authority figures who acted in loco parentis. While such fears and reservations prevented many of them from taking a role in the movement, hundreds more decided that here was a personal and communal defining moment to engage in the struggle. Perhaps it was their youthful exuberance and innocence that convinced many of them to participate. It is not quite clear why students "acted out" against the establishment when they did, nor is it certain what prompted such a collective show of force. However, it is evident that something about the shelter of black colleges made them the launching point for the black student movement in America. On March 28 Jackson State students continued their defiance of authority and their show of solidarity with Tougaloo by boycotting classes.

Word of an impromptu rally spread quickly as students gathered on the campus lawn to decide their next move. A small band of students thought it prudent to march downtown to the city jail, where the Tougaloo students were being held. This was an enormous step. Advancing upon the local white power structure was sure to heighten the wrath of the campus administration. A suggestion to march into the jaws of white authority was undoubtedly enough to give even the boldest campus activists considerable pause. When the call for marchers went out, only fifty students joined the ranks of those willing to make the short trek downtown.

Among those was Dorie Ladner. Both Ladner sisters were struggling in their adjustment to college life. Chief among their dislikes at Jackson State were the numerous social restrictions administrators placed upon the student body. Students were expected to observe curfews and attend mandatory vespers on campus. When students did gain free time, it was allotted in small doses under the sharp observation of dorm mothers and chaperones. Like many college students, the Ladner sisters expected the excitement of freedom from home and the relinquishing, if not relaxing, of the strict rules that stifled the social aspirations of young men and women ready to discover themselves—and each other. Most students coped with the social limitations found at Jackson State. If not, they certainly found sly ways to subvert the rules to make their environment more palatable. Social stimulation was not, however, the only thing important to the Ladner sisters, and if Jackson State offered anything to them, it was the close proximity of the local NAACP headquarters located on Lynch Street.

It was there that the two sisters formed a close relationship with a man who inspired many of Jackson State's politically frustrated students. In his small second-story office, Medgar Evers spent numerous hours counseling Mississippi's black youth and speaking to them about a freedom that he envisioned for the future and the distinct role they could play in helping to usher in that new era. Perhaps it was those moments conversing with Evers that convinced the Ladner sisters and others to march into downtown Jackson in support of the Tougaloo students.

Leaders of the local power structure in Jackson also had strong convictions. They wanted to send a clear message to Jackson State and Tougaloo students that Mississippi would not become the next staging ground for the student movement. The day before the students' decision to march downtown, Jackson's law enforcement officers invaded Jackson State's campus, bringing police attack dogs to dissuade students from future campus rallies. "Within two hours they brought dogs in," recalled Dorie Ladner. "They had dogs running up and down the dorm on Jackson State's campus."[51] As students entered downtown Jackson, they were greeted by the same attack dogs. In addition, police were armed with clubs and tear gas to disperse the students when they refused to turn back.

The brutal tactics of local law authorities were bitter experiences for idealistic youth. As students became disoriented by the toxic fumes and attack dogs, they were enveloped and protected by those who were most invested in their success: the black community. The histories of black colleges bear out the fact that any separation between town and gown was superficial. Black colleges were beacons of hope to the impoverished communities that often surrounded them. The academy seemed distant to those who could never muster the time or money to attend, but they realized that within the shelter of black colleges an important component of the future of the race was being formed and fashioned. In the early stages of the movement, many could only afford to offer advice or temporary shelter from white terrorism. As black youth ran throughout the streets of Jackson seeking refuge, kind and familiar voices began to call out to them. "And I now know how strange people felt, because we were running and trying to hide," recalled Dorie Ladner. "And one Black woman said, 'Come into my house,' and she cleaned my face off and she said 'Come out and sit on the porch.'" Dorie's rescuer opened her home to her like she was one of her own, and together they watched the terror unfold before them. As evening fell, both Dorie and her anonymous Good Samaritan realized they had witnessed the dawning of the civil rights movement in Jackson: "I sat on the porch and saw folks running up and down the alley and all around with the dogs," Dorie recalled. "I sat there like I lived there, and by nightfall I went back to campus."[52]

As the smoke literally settled on the streets of Jackson, those who witnessed the events of the last few days realized that the collision of different worlds and interests had set in motion an irreversible chain of events. The Tougaloo Nine were given suspended jail sentences, and the case was later thrown out on appeal. They returned to campus as heroes of the movement. Local whites' frustration with Tougaloo and its seemingly renegade students was rapidly increasing. Restraining the impulse of protests at Tougaloo would require more imaginative and clandestine approaches, but suppressing protests at Jackson State would prove much easier. President Reddix's ego was severely bruised by the defiant actions of his students, a fact that led to even tighter demands upon his faculty and an even harsher working environment. The buck stopped with him, and if the state came calling, then it was he who was subject to immediate reprisal. In her journal, Margaret Walker noted,

> He cracks the whip and rattles his saber and struts across the stage a pompous and tyrannical jackass. The faculty meetings at Jackson College have deteriorated into ludicrous puppet shows where the president performs in a ridiculous manner. The trustee board downtown calls him in to lay down the law of how to keep his Negras "in line." And he comes down the freight elevator with the garbage and slips out at the back door for fear some of us have seen that he has been to see the governor and that he swells up on the campus and knocks the student to the ground. And then intimidates the mother of the girl, with the threat of expulsion so that she will deny he struck her down, despite the obvious accounts of students, teachers and of average citizens in town.[53]

For a brief moment, Jackson State students broke away from their conservative bonds and the expectations of their enraged president and allowed the second curriculum to breathe free. Jackson State students helped to set the tone of activism in the state by rallying to Tougaloo's side. After all, Tougaloo's cause was theirs also. With the sultry Mississippi summer quickly approaching, the citizens of the nation's most totalitarian state prepared themselves for a movement that was assured to make life in Mississippi hotter than normal.

The dawning of the 1960s illuminated fissures in America's foundation. The collective student assault against the hypocrisies of society emboldened even those who fear still marginalized them. In her journal, Margaret Walker declared, "I still was not sure of my mission, but mission I knew I had. . . . When shall I cease merely to live and begin to BE?"[54] Jackson State administrators hoped that the development of student insurgency would remain confined to Tougaloo's campus, and perhaps had Reddix and others had the courage to create an open dialogue with the students, it would have done so. However, in the autocratic manner that defined his administration, Reddix dissolved the Student Government Association (SGA) when students returned that fall, a move that re-ignited the anger and wrath still smoldering from the incidents in the spring.

In this new decade, students at Jackson State had very little room to articulate their concerns on campus. There were, however, various campus organizations, fraternities and sororities, and athletic teams that helped to create a bond and identity among students. When Reddix dissolved the SGA as payback for the spring uprising, it struck a blow at one of the chief outlets for student self-expression. Reddix said he acted because the actions of the students had "embarrassed" the school. "I just had to put my foot down," he declared. A more likely scenario is that Reddix caved to local and state government pressures. His decision, though, caused backlash among the student body of Jackson State. Four hundred students boycotted classes in protest. Later, the students gathered at the college stadium and "paraded around the campus."[55]

Despite the outcry and decision to boycott classes, the atmosphere at Jackson State was far from that of Tougaloo, a fact that continued to frustrate would-be organizers and activists. The environment was simply not conducive to sustaining overt protest against the state that ultimately decided whether the doors of the institution should remain open. In addition, the background of many Jackson State students differed from their counterparts at Tougaloo. Many of Tougaloo's students came from educated parents, and the student body was comprised of students who represented, in many cases, the aspirations and expectations of the black middle class. The typical Jackson State student was more often the first of his or her family to attend college. They represented the hopes of sharecroppers and domestic laborers who saved all that they could just to enable their son or daughter to have an opportunity to attend college. For generations, African Americans invested heavily in the concept that education was a passageway that would lead to the collective uplift of the race. The fact that many of these youth were now seemingly flinging this opportunity to the wind was a risky proposition, even if those actions were motivated by desires to achieve black liberation. Abandoning that dream and risking expulsion was a sacrifice that many Jackson State students were not yet willing to make.[56]

In fact, discarding the dream of college was something that many Tougaloo students were not willing to risk either. Those daring enough to become engaged in student protests took heavy tolls upon themselves and in some cases their families. The hesitation of many black students to play active roles in the movement placed them in the same company as most African Americans during the 1960s who found the most pragmatic ways to survive the overt oppression that characterized their lives. Although Reddix later suggested that his major contribution to the black struggle was the granting of over 5,000 degrees during his tenure as president, there were still several students and a few faculty in his midst who wondered the extent to which those degrees mattered if Jackson State graduates could not become full participants in the democracy he claimed to prepare them for. Unknown to Reddix, one of his best and brightest students had already put in motion a series of events that would serve as a litmus test for democracy and rock the very foundation of the state.

James Howard Meredith was in his first year as a student at Jackson State when he wrote to the University of Mississippi to inquire about admission. A native of Kosciusko, Mississippi, Meredith clearly understood the rules and boundaries of Jim Crow. Clyde Kennard, dying from cancer in Parchman Penitentiary after his attempt to integrate the University of Southern Mississippi, offered a solemn reminder of just how far previous struggles to break the racial barriers in education had gone. Nevertheless, by January 1961, when Meredith made his first contact with Ole Miss, the dawning of a black student movement was in full swing, and black youth across the country increasingly questioned the restrictions white supremacy forced upon them. Fewer black students were heeding the prescriptive observations of men like Jimmy Ward, columnist and editor of the *Jackson Daily News*, who noted, "It would appear by now that prudent people will not wantonly toy with traditions or tamper with the soul of a civilized society."[57] Although Meredith's attempt to desegregate the campus of Ole Miss lacked the massive frontal attack that defined the direct action tactics of other activists, his lone struggle caused one of the most fierce and hateful backlashes that Mississippi had ever seen.

In 1961 Governor Ross Barnett appeared in a movie production produced by the Sovereignty Commission entitled *Message from Mississippi*, in which he declared, "No student can get a better education than is offered the Negro children in Mississippi."[58] Both Meredith and Barnett knew this to be false. The legacy of black colleges had successfully produced generations of local and national leaders, activists, and professionals, and a talented working class that waited patiently for America to live up to what it professed in its founding documents. Yet a stigma of inferiority hung over black education that was caused by segregation and was further reinforced by the paucity of resources made available to black educators.

After numerous creative attempts on behalf of the University of Mississippi Board of Trustees to bar Meredith from enrolling, the federal courts finally upheld Meredith's constitutional right to become the first African American student at the state's most elite institution of higher learning.

Meredith confronted both solitude and hostility, and his tormented nights at Ole Miss were not without the constant reassurance and encouragement of a familiar voice he knew all too well at Jackson State, Jane McAllister. McAllister remained in contact with Meredith during his ordeal and gave him the tutoring, advice, and nurturing to which he was accustomed at Jackson State. Indeed, McAllister kept in contact with most of her former students, signing her correspondence with them as their "teacher and friend." More than anything, Meredith needed a friend in the moments when he felt most abandoned, and in his most desolate and darkest hours at Ole Miss he reached out to his "teacher and friend." McAllister wrote to a colleague, "Your letter came soon after I had a telephone conversation with James Meredith who was one of our students. He asked me if I could hear the noises of the cherry bombs as he was trying to study. When students act in mobs, I almost lose my faith in the power of education."[59]

But McAllister never lost faith in education. She understood that even the constraints Jackson State placed upon her could not prevent her from edifying students who sought her counsel, wisdom, and love. Behind the closed doors of her classroom, in her private office hours, or through her correspondences with current and former students, she never stopped investing in those she believed capable of changing the world. In a letter to a troubled former student she wrote, "keep in mind that only when a man's fight begins with himself is he worth anything. Begin your fight with yourself and begin now."[60]

McAllister knew that the personal was—and had to be for blacks—political. Indeed, as the battle for America's soul spilled over into Jackson, young men and women were forced to come face to face with racialized demons that had perplexed the souls and consciousness of generations before them. McAllister's former student James Meredith began this fight with himself and concluded that the time was right to trouble the waters of segregation. When the smoke settled in Oxford and the long road to healing began, McAllister wrote to J. D. Williams, the president of the University of Mississippi, to convey her support for Williams, who attempted literally to rebuild Ole Miss in the wake of the riots. McAllister lent her creed to Williams: "In the 42 years of my teaching in Mississippi and Louisiana colleges and in travel in various countries; students, faculty and I, regardless of race, color, or creed have met on the common ground of ideas. . . . May I congratulate those students to whom you pay tribute, for it is upon such as they—and again I say regardless of race, creed, or color—on whom will depend the salvation of our state."[61]

Conclusion

While it is true that students had crossed a deep river of fear by engaging in direct action protest, navigating that blood-filled stream and convincing an older black generation that it was necessary was a chore unto itself. Dorie Ladner recalled her tragic experience in confronting the parent of a former classmate at Jackson State who was shot in the head after she became involved in voter registration activities in the Delta. She noted, "After being informed about Marylene being shot, I went to visit her at a local hospital in Jackson and her mother started screaming at me and accusing me of her daughter getting shot, saying if it hadn't been for me, her daughter wouldn't have gotten shot. I had never been so hurt and I was overcome with grief."[62]

This generational divide posed a serious problem for movement organizers seeking a unified front in the struggle against white supremacy. However, in a culture where deference to one's elders still mattered, the relationship between black youth and the adults who cared for their well-being never withered. Dave Dennis recalled:

> But underground that is, there was really the adult and elders who gave
> support to the movement, who provided all kinds of stuff. Made everybody
> food, food came out of nowhere. . . . I mean they [students] were housed in
> private homes, they were our hotels. . . . You had kids out there because they
> were trying to keep their jobs. . . . And a lot of the meeting places we had
> was in churches you see, and even when the ministers couldn't come out
> front, they would turn their back, because the deacons would take over the
> church, you know and say you gone meet at the church. . . . So you had this,
> but none of that could have happened without adult participation.[63]

The strong presence of an elder black community that quietly supported the actions of black youth was a strong component of the movement. They fed the hungry, they gave guidance to those venturing down dangerous pathways, and they provided shelter in a time of storm. Nevertheless, student activists questioning the authority figures that appeared to be in lockstep with the white power structure was an increasing theme within the movement. Although many found support among members of the older generation, others progressively raised serious doubts about the policies, programs, and actions of the black conservative establishment.

For the handful of Jackson State students who were taking notice and playing more active roles in the local movement, their ability to engage openly with students and faculty who were pondering the same questions was extremely important in the development of their political consciousness. From the shelter of black colleges such as Jackson State, they were free to explore and express their doubts, feelings, and pent-up frustrations with the political structure that sought to mute their latent hatred of the system. In reference to an incident that took place in her classroom, Jackson State professor Jane McAllister noted, "Students found the Rebel Antigone quotation which had so intrigued them; only they changed "king" to governor. (I know Barnett would never appreciate that.) The quotation was: "The Rebel Antigone, who defied a king rather than betray her own conscience."[64] Such subtle forms of protest suggest students comfortable enough to engage these ideas in the campus setting, but still too hesitant to lay their dissatisfaction with white supremacy at the feet of the king/governor himself.

The continued anguish of Jackson State professor Margaret Walker further illustrates the personal confrontations that many faced. In her journal she wrote, "I have written an article that's both a tribute to Medgar Evers and an exposé of the whole Mississippi story but I dare not to print it now that I have written it. My family would be in danger, there might be all kinds of reprisals. I seem to be too vulnerable, too fearful and too cowardly."[65] As Alexander dealt openly and honestly with her angst, she was not alone. The sidelines were filled with bystanders and onlookers, a fact that debunks the characterization and romanticization of a movement supplied with the steady participation of the masses. With the death of Medgar Evers, the political sails of the Jackson movement fell limp. The questions that penetrated the hearts and minds of hopeful but inactive black folks across Mississippi pressed on. Alexander noted:

> One asks himself daily, where am I? Am I out there in the thick of the struggle? In the middle of the fight? Am I doing something for the call of freedom? Going to jail, demonstrating, boycotting, sitting in, campaigning and lobbying, or what am I doing? Am I standing on the sidelines cheering but still doing nothing? Am I obstructing the movement? Am I fearful and silent? Have more concern with my own security than with the plight of the Negro masses? Am I a traitor to my people, a segregationist and an intellectual Uncle Tom? . . . How many of us are purged of hate and have strength to love? Strength to be kicked but not kick back. Strength to love and not retaliate, can go to jail, can be able to stand before hate and forgive. Where am I, and where do I stand?[66]

The struggle for black liberation would soon begin to take different directions both in the state of Mississippi and across the nation. But throughout the 1960s, black colleges proved themselves as the most radical incubators of insurgency. Young activists that demanded equal access to political accommodations in the first half of the decade began to question the lack of economic empowerment in the black community, the absence of black elected officials, and the historical shortcomings in the housing industry. Black colleges provided a forum in some shape or form through every turn. By 1967 Jacob L. Reddix was ready to transition to retirement. Indeed, the tone of his administration during the turbulent decade caused former governor Ross Barnett to thank Reddix in a personal letter for cooperating in "every way."[67] Unquestionably, Reddix, like numerous other black college presidents, resented the pull and tug of the puppet strings as those who have no personal control or voice so often do. Their emasculation resulted in a professional atmosphere that was paternalistic and domineering in fashion. Nevertheless, in the first twenty years of his tenure, Reddix must be credited for supporting an environment that could produce students who went on to become thoroughly engaged in their own local movement for black liberation. Such was the case for countless other alumni of Jackson State. A second curriculum put wind in their sails and strengthened their resolve. Yet the world was changing at a rapid pace around them, convincing many students to drop their anchors in the burgeoning civil rights movement.

Trouble continued to mount for African Americans seeking justice through the conformity of the Cold War era to the dawning of the modern civil rights movement. Their pursuit of reprieve from the stinging effects of white supremacy was extremely diverse and resulted in a multitude of tactics that were used to confront their troubles. From the shelter of black colleges, students entered society as teachers, ministers, doctors, insurance agents, lawyers, and law-abiding citizens yearning and fighting for the day when the laws would shift to favor all Americans. This had been their training for years at black colleges, and in spite of the trouble in their way, alumni, students, and common black folk continued to press toward the realization of their freedom rights.

NOTES

1. George Swan, "College Represented at Youth Congress," *The Blue and White Flash*, December 1946, Jackson State University (JSU) Archives.

2. Students at both Jackson State and Tougaloo College established chapters of the SNYC on their respective campuses. However, by the end of the 1940s the SNYC

folded under the increasing pressure and scrutiny of the conservative Right and the increased intimidation of white supremacists organizations. For more information on the SNYC, see C. Alvin Hughes, "We Demand Our Rights: The Southern Negro Youth Congress, 1937–1949" *Phylon* 48, no. 1 (1987); Johnetta Richard, "The Southern Negro Youth Congress: A History" (Ph.D. diss., University of Cincinnati, 1987); "Report of the Youth Section of the National Negro Congress," February 14–16, 1937, Reel 2, Part I, Papers of the National Negro Congress, Library of Congress, Washington, D.C.; "Report of Committee on Permanent Organization," Papers of the National Negro Congress, Reel 2, Part I, 29 Collections of the Manuscript Division, Library of Congress.

3. In an e-mail message to the author on February 8, 2010, George Swan III revealed that correspondence from his parents indicated that a trunk being mailed to his father was packaged with extra care. That trunk was subsequently broken into and searched during its transit, and the Swans kept a copy of the claim and receipt of payment from the insurance company, documentation of which was provided to the author. This perhaps corroborates the Swans' fears that their correspondence was under surveillance.

4. "The Younger Generation," *Time*, November 5, 1951.

5. John Peoples is a 1950 graduate of Jackson State College and served as student government president and captain of the football team.

6. John Peoples, interview by author, July 21, 2004.

7. David Hoffman, *Making Sense of the Sixties: We Can Change the World*, VHS (PBS Video, 1991).

8. Useful book-length studies underscoring the diversity, purpose, and mission of black college faculty include James D. Anderson, *The Education of Blacks in the South, 1860—1935* (Chapel Hill: University of North Carolina Press, 1988); Charles Payne and Carol Strickland, *Teach Freedom: Education for Liberation in the African American Tradition* (New York: Teachers College Press, 2008); Adam Fairclough, *A Class of Their Own: Black Teachers in the Segregated South* (Cambridge, Mass.: Harvard University Press, 2007); and Gabrielle Edgcomb, *From Swastika to Jim Crow: Refugee Scholars at Black Colleges* (Malabar, Fla.: Krieger, 1993).

9. Joy Ann Williamson, *Radicalizing the Ebony Tower: Black Colleges and the Black Freedom Struggle in Mississippi* (New York: Teachers College Press, 2008), 34.

10. Margaret Walker Alexander, interview with Ann Allen Shockley, July 18, 1973, Fisk University Archives, John Hope and Aurelia Franklin Library, Fisk University, Nashville, Tenn.

11. Susie Baughns, "Join the Youth Council," *The Blue and White Flash*, November 1942, JSU Archives.

12. "Jackson College Represented at NAACP Conference," *The Blue and White Flash*, November 1942, JSU Archives.

13. Fairclough, *Class of Their Own*, 137.

14. Onezimae Clark, "A Prayer for the Class of '45," *The Blue and White Flash*, May 1945, JSU Archives.

15. Johnny Edwards, "Moving Forward to Serve Humanity," *The Blue and White Flash*, May 1949, JSU Archives.

16. "This I Believe," *The Blue and White Flash*, March 1956, JSU Archives.

17. "Columbia's First Negro Woman Ph.D. Joins Faculty Here," *The Blue and White Flash*, January 1951, JSU Archives.

18. Jane McAllister to Mark Starr, December 14, 1951, Box 2, Jane McAllister Collection, JSU Archives.

19. Jane McAllister to Charles Hunt, January 15, 1952, Box 1, Jane McAllister Collection, JSU Archives.

20. Rita Kinard, interview by author, July 31, 2005.

21. Dorie Ladner, interview by author, June 23, 2004.

22. Jane McAllister to Arthur Gray, March 15, 1957, Talladega College file, Jane McAllister Collection, JSU Archives.

23. Margaret Walker Alexander, journal entry, July 22, 1949, Box 5, Folder 34, Margaret Walker Alexander Research Center (MWARC), Jackson State University (JSU), Jackson, Miss.

24. Margaret Walker Alexander, journal entry, September 27, 1949, Box 5, Folder 36, MWARC, JSU.

25. Margaret Walker Alexander, journal entry, January 12, 1950, Box 5, Folder 38, MWARC, JSU.

26. Margaret Walker Alexander, journal entry, October 9, 1955, Box 9, Folder 51, MWARC, JSU.

27. Ibid.

28. Alexander's own life may have had some bearing on the main character, Vyry, in her acclaimed novel *Jubilee*. In the novel, Vyry makes the conscious decision not to escape the horrors of slavery in order to remain with her family. See Margaret Walker Alexander, *Jubilee* (Boston: Houghton Mifflin, 1966).

29. Margaret Walker Alexander, journal entry, August 12, 1957, Box 9, Folder 53, MWARC, JSU.

30. Gloria Douglas, interview by author, July 31, 2005.

31. Rita Kinard, interview by author, July 31, 2005.

32. Douglas interview.

33. Margaret Walker Alexander, journal entry, June 24, 1958, Box 9, Folder 54, MWARC, JSU.

34. Fairclough, *Class of Their Own*, 378.

35. Jacob L. Reddix Papers, JSU Archives.

36. Ibid.

37. Ibid.

38. Ibid.

39. Jacob Reddix was the first president to preside over Jackson College after the state assumed control of the institution in 1940, ending sixty-three years of control by the American Baptist Home Mission Society (ABHMS). The ABHMS noted that Tougaloo College was adequately meeting the educational needs of African Americans in the area, therefore relinquishing its financial support for Jackson College. For more on the transition of Jackson College to state control, see Jacob L. Reddix, *A Voice Crying in the Wilderness: The Memoirs of Jacob L. Reddix* (Jackson: University Press of Mississippi, 1974); and Lelia Rhodes, *Jackson State University: The First Hundred Years* (Jackson: University Press of Mississippi, 1979).

40. Reddix, *Voice Crying in the Wilderness*, 222.

41. John Peoples, interview by author, July 21, 2004.

42. For more on the Tougaloo Nine incident and the legacy of activism at Tougaloo, see Clarice Campbell and Oscar Rogers Jr., *Mississippi: The View From Tougaloo* (Jackson: University Press of Mississippi, 1979); John Dittmer, *Local People: The Struggle for Civil Rights in Mississippi* (Urbana: University of Illinois Press, 1994); David G. Sansing, *Making Haste Slowly: The Troubled History of Higher Education in Mississippi* (Jackson: University Press of Mississippi, 1990); and Williamson, *Radicalizing the Ebony Tower*.

43. Hattiesburg's most famous freedom fighters were local NAACP leader Vernon Dahmer and activist turned political prisoner Clyde Kennard, both of whom worked vigorously for change in Mississippi. Dahmer fought tirelessly for change in Hattiesburg until his assassination in 1966. Kennard's demise was equally upsetting to black Mississippians. Kennard attempted to become the first black to enroll in Mississippi Southern College (now the University of Southern Mississippi). Kennard's attempts were unsuccessful, as he was continually harassed by local and state law officials and was finally arrested and sentenced to a seven-year prison term at the state penitentiary on trumped-up charges of theft. During his incarceration, it was discovered that Kennard was suffering from cancer. Kennard was eventually released but succumbed to cancer shortly afterward. Both men played critical roles in shaping the political conscious of numerous young men and women, namely Dorie Ladner and Joyce Ladner. For more on both Vernon Dahmer and Clyde Kennard, see Dittmer, *Local People*; Charles Payne, *I've Got the Light of Freedom: The Organizing Tradition and the Mississippi Freedom Struggle* (Berkeley: University of California Press, 1995); and Sansing, *Making Haste Slowly*, 148–154.

44. Dorie Ladner, interview by author, June 23, 2004.

45. "Jackson State College Students Stage Protest," *Clarion-Ledger*, March 28, 1961.

46. Ibid.

47. Ladner interview.

48. "Jackson State College Students Stage Protest."

49. Jacob L. Reddix to Albert Jones, April 1, 1961, Mississippi State Sovereignty Commission Files, Mississippi Department of Archives and History, Jackson.

50. Ladner interview.

51. Ibid.

52. Ibid.

53. Margaret Walker Alexander, journal entry, July 9, 1961, Box 10, Folder 61, MWARC, JSU.

54. Margaret Walker Alexander, journal entry, May 1, 1960, Box 10, Folder 58, MWARC, JSU. MWARC, JSU.

55. "Report Classes Boycotted at Jackson State," *Jackson Daily News*, October 7, 1961.

56. One can easily conclude that environmental factors played a large role in both Tougaloo and Jackson State students deciding not to become involved in the movement. The class factor represents a somewhat plausible theory in comparing Jackson State and Tougaloo but does not hold up in comparison to other institutions involved in the black student movement, most notably North Carolina A&T State University, where the movement started. As a state institution, students involved in the movement there came from the same working-class background as many Jackson State students, yet they became the pioneers of black student activism. The less-threatening political and social climate can perhaps be attributed to the boldness of the students from Greensboro. For more on the student movement in Greensboro, see William Chafe, *Civilities and Civil Rights: Greensboro, North Carolina, and the Black Struggle for Freedom* (Oxford: Oxford University Press, 1980); and Miles Wolff, *Lunch at the 5 & 10* (Chicago: Elephant Press, 1970).

57. Silver, *Mississippi*, 34.

58. Ibid., 8.

59. Jane McAllister to Miss Briffault, November 12, 1962, Dr. Jane McAllister Papers, JSU Archives.

60. Jane McAllister to Rosalie, March 4, 1963, Dr. Jane McAllister Papers, JSU Archives.

61. Jane McAllister to J. D. Williams, November 8, 1962, Dr. Jane McAllister Papers, JSU Archives.

62. Ladner continues to say in the interview that although she was hurt by Burke's accusation, she did not take it personally. She contends that it was part of a larger web

of ignorance on the part of a few of the older generation who blamed activists and not the culture of intolerance and terrorism in which they lived. Ladner interview.

63. Dave Dennis, interview by author, August 11, 2004.

64. McAllister's students were referencing a speech that was delivered on campus by James Colston, president of Knoxville College, a small historically black college in Tennessee. During his speech, Colston keenly relayed the ancient Greek story of Antigone to students. The classic tale speaks of Polynices, a rebel who has been killed in battle. Polynices has been denied proper burial by Creon, ruler of Thebes, and Polynices's sister Antigone has decided to defy Creon and bury her brother anyway. The story concludes with the gods punishing Creon for being on the wrong side of righteousness. Colston's delivery of such a story in the wake of Medgar Evers's assassination and the turmoil following his funeral was not lost upon Jackson State students, who embraced the metaphors. Jane McAllister to James A. Colston, July 27, 1963, Box 1, Jane McAllister Collection, JSU Archives.

65. Margaret Walker Alexander, journal entry, February 1964, Box 11, Folder 68, MWARC, JSU.

66. Margaret Walker Alexander, journal entry, July 28, 1963, Box 11, Folder 69, MWARC, JSU.

67. Jacob L. Reddix Papers, JSU Archives.

"Hell Fired Out of Him"

The Muting of James Silver in Mississippi

Robert Luckett

Members of the Southern Historical Association (SHA) who attended the 1963 annual meeting in Asheville, North Carolina, witnessed one of the most significant addresses ever made to that organization. As president of the SHA that year, James Silver delivered a damning blow to the Jim Crow South, where he had lived since joining the history department at the University of Mississippi (Ole Miss) in 1936. Not much more than a year after the riots that accompanied James Meredith's integration of Ole Miss in October 1962, Silver characterized white Mississippi as a "Closed Society" committed to thwarting the cause for racial equality at all costs.[1]

The impact of Silver's words went well beyond the walls of that academic gathering and led to his exile from the South. For his part, Silver could no longer hold his tongue in the face of massive resistance to the civil rights movement, and white Mississippians could not stomach such blatant criticism from a state employee even if he did have tenure. More notably, those whites could not engage any honest discussion about their racist social system. To do so would compel them to recognize that the efforts of activists had increasingly weakened Jim Crow and forced a reluctant federal government to act on behalf of civil rights, especially in the face of continued white violence and demagoguery as seen in Oxford during the Meredith crisis. Many segregationists saw that they had less and less ground to stand on and looked to craft a more effective brand of conservative politics that avoided issues of race while maintaining white power.

Due to the events surrounding Meredith's integration of Ole Miss that left two people dead, a growing number of whites recognized that in order to protect their prerogatives they needed to ditch the old line-in-the-sand defiance that had characterized massive resistance to black advancement. If they were to retain their power, they needed to abandon unconcealed racism and acquiesce to some activist demands. Historian Joseph Crespino claims that this "strategic accommodation" of the movement by segregationists in turn fueled the rise of a new version of "color-blind" politics in Mississippi, which was implicitly about racial power but explicitly spoke to individual freedom. By so doing, the advocates of white supremacy created the illusion for the federal government and other observers that they had changed their ways and rejected explicit resistance to racial progress.[2]

Those southern whites who proffered such color-blind tools as "freedom of choice" plans for the desegregation of public schools became quite effective at preserving white power. Of course, the "freedom" to send a child to any school within a district obscured the reality that few black parents were willing to "choose" an all-white school for their children despite the fact that it may have had better resources. Most black parents would not take the physical, social, and economic risks that such a stance would mean for them or their children.

Although it is not shocking that James Silver saw himself ostracized by white southerners in 1963, the nature of the white response to him is a bit more surprising in the light of popular conceptions about resistance to the civil rights movement in Mississippi. While he was chased from the state, he did not run from a lynch mob. Instead, white powerbrokers, who could no longer tolerate his ideas, created an untenable atmosphere, and Silver ostensibly left on his own accord. Those whites had no answer to his direct assault, but in the wake of the Meredith crisis, they recognized that a violent confrontation would not serve the cause of Jim Crow due to the potential bad press in the international media and possible federal government intervention, which in turn would further fuel the civil rights movement.

Silver had had a topsy-turvy relationship with segregationists long before his SHA address. Historian Charles Eagles profiled Silver in his book *The Price of Defiance: James Meredith and the Integration of Ole Miss*, and noted that, by the early 1940s, Silver had developed an "image as a fomenter of dissent." At one point in 1949, he faced accusations of being a Communist from the General Legislative Investigating Committee (GLIC)—the state's version of the House Un-American Activities Committee (HUAC). Cleared of all charges, Silver did not retreat into anonymity but continued to capitalize on his academic freedom as a college professor even if that meant finding some unlikely allies.[3] For some time, he had been close friends with former attorney general and governor of Mississippi James P. Coleman, who had his own complicated association with hard-line racists.

When the state legislature asked the newly elected governor to speak about the philosophy of nullification for the upcoming 1956 session, Coleman turned to Silver for assistance and revealed his feelings on the matter: "If you can help me again lay this ghost [to rest], now almost a hundred years after its final death, I shall be deeply grateful." Silver responded the next day that he was happy to help.[4] Coleman's uneasiness with interposition was not entirely unusual for a man in his position. Many segregationists saw little hope in notions that the South could somehow reprise the Civil War and this time win a confrontation with the federal government. Thus they recognized the need for color-blind politics, but Coleman's relationship with Silver still would have raised some eyebrows.

A few months after Coleman's address, Silver appeared on the Mississippi State Sovereignty Commission's radar following racially progressive remarks he made at an October 1956 speech in Jackson, Tennessee. The state legislature had created the Sovereignty Commission soon after the *Brown v. Board of Education* decision "to protect the sovereignty of . . . Mississippi . . . from encroachment thereon by the federal government"—a century-old states' rights mantra that hardly concealed its dedication to massive resistance.[5] As governor, Coleman was the commission's ex officio leader, and, when it released its report on Silver's speech, he was put in an awkward position.

In a letter to Joe Patterson, the state's attorney general, H. B. Abernethy asked for a full accounting of Silver's actions in Tennessee. Not mincing words, Abernethy, who was the brother of U.S. congressman Thomas Abernethy, pointed out that

> James W. Silver HEADS the history department at the University, he does not only teach there, but HEADS the department. WHO HIRES MONKEYS LIKE HIM? And we pay our tax money to have his "tripe" taught to our children. What can we expect of our children and grand-children if we continue to allow these misplaced "monkeys" to teach in our schools? Someone is responsible for the employment of such people, and I for one think that some investigation should be made of the people who do the employing.[6]

Patterson agreed and had "been awaiting an opportunity to discuss this matter with the governor. In the language of former Governor Bilbo, I think that anyone connected with a state institution who makes remarks like this about the state 'should have hell fired out of him on the spot.'"[7] Indeed, a Sovereignty Commission investigation was already under way with noteworthy assistance.

The state's Board of Trustees of Institutions of Higher Learning, which governs colleges and universities in Mississippi, had resolved earlier in the year "to confer with the State Sovereignty Commission . . . [and] to cooperate in any way possible with the new Commission." This resolution apparently included funneling information about the Ole Miss historian to the state's segregationist watchdog.[8] In the end, not much came of the investigation, but, as Silver told his friend and editor of the *Delta Democrat Times*, Hodding Carter III, he was forced to explain himself and his comments to his boss, University Chancellor J. D. Williams.[9] Nonetheless, those facts did not dissuade Governor Coleman from looking to Silver for analysis on another controversial topic that no doubt stood in stark contrast to what many whites wanted to hear.

Just a month later, Coleman asked Silver about a speech on "the origins of the constitution of 1890" that the governor was set to present before the Mississippi Historical Society. The next day, Silver expressed gratitude that someone in the governor's position would give such a professional academic paper. He told the governor that he had already talked to Charlotte Capers, director of the Mississippi Department of Archives and History (MDAH), and that they were putting materials together for him to look over.[10] When Silver wrote back a week later, he explained how "corruption among the whites, dangling for Negro votes, from 1875 to 1890 . . . was the basic cause of the calling of the convention." As Silver saw it, when a farmer's movement came about along with populism, the one-party system of southern politics was threatened, and black voters became important. The constitutional convention of 1890 was meant to suppress their votes.[11] While that view of Reconstruction history is generally accepted today, it would have been much more controversial in Mississippi in 1956.

Governor Coleman knew that Silver's historical analysis was going to vastly differ from that of more popular opinions among white Mississippians. In all his years in public life, Coleman never backed down from his commitment to Jim Crow, but he did utilize color-blind language to advance the cause of white power and to show how interposition was a dead strategy. He realized that Silver could help craft an argument that avoided the implications of massive resistance, especially the notion that state governments were willing to deny the authority of the federal government when it came to the enforcement of judicial decisions that furthered the cause of civil rights.

Over the next decade, Silver continued to make a name for himself as an "agitator" among segregationists despite his close relationship with the governor. In 1960 Silver was linked to Billy Barton, an Ole Miss senior who was nominated to be the editor of the *Daily Mississippian*, the school's newspaper. The Citizens' Council was the leading private segregationist organization in the state, and its leader, William J. Simmons, reported to the director of the Sovereignty Commission that Barton was possibly part of a radical conspiracy to invade southern campuses. Along with participating in several sit-ins in Atlanta, Barton had been working for the *Atlanta Journal* under the auspices of its editor, Ralph McGill, which in Simmons's opinion proved "that Barton is well regarded in left-wing circles as a promising young man, and has been selected for advanced training." Not only that, but Barton "has the strong support of Dr. James Silver along with several other faculty members whose names are not known at the present time."[12] The Citizens' Council was a powerful defender of Jim Crow, and accusations like those by Simmons carried a lot of weight. It all fueled Silver's desire to speak out against the injustices he saw around him.

Early in 1962 Silver pleaded with Coleman to run again for office, as the regime of Governor Ross Barnett had entrenched uncompromising racists in power. Mississippi law at the time prohibited back-to-back terms in state office, so Coleman had not been able to run for reelection, but he could run for another term in 1964. Silver saw it as Coleman's "duty" to reenter public life because he was "the one possible ray of hope in a very dismal situation" in Mississippi. Silver even declared that he would leave Ole Miss and the state if Coleman did not run or was not elected, and he pledged his support "in every way possible except openly—for obvious reasons."[13] Before the events at Ole Miss that fall and at the SHA the following year, Silver knew that he would be a political liability for Coleman, but, as he began to prepare his remarks for the SHA, he could not have foreseen that his promise to leave Mississippi would become a reality in short order.

Looking for advice from Hodding Carter in the spring of 1962, Silver told the editor about his proposed speech in Asheville. Months before Meredith arrived on campus, Silver confided that he planned to compare Governor Ross Barnett to John Jones Pettus, who had led the state 100 years earlier. In Silver's view, they were almost identical and stood as bookends for a period of Mississippi history from 1860 to 1960 that had seen little to no social progress. "But the paper will be bigger than this. . . . [It] will include attempts to control education, speakers coming into the state, vigilante (citizens' council) action, etc." Carter approved of Silver's planned attack on the likes of the Citizens' Council and Ross Barnett, who had once attempted to mock Carter by describing him as "a moderate by his own admission."[14] For those segregationists who were not willing to budge on the issues surrounding black civil rights, any concessions showed intolerable weakness, but Silver's remarks and the tone they took in the aftermath of the Meredith crisis were unforgivable.

A staunch defender of James Meredith's right to an education at Ole Miss, Silver witnessed the riots on campus the night Meredith enrolled, and he provided written testimony to the U.S. Justice Department about what he saw— a definite taboo in white southern society. Silver detailed specific instances of violence and knew that "many who were present that night are willing to testify to their accuracy." Perhaps most important, Silver emphasized the fact that the riots took place "*before* the firing of tear gas by the marshals."[15] Thus federal troops were justified in their use of force in reaction to the violence perpetrated by both Ole Miss students and outsiders that night—a version of events that stood in stark contrast to the picture of federal aggression painted by white officials in the state.

Silver's efforts did not end there. He committed himself to helping Meredith stay enrolled at Ole Miss. With the prodding of the famed southern historian C. Vann Woodward, Silver pushed Meredith to write a book about his experiences, and, in the process, Silver further formulated his own ideas about Mississippi.[16] Edward Kuhn, editor-in-chief of the trade book department at McGraw-Hill, encouraged Silver and Meredith to explore their stories, but, ultimately, Kuhn thought Silver "probably should not be the official collaborator" with Meredith. Silver could be of great help, especially in providing direct quotations, but Meredith's lawyers proposed a journalist-editor who would be named later but who would not appear on the jacket of the book. Meredith insisted that the book would be better if it was "entirely his," and Kuhn agreed with that assessment.[17] Beyond Meredith's memoir, though, Silver showed great concern over Meredith's academic standing.

Many people who knew Meredith could see that he was having a hard time adjusting to his status as a pariah at Ole Miss. Kuhn told Silver that he thought Meredith might have just been happy to get in. Kuhn had seen some indications that Meredith might flunk out, but that was not exactly the storybook ending the editor was looking for.[18] More distressing was a letter that Silver got from C. Vann Woodward after Meredith had gone to visit the Yale campus for a few days.

Encouraged by National Association for the Advancement of Colored People (NAACP) attorney Constance Baker-Motley, Meredith had traveled to New Haven, Connecticut, for special tutoring and rest. Woodward and Meredith did not get to meet because Woodward had to attend his mother's funeral, but the Yale professor had heard that Meredith was depressed while he was there. According to Woodward's sources, Meredith was concerned that he was not going to pass algebra and French, and, if he failed, Meredith told people at Yale that "he was determined to 'get himself killed,' meaning that he intended to provoke violence against himself deliberately in Mississippi. . . . My friends were convinced he meant it."[19] Silver took those concerns to heart and, despite great personal threat, sought out Meredith to help shepherd him through his time in Oxford.

Letters poured in, both condemning and praising Silver's efforts. Historian and civil rights activist Connie Curry worried about how Silver was handling all of the stress, while U.S. Attorney General Robert Kennedy thanked him for telling people the truth about what happened during the entire ordeal. And again Chancellor Williams called him in and confided, "You do give me fits at times, but I love you just the same."[20] Through it all, Silver's disenchantment with racial politics in the South was only growing, and, in that context, he continued to prepare his SHA remarks, seeking assistance from sympathetic friends.

Over the summer of 1963, as Silver worked on his speech, he got help from a number of sources, including Rabbi Perry Nussbaum. Silver told Nussbaum about his proposed SHA address and its tentative title, "Mississippi: The Closed Society." He asked for Nussbaum's opinion on "the reasons for Mississippi being at least a little different than most of the rest of the states." Nussbaum penned his reply at the bottom of Silver's letter and argued that "the doctrine of States Rights has been a rationalization for an inferiority-complexed individualism that has found expression in automatic rejection of ideas and values which originate elsewhere. Our State is a half-century behind modern historical forces. Our resistance in the Race Issue is a *facet* of such backwardness." Nussbaum blamed the church for not being a greater force for positive change in Mississippi and compared the state to Nazi Germany, fearing a repeat of that history.[21] With help like that, there can little wonder that Silver's speech engendered hard feelings among segregationists.

Even before the conference, Silver's remarks were stirring the Jim Crow pot. John Pemberton of the American Civil Liberties Union (ACLU) wrote to Silver to warn him that he had heard about threats of retribution. Pemberton asked for an advance copy of the text and offered the help of the ACLU, particularly when it came to Silver's right to free speech. Silver was somewhat perplexed and did not know what to say to Pemberton. He realized that there would be a backlash because southern "society cannot tolerate the kind of criticism which I shall level at it." Silver doubted that he would be fired since Ole Miss was being watched closely for accreditation in the aftermath of its integration controversy, but Silver would not try to predict what would happen otherwise. "I do expect trouble, serious trouble. . . . Beyond that all I can say right now is that I plan to try to weather the storm and stay here."[22] In spite of those threats, Silver was not going to pull any punches when it came time for his speech.

Silver's address and future book were an acerbic examination of the state's racial climate. He painted a picture of continuity in the segregationist order, where "the voice of reason is stilled and the moderate either goes along or is eliminated. Those in control during such times of crisis are certain to be extremists whose decisions are determined by their conformity to the orthodoxy."[23] As Silver saw it, Mississippi society was governed by white, monolithic extremists who crafted a power structure that protected their authority through any means necessary. Partly due to the proximity of the Meredith crisis, which colored his opinion, Silver's message glossed over many nuances, but it still contained much truth. The trauma inflicted upon black Mississippians and civil rights activists could not be denied, nor could the extremism of many white southerners.

Newspapers quickly picked up the story. The *Memphis Commercial-Appeal* covered Silver's attacks and remarked that white denunciations were quick and clear. One of the state's U.S. Representatives, John Bell Williams, not only criticized Silver but called for him to be fired. In a rather nasty metaphor, Williams pushed for the "fumigation" of Ole Miss in order to get rid of pests like Silver.[24] Some people did come to Silver's defense though. The president of the Mississippi American Federation of Labor and Congress of Industrial Organizations (AFL-CIO), Claude Ramsey, said that his organization might demand Williams's resignation for threatening Silver. Although Silver did not always support labor unions, Ramsey defended him: "Dr. Silver, a historian, must deal in facts, while Representative Williams can display his usual brand of demagoguery." Ramsey did not think that Silver's right to free speech should be impinged upon by someone he saw as the worst member of Congress who only represented "lunatic-fringe groups that appear hell-bent on destroying all semblance of freedom and democracy in our state and nation."[25] Most whites had a harder time coming to grips with Silver's words.

In an editorial, the *Commercial-Appeal* tried to grapple with the problem and urged that the issues raised by Silver

> be publicly discussed. But it is difficult to discuss it with clarity because
> of three reasons: First, the general reaction to it is charged with explosive
> emotionalism; second, Dr. Silver's personal bitterness, resentment and lack

of sympathy for a problem that is basically historic impairs his own position; and third, the documentation of events, pro and con, are [*sic*] so much
in dispute as to make it difficult to establish exactly what happened at Ole
Miss.

The editorial did criticize Ross Barnett and John Bell Williams for saying that
Silver ought to be fired. In the view of the *Commercial-Appeal*, such attacks
only proved Silver's point: "This official comment was a monumental example of what constitutes the antithesis of academic freedom." Instead, southerners should openly discuss whether Mississippi was a "closed society" and
"venture self analysis. Will we challenge his position, be challenged by it or
ignore it?"[26] For a growing number of whites, the best option was to ignore it
by attempting to mute Silver within the state.

The Board of Trustees of Institutions of Higher Learning began immediately to look for ways to silence the historian and informed him of its official
efforts in the spring of 1964. E. R. Jobe, who headed the board, laid out fifteen
areas of inquiry and told Silver that a special three-member subcommittee
had been established to investigate his actions. Jobe asked that Silver appear
before the subcommittee in Jackson to address concerns, which were mostly
related to statements Silver had made at various times in relation to the culpability of university officials in fomenting the riots at Ole Miss. In addition,
Jobe asked that Silver answer a broad array of questions, some without any
obvious pertinence. He wanted to know about Silver's actions on the night of
the riot as well as when, where, and on what topics Silver had given speeches
in the recent past. Yet Jobe also queried Silver on the number of dissertations
he had overseen, what other materials he had published, and if there had
been other times that he had been in trouble with the board.[27] Such questions
indicated the seriousness with which the board and white leaders in the state
took Silver's words; they were looking for any angle to get rid of him.

Caught a bit off guard, Silver prepared a letter to Jobe that expressed his
confusion; all he could figure out was that the board was thinking about firing him. He also wondered why, after he got Jobe's letter, he received a phone
call asking that he testify about the board's accusations; precedent held that
all faculty communication with the board take place through the chancellor.
Silver wanted to know exactly what the board expected to hear because he
was willing to call "a hundred witnesses" to testify to the accuracy of all of his
comments. Rather than start an investigation, Silver thought the subcommittee ought to wait for the publication of his book, *Mississippi: The Closed
Society*, because it would answer many of their questions. But Silver had his

lawyers read that version of the letter first, and they convinced him to send another that simply said he was preparing his legal defenses.[28]

Three weeks later Silver's attorney, Landman Teller, sent an official response to Jobe. Teller indicated that the subcommittee formed to investigate Silver was not authorized by the bylaws of the board of trustees to conduct examinations concerning employment, tenure, and faculty dismissal. Having reviewed the minutes and policies of the board, Teller bolstered Silver's case with the official policies of the American Association of University Professors (AAUP) in regards to such matters. If there were other rules, Teller asked that Jobe forward them to him and spell out specific charges as well as what rights Silver had to defend himself.[29] Jobe waited two and a half months to reply to Teller's letter.

In the intervening time, the board of trustees approved a leave of absence without pay for Silver at its meeting on June 18, 1964. Silver had accepted a position as a visiting professor of history at Notre Dame for the 1964–1965 school year. He wanted out of a situation that was increasingly untenable both personally and intellectually, and the board was all too happy to oblige. It was only going to be a one-year appointment, and Silver pledged to come back to the state. Still, the board's approval of his departure did not end its investigation into Silver's supposed "contumacious conduct."[30] At that point, the threat of an investigation against Silver was mostly an idle one, and Silver's attorney knew it and sought clarification.

Claiming that the subcommittee had not required Silver to appear before it to face any charges, Jobe remarked that it had just asked for his help in the investigation. There were no formal charges. Jobe assured Teller that the board would follow its own guidelines and that there was no other "procedural information" that Jobe knew of that would be pertinent. If any formal charges were to arise, then Silver would have the opportunity to defend himself.[31] Perhaps the board was just glad to see Silver leave Mississippi, but, either way, Teller realized the delay in Jobe's response was purposeful. The board wanted Silver out of town and recognized that its investigation was at best misguided and at worst illegal. With Silver gone, Teller insisted that the historian would not appear before the subcommittee and demanded that the charges against him be dropped due to their bogus nature.[32]

Nothing came of the board's accusations against Silver, and two years later he tendered his resignation from Ole Miss. Silver had received an additional year for his leave of absence and recognized that it would do him little good to return to Mississippi. Chancellor Williams, who had been engaged in a nationwide campaign to rehabilitate his institution's image, accepted Silver's resignation as of June 5, 1966. Williams wished him good luck at Notre Dame: "You and your family will be missed by your friends in Oxford and at the University. I hope you will come back to visit us, and be sure to stop by to see me when you do."[33] The tone was conciliatory, but, like most whites who were not as gracious, Williams must have been glad to see Silver gone. It certainly made his job easier as chancellor.

Not everyone wanted to see Silver leave, however. Longtime Mississippi NAACP activist Aaron Henry was an old friend, and he and Silver shared an extensive correspondence. Henry had recently returned from the 1964 Democratic National Convention in Atlantic City, New Jersey, where the Mississippi Freedom Democratic Party (MFDP) had unsuccessfully challenged the seating of the state's all-white delegation. Upon hearing the news of Silver's initial leave, Henry was glad to know that it was for just one year and told Silver that he would stay in touch to "make damn sure" that Silver returned to the state.[34] However, that never came to pass, in large part due to the publication of *Mississippi: The Closed Society* in 1966.

Without a doubt, the appearance of *Mississippi: The Closed Society* only heightened the relief the board of trustees and other white leaders felt when they learned that Silver had resigned from Ole Miss. While writing it, Silver sought the assistance of people who had little sympathy for the Jim Crow regime of Mississippi. Burke Marshall and John Doar, both assistant U.S. attorneys general for civil rights, read multiple chapters and offered their thoughts. Marshall even went so far as to write a positive review of it in the *Georgetown Law Journal*.[35] Help and praise like that assured Silver's fate in the state of Mississippi and made his resignation a logical step. With Silver gone, there were few white voices within the state to challenge the existing order of things, at least voices with any significant platform from which to be heard.

There were some weaknesses in his argument. Silver's attack rightly condemned the racist intentions of white leaders, but it obscured the reality of how politicians and others were shaping a brand of "color-blind" politics. Silver bolstered a paradigm that has seen many people, historians included, write off all segregationists as one and the same—dedicated to their "Closed Society" at all costs. Yet he missed the nuances of a changing atmosphere in the state even as he was directly affected by it, and, in reality, he may have been too close to establish objective distance. Although his move to Notre Dame preempted the potential for violent repercussions, the circumstances surrounding his departure provide some indication of the growing power of color-blind politics in the state.

Rather than a monolithic "Closed Society," the predominant system of white power tried to ignore issues of race because of its growing weakness on those topics. Interposition was the only option left for hardcore segregationists, but most white leaders recognized that was a dead end. Instead, they worked to implicitly prop up a social and political system based on white supremacy by giving lip service to individual "freedom." It was still a "Closed Society" in the sense that it could not tolerate a legitimate discussion of race, but the response to Silver was not a physical, violent rejection in the name of Jim Crow. An environment was created whereby Silver "chose" to leave, and his absence meant that these white leaders were able to more easily craft a system of hegemony without as much dissent from within.

These responses were not necessarily new, but, for the first time they were the primary course of action for segregationists. That did not mean that violent racists disappeared in Mississippi, and, in fact, it remained the most dangerous state in which to be a civil rights activist or even a moderate supporter of racial equality. Still, massive resistance no longer dominated the entire discourse on race in the state. Most of that had to do with the advancing civil rights movement itself, which offered a stout challenge to white supremacy and provoked a need for different kinds of responses. By 1966 whites were better equipped with color-blind strategies to face what defiance was left. They were able to keep attention off a power structure that maintained white supremacy by supposedly giving each person an equal and free opportunity to make his or her own choices regardless of race. In that sense, the effort to mute James Silver in Mississippi was a natural extension of the racist discourse that had come to forefront in the state after the Meredith crisis in 1962.

NOTES

1. James Silver, "'Mississippi: The Closed Society,' Presidential Address Before the Southern Historical Association, Asheville, North Carolina, 7:00 p.m., November 7, 1963," "Silver, James W. 1963" Folder, Box 13, Wilson Minor Papers, Mississippi State University (MSU).

2. Joseph Crespino, *In Search of Another Country: Mississippi and the Conservative Counterrevolution* (Princeton, N.J.: Princeton University Press, 2007), 4, 19, 30.

3. Charles W. Eagles, *The Price of Defiance: James Meredith and the Integration of Ole Miss* (Chapel Hill: University of North Carolina Press, 2009), 142, 148–149.

4. J. P. Coleman to James Silver, December 19, 1955, "Correspondence w/ J. P. Coleman," Folder 12, Box 23, James W. Silver Papers, University of Mississippi (UM); James

Silver to J. P. Coleman, 20 December 1955, "Correspondence w/ J. P. Coleman," Folder 12, Box 23, James W. Silver Papers, UM.

5. Yasuhiro Katagiri, *The Mississippi State Sovereignty Commission: Civil Rights and States' Rights* (Jackson: University Press of Mississippi, 2001), 6.

6. H. B. Abernethy to Joe Patterson, November 9, 1956, "Attorney General Correspondence: Joe T. Patterson State Sovereignty Commission 1956" Folder, Box 7516, Mississippi Attorney-General's Office Files, Mississippi Department of Archives and History (MDAH), Jackson.

7. Joe Patterson to H. B. Abernethy, November 13, 1956, "Attorney General Correspondence: Joe T. Patterson State Sovereignty Commission 1956" Folder, Correspondence—Subject, 1931–1980, Box 7516, Mississippi Attorney-General's Office Files, MDAH.

8. Minutes of the Board of Trustees of Institutions of Higher Learning, May 17, 1956, "*Board of Trustees v. Silver* 1964 Related Correspondence, Misc.," Folder 4, Box 20, James W. Silver Papers, UM; Minutes of the Board of Trustees of Institutions of Higher Learning, October 18, 1956, "*Board of Trustees v. Silver* 1964 Related Correspondence, Misc.," Folder 4, Box 20, James W. Silver Papers, UM.

9. James Silver to Hodding Carter, October 29, 1956, "Hodding Carter: Correspondence: 1956: S. (April–December)" Folder, Box 15, Hodding Carter Papers, MSU.

10. J. P. Coleman to James Silver, December 10, 1956, "Correspondence w/ J. P. Coleman," Folder 12, Box 23, James W. Silver Papers, UM; James Silver to J. P. Coleman, December 11, 1956, "Correspondence w/ J. P. Coleman," Folder 12, Box 23, James W. Silver Papers, UM.

11. James Silver to J. P. Coleman, December 18, 1956, "Correspondence w/ J. P. Coleman," Folder 12, Box 23, James W. Silver Papers, UM.

12. W. J. Simmons to Director State Sovereignty Commission, August 16, 1960, "Attorney General's Correspondence: Sovereignty Commission 1957–1960" Folder, Correspondence—Subject, 1931–1980, Box 7516, Mississippi Attorney-General's Office Files, MDAH.

13. James Silver to J. P. Coleman, January 2, 1962, Folder 12, Box 23, James W. Silver Papers, UM.

14. James Silver to Hodding Carter, March 20, 1962, "Hodding Carter: Correspondence: 1962: S. (January–June)" Folder, Box 22, Hodding Carter Papers, MSU; Hodding Carter to James Silver, April 4, 1962, "Hodding Carter: Correspondence: 1962: S. (January–June)" Folder, Box 22, Hodding Carter Papers, MSU.

15. James Silver, "Statement by James W. Silver Regarding the Events at the University of Mississippi, September 30, 1962, October 31, 1962," 1–2, Folder 6, Box 3, Russell Barrett Papers, UM; "Statements by Barrett RE: Enrollment of James Meredith & Subsequent Riots, Oct. 1962," Folder 6, Box 3, Russell Barrett Papers, UM.

16. C. Vann Woodward to James Silver, October 15, 1962, "Correspondence 1962

A–Z Inc. Arthur Schlesinger, Frank Smith," Folder 3, Box 7, James W. Silver Papers, UM.

17. Edward Kuhn to James Silver, November 12, 1962, "Correspondence 1962 A–Z Inc. Arthur Schlesinger, Frank Smith," Folder 3, Box 7, James W. Silver Papers, UM; Edward Kuhn to James Meredith, November 15, 1962, "Correspondence 1962 A–Z Inc. Arthur Schlesinger, Frank Smith," Folder 3, Box 7, James W. Silver Papers, UM; Edward Kuhn to James Silver, December 10, 1962, 1–2, "Correspondence 1962 A–Z Inc. Arthur Schlesinger, Frank Smith," Folder 3, Box 7, James W. Silver Papers, UM.

18. Edward Kuhn to James Silver, November 15, 1962, "Correspondence 1962 A–Z Inc. Arthur Schlesinger, Frank Smith," Folder 3, Box 7, James W. Silver Papers, UM.

19. C. Vann Woodward to James Silver, December 28, 1962, "Correspondence 1962 A–Z Inc. Arthur Schlesinger, Frank Smith," Folder 3, Box 7, James W. Silver Papers, UM.

20. Connie Curry to James Silver, October 15, 1962, "Correspondence 1962 A–Z Inc. Arthur Schlesinger, Frank Smith," Folder 3, Box 7, James W. Silver Papers, UM; Robert Kennedy to James Silver, November 7, 1962, "Correspondence 1962 A–Z Inc. Arthur Schlesinger, Frank Smith," Folder 3, Box 7, James W. Silver Papers, UM; J.D. Williams to James Silver, November 2, 1962, "Correspondence 1962 A–Z Inc. Arthur Schlesinger, Frank Smith," Folder 3, Box 7, James W. Silver Papers, UM.

21. James Silver to Perry Nussbaum, June 19, 1963, "Correspondence—1963 H–Q," Folder 6, Box 7, James W. Silver Papers, UM; Perry Nussbaum to James Silver, July 2, 1963, 1–2, "Correspondence—1963 H–Q," Folder 6, Box 7, James W. Silver Papers, Box 7, UM.

22. John Pemberton to James Silver, October 9, 1963, "Correspondence—1963 H–Q," Folder 6, Box 7, James W. Silver Papers, UM; James Silver to John Pemberton, October 17, 1963, "Correspondence—1963 H–Q," Folder 6, Box 7, James W. Silver Papers, UM.

23. James W. Silver, *Mississippi: The Closed Society* (New York: Harcourt, Brace & World, 1966), 6.

24. Kenneth Toler, "Williams Blasts Professor's Talk on Racial Issue: Mississippi Representative Says Some College Staffs 'Need Fumigating,'" *Commercial Appeal*, November 7, 1963, "Ole Miss, James Meredith 1962–1963," Folder 50, Box 2, Kenneth Toler Papers, MSU.

25. Kenneth Toler, "Hi Ho Silver," *Commercial Appeal*, November 12, 1963, "Ole Miss, James Meredith 1962–1963," Folder 50, Box 2, Kenneth Toler Papers, MSU.

26. "Dr. Silver's Speech and Reactions to It," *Commercial Appeal*, November 15, 1963, "Ole Miss, James Meredith 1962–1963," Folder 50, Box 2, Kenneth Toler Papers, MSU.

27. E. R. Jobe to James Silver, April 27, 1964, 1–4, "*Board of Trustees v. Silver* 1964 Related Correspondence, Misc.," Folder 4, Box 20, James W. Silver Papers, UM.

28. James Silver to E. R. Jobe, May 1964, 1–3, "*Board of Trustees v. Silver* 1964 Related Correspondence, Misc.," Folder 4, Box 20, James W. Silver Papers, UM; James Silver to E. R. Jobe, May 6, 1964, "*Board of Trustees v. Silver* 1964 Related Correspondence, Misc.," Folder 4, Box 20, James W. Silver Papers, UM.

29. Minutes of the Board of Trustees of State Institutions of Higher Learning, November 15, 1962, "*Board of Trustees v. Silver* 1964 Related Correspondence, Misc.," Folder 4, Box 20, James W. Silver Papers, UM; Board of Trustees of State Institutions of Higher Learning, *Employment and Tenure of Faculties of Institutions of Higher Learning of Mississippi*, "*Board of Trustees v. Silver* 1964 Related Correspondence, Misc.," Folder 4, Box 20, James W. Silver Papers, UM; American Association of University Professors, "Statement on Procedural Standards in Faculty Dismissal Proceedings." *Bulletin* 4, no. 1 (Spring, 1958), "*Board of Trustees v. Silver* 1964 Related Correspondence, Misc.," Folder 4, Box 20, James W. Silver Papers, UM; Landman Teller to E. R. Jobe, May 30, 1964, 1–2, "*Board of Trustees v. Silver* 1964 Related Correspondence, Misc.," Folder 4, Box 20, James W. Silver Papers, UM.

30. Eagles, *Price of Defiance*, 433. Memorandum by J. D. Williams to James Silver, June 19, 1964, "*Board of Trustees v. Silver* 1964 Related Correspondence, Misc.," Folder 4, Box 20, James W. Silver Papers, UM.

31. E. R. Jobe to Landman Teller, August 14, 1964, 1–2, "*Board of Trustees v. Silver* 1964 Related Correspondence, Misc.," Folder 4, Box 20, James W. Silver Papers, UM.

32. Landman Teller to E. R. Jobe, September 3, 1964, "*Board of Trustees v. Silver* 1964 Related Correspondence, Misc.," Folder 4, Box 20, James W. Silver Papers, UM.

33. J. D. Williams to James Silver, April 14, 1966, "Correspondence—1965 N–Z Inc. Arthur Schlesinger, Wm. Winter," Folder 2, Box 10, James W. Silver Papers, UM.

34. Aaron Henry to James Silver, September 14, 1964, "Correspondence–1964– Unclassifiable," Folder 2, Box 9, James W. Silver Papers, UM.

35. James Silver to Burke Marshall and John Doar, January 13 1964, "Correspondence—1964 A–B," Folder 1, Box 8, James W. Silver Papers, UM; Burke Marshall, "Book Review," *Georgetown Law Journal* 53 no. 1 (Fall 1964): 262–265, "'*Mississippi: The Closed Society' Fall 1964 Georgetown University Law School*" Folder, Box 13, Burke Marshall Papers, John F. Kennedy Library, Boston.

"Doing a Little Something to Pave the Way for Others"

Participants of the Church Visit Campaign to Challenge
Jackson's Segregated Sanctuaries, 1963–1964

Carter Dalton Lyon

For ten months beginning in June 1963, the entrances of white churches in Mississippi's capital city became some of the key battlegrounds in the national struggle over civil rights. On most Sundays, integrated groups attempted to attend worship services at all-white Protestant and Catholic churches in Jackson. By challenging one of the remaining bulwarks of racial segregation, faculty and students at Tougaloo College, under the leadership of their chaplain, Rev. Edwin King, aimed to provide a palpable testimony to Christian teachings of the oneness of humankind. Even if ushers rejected them, the activists hoped their presence and their conversations would stir the consciences of white Christians into recognition that racial segregation was contrary to the will of God. The tactic of church visitation was just one of the many forms of direct action techniques employed by civil rights activists to test access to public spaces during the 1960s, but the approach held special meaning for the Tougaloo students, the laypeople, and the dozens of ministers who traveled to Jackson to join in the effort in 1963 and 1964. Participants came to the campaign with distinct experiences that framed their understandings on race, but they shared a sense of the potential usefulness in trying to interact with white Christians in dialogue and worship. Many who recalled their involvement in the campaign forty-five years later saw it as a decisive moment in their life and a turning point in spurring activism in race and other social issues.

Tougaloo activists initiated the church visit campaign on June 9, 1963, in the wake of a boycott, sit-in, and picketing effort against Jackson businesses and public accommodations and a new injunction prohibiting them from engaging in any future demonstrations and acts of civil disobedience. Before commencing these direct action tactics, Jackson movement leaders attempted to engage white church leaders and ministers by encouraging a series of interracial ministers meetings, but those secret gatherings did little except reveal a series of fundamental disconnects: between the motives within the black Jackson community and the false assumptions within the white Jackson community and between the stated Christian beliefs each shared and the exclusionary practices of the white congregants. In the preceding months, the Tougaloo activists discussed attempting to attend white churches, a tactic employed by civil rights activists in other southern cities since at least 1960. Beginning in June—and fully expecting police to arrest them—the Tougaloo activists finally put those plans into action. They attempted to attend churches spanning the denominational spectrum, including First Baptist Church, where Governor Ross Barnett arrived just as a deacon told the students that their presence "would disrupt the worship of all our people."[1] Those students then proceeded around the corner to Galloway Memorial Methodist Church, where ushers explained that the congregation maintained an all-white attendance policy. Though the Official Board of Galloway first voted on this policy two years earlier, they did so over the objection of their long-tenured and respected senior pastor, W. B. Selah. He privately determined to step down if ushers ever proceeded to bar black visitors from worship services, and followed through with his promise upon learning of the incident outside. Just minutes after the turning away of the students, Selah announced to his congregation that "there can be no color bar in a Christian church" and then tendered his resignation, with his assistant, Rev. Jerry Furr, quickly following suit.[2] Selah and Furr were just the first of several pastors who would have to leave their pulpits in Jackson in the succeeding years because of their convictions on race. Though only the Catholic Cathedral of St. Peter the Apostle admitted the black visitors on this first Sunday of visits, police restraint that day convinced the activists that the steps of white churches could continue to be a space to contest racial discrimination without government interference.

Following the murder of one of their leaders—Medgar Evers—just days after he drove students to several white churches on June 9, Tougaloo students and volunteer activists on campus returned to some of the same churches but broadened their scope to include other denominations through the summer. On June 16 St. Andrew's Episcopal, guided by Rev. Christoph Keller and a majority of lay leaders who favored his vision of racial moderation, became the first Protestant church to allow black visitors inside. Ushers there, and at other Episcopal churches in the city, routinely admitted integrated teams in subsequent weeks, though many church members did not exactly welcome their presence. At other Protestant churches, however, the weekly visits sparked extensive internal debates and turmoil.

At First Christian Church, the flagship church for the Disciples of Christ in Mississippi, ushers barred Anne Moody and another black student on June 16 in keeping with a two-year-old closed-door policy. The incident shocked the church's longtime pastor, Rev. Roy Hulan, who had been laboring to guide his church toward greater inclusiveness. The following Sunday he condemned his congregation for not understanding Christ's teaching and the gospel of reconciliation. Elders in the church then decided to put the board's earlier policy of racial exclusion up for a congregation-wide vote in late July. When the vote resulted in an overwhelming affirmation of the closed-door policy, some members succeeded in putting forward another churchwide referendum for late August—a vote on whether to retain Rev. Hulan as pastor. For some members, Rev. Hulan's denunciations of segregated worship were just the latest in a series of stands and activities—ranging from his involvement with the Mississippi Council on Human Relations to his participation in the interracial ministers' meetings the previous May—in which he stood apart from a segment of his congregation. The vote went against him, and he joined Selah and Furr as another minister exiled from Jackson.[3]

At Trinity Lutheran Church, the largest Lutheran congregation in Mississippi, the barring of black visitors also sparked a reevaluation of the admittance policy of the church, but in this instance the Mississippi State Sovereignty Commission weighed in to help ensure a satisfactory outcome. The pastor of the church was Rev. Wade Koons, who, like Rev. Hulan, joined in the interracial dialogue efforts earlier in the year and had been working to steer the church community toward racial moderation in the proceeding decade. Unlike First Christian, however, Trinity's lay board maintained an explicit open-door policy to African Americans. Nevertheless, church members acting on their own power rejected an integrated group on June 30. After once again voting to reaffirm Trinity's policy of inclusion, the Church Council—over Rev. Koons's advice—then moved to put the admittance policy to a churchwide vote set for late August. In the meantime, the doors were officially open and integrated groups succeeded in worshipping at Trinity, though some church members again took it upon themselves to reject those they encountered.[4]

Ahead of the vote, both sides in the debate over segregated worship at Trinity Lutheran turned to outside help to leverage influence. A lay leader at the church contacted Raymond Wood, the president of the Southeastern Synod of the Lutheran Church of America, who wrote a letter that the layman then mailed to all members. The letter explained the stance of the denomination, that Lutheran churches were open to all regardless of race. Another layman responded by contacting an investigator with the Mississippi State Sovereignty Commission to see if director Erle Johnston could furnish the church with the viewpoint of the state government. Johnston sent back a letter, which the layman forwarded on to church members, that argued that the church visitors were insincere and that Mississippi law considered a church to be private property belonging solely to the individual congregation. Additionally, Sovereignty Commission investigators spent time monitoring the activities of the visitors to Trinity who came from the Tougaloo campus.[5] To reinforce the position of the government even more, one of Jackson's two city commissioners—church member D. L. "Dock" Luckey Sr.—wrote his brethren an ominous note on official city letterhead just days before the vote. He urged members to vote against "mixing," but then added that the outcome was beside the point since any mixing would constitute a breach of peace that would result in an arrest.[6] On August 25 Trinity's members voted two to one to not allow "members of the Negro race to attend any or all of [church] activities."[7] Rev. Koons resisted calls for his resignation as he continued to insist that the vote was irrelevant given the denomination's stance. Later in the year Wood arrived in Jackson to lend his support to Rev. Koons. Wood spoke before the church members and demanded that they renounce the previous vote within a month or the congregation would face expulsion from the denomination. When a majority in the church failed to reverse course, Rev. Koons announced his resignation, and many of his supporters left the church for new start-up Lutheran congregations in the city.[8]

Though segregationists succeeded in closing the doors at First Christian and Trinity Lutheran by late summer 1963, the reality of open doors at the city's Episcopal and Catholic churches exposed cracks in the closed society of Jackson. Sensing that other churches might capitulate in the face of even more visits, especially following the bombing at the Sixteenth Street Baptist Church in Birmingham, Alabama, the Jackson Citizens' Council announced a plan on September 21, 1963, to "save these churches from integration." The local council never publicly explained what its new strategy entailed, but Rev. Ed King determined that the meaning and timing were clear, that "in the wake of the Birmingham tragedy, the soul of the white Christian had been touched" and that the climate now existed to change the closed-door policies of the city's churches.[9] Less than two weeks after the announcement by the

Jackson Citizens' Council, the city police ended their policy of nonintervention and began arresting church visitors. On October 6, 1963—World-Wide Communion Sunday—Jackson police detained two black students, Bette Anne Poole and Ida Hannah, and one white student, Julie Zaugg, after ushers at Capitol Street Methodist Church turned them away. With the initial arrests occurring outside of a Methodist church, denominational leaders stepped in to provide the bail money for the three, and liberal Methodist ministers throughout the East organized "witness" trips to Jackson to join the students in their campaign. Like the Tougaloo activists, these pastors intended to engage in dialogue with local Christians, setting up meetings with white clergy and laypeople on the Saturday of their visit. Then the ministers paired up in small groups with a Tougaloo student and attempted to attend worship on Sunday. Though the church visit campaign began as an effort to hold all the city's white churches accountable for their Christian beliefs, the first arrests at a Methodist church and the subsequent interest of Methodist clergy to expose the problem of segregation within their own denomination refocused the campaign on the city's Methodist congregations.

From the initial arrests in early October 1963 through the end of the formal campaign the following March, over fifty clergy and laypeople joined over a dozen Tougaloo students and faculty in their weekly visits to white churches. Though choosing not to intervene every Sunday, Jackson police arrested a total of thirty-seven individuals, twenty-two of whom were Methodist ministers. Most of the arrests occurred at Galloway Memorial Methodist and Capitol Street Methodist Churches when an integrated group insisted upon remaining on the church steps after being barred. As one of the visiting ministers stated, the witness teams declined to leave the premises simply because the group "had to say NO to the church's assertion of the right to turn us away." The church had the power to do so, but he reasoned that "we would have to deny that it had the right" and "would take the consequences."[10] When the Methodist General Conference, meeting in Pittsburgh in late April 1964, failed to bring an end to segregation within its own structures and congregations, Rev. King and the Tougaloo activists turned their attention to preparing for the Mississippi Summer Project. The visitation campaign failed to unlock most of the white church doors in the city, but, as Rev. King later wrote, they had "the satisfaction of knowing that the question of any possible significant action by the white moderates was settled." He thought that "it was good that the effort had been made" to confront white Christians with the immorality of segregation, and now they could turn to more drastic action.[11]

Though many of the Tougaloo activists who joined in the church visit campaign participated in concert with other local efforts to break down the barriers of racial discrimination, the uniqueness of the tactic—trying to attend white-only churches in small groups—provided the students a direct and unambiguous means through which to apply religious convictions. One of the prevailing themes that the students emphasized was that they visited white churches simply because the notion of segregated worship was so unfamiliar to their understanding of Christianity. Thomas Armstrong, who participated frequently in the campaign, recalled that because he grew up in the Holiness Church, he had a very personal reason for joining in the visitation effort. He held that the "segregated church just went against everything I knew and believed," and being turned away from white churches totally confused him. Though it was just one aspect of what the local movement was doing, Armstrong maintained that "the idea of it was great." He believed that "the religious element of segregated society should be the one to change" and that one "would think that it would be the first to get good people speaking up."[12] Bette Poole's father, who was a Baptist preacher, taught her from the cradle that no one was better than she. Poole, whom police arrested twice for attempting to worship at Capitol Street Methodist Church in October 1963, remembered always suffering from cognitive dissonance when in a segregated environment and felt called to be an agent of change. She joined the church visit effort because it was a clear way to expose the immorality of segregation. Poole saw that by turning her and other activists away, the white churches were essentially saying that they would only admit church members into their services, which seemed to be a backward mission for a congregation proclaiming Christ. Together with other movement activities in which she participated during that period—she worked to register voters in the Delta the summer of 1964—she regarded the whole experience as one of empowerment. She recollected not feeling weak anymore. She believed that an individual could effect change.[13]

Ida Hannah, another two-time church arrestee with Poole, also grew up in the Baptist church, where her parents and others taught her that all people were God's children. She recalled that in one sense, she wanted to attend a white church out of inquisitiveness. She saw how whites treated blacks outside of church, and she aimed to see if it was any different inside a church. Yet she also wanted to worship in a white church because she believed that if people from two races could worship together, then they would understand each other. Whites would understand that "we are all seeking salvation together." She participated in other movement activities, such as canvassing for voters, but for her, nothing demonstrated the goal of interracial brotherhood as clearly as the church visit campaign. Though her religious motive was at the forefront, she desired to change her home state, particularly so that her younger siblings and future children could "enjoy all the freedom they could." During one of her arrests, the detective, recognizing that she was the only one in the group from Mississippi, asked her if she planned on remaining and rearing her children in the state. She replied, "Of course, but first I've got to help clean Mississippi before I bring a child in this state." Like many of the activists, Hannah worried how her family would react if they ever found out about her involvement in the movement, so she kept quiet about it as long as she could. Her parents learned of her activism when most others did, by seeing a national television news broadcast highlighting her arrest at Capitol Street Methodist Church. Hannah's parents expressed shock, reminding her that she should have thought differently about doing such a thing because of where she lived—in Leake County. One of her neighbors told her bluntly that she was not reared to behave like that. Fortunately, her parents never received any threats, something she credits to the respect and independence they enjoyed in the community. Though she admitted being a private person—she never publicly mentioned her involvement in the church visits or the movement in her thirty-five years as a teacher—she talked about it with her children. More recently, some of her grandchildren wrote in school essays that she was their hero. Hannah felt uncomfortable with such a tribute, believing instead that she was merely "doing a little something to pave the way for others."[14]

While many of the Tougaloo students saw their participation in the church visits as an extension of other movement activities and protests in which they engaged, for some, enlisting in the campaign was the extent of their activism. These students emphasized that the tactic of trying to go to church seemed more acceptable than other direct action methods, especially in the eyes of their parents. Joan Trumpauer, who helped coordinate the visits, recalled trying to underscore this point when she stood before the school during chapel and at various meetings trying to recruit others to the campaign.[15] One of the students who wanted to take part in the movement and decided upon church visitation as the means was Doris Browne. She did not aim to tell her parents about her involvement at the time—and did not until years later—but she thought that if police arrested her at a church, her actions would meet the approval of her parents in Biloxi, for they were particularly religious. Browne sensed that her family would understand that she was doing more than just demonstrating. Like her parents, she believed in one God and was really just trying to worship.[16] Another student who became involved in the campaign but eschewed other protest activities was Camille Wilburn. She wanted to participate more in the movement, but feared repercussions on her parents who were educators in Okolona. She answered the call to go on visits to St. Andrew's Episcopal Church, namely because she was the only Episcopalian and knew that the Episcopal churches in Jackson were more accepting than others. Yet the negative reactions from some of the members of St. Andrew's surprised her and triggered a reevaluation of the Episcopal church, though she ultimately reasoned that the members' behavior was more indicative of being Mississippians than being Episcopalians.[17] For Browne and Wilburn, the church visit campaign was their entryway into the movement. Though being arrested would have changed how their parents and home communities viewed them, at the time visiting churches was a comfortable way to be involved while remaining true to their convictions.

The church visit campaign gave many students an opportunity to affirm their Christian beliefs, but the effort steered at least one nonreligious student, Austin Moore, more toward the faith. Moore's involvement in the campaign was more peripheral, driving students to churches on a few Sundays. He was busy spearheading the effort to discourage artists from performing to segregated audiences in Jackson. His role as a local movement leader brought him to the General Conference of the Methodist Church in Pittsburgh in May 1964, an event that changed everything for him. His father, like other newspaper readers throughout the country, saw a picture of Moore carrying the charred cross during the Living Memorial. Moore's father immediately ordered his son to leave Mississippi and move to California, where Moore has lived ever since. Participating in such a public way in the Prayer Pilgrimage and having to explain it to his father caused Moore to reevaluate his own spirituality. In addition to other pursuits, Moore became an ordained minister.[18]

Like most of the Tougaloo activists, the ministers who traveled to Jackson to participate in the church visit campaign and joined the students in Pittsburgh for the Living Memorial saw their effort as a Christian "witness," a word the pastors used repeatedly in discourse with each other at the time and when they recalled the events forty-five years later. They meant to testify to Christ's teachings—and the principles of the Methodist Church—that all men were brothers, that Christ offered himself for the sins of the whole world, and that the House of God was open to the whole family of God. They believed, as one of them recalled, that the church needed to move more openly toward equality. The church visits were one of the forms in the overall effort to change the denomination, but the campaign was essential because it was trying to move the church from the bottom up.[19] By witnessing in Jackson, the ministers aimed to elucidate and simplify the crucial issues ahead of the General Conference, beginning with the recognition by all that racial discrimination was a reality in local churches. For Rev. David James Randolph, who police arrested at Capitol Street Methodist on Easter Sunday, this was one of the main accomplishments of the church visit campaign. The actions of the white Methodist churches in Jackson demonstrated that if one intended to worship interracially, one would have to go to jail. The Methodist Church had to choose sides: either affirm the beliefs of the Methodist Church or the discriminatory practices of the white Mississippi Methodist churches.[20] As Rev. Ed Hiestand, a participant in an early November 1963 weekend, and Rev. Paul Minus, a cellmate of Randolph's, remembered, the church visits helped Methodists face the problem that sickness existed in the church. Because of the nationwide press coverage of the campaign, the white delegates from the Southeastern Jurisdiction could no longer claim that their churches were open.[21] For Rev. Paul Lowley, who joined in a mid-November witness effort, the disease of racial discrimination festered because local churches believed they had the liberty to form their own policies. The visits therefore helped expose a structural problem in the church that the denomination needed to correct. Rev. Lowley believed that "if the local church is made to feel that they have control over polity, they will think that they have control over their theology."[22]

After traveling to Jackson, conversing with local people, and trying to attend churches in integrated groups, visiting ministers returned home to find new opportunities to discuss the issue of race and the social conditions in Mississippi's capital city. Several of the groups, such as the teams from Chicago and the seminary professors from the Methodist Theological School in Ohio, discussed their witness during special assemblies held soon after their return. Many of them talked about their experience from the pulpit, trying to defuse misunderstandings about their motivations for going and using the visit as a chance to focus parishioners on the racial problems in their own cities. Rev. Al Bamsey of St. Claire Shores, Michigan, a participant in a mid-November witness, wrote back to the Tougaloo activists that he and the others from the Detroit area were "carrying on the fight" in their own segregated communities. He said that on Race Relations Sunday, he and others leveled with the congregations again. Rev. Bamsey reported that more parishioners were willing to get involved in the struggle and that the entrenched opposition in the churches was not as powerful as it once was.[23] When Rev. Bill

Martin came back to his church outside of Nashville, Tennessee, after being turned away from Capitol Street Methodist in early December 1963, he preached more on race to his congregation, though he recalled "not trying to slap them in the face with it" too much. He used the visit as a springboard to focus more on Race Relations Sundays, inviting Southern Christian Leadership Conference leader Rev. Joseph Lowery to his church just two months after his trip to Jackson.[24] Like Rev. Martin, Rev. Richard Teller tried not to overwhelm his congregation with sermons on race following his return to Ohio in late November 1963, thinking that some ministers closed the doors of communication with the church if they talked too exclusively on the matter. Yet Rev. Teller remembered preaching about his trip the first Sunday after he returned, and, as news filtered through the mostly Republican suburb of Tipp City, Ohio, he sensed that his involvement made the issue of racial discrimination more visible.[25] Rev. Ed Hiestand remembered that he tried to emphasize to his congregation outside of Chicago that he and the other ministers were trying to help the church face the problem, and that Jackson was just a symbol and a particularly clear example.[26] Rev. Randy Lunsford wrote to the Tougaloo activists of the wide range of reactions that people in Indiana, Pennsylvania, were having to his visit to Galloway Memorial Methodist Church in February 1964. Yet he reported that one tangible outcome was the creation of a new local Christian-based group to combat racial prejudice and said that the organization planned to lead the effort to desegregate the town's swimming pool.[27] Rev. Sally Smith wrote that her group's visit in mid-January 1964 received extensive local news coverage in Iowa City and Cedar Rapids, Iowa, and they appeared as guests on radio programs and were set to speak to several local groups about the situation in Jackson. Moreover, she said that all of the churches in Iowa City would be emphasizing human relations in programs the following Sunday, with members of the group preaching at most of them.[28]

The ministers and laymen from Ohio who participated in the Jackson witness in late November 1963 were also eager to talk about their involvement back home. In the days following Rev. Al Tomer's arrival back in Kenton, he recognized that many people throughout the small town were discussing his role in the Jackson witness. To dispel any more gossip, he contacted the local newspaper, the *Kenton Times*, and convinced the paper to allow him to write a series of articles about what he experienced in Jackson.[29] Rev. John Wagner returned to Ohio to find strong interest in his trip and estimated that he spoke to fifteen church groups and clubs in the succeeding weeks. Rev. Wagner thought that most people were simply eager to hear an accurate description of what was occurring in Jackson, regardless of whether they approved of his role.[30] Robert Meeks, a layman, wrote Rev. King after his arrest in Jackson explaining that the campaign gave him a unique opportunity to witness at home. In January 1964 he was helping a young Arab friend apply for American citizenship, and the federal officer, who was black, asked Meeks if he had ever been arrested. He said yes, that in fact he was arrested two months earlier in Mississippi for trying to go to church with a black minister. The officer smiled, and he and Meeks made arrangements to attend Meeks's Methodist church together in Lakewood, Ohio. Meeks also remained in touch with Rev. Frank Dement, the pastor of St. Luke's Methodist in Jackson, the church where Meeks, Rev. Donald E. Hall, and Rev. Woodie White were arrested. Meeks passed along the sentiments of Rev. Dement, who wrote him explaining that members of his Official Board were suggesting an end to the church's closed-door policy.[31] Ed Craun, another layman, wrote to the Tougaloo activists that the involvement of the group from Ohio produced discussions in a number of churches in the Cleveland district and that he and others received dozens of phone calls and letters from people inquiring about the witness. Craun said that "one result of this trip in my life has been a very great internal pressure to speak forth at every opportunity on the power of prayer and the Holy Spirit."[32] Yet at least one minister found that many adults reacted the same way as their counterparts in Jackson, denying that there was a problem in the first place. Arthur Jeffrey Hopper, a seminary professor at the Methodist Theological School in Delaware, Ohio, found that his church's youth group was the only one that wanted to hear from him.[33]

The ministers welcomed the opportunities to talk about the problem of race in their communities and within the denomination, but the discussions with parishioners for at least a few of them centered upon defending their involvement in the witness in the first place. When Rev. Elmer Dickson returned to Westchester, Illinois, after being released from jail in Jackson for trying to attend Sunday school at Galloway Memorial Methodist with a black student on October 20, 1963, church members called a special board meeting. His lay leaders then asked him to promise the church would not engage in that type of activism again. Rev. Dickson replied that he had no plans for such a similar witness, but insisted that he could not make such a promise. He told them that he "would be guided by what God's Spirit called me to do at a time when America was in the midst of significant change." He and several of his cellmates from Chicago decided that their own churches needed to experience a visitation exchange, so a team of black Methodists came to Rev. Dickson's church, and he later recalled that the visit did not cause any significant problems.[34] Rev. Richard Raines returned to his church on the outskirts of Detroit, following his participation in a mid-November 1963 witness, to find that members called a special meeting in his absence to decide whether to ask for his removal. Though his trip to Jackson triggered the emergency meeting, many were already upset over his earlier move to put up a poster in front of the sanctuary that welcomed people of all races to worship services. The church recently relocated out of downtown Detroit after trying to avoid much interaction with the growing black community in the neighborhood. Rev. Raines learned later that he survived the vote from this meeting because one of the church's most respected members—an elderly woman—spoke convincingly in support of him. Though the incidents resulted in more conversations about race and with African Americans in the church, Rev. Raines remained skeptical that his participation in the witness impacted any members greatly.[35]

When the four seminary professors from the Methodist Theological School in Ohio returned following their arrest at Capitol Street Methodist Church on Easter Sunday, some on the school's board of trustees called for the dismissal of one of them, the school's dean, Van Bogard Dunn, though support for the professors was more widespread among the student body and other faculty. One trustee, Ed Crouch, recalled that he was one of those wanting Dunn fired. A native southerner, Crouch thought that the professors were unnecessarily intruding on a local problem that would best be solved by local people. He saw Dunn as the ringleader, someone who needed to take responsibility for the group's actions.[36] Dunn later emphasized that the controversy with the trustees stemmed from his decision before the trip to avoid seeking the approval of the president of the seminary, Walter Dickhaut. Though he admitted to lacking sensitivity to this years later, Dunn remembered that he simply assumed that taking part in the witness was the right thing to do and that it never occurred to him to ask the president or anyone else whether the group could go.[37] Another one of the four, Arthur Jeffrey Hopper, recalled that Dickhaut was a little upset about their involvement, but bore the brunt of the attacks on the professors and ultimately resisted calls for rebukes or for anyone's dismissal.[38] Dickhaut later presided over an assembly at the school's library where each of the four shared different aspects of their witness in Jackson. Dickhaut said that "we are grateful and we are proud" that "these men have walked right into the middle of trouble and suffering which will involve every single one of us before this chapter is concluded."[39]

While the involvement of the four professors from the Methodist Theological School in Ohio offended some of the school's trustees, their witness inspired at least a few students and opened up opportunities for others to get involved in the southern movement. Walter Dickhaut, a nephew of the school's president, recalled being rather indifferent to the issue of civil rights during his early time as a student. He remembered hearing Everett Tilson constantly preach on the issue of race during chapel services, and, at one point, he thought that if he heard Tilson give another sermon on civil rights, then he would quit. He gradually came to understand the relevance of the Christian faith to civil rights and saw that what the professors did in Jackson was merely the natural product of what the professors were trying to get students to understand in class. Months later, Dickhaut helped organize a busload of students to take part in the protests in Selma, Alabama.[40] Another student, Joseph Sprague, was already heavily involved in various movement activities and joined Van Bogard Dunn on a return trip to Jackson just a few weeks after the conclusion of the General Conference in Pittsburgh. A group of a half-dozen students and professors from the Methodist School of Theology came to Jackson at the invitation of local black leaders who wanted help keeping public facilities integrated that activists succeeded in opening earlier. Sprague recalled that they were in Jackson for nearly two weeks, attending nightly rallies and interacting with the black community. One of the other professors on the trip was a Hebrew scholar, and, in several visits with black clergy, he used his expertise to debunk many of the biblical myths, such as the curse of Ham, that white supremacists often pointed to in defending racist ideologies. Yet years later what Bishop Sprague remembered most was the truly interracial aspect of the whole experience. He sensed that during many of these activities, such as on the basketball court playing with youth, these interactions represented the first times that the young people intermingled this way with white people. Bishop Sprague remembered in awe the determination of the black community, especially those who opened their homes to the groups at great physical danger, and the courage of men like Rev. Ed King, who had such a deep theological understanding that he put into everyday action.[41]

Though most of the visiting ministers were already actively involved trying to steer their own churches and communities toward greater inclusiveness before they traveled to Jackson—and many considered themselves to be movement activists—some saw their experience as a turning point in their own ministries and their concern for race issues at home. Rev. Al Tomer called his participation in the Jackson witness in late November 1963 a "trigger event" for confronting racial discrimination at home. Shortly after his return to Kenton, Ohio, he and a Presbyterian layman—the two constituted the social action committee for the town's council of churches—tried to convince the eight barbers in the town to cut the hair of black men, who had to travel thirty miles to get their hair cut. Rev. Tomer found that this incident provoked more controversy than his trip to Jackson. All of the barbers, including three who were members of Rev. Tomer's church, refused. The district superintendent was eager to move him out of the church, so he placed him at an inner-city church in Toledo, where Rev. Tomer became active in open housing legislation. Like other ministers involved in the Jackson witness, Rev. Tomer worked to encourage cross-racial appointments in Methodist churches. In the early 1980s he became the first district superintendent in his conference to appoint an African American to a white church.[42] Rev. John Wagner, who traveled to Jackson with Rev. Tomer, recalled that the Jackson witness was a defining moment for his ministry, for he was not involved in social justice issues in the conference before the trip. He remembered that he joined the effort because he felt called to do so, not because he was trying to help desegregate the denomination. Yet his outlook changed significantly upon his return, for the campaign gave him a chance to be in the midst of a social justice campaign. He believed that it was now part of his heritage. He participated in several sit-ins at federal courthouses and, as an elected delegate to jurisdictional conferences, labored to put together interracial slates of clergy and laity.[43] Rev. Bill Wells, who admitted his reluctance to participate in the church visit campaign in early December 1963, returned to North Carolina feeling "more committed than ever to doing something to integrate our lives." As the state director for campus ministries, he worked to ensure the desegregation of all the state conferences and activities and drove a few students to the marches and voter registration drives in Montgomery, Alabama.[44]

Participation in the Jackson witness, and the notoriety that came with it, catapulted some to positions of leadership on civil rights issues in their communities and within the Methodist Church. Rev. John A. Collins, who was chair of the social action committee while in seminary and was organizing a mostly black East Harlem church, returned to New York to find that his involvement in the effort and arrest at Galloway in December made him even more of a leader on social justice issues in his conference. He regarded his participation as a watershed event, firming up his own commitment to racial issues while he served in the congregation for another five years and when he became program director for social concerns in the conference in the succeeding years.[45] Rev. Ed Hiestand recalled that the experience gave him credibility as a civil rights leader in his town and especially within the black community. He believed that the Jackson witness helped him feel the vulnerability of blacks so he could better minister to African Americans.[46] Rev. Richard Raines echoed Rev. Hiestand's sentiments, remembering how the witness educated him on how much he did not know about racism. Until he saw racial discrimination firsthand and experienced it with a black man, he thought that he did not truly know the world and feelings of African Americans. The experience taught him to seek out all of the other unfinished justice questions in the country, a lesson he continues to try to apply.[47] Rev. Woodie White, a black minister who served a mostly white congregation in Detroit, saw his involvement in the campaign and his arrest at St. Luke's Methodist Church on November 17, 1963, as a defining moment in his life. Up to that point, he worked vigorously to combat northern-style racism and welcomed the invitation from his friend from seminary, Rev. Ed King, to come to Mississippi. The experience broadened his perspective and gave him insight into linking the struggle between the North and the South. When the denomination finally moved decisively to end segregation in the church in 1968, he became head of a new Methodist agency, the Commission on Religion and Race. Though recognized as a civil rights leader within the denomination by that time, he believed that Methodists elected him to this position because of his involvement in the Jackson witness.[48]

Unlike so many of the other battles of the civil rights movement, the Jackson church visit campaign failed to achieve its primary objective—to desegregate the white-only churches of Mississippi's capital city. Participants aimed to unlock the closed society of Jackson by going through the doors of white churches, thereby demonstrating the oneness of humankind through interracial dialogue and worship. A few white churches recognized that discriminatory attendance policies undercut fundamental Christian beliefs and denominational practices, but most churches did not. The campaign yielded few victories, yet it succeeded in making segregation visible in the Christian church, an uncontested social space up to that time. Church people who affirmed white-only policies now had to defend them on a near-weekly basis. The persistence of the integrated teams ensured that segregationists had to fight to keep their doors closed. The confrontations outside of the churches sparked debates within the congregations, and some pastors had to step down or were dismissed from their pulpits after refusing to preach before a closed church. While many blamed the Tougaloo activists and their supporters for causing turmoil inside the churches, the visitors merely shook white Christians from their comfortable but unstable moorings and brought to light the moral crisis that was previously flickering out of view. The participants in the Jackson church visit campaign felt frustrated by the repeated rejections and police interventions at the time, but they did not feel defeated. Most carried on the fight elsewhere and by other means. Recalling their involvement years later, an overwhelming sense of pride dominates their memory. They were unable to worship at most of the churches they visited, but they asserted a belief that is now accepted practice within the Methodist Church and the formerly all-white churches in Jackson.

NOTES

1. "Negroes Attempt to Visit Six Jackson Churches," *Baptist Record*, June 13, 1963, 1, 2; "Six Churches Turn Away Negroes," *Clarion-Ledger*, June 10, 1963, 1, 10.

2. "Six Churches Turn Away Negroes"; Ed King, "Prophet and the Preacher," manuscript, 162–163, Ed King Private Papers; W. B. Selah, "Galloway and the Race Issue," manuscript, Box 2, Folder 2, Selah Papers, J. B. Cain Archives of Mississippi Methodism, Millsaps College, Jackson, Miss.; Ray E. Stevens, *Galloway Church History: Book I* (Jackson, Miss.: Ray E. Stevens, 1996), 113. Lay leaders at Galloway initiated the closed-door policy in June 1961 after Mayor Allen Thompson informed them that Freedom Riders might try to attend worship services there. The policy specifically stated that "ushers of the church are herby instructed to decline to admit any person or persons, white or colored, who, in the judgment of the greeters or ushers, seek admission for the purpose of creating an incident, resulting in a breach of peace." Though the policy seemed to only apply to demonstrators, Galloway ushers—and Selah—understood it to apply to all African American visitors. See W. B. Selah, "Freedom Riders," undated sermon, 1–2, Selah Scrapbook, Box 2, Folder 9, Mississippi Department of Archives and History (MDAH); Stevens, *Galloway Church History*, 92.

3. Roy S. Hulan, "A Local Minister's Experience in Revolution 1961," 1–4, Roy S. Hulan Papers, Disciples of Christ Historical Society, Nashville, Tenn.; Roy S. Hulan, "A Statement from Roy S. Hulan to the Members of First Christian Church, Jackson, August 20, 1963," 1–2, Richard H. Hulan Private Collection; Roy S. Hulan, "When Men Are at Odds," *The Christian*, September 22, 1963, 4–5. Rev. Hulan's sermon on June 16, 1963, is reprinted in this issue of *The Christian*.

4. Fred Patton to "All Members of Trinity Lutheran Church," July 24, 1963, SCR ID # 3-79-0-1-2-1-1, Sovereignty Commission Online; Charles W. Koons, interview by author; Wade Koons, "The Jackson, Mississippi Problem," 1, n.d., Fry–Southeastern Synod 1963–1964, Re Trinity Jackson, Mississippi, Archives of the Evangelical Lutheran Church in America (AELCA), Elk Grove, Ill.

5. "Activity Report for Month of July, 1963, Virgil Downing, Investigator," SCR ID # 7-4-0-104-4-1-1, Sovereignty Commission Online; Memo from Virgil Downing to Erle Johnston, July 30, 1963, SCR ID # 3-79-0-3-1-1-1, 3-79-0-3-2-1-1, Sovereignty Commission Online; Erle Johnston Jr. to O. F. Schluetter, August 19, 1963, SCR ID # 3-79-0-4-1-1-1, 3-79-0-4-2-1-1, Sovereignty Commission Online.

6. D. L. Luckey, August 22, 1963, memo, Fry–Negro Question 1963–1964, Re Trinity Jackson, Mississippi, AELCA; "Conflicts Over Segregation Arise in Mississippi's Churches," *New York Times*, January 5, 1964, L71.

7. Koons, "Jackson, Mississippi Problem," 1–2.

8. "Koons Resigns as Pastor of Jackson Church," *Jackson Daily News*, January 27, 1964, 7; "Synod President's Message to Trinity Lutheran Church, Jackson, Mississippi, December 8, 1963," 1–3, Fry-Southeastern Synod 1963–1964, Re Trinity Jackson, Mississippi, AELCA; Wade Koons to Raymond Wood, January 20, 1964, 1–2, Fry–Southeastern Synod 1964–1964, Re Trinity Jackson, Mississippi, AELCA.

9. "Aspect, A Project of the Information and Education Committee, Jackson Citizens' Council," September 1963 Bulletin, Vol. 1, no. 2, 2, Archives and Special Collections, J. D. Williams Library, University of Mississippi; "Council Plans Fight against Church Mixing," *Clarion-Ledger*, September 22, 1963, A16; Ed King, "White Church, Part I," manuscript, 16, Edwin King Private Papers. W. J. Simmons, interviewed by the author on February 8, 2006, could not recall the specific reasoning behind the timing of the announcement or what the specific plan entailed. Asked if the Citizens' Council members thought that Jackson churches were in danger of opening their doors because of the church bombing and the fact that several churches had recently admitted blacks, Simmons said "that seems like a logical conclusion." Asked whether he or other Citizens' Council leaders pressured Jackson police to arrest church visitors, Simmons replied that they consistently pressured the police to intervene against civil rights protestors.

10. Tyler Thompson, "A Communication: Another Pilgrimage to Jackson," *Christian Century*, April 22, 1964, 512.

11. Ed King, "White Church: Part IV," manuscript, 192–194, Edwin King Private Papers.

12. Thomas Armstrong, Chicago, telephone interview by author, August 21, 2008; Thomas Armstrong, "Panel: How Did These Events Change You?" Church Desegregation and the Jackson, Miss., Witness, First Methodist Church, Chicago, October 4, 2008.

13. Bette Anne Poole Marsh, Chicago, telephone interview by author, September 17, 2008; Bette Anne Poole Marsh, "Panel: How Did These Events Change You?" Church Desegregation and the Jackson, Miss., Witness, First Methodist Church, Chicago, October 4, 2008.

14. Ida Hannah Sanders, Jackson, Miss., interview by author, July 20, 2009.

15. Joan Trumpauer Mulholland, Jackson, Miss., interview by author, June 12, 2009.

16. Doris Browne, Washington, D.C., telephone interview by author, June 4, 2009.

17. Camille Wilburn McKey, Jackson, Miss., interview by author, June 19, 2009.

18. Austin Moore, Pomona, Calif., telephone interview by author, January 29, 2009.

19. Al Bamsey, Ann Arbor, Mich., telephone interview by author, June 2, 2009.

20. David James Randolph, Albany, Calif., telephone interview by author, February 13, 2009.

21. Ed Hiestand, Oak Park, Ill., telephone interview by author, June 5, 2009; Paul Minus, Claremont, Calif., telephone interview by author, September 19, 2008.

22. Paul Lowley, Petoskey, Mich., telephone interview by author, May 21, 2009.

23. Al Bamsey to Joan Trumpauer, February 13, 1964, Box 9, Folder 446, Ed King Collection, MDAH.

24. Bill Martin, Lubbock, Tex., telephone interview by author, June 22, 2009.

25. Richard Teller, Delaware, Ohio, telephone interview by author, June 11, 2009.

26. Hiestand interview.

27. Randy Lunsford to Joan Trumpauer, March 6, 1964, Box 9, Folder 444, Ed King Collection, MDAH.

28. Sally Smith to Ed King, n.d., Box 9, Folder 446, Ed King Collection, MDAH.

29. Al Tomer, Cincinnati, telephone interview by author, June 16, 2009. For Rev. Tomer's articles, see "Two Worlds Behind a Magnolia Curtain, Part I, The Curtain Makers," *Kenton Times*, December 4, 1963, 1, 5; "Two Worlds Behind a Magnolia Curtain, Part II, The Plight of the Moderate," *Kenton Times*, December 5, 1963, 1; and "Two Worlds Behind a Magnolia Curtain, Part III: The Events of Sunday and Conclusions," *Kenton Times*, December 7, 1963, 1.

30. John Wagner, Westerville, Ohio, telephone interview by author, June 3, 2009.

31. Robert L. Meeks to Mr. and Mrs. King, January 27, 1964, 2, Box 9, Folder 446, Ed King Collection, MDAH; Robert Meeks to Grover Bagby, n.d., Box 1433-6-7, Folder 2, Jackson Arrest Cases, 1963–1967, Administrative Records of the Division of Human Relations and Economic Affairs of the General Board of Church and Society, General Commission on Archives and History (GCAH), Drew University, Madison, N.J.

32. Ed Craun to Joan Trumpauer, December 31, 1963, Box 9, Folder 446, Ed King Collection, MDAH.

33. Arthur Jeffrey Hopper, Westerville, Ohio, telephone interview by author, September 10, 2008.

34. Elmer. A. Dickson, "Civil Rights Memories," January 21, 2008, 4, Gerald Forshey Project, First Methodist Church, Chicago.

35. Richard C. Raines Jr., Redwood City, Calif., telephone interview by author, May 26, 2009.

36. Ed Crouch, interview by Paul Grass, Winter 1994, Rev. William H. Casto Jr., Personal Collection.

37. Van Bogard Dunn, interview by Paul Grass, Winter 1994, Rev. William H. Casto Jr., Personal Collection.

38. Arthur Jeffrey Hopper, interview by Paul Grass, Winter 1994, Rev. William H. Casto Jr., Personal Collection.

39. Van Bogard Dunn, Arthur Jeffrey Hopper, Paul M. Minus, and Everett Tilson, "Report on Trip to Jackson, Mississippi, Easter 1964," transcript, 1964, Methodist Theological School in Ohio Library, Delaware, Ohio.

40. Walter Dickhaut, Bangor, Me., telephone interview by author, September 13, 2008.

41. Joseph Sprague, London, Ohio, telephone interview by author, September 26, 2008.

42. Tomer interview.

43. John Wagner, Westerville, Ohio, telephone interview by author, June 3, 2009.

44. Bill Wells, Laurinburg, N.C., telephone interview by author, June 15, 2009.

45. John A. Collins, New Rochelle, N.Y., telephone interview by author, September 26, 2008.

46. Hiestand interview.

47. Raines interview.

48. Woodie White, Atlanta, telephone interview by author, September 22, 2008. Significantly, Woodie White and Fitts Herbert Skeete, two of the black Methodist ministers who participated in the Jackson witness, went on to become bishops of the Methodist Church.

"Born of Conviction"

White Mississippians Argue Civil Rights in 1963

Joseph T. Reiff

Imagine you are a white Methodist preacher in Mississippi in the early 1960s. You grew up in the 1930s and 1940s in a segregated world and simply accepted it as reality. Then as a Methodist teenager or college student at Millsaps or Mississippi Southern, you were exposed to a few speakers, religious life leaders, or professors who gently but persistently pushed you to ask questions about that segregated world. As a college student involved in religious life, you had the opportunity in the late 1940s to meet with a few students from black colleges in Mississippi at occasional events sponsored by religious life leaders at the schools, or in the late 1950s you participated in an interracial forum at Tougaloo College, or you heard Tougaloo professor Ernst Borinski publicly calling segregation into question at Millsaps in 1958.[1]

Feeling a genuine call to the ordained Methodist ministry, you attended seminary (at Emory or Vanderbilt or Yale or Southern Methodist University [SMU] or Duke or Drew) and were challenged to think in new ways about race relations and the role of the church in society. Now back in southern Mississippi, you have begun your service as a local church pastor in the Mississippi Conference, more conscious of the evils of the "Closed Society," but not sure what you can do to change things. In spite of the national Methodist Church's call for a new day in race relations, it still maintains a segregated structure: in addition to the state's two white annual conferences, Mississippi and North Mississippi, there are two black Mississippi conferences (part of the larger Central Jurisdiction), and there is little interaction between white and black Methodists, even those who live in the same town.[2]

This was the situation for the twenty-eight white Methodist ministers of the Mississippi Conference (hereafter referred to as "the 28") who signed "Born of Conviction," the second-best-known white clergy statement in the civil rights era. Written in the wake of the September 1962 riot at the University of Mississippi and appearing in the *Mississippi Methodist Advocate* (the weekly newspaper for the two white conferences) on January 2, 1963, the statement called for freedom of the pulpit, reminded readers of the Methodist *Discipline*'s (the denomination's official book of doctrine and polity) claim that the teachings of Jesus "[permit] no discrimination because of race, color, or creed," expressed support for the public schools and opposition to any attempt to close them, and affirmed the signers' opposition to Communism.[3]

"Born of Conviction" caused a firestorm of controversy, and I propose that its publication three months after the insurrection at Ole Miss, along with the range of public and private responses to it, can be understood as a full-fledged argument among whites in Mississippi about the civil rights movement and its increasingly persistent call for an end to the segregated system and white supremacist ideology. This early 1963 debate reveals the complexity of attitudes as white Mississippians were confronted with the possibility that their segregated world might need or have to change, and attending to these voices supports my contention that the publication of "Born of Conviction" was a catalyst for this argument in both public and private theaters. Forcing this debate into the public arena and into the smaller but important local congregational publics of white Mississippi Methodism served a small but important role in bringing about change in Mississippi race relations.[4]

A Time to Speak

After the Ole Miss riot, some whites who had kept silent out of fear believed the time had come to speak against massive resistance to desegregation. Leaders who could not be dismissed as radical outsiders needed to break the pattern of rigid conformity to the Closed Society. An ecumenical group of white ministers in Oxford responded by publicly calling for repentance "for our collective and individual guilt in the formation of the atmosphere which produced the strife at the University of Mississippi." The white North Mississippi Conference district superintendents "whole-heartedly endorse[d]" the Oxford ministers' statement and said, "We affirm the freedom of the pulpit. We . . . support [our ministers] in the preaching of the whole Gospel in the Spirit of Christ." This response made the silence of Bishop Marvin Franklin and the district superintendents of the Mississippi Conference (which covered the southern half of the state) more glaring. The North Mississippi endorsement in the *Advocate* was not reported in the secular press, and it caused no noticeable controversy.[5]

North Mississippi Conference minister Sam Ashmore, editor of the *Mississippi Methodist Advocate*, was sixty-eight years old and approaching the end of his career in October 1962. He had not been known as a particularly prophetic or liberal minister when he took the editor's position in 1955, but subsequent events led him to speak with uncommon boldness. In an editorial published ten days after the riot, Ashmore said the blame for the rioting belonged to "all of us." "Yes, the church is partly responsible for what happened at Ole Miss," he concluded, because church people failed to speak out forcefully enough and "were not true to our Christian convictions." Even mild protest against the massive resistance juggernaut elicited accusations of betrayal of the sacred cause of white Mississippi and assertions that "the church had no business being concerned with political matters." Now, he said, "the Church will lose her life whatever she does," and the choice facing the white Mississippi Methodist Church is "whether she loses her life for Christ's sake and finds it in this hour of crisis or whether she really loses her life in pious platitudes and innocuous activity in a day which demands courageous witness."[6]

Some Mississippi Conference ministers became increasingly frustrated that none of their leaders were saying anything publicly in response to the current turmoil. In late October or early November four of them—Maxie Dunnam of Gulfport, Jerry Trigg of Jackson County, Jerry Furr of Jackson, and Jim Waits of Biloxi—gathered for a retreat at Dunnam's fishing cabin near Richton. It was time for some "courageous witness" in response to Ashmore's editorial. In that marathon session, the four settled on a manifesto of about 600 words with four main points:

- *Freedom of the pulpit*: "The Church is the instrument of God's purpose. . . . It is ours only as stewards under His Lordship." Clearly it was not to be used simply as a tool to prop up the Closed Society, where many ministers felt severely restricted in what they could say in churches because of widespread resistance to any questions raised about the Closed Society orthodoxy. Preachers should be free to speak their true convictions.
- *Affirmation of faith in "the official position of The Methodist Church on race"* as found in the 1960 *Discipline*. Statements quoted included "Our Lord Jesus Christ teaches that all men are brothers. He permits no discrimination because of race, color, or creed," and "God is Father of all people and races."
- *Support for public schools and opposition to their closing when desegregation comes*: "The Methodist Church is officially committed to the system of public school education and we concur. We are unalterably opposed to the

closing of public schools on any level or to the diversion of tax funds to the support of private or sectarian schools."

• *Affirmation of "an unflinching opposition to Communism"*: "In these conflicting times, the issues of race and Communism are frequently confused." The Closed Society rigidity meant that anyone who dissented was routinely labeled a Communist.[7]

The statement began with these words: "Confronted with the grave crises precipitated by racial discord within our state in recent months, and the genuine dilemma facing persons of Christian conscience, we are compelled to voice publicly our convictions. Indeed, as Christian ministers and as native Mississippians, sharing the anguish of all our people, we have a particular obligation to speak." The four writers, along with the twenty-four other ministers who signed the statement in late 1962, believed they spoke for many Mississippi Christians struggling with a "genuine dilemma" of Christian conscience. Speaking as natives of Mississippi and therefore avoiding suspicion as "outside agitators," the 28 sought to address the "anguish" of all who were deeply troubled by what had been happening but felt powerless to do or say anything in response. The Closed Society orthodoxy admitted no dilemma, agreeing with Alabama governor George C. Wallace's inaugural decree on January 14, 1963: "Segregation now, segregation tomorrow, segregation forever!"

When "Born of Conviction" appeared in the *Advocate* on January 2, 1963, every Mississippi daily newspaper—plus the Memphis, Mobile, and New Orleans papers—reported it on January 3. By that afternoon Bishop Marvin Franklin had declined comment. When told by a reporter that "another Methodist minister in Meridian had declined comment on the statement and said he didn't even want his name near the story," signer Ed McRae called that reaction "typical of the type of fear of free expression that the statement is attacking." All four of the signers quoted in a *Meridian Star* story said the statement simply reflected the position of the Methodist Church. Wilton Carter explained, "This is not a rabid stand a few preachers have taken but what Methodists have believed all along. It is the position of the officials of the church." McRae said the 28 had signed the statement "in order to open the door to discussion of the issues . . . without fear of recrimination."[8]

Lots of discussion and recrimination resulted. Responses to the 28 demonstrate a spectrum of attitudes and action among white Mississippians falling between the activism of the hundreds of Mississippi civil rights movement leaders and volunteers on one end and the bitterly opposed activism of violence, fear, and terror of the Ku Klux Klan and similar groups on the other. I propose four categories for that response, beginning short of participation in the movement and proceeding farther away toward the most vocal and active representatives of massive resistance: Voices for Change, Sympathetic but Silent, Protect the Institutional Church/Don't Rock the Boat, and Segregationists. Let us examine them in turn (and not in that order), both on the public and private levels.

Public Responses: Voices for Change

Public expressions of support came from Conference Lay Leader J. P. Stafford of Cary, Associate Lay Leader Francis Stevens of Jackson, a group of twenty-three ministers in North Mississippi's Tupelo District, and W. B. Selah. Stafford "heartily endorse[d] and applaud[ed]" the statement and said, "It is hard for many of us to go along with the great Methodist Church and changing times, in matters of race, but this is an adjustment *Christians can make.* Let's face it; brotherhood is as much a part of the teachings of Jesus Christ as salvation and faith." In a January 3 letter to the 28 that he made public, Stafford began, "Welcome to the fold of those who are willing to stand up and be counted." He also invoked the Old Testament prophet Elijah, rejoicing that the 28 had "not 'bowed the knee to Baal,'"—that is, had publicly rejected the Closed Society idolatry.[9]

The boldest endorsement—a stronger statement than "Born of Conviction" and quoted in full in the *Clarion-Ledger*—came from W. B. Selah, pastor of Galloway Memorial, white Mississippi Methodism's flagship church in downtown Jackson. Insisting that "for seventeen years I have preached the law of Christian love from the pulpit of Galloway Methodist Church," he proclaimed, "we must seek for all men, black and white, the same justice, the same rights, and the same opportunities that we seek for ourselves. Nothing less than this is Christian love. To discriminate against a man because of his color or his creed is contrary to the will of God. Forced segregation is wrong. We should voluntarily desegregate all public facilities." He added, "As Christians, we cannot say to anyone, 'You cannot come into the house of God.' No conference, no preacher, no Official Board can put up a color bar in the church," because Christianity is "an inclusive fellowship." Echoing the 28's call for pulpit freedom, he asserted, "The preacher must get his message not from the community but from Christ."[10]

A *Delta Democrat Times* editorial, "The Veil Is Lifted," praised the 28 and said that individual ministers who had "raised their lonely voices of protest" were "no longer so lonely." The weekly *Jackson Times* ran a front-page editorial under the headline "Preachers Should Always Speak Out." A few other state editors eventually expressed praise or respect for the 28, including Hazel Brannon Smith in Lexington, Ira Harkey in Pascagoula, P. D. East in Petal, and Oliver Emmerich in McComb.[11]

Public Responses: Segregationists in the Press

Moving to the other end of the spectrum, segregationist critics went public in greater numbers and with louder voices. State senator John McLaurin, a member of "Born of Conviction" signer James Conner's church in Brandon, asked Mississippians "not to judge the membership of the Methodist Church by these spokesmen." "Born of Conviction," he charged, was "calculated to stir racial strife and to destroy the society in which we are accustomed to living." He urged Mississippi Methodists not to "let a few men destroy our great church." The Mississippi Conference's Jackson District Lay Leader Spencer Sissell echoed the call for freedom of the pulpit, but said *"there should likewise be freedom of the pew."* While agreeing with the call to brotherhood, he added that if "they advocate the mixing of the races in the local church, in the school room or socially, then I vehemently disagree with them." He also supported the public schools, "but if the statement is meant to imply that there should be mixing of races in the schools, then we are miles apart in our belief."[12]

Several newspaper editors attacked or dismissed the 28, including the notorious Mary Cain of the weekly *Summit Sun*, who praised the Official Board of Summit Methodist Church for publicly condemning both "certain ministers" for "promot[ing] racial integration in our churches, schools and society" and J. P. Stafford, who "does not represent our laymen with his thinking." The church board said, "God will not smile on a mongrelized people. . . . We are at peace and need to be left alone by those who would attempt to cause friction among us. 'God help us maintain this peace' is our prayer." Cain saluted the Summit Methodists: "Their clearly presented statement leaves no doubt that our local church is blessed with real leaders." The *Meridian Star* said the 28 were meddling in politics: "This meddling, termed by the clergy, 'The Social Gospel,' is deplorable."[13]

The most influential dailies in the state were the two Jackson papers owned by the Hederman family, with a combined circulation over three times as large as their closest competitor and accounting for almost 50 percent of the daily newspaper sales in south Mississippi, the area covered by the

Mississippi Conference. Jimmy Ward of the *Daily News* followed his January 3 comment about "noisy" preachers who were "about to get out of hand" with an editorial questioning whether Mississippi preachers truly lacked freedom of the pulpit and suggesting that progress might be "better achieved with a return to old fashioned religion distinctly separated from the frills of new-fangled social and complex political theories." Tom Ethridge criticized Selah and the 28 with a sarcastic piece asking, "Just where does Christian practice of 'equality' cease and un-Christian 'discrimination' end in a church, community or family? Can the Christian who sincerely advocates 'equality without regard for race or color' draw a color line anywhere without some degree of 'prejudice' and 'discrimination' which allegedly is sinful?" Ward later criticized the 28 for abandoning "the state's efforts to maintain racial integrity" and giving in to "politically-inspired, plate-passing agitators" who were trying to "[destroy] Mississippi's peaceful society and [convert] the state into one more integrated jungle of mahem [*sic*], rape and murder."[14]

These standard Closed Society views—that the 28 were meddling in politics and secular matters and straying from their calling to preach the Gospel and save lost souls, that segregation and the supposedly historically peaceful race relations in Mississippi (now stirred up only because of outside influence) were ordained by God, and that the 28 were betraying the holy cause of white Mississippi—were repeated frequently in January letters to the editor. Of twenty related missives published in the Jackson papers that month, all but one were critical of the 28 (and occasionally Selah), with another five negative responses in the Meridian paper. The positive letter did not mention the 28 ministers but disagreed with the claim "that preachers should just stick to winning souls to Christ," insisting rather "that if preachers cannot preach in a way that our daily lives are helped they might as well stop preaching." The only letter specifically supportive of the 28 in any Mississippi daily that month appeared in the Gulf Coast *Daily Herald*, written by Clara Mae Sells, a retired Methodist deaconess and daughter and sister of Mississippi Conference ministers. She fully endorsed the statement and called for more open communication between the races.[15]

Some letter writers claimed Christian brotherhood was spiritual, not physical or social, and thus did not entail any race mixing; one linked "spiritual purity" with "uphold[ing] racial integrity." Several also blamed the Methodist Church, its "integrationist" Sunday school literature and other publications, and the National Council of Churches, with a few explaining that these factors had led to their leaving the denomination for spin-off Methodist groups like the Southern Methodist Church. Some claimed the Bible clearly teaches segregation and distinguished between "Biblical truths" and the "personal opinions" of the 28. One suggested the ministers should be more concerned about the recent banning of prayer in public schools than any supposed racial injustice.[16]

The 28 were accused of betraying the trust of "those who look to them for spiritual guidance" and of being Communist dupes. A writer suggested the churches of the ministers demanding freedom of the pulpit "should rise as one man and 'free them of the pulpits' they now hold." This sentiment was echoed in another letter: "We may have to put up with a Negro in our university, but God have mercy upon a congregation who hasn't got enough of the spirit of God left in it to rid its pulpit of these sheep in wolves clothing [sic] who have openly denied the teachings of God's holy word." A ministerial colleague of the 28 wrote that if pulpit freedom "means that laymen should be forced to pay a man's salary to stand Sunday after Sunday and shove integration down their throats, I do not believe in a 'free pulpit.' If it means to uncompromisingly proclaim the truth of God's Holy Word, I do believe in a 'free pulpit.'"[17]

Another attack came from the segregationist Mississippi Association of Methodist Ministers and Laymen (MAMML). In its "Methodist Declaration of Conscience on Racial Segregation," released on January 10 in response to "Born of Conviction," MAMML charged that it is not Christian to "endanger" segregation, an institution "which has protected both races and allowed both their fullest development." It claimed there would be no problems of marriage, economics, death, or racial segregation in the Resurrection, "but on this earth we have all those problems, and segregation is a means of solving problems of relations between the races, just as marriage is a means of solving problems of relations between men and women, and as the division of labor is a means of solving economic problems."[18]

Segregationist Responses in Congregations

Segregationist responses also came in local Methodist churches. The 28 had quoted statements from the *Discipline* about the teachings of Jesus not permitting discrimination, thinking that the "expressed witness" of the Methodist Church would influence their church members. But to many church readers, it was scandalous for ministers in their conference to call for a change in race relations in such a public way and to upset so many white Mississippians. The range of views expressed in the media represented a public argument about the meaning of "Christian brotherhood," appropriate relations among human beings, and the purpose of the church itself, and this debate extended into local Methodist congregations. For many Methodist church members and some pastors, the Closed Society orthodoxy and commitment to "our Southern way of life" trumped the church's "expressed witness" as interpreted by the 28, who by publicly advocating change in race relations had betrayed their families and their Church (the Conference and their congregations), "barter[ing] their loyalty to their own race, their state and to those who look to them for spiritual guidance." Most of the 28's vocal critics saw no tension between the segregated system and the Christian faith.[19]

The 28 offended many members of their own churches. On January 10 the members of the Official Board of Oakland Heights Church in Meridian voted down (19-13) an attempt to dismiss their pastor, Ed McRae. A member of the anti-McRae faction quoted in the press gave this reason for his opposition:

> We do not believe in integration. We do not believe that all races are brothers as stated in the document signed by the 28 pastors. We believe in the freedom of worship and feel that we do not have this if we are forced to listen to a minister who has shown by his actions that he does not care about our Southern way of life but will betray part of his membership by signing what we believe is a politically inspired document.

In February the same board formally requested a change in pastors in June and declared "we do not want one of the twenty-seven Ministers that signed this resolution."[20]

Several other congregations passed resolutions, some echoing the request not to have any of the 28 as pastor. At Wesson and Galloway, served by signers Rod Entrekin and Jerry Furr, respectively (and vocal supporter Selah at Galloway), more polite resolutions were passed, agreeing to disagree with their pastors by expressing respect for their "integrity of opinion" and leadership, but claiming the published statements of their pastors were "not necessarily the views and opinions of the individual members." Both churches asserted, "It is not un-Christian that we prefer to remain an all-white congregation" and cited "time-honored tradition," hoping its "perpetuation . . . will never be impaired." Other churches passed resolutions expressing shock and profound disagreement with "Born of Conviction." One insisted that the words of the 28, Sam Ashmore, and Selah were a "minority report" and called on the bishop or cabinet to publish the "majority report" in the media. A cluster of five churches in Rankin County claimed "recent actions and statements in the press by certain ministers and leaders have done incalculable harm to our Church" and "earnestly solicit[ed] our Church leaders and ministers to provide that leadership and spiritual guidance that will enable our Church to fulfill its great destiny"; presumably, such leadership meant no more "integrationist" statements to the press.[21]

Churches served by three of the 28 entered the public argument by rejecting and ejecting their offending pastors immediately. Within a week of the statement's publication, at a chargewide meeting of Neshoba County's Philadelphia Circuit, signer James Rush was asked to recant and publicly remove his name from the statement, which he refused to do. Someone said, "If the Methodist Church can't get rid of a nigger-lovin' pastor, we know how to do it." The persons present voted 70–4 to remove him as their pastor. One of the seventy was Lawrence Rainey, elected later that year as Neshoba County Sheriff and acquitted in 1967 of violating the civil rights of 1964 slaying victims James Chaney, Andrew Goodman, and Michael Schwerner.[22]

At Byram, James Nicholson also lost his pastorate. Nicholson had preached an antisegregation sermon in October after the Ole Miss riot, and most of the congregation had boycotted worship services since then. When he went public in January as one of the 28, church members again asked District Superintendent J. W. Leggett for their pastor to be removed, saying they would continue the boycott and would not pay his salary. Leggett agreed to the request.[23]

At Pisgah in Pike County, a local Citizens' Council member appeared in Bill Lampton's office on Thursday, January 3, carrying a copy of the New Orleans paper and announcing, "You've messed yourself up real good, boy." He told the pastor a church meeting would be held that evening to "throw [him] out." District Superintendent Norman Boone had other ideas as he presided at the "lively affair." No vote was taken; a few members said they would be at worship Sunday, but others "swore that as long as [Lampton] was the pastor they would refuse to support the church in any way." One person said, "If this is what the churches are teaching, then I won't go to any church at all." The next night two tires on Lampton's car were slashed, and on Saturday two church members informed him of "rumors of a mob, with possible threats to the church or parsonage," and asked him not to be at worship on Sunday. "Fearing," Lampton said, "that the eruption of violence might spread like measles," he took his family fifty miles away to his hometown of Columbia and did not return. In explaining his departure to the press, he said, "It looked like I had another Ole Miss on my hands."[24]

With twenty-eight ministers involved, there was a wide range of experience, and some received much worse treatment than others. In some churches, signers succeeded in having some honest and forthright dialogue with a few church members. But in several of the congregations served by the 28, many church members gave their pastors and pastoral family members the silent treatment, and some who spoke did so only in anger and rejection. There was some ostracism from people in the towns where the 28 and their families lived, as well as rejection from some fellow ministers. Most signers received anonymous threatening phone calls and some hate mail. There were isolated incidents of property damage, and crosses were burned in the yards of three signers.[25]

A couple of the 28 were told by the bishop or their district superintendent that "there is no church in the Conference that will accept you as their pastor." Summer Walters, associate pastor at Jefferson Street Church in Natchez, was told publicly at a church meeting that he was no longer welcome in a prominent church member's home. Elton Brown learned that some members of his church in Natchez were getting pressure from acquaintances of another denomination who called to say, "I saw that your preacher signed the statement in the paper. What are you all going to do about it?" A member of Powell Hall's church at Scooba interrupted the sermon one Sunday to ask Hall if he wanted "them" to come to "our church." After Ed McRae visited a church member in the hospital, the patient's angry husband, no longer recognizing McRae as his family's pastor, accosted Ed and his wife, Martina, in their parsonage driveway. The assailant told Martina to go in the house, but she refused, fearing that he meant to do harm to Ed.[26]

Some Methodist pastors opposed to the 28 used their pulpits to weigh in on the argument. At Jackson's Broadmeadow Methodist Church, Charles Duke preached a sermon entitled "Born of the Spirit," claiming Christians are "born of the spirit and not of convictions," because the latter without the former destroys the unity of Christian people. Like other critics, Duke expressed puzzlement at the 28's claim of lack of freedom in the pulpit. He claimed he had always enjoyed "complete freedom" in the pulpit but would never "take advantage of the protection of this pulpit to air my personal opinions or debate any issue." He resented the claim that those who supported "Born of Conviction" were courageous "while the rest of us are afraid to take a stand." He explained his central disagreement with the 28 by saying,

> I am not willing . . . to accept as the Christian position on race relations the theory that the Negro advances only in relation to his ability to force himself into social relations with the white race. I do not accept integration as an advancement for the Negro and I do not accept segregation as discrimination against the Negro.[27]

Then came a common segregationist argument: "Animals maintain their identity by nature and by nature each associates with its own kind." Birds of different species do not mix; different dog breeds are not improved by mating with each other. It is not "discrimination" to keep dog breeds separate and allow them "to become their best in the area for which they are best suited by nature." In human relations, "forced integration is unchristian since it inevitably results in abnormal conditions in which both races suffer and become less than their best." Christians, therefore, should "strive for conditions that will provide for the development of the best in all individuals. We know that nothing works contrary to its nature and, when force is attempted, tragedy results."[28]

Private Responses: Sympathetic but Silent

There were church members and pastors who supported the 28, but they were not nearly as vocal as the segregationists. At Capitol Street Methodist in Jackson, Pastor Roy Clark, a supporter of the 28, addressed this phenomenon in a January 13 sermon on freedom of Christian conviction and its expression. He linked his text from Acts 5:29 ("We must obey God rather than men") to another claim: "Each individual is personally responsible before God." Clark acknowledged that most of the laity with whom he had spoken since January 2 had said "they think they can sincerely follow the light they now have in Christ . . . and support segregation." He had responded to them, "Support segregation as long as the *Lord* will let you." But he reminded his listeners that not all Mississippi Methodists, including himself, saw it that way:

> The most pressing moral issue before us is: Do I and others like me, who sincerely believe by our light from Christ that justice and love require modification in the segregated way of life, have the same right to believe as we do and to express this belief and to work for it in appropriate ways without prejudice or reprisal against ourselves or our families?[29]

This fear of reprisal caused many who supported the 28 to remain "sympathetic but silent." Another Methodist pastor, Bill Lowry, had privately agreed in December to sign "Born of Conviction," but his name was not included. At an Official Board meeting of his church in late January, church members spent several minutes criticizing the 28, and then one member said, "I'm so proud our preacher did not sign that statement," followed by exuberant applause. Lowry did not feel free to tell his church members that he supported and had intended to sign "Born of Conviction," and years later he termed it "the most embarrassing moment of my ministry."[30]

In addition to all the public hoopla in response to "Born of Conviction," hundreds of private letters were sent to the 28, running four to one on the supportive side—quite different from the near unanimity of negative responses in letters to the editor in the secular press. The difference is explained in J. P. Stafford's letter to the 28: "When the shooting starts and you are far apart, maybe it will help to know that hundreds of consecrated laymen will applaud you, and countless others will wish you well in secret—that lack the courage and fortitude to come out into the open." About two-fifths of the positive and almost all of the negative letters came from Mississippi.[31]

The *Advocate* received many supportive letters from Methodists within and outside of the state, including praise for Ashmore's editorials, but these remained private, as the *Advocate* did not publish letters to the editor. A Gulfport layman predicted that "Born of Conviction" and Selah's statement would result "in awakening a great many people who have been afraid to speak out," and he was happy that "decent and responsible leadership" had risen to "replace the wrong kind that unfortunately has prevailed in recent months." A Memphis layman referred to the witness of the 28 and Selah as "'standing up for Jesus,'" while the executive director of the Methodist United Nations Office requested copies of the January 2 *Advocate* for some United Nations friends "who need to have their hearts warmed by your courage." Victoria Gray, a black Methodist civil rights activist from Hattiesburg (and definitely not silent), responded to a Methodist pastor's published attack on the 28 by writing him to express admiration for those who spoke out against racial injustice even though they well knew the price of taking such a stand in Mississippi. To her, to be "Born of Conviction" meant that one had to speak out. A pastor wrote, "Some are saying that Bishop Franklin should either say something or resign. He should represent THE METHODIST CHURCH, and if he lets these boys suffer because they have convictions, then he has lost the respect of all of us."[32]

Bishop Franklin also received positive letters, including three from members of Maxie Dunnam's Gulfport congregation, all writing to praise their pastor's stand. Dunnam also heard from Henry Clay of Laurel, a black Methodist pastor whom he had known and worked with in Gulfport a couple of years earlier, expressing appreciation for "Born of Conviction." Another church member wrote Dunnam, admitting, "I am ashamed of my own silence, but my husband and I have tried not 'to rock the boat' since we chose to live here. So, I cannot tell you what it means to me to know that you and others like you are saying what I feel but do not have the courage to say."[33]

Public and Private Responses:
Protect the Church and Don't Rock the Boat

Some avoided rocking the boat to protect themselves, but others criticized the 28 for hurting the church. Associate Conference Lay Leader Bert Jordan of Jackson said, "I do not understand why, in the face of magnificent progress, unparalleled growth in stewardship and unlimited opportunities, that we would bring down upon ourselves an unnecessary social crisis that lashes a staggering blow to the church and the unity of our people." Speaking from the lay perspective, Jordan wondered why ministers considering making controversial public statements would not first consult their church members or Official Board, "since they too strive to be Christian and are interested in any issue that involves the church they love."[34]

Though the claim of an "unnecessary social crisis" denied the reality of the situation to which the 28 had responded, Jordan's critique was not necessarily segregationist. Concerns at the "incalculable harm" that "Born of Conviction" would cause the church may have been a smokescreen for segregationist views, but some critics responded to the 28 out of their intense (though misguided) love for the Methodist Church in Mississippi. Old friends of Maxie Dunnam wrote him a thank-you note for an expression of sympathy they had received from him, but also voiced disappointment at his "recent 'extracurricular' clerical activities," which had done "a great deal of harm to the Methodist Church."[35]

The response of Bishop Franklin and the Mississippi Conference Cabinet appeared in the January 16 issue of the *Advocate*. Avoiding any mention of "Born of Conviction," the conference leaders said without elaboration, "We each declare anew our support of the doctrines and historic positions of the Methodist Church" but also assured Mississippi Methodists that "integration is not forced upon any part of our Church." They closed by saying, "Our Conference has a great program in evangelism, education, missions and other areas. Let us move on to do the work of the Church, loving mercy, doing justly, and walking humbly with our Lord, pressing toward the mark of the prize of high calling of God in Christ Jesus." Was this what Sam Ashmore feared when he warned in October 1962 that the church might lose its life in "pious platitudes" when "courageous witness" was needed? Did the "Let us move on to do the work of the Church" mean that public clergy response to social crisis was not the work of the church? Were they saying, "Let's put this Born of Conviction embarrassment behind us"? Signer Bufkin Oliver told James Silver that the 28 considered the bishop's and cabinet's statement "a repudiation of what we had done."[36]

Before January 1963 some of the 28 had been fairly open with their congregations about their views on race relations without much difficulty. Two ministers who agreed to sign "Born of Conviction" and then withdrew before publication claimed their congregations knew where they stood on the issue and were still willing to hear them, but would be more upset if their pastors' views were more publicly known by signing the statement. Jack Loflin was in his fourth year as pastor at Bude in Franklin County in January 1963. After the statement appeared, a church member asked, "Boy, why didn't you sign that statement?" Loflin replied, "They didn't ask me." The church member inquired, "If they'd asked you, what would you have done?" Loflin said he probably would have signed. The reply: "I love you like a son, but [if you had signed it,] your ass would have been gone!" This man knew his pastor's views on the race issue and could live with them, but it was not acceptable for those views to be made public.[37]

A member of Laurel's Franklin Church who referred to his congregation's founding pastor, signer N. A. Dickson, as "one of the dearest personal friends I have" disagreed with Ashmore's claim that the 28 spoke for "the vast majority of the clerical members of the conference." He had consulted several pastors and reported, "I won't say 'a vast majority' of all the ministers were opposed to the statement. But everyone with whom I have spoken did or indicated they would have declined the opportunity to affix their signature. None felt that it was good for the Church."[38]

Private Responses: Segregationist

The *Advocate* received some private negative responses. One Jackson Methodist pastor insisted that God "created every race and color and intended for man to stay that way" through "race purity." Another writer claimed the message of the Tower of Babel story in Genesis 11 was that "God created the races distinct from one another, and he scattered them all over the earth when they attempted to integrate and become as one."[39]

The 28 also received critical letters from individuals. Inman Moore heard from an acquaintance who urged him to not let the Communists "make you think you are 'going all the way' to be real Christian, when really this false teaching of theirs helps them to create a civil war in the U.S. and meantime they will take over and all Christians will be imprisoned or beheaded, etc." She knew he would recant publicly "when you see the true Bible teachings." Moore responded that "Born of Conviction" was "thoroughly in keeping . . . with the teachings of the New Testament and the Spirit of Jesus Christ."[40]

A member of signer Summer Walters's church wrote him that the statement could "accomplish no good for our church. It should have been left unsaid." Echoing arguments that "Born of Conviction" was "political" and Christians would not be damned to hell if they sought alternatives to integrated schools, he added, "If my choice for my children is immorality or illiteracy I won't hesitate to choose the latter. If this deluge of filth and hatred that is being thrust upon us by every known medium of communication is Christianity in any form, I don't even know my savior." Signer Wilton Carter received a sarcastic anonymous letter that began, "Your recent action does not merit your being address Mr. or Rev [sic]." It attacked various statements Carter had made to the press, and concluded, "We are interested in seeing later reports along from you and other *sheep* (signers) of the *Methodist discipline resolution.* . . . Not once did any of you mention the *Bible*, which lays bare the fact that woe be unto them that sow *dissention* [sic] and the little 28 did just that and the harvest will be great with turmoil and hate."[41]

Results of the Argument?

Did the 28 and those on their side lose this 1963 argument about race relations in Mississippi? The public segregationist voices were louder and more numerous, and by the summer, thirteen of the 28 had left Mississippi; five more left in the next year, and two left later. A few were truly forced out, while the others chose to leave for a variety of reasons related to the response to "Born of Conviction" but also involving other factors. The power structure in the conference capitalized on the negative response to "Born of Conviction" and secured a tighter hold on leadership over the next few years, and most who publicly supported the 28 also suffered in some way. When the 28 are mentioned in historical treatments of this period, it is usually "the twenty-eight ministers spoke out and were forced out of Mississippi"—end of story.

But other facts tell a different story. After the Mississippi Annual Conference meeting in late May 1963, ten of the 28 returned to the same church appointment for another year, meaning their congregations were willing to keep them. Eight of the 28 remained in Mississippi for the rest of their ministerial careers, several of them achieving positions of significant leadership in the conference, and two of those who left returned to Mississippi to serve in the North Mississippi Conference within three or four years of their departure. All these ministers worked in the churches and communities where they served—both publicly and privately—toward the hope of a new post–Closed Society Mississippi.

The results of the argument would be clearer if more supporters of the 28 had been willing to speak out, but the many private expressions of support and conversations the 28 and others had with church people, friends, and family played a role in pushing other white Mississippians to think about what they had simply assumed. In response to bewildered questions from his mother (Governor Ross Barnett's cousin), Jack Troutman wrote her to explain his signature on "Born of Conviction":

> I *will not* have to stand before the judgment bar of God and answer for anyone's soul but my own. I will have to answer for my own convictions and how I lead others . . . to rid themselves of hatred and malice toward others regardless of race, color, or creed. . . . In all of Christian history, it is not for the Christian to conform to public opinion but to let the love of God transform them into the personality of Jesus Christ who looked upon *all peoples* as of infinite worth. . . . Who are we to blame for such "radical" beliefs? Jesus Christ, who was the most radical and unpopular preacher that ever lived.[42]

The "Born of Conviction" story reveals part of the larger "ecology" of the Mississippi civil rights era by examining the roles played by some white liberal/moderate ministers and the white Methodist Church in the early 1960s. The 28 were not civil rights workers; they did not take the same risks or suffer as much as most movement folks did. But they did pay a price, because they dared to say something prophetic to the church in the Closed Society. What they said was labeled "the strongest, most carefully thought out statement by any group of white Mississippians up to that time about the racial problems of the state" by Rev. Ed King, a native Mississippian and white Methodist minister who became a leader in the Jackson movement after he arrived as chaplain at Tougaloo College in January 1963.[43]

For any mainstream white leaders to speak out like this at that moment was important. In January 1963 most Mississippi whites could still dismiss movement activists as either outside agitators or local blacks who had forgotten their place. But the 28 and those who publicly supported them could not be written off so easily; they were part of "us" and had to be answered. They spoke for a significant minority of silent white Mississippians who agreed with them, and they got people talking more publicly about civil rights, both in the larger publics of the press and Mississippi Methodism, and in the hundreds of smaller community and congregational publics. Forcing people to explain more fully why they were against a change in race relations enabled more whites to move away from simple acceptance of the Closed Society orthodoxy as the way things had to be toward an increasingly genuine struggle with the questions raised by the civil rights movement.

NOTES

The author gratefully acknowledges partial funding for this research from the Louisville Institute, the Virginia Foundation of Independent Colleges, and Emory & Henry College. Portions of this essay appeared in different form in L. Edward Phillips and Billy Vaughan, eds., *Courage to Bear Witness: Essays in Honor of Gene L. Davenport* (Eugene, Ore.: Wipf and Stock, 2009). Used by permission of Wipf and Stock Publishers.

1. Rod Entrekin, "My Journey in Ministry," Rod Entrekin Private Papers (the author has copies of all unpublished documents cited in this essay); *Clarion-Ledger* (*CL*), March 7, 1958; *Jackson Daily News* (*JDN*), March 4, 1958.

2. This characterization of the experiences of the 28 "Born of Conviction" signers is drawn from author's interviews with them; in January 1963 the twenty-eight ranged in age from twenty-five to fifty-six, but half were still in their twenties, and three-fourths were thirty-five or younger. Sixteen were Millsaps graduates; ten more were graduates of Mississippi Southern College (MSC) (now the University of Southern Mississippi), where they came under the remarkable influence of Sam Barefield, director of the Wesley Foundation at MSC in the 1950s. Nineteen went to Emory to seminary, and eight attended the other schools mentioned. Beginning in the 1940s the Social Creed in the *Discipline of the Methodist Church* called for racial equality, but the Central Jurisdiction, created in 1940 when Northern and Southern Methodists reunited as a new denomination, kept black Methodist churches in separate annual conferences and in a separate racial jurisdiction until 1968. It took Mississippi Methodists until the mid-1970s to merge their black and white conferences; for an account of that process, see Ellis Ray Branch, "Born of Conviction: Racial Conflict and Change in Mississippi Methodism, 1945–1983" (Ph.D. diss., Mississippi State University, 1984), chapters 8–10. For an account of Methodist race relations struggles on the denominational level, see Peter C. Murray, *Methodists and the Crucible of Race, 1930–1975* (Columbia: University of Missouri Press, 2004).

3. *Mississippi Methodist Advocate* (*MMA*), January 2, 1963. The best known is the April 1963 statement issued by eleven Alabama white clergy, to which Martin Luther King Jr. responded in "Letter from Birmingham Jail." See S. Jonathan Bass, *Blessed Are the Peacemakers: Martin Luther King, Jr., Eight White Religious Leaders, and the "Letter from Birmingham Jail"* (Baton Rouge: Louisiana State University Press, 2001). The names of the twenty-eight signers are Jerry Furr, Maxie Dunnam, Jim L. Waits, O. Gerald Trigg, James B. Nicholson, Buford A. Dickinson, James S. Conner, J. W. Holston, James P. Rush, Edward W. McRae, Joseph C. Way, Wallace E. Roberts, Summer Walters, Bill Lampton, Marvin Moody, Keith Tonkel, John Ed Thomas, Inman Moore Jr., Denson Napier, Rod Entrekin, Harold Ryker, N. A. Dickson, Ned Kellar, Powell Hall, Elton Brown, Bufkin Oliver, Jack Troutman, and Wilton Carter.

4. For more general discussions of white church and clergy response to the civil rights movement, see Samuel S. Hill, *Southern Churches in Crisis Revisited* (Tuscaloosa: University of Alabama Press, 1999); Michael B. Friedland, *Lift Up Your Voice Like a Trumpet: White Clergy and the Civil Rights and Antiwar Movements, 1954–1973* (Chapel Hill: University of North Carolina Press, 1998); David L. Chappell, *A Stone of Hope: Prophetic Religion and the Death of Jim Crow* (Chapel Hill: University of North Carolina Press, 2004), especially chapter 6; and Paul Harvey, *Freedom's Coming: Religious Culture and the Shaping of the South from the Civil War through the Civil Rights Era* (Chapel Hill: University of North Carolina Press, 2005). For a specific discussion of the situation in Mississippi and white Christian responses, see Joseph Crespino, *In Search of Another Country: Mississippi and the Conservative Counterrevolution* (Princeton, N.J.: Princeton University Press, 2007), 59–74, 144–172. For discussions of specific denominational struggles, see Murray, *Methodists and the Crucible of Race*; Gardiner H. Shattuck Jr., *Episcopalians and Race: Civil War to Civil Rights* (Lexington: University Press of Kentucky, 2000); Mark Newman, *Getting Right with God: Southern Baptists and Desegregation, 1945–1995* (Tuscaloosa: University of Alabama Press, 2001); and Joel L. Alvis Jr., *Religion & Race: Southern Presbyterians, 1946–1983* (Tuscaloosa: University of Alabama Press, 1994). On the role of Jewish rabbis, see Mark K. Bauman and Berkley Kalin, eds., *The Quiet Voices: Southern Rabbis and Black Civil Rights, 1880s to 1990s* (Tuscaloosa: University of Alabama Press, 1997). On the responses of Methodists in one state or annual conference, see Donald E. Collins, *When the Church Bell Rang Racist: The Methodist Church and the Civil Rights Movement in Alabama* (Macon, Ga.: Mercer University Press, 1998); and James T. Clemons and Kelly L. Farr, eds., *Crisis of Conscience: Arkansas Methodists and the Civil Rights Struggle* (Little Rock: Butler Center for Arkansas Studies, 2007).

5. *MMA*, October 17, 1962 (the endorsement was dated October 8). Bishop Franklin presided over both conferences and was on a trip to Asia when the North Mississippi Cabinet (the Methodist name for the group of district superintendents in an

annual conference) endorsement was released. He never commented publicly on Ole Miss. The Oxford ministers' statement was issued less than a week after the riot and was later published in *Christianity Today*, October 26, 1962, and *New South*, March 1963.

6. *MMA*, October 10, 1962, 3.

7. None of the participants remembers the date of the retreat, and I have found no written evidence to pinpoint it conclusively. The four writers and others were recruiting signers for the statement by late November. Author's interviews with each of the four creators of the statement and Rayford Woodrick; *MMA*, January 2, 1963; *Discipline of the Methodist Church* (1960), Paragraphs 2026 ("The Methodist Church and Race") and 2020 ("The Methodist Social Creed"). For a discussion of accusations of Communism in this era, see Yasuhiro Katagiri, *The Mississippi State Sovereignty Commission* (Jackson: University Press of Mississippi, 2001), 88–89, 93–94.

8. *MMA*, January 2, 1963; *CL*, January 3, 1963; *JDN*, January 3, 1963; *Meridian (Miss.) Star (MS)*, January 3, 1963. Ironically, in 2004 McRae remembered that he himself was upset that the reporter had quoted his comments more extensively than he expected in the story.

9. *MMA*, January 9, 1963; *CL*, January 4 and 6, 1963; *JDN*, January 4, 1963. A copy of Stafford's letter is in Box 1, Folder 3, Summer and Betty Walters Papers, J. B. Cain Archives of Mississippi Methodism, Millsaps College, Jackson, Miss.

10. *CL*, January 7, 1963.

11. *Delta Democrat Times*, January 6, 1963; *Jackson Times*, January 10, 1963; *Lexington Advertiser*, July 18, 1963; *Pascagoula-Moss Point Chronicle*, May 15 and 22, 1963; *Petal Paper*, February 1963; and *McComb Enterprise Journal*, January 11 and 18, 1963; see also *Deer Creek Pilot*, January 18, 1963.

12. *CL*, January 8, 1963; *JDN*, January 8, 1963; *MMA*, January 16, 1963.

13. *Summit Sun*, January 17, 1963, see also January 10, 1963; *MS*, January 10, 1963.

14. Susan Weill, *In a Madhouse's Din* (Westport, Conn.: Praeger, 2002), 256; *JDN*, January 3, 4, and 25, 1963 (Ward was Methodist); *CL*, January 10, 1963.

15. The letters date from January 6 to January 29, 1963, with seventeen in *CL*. Ruth A. Wallace of Jackson wrote the positive letter (*CL*, January 24, 1963). The clearest examples echoing the editorial arguments outlined here are found in *CL*, January 18 and 23, 1963, and *JDN*, January 9, 1963; *Gulf Coast Daily Herald*, January 7.

16. *MS*, January 8, 1963; *JDN*, January 9 and 16, 1963; *CL*, January 9, 10, 11, 18, 24, and 29, 1963.

17. *CL*, January 10, 23, and 24, 1963 (either the writer meant "wolves in sheep's clothing" or intentionally reversed it to imply that they were both brainwashed and dangerous); Charles Hills's "Affairs of State" column, *CL*, January 8, 1963 (obviously

to this Methodist minister, the "truth of God's Holy Word" meant segregation of the races).

18. *CL*, January 11, 1963. The statement was written by Medford Evans, a Yale Ph.D. in literature, the son of a Methodist minister, and part of the "chain of seniority" in the Citizens' Council who pursued a career in "organized racism." Neil McMillan, *The Citizens' Council* (1971; repr., Urbana: University of Illinois Press, 1994), 125–126. It was also published in the January 1963 editions of MAMML's "Information Bulletin" and the Citizens' Council's *The Citizen*; MAMML had no official relationship with Mississippi Methodism.

19. "Born of the deep conviction of our souls as to what is morally right, we have been driven to seek the foundations of such convictions in the expressed witness of our Church." "Born of Conviction" statement, *CL*, January 23, 1963.

20. *MS*, January 11, 1963 (the vote was out of order, as Methodist polity does not allow churches to fire their pastors); H. H. Buchanan to Bishop Franklin, February 11, 1963, Box 1, Folder 19, Bishop's Office Papers, J. B. Cain Archives, Millsaps College.

21. Pine Springs (*CL*, February 16, 1963) and Meridian Wesley (Louis R. Wolfe to Bishop Franklin, February 22, 1963, Box 1, Folder 19, Bishop's Office Papers); *CL*, January 15 and 31, 1963, (the Wesson resolution copied Galloway's almost verbatim, and a copy of the Galloway document and other resolutions are found in Box 1, Folder 19, Bishop's Office Papers); T. V. Nichols Jr. to Bishop Franklin, January 20, 1963, Box 1, Folder 19, Bishop's Office Papers; Gulde, Shiloh, Lodebar, Holly Bush, and Pelahatchie Churches, n.d., Box 1, Folder 19, Bishop's Office Papers (see *CL*, January 24, 1963).

22. *Neshoba Democrat*, January 10, 1963; James Rush and Libby Rush, interview by author; handwritten vignette in Maxie Dunnam Private Papers (the Mars Hill Church gave Rush a vote of confidence). A portion of Rush's account is included in James Silver, *Mississippi: The Closed Society* (New York: Harcourt, Brace & World, 1966), 59–60; *Journal of the Mississippi Conference* (1963): 113; Rush to Silver, January 17, 1963, Box 23, Folder 9, James W. Silver Papers, Department of Archives and Special Collections, J. D. Williams Library, University of Mississippi.

23. James Nicholson, "Real Issues for These Times," *New South* (March 1963) (unlike those of Rush and Lampton [see below], Nicholson's dismissal was not reported in the Mississippi press in January, though it was mentioned in Claude Sitton's *New York Times* story on January 19, 1963); James Nicholson, "My Mississippi Experiences," unpublished, Nicholson Private Papers; J. W. Leggett Jr. to James Nicholson, January 11, 1963, Nicholson Private Papers; James Nicholson, interview by author.

24. Bill Lampton to James Silver, January 30, 1963, Box 23, Folder 9, Silver Papers; *McComb Enterprise Journal*, January 7, 1963; *CL*, January 9, 1963. Lampton declined to be interviewed by the author.

25. Joseph C. Way to James Silver, June 17, 1963, Box 23, Folder 9, Silver Papers; Way to author, April 21, 2004; Keith Tonkel, Elton Brown, and Jim Waits, interviews by author; Furr response to Waits 1965 questionnaire, Box 1, Folder 14, James L. Waits Papers, Pitts Theology Library Archives, Emory University, Atlanta; Ed and Martina McRae, and Jerry and Rose Trigg, interviews by author.

26. Way to author, April 21, 2004; interview with Summer and Betty Walters and "My Ministerial Experiences in Mississippi 1961–1963," Box 2, Folder 3, Walters Papers; Brown to Silver, January 29, 1963, Box 23, Folder 9, Silver Papers; Powell Hall, interview by author; Ed and Martina McRae interview.

27. Charles Duke, "Born of the Spirit," preached January 20, 1963, enclosed with March 1963 letter, John and Margrit Garner Letters, Mississippi Department of Archives and History (MDAH). There was no news coverage of this sermon, but it was reproduced and distributed fairly widely, as I have run across several copies.

28. Ibid.

29. Roy C. Clark, "Coming to Grips with the Real Issue," January 13, 1963, enclosed with March 1963 letter, John and Margrit Garner Letters, MDAH; a UPI story on Clark's sermon ran in the Meridian and Jackson dailies on January 15, 1963. Clark was not invited to sign "Born of Conviction."

30. Bill and Barbara Lowry, interview by author.

31. J. P. Stafford to "Dear Brothers," January 3, 1963, Box 1, Folder 3, Walters Papers. Stafford's assertion that hundreds of laymen would (publicly) applaud the 28 was mistaken. The 28 received national press coverage, both in church press (for example, "Methodist Ministers Shatter Vacuum," *Christian Century*, February 20, 1963, 229–230) and secular press (*New York Times*, January 19, 1963). The 4–1 positive ratio is based on all the letters I have found in archives and the private papers of ten of the signers, with approximately 108 different positive missives and 26 negative (of the latter, over half were sent to the *Advocate* and are found in Box 1, Folder 1, Ashmore Papers, J. B. Cain Archives).

32. J. L. Henderson to Ashmore, January 8, 1963; Ensley Tiffin to Ashmore, January 24, 1963; Carl David Soule to Ashmore, January 13, 1963; Victoria J. Gray to Rev. Bertist C. Rouse, January 14, 1963 (for more on her role in the movement, see John Dittmer, *Local People: The Struggle for Civil Rights in Mississippi* [Urbana: University of Illinois Press, 1994], 127, 148, 181–184); R. Glenn Miller to Ashmore, January 10, 1963, all in Box 1, Folder 4, Ashmore Papers.

33. Louis Doleac Family to Franklin, February 15, 1963; James Lawrence James to Franklin, January 11, 1963; and Nettie Beeson to Franklin, n.d. (January 1963); see also Tex S. Sample to Franklin, January 11, 1963; Arthur M. O'Neil Jr. to Franklin, January 16, 1963; and William M. Justice to Franklin, March 21, 1963; all in Bishop's Office

Papers Box 1, Folder 19; Henry C. Clay Jr. to Dunnam, February 27 1963; and Meg Marcow to Dunnam, January 6, 1963, both in Dunnam PP.

34. *MMA*, January 16, 1963.

35. Gulde, Shiloh, Lodebar, Holly Bush, and Pelahatchie Churches, n.d., Bishop's Office Papers, Box 1, Folder 19; Martha and Grady Jackson to Dunnam, January 5, 1963, Dunnam Private Papers.

36. *MMA*, January 16, 1963; see also Gulf Coast *Daily Herald*, January 15, 1963; and *CL*, January 15, 1963 (that while the Hederman papers buried the January 3 stories on "Born of Conviction" on page 12A [*CL*] and 3D [*JDN*], they saw the bishop's statement as a repudiation of the 28 and featured it on page 1); *MMA*, October 10, 1962; Bufkin Oliver to Silver, April 9, 1963, Box 23, Folder 9, Silver Papers; see also Jim L. Waits, "To Live in Controversy," *Concern*, March 1963, 10. For similar claims, see Ray Branton to Franklin, January 16, 1963, Box 1, Folder 3, Walters Papers; James McKeown to Franklin, January 15, 1963, and Dean M. Kelley to Franklin, February 20, 1963, both in Box 1, Folder 19, Bishop's Office Papers.

37. Roy Eaton to Dunnam, December 24, 1962, and Hubert Barlow to Dunnam, December 25, 1962, both in Maxie Dunnam Private Papers; Jack Loflin, interview by the author.

38. E. U. Parker Jr. to Ashmore, January 5, 1963, Box 1, Folder 1, Ashmore Papers.

39. Roy Wolfe to Ashmore, January 3, 1963; and J. N. Harris, Olive Branch, Miss., to Ashmore, January 17, 1963, both in Box 1, Folder 1, Ashmore Papers. Again, these letters were not published in the *Advocate*.

40. Grace Jones to Moore, n.d. [early January 1963] and his January 17, 1963, response, Moore Private Papers.

41. Robert B. Haltom to Walters, January 9, 1963, Box 1, Folder 3, Walters Papers; Anonymous to Wilton Carter, postmarked Hattiesburg, January 9, 1963, Carter Private Papers.

42. Jack Troutman to "Dear Mother," February 8, 1963, J. Troutman Private Papers.

43. R. Edwin King, "The White Church in Mississippi" manuscript, Part 3, 7–8 (used by permission of R. Edwin King). As a native white Mississippian, Ed King was an anomaly among Mississippi movement leaders but had already made a reputation as a civil rights activist while in seminary. Most white Mississippi Methodists regarded him with suspicion, but he was a friend of several of the 28 from his years as a Millsaps student.

Shades of Anti–Civil Rights Violence

Reconsidering the Ku Klux Klan in Mississippi

David Cunningham

There is no more resonant embodiment of southern white resistance to racial integration than the Ku Klux Klan (KKK). White hoods, burning crosses, and other KKK iconography are familiar even to the most casual student of civil rights–era racial struggles. Popular accounts of anti–civil rights action, in particular those that focus on Mississippi, frequently portray the klan as a ubiquitous vigilante force, standing apart from mainstream institutions. Recent scholarship has usefully adopted a mild revisionism, recognizing the KKK as part of the web of institutional efforts to, with varying degrees of coordination, massively resist civil rights reforms.

Klan historiography has evolved largely through studies of the civil rights movement, a phenomenon that has both helped and hindered its progress. KKK-perpetrated cross burnings, beatings, and murders figure prominently in many emblematic episodes of the civil rights struggle.[1] While the tragic costs of anti–civil rights violence have been borne most fully by its victims, civil rights historians have noted that militant white supremacist action had broader reverberations as well. For instance, Michael Klarman's influential "backlash thesis," in which segregationist violence provided the impetus for federal support of civil rights provisions, suggests that white vigilantism had a profound effect on the trajectory of the movement. By underscoring klan members' willingness to engage in violent extralegal tactics to suppress civil rights activism, existing portraits of the KKK encapsulate a key dimension of the klan's role in twentieth-century civil rights struggles.[2]

They also, however, flatten our understanding of the group's structure, orientation, functions, and impact. By invoking "the klan" as a unitary organizational force, unyieldingly committed to violence and terror, the KKK's contours and significance are generally treated, at least implicitly, as self-evident and unvarying. But in fact, as we know, multiple klan organizations operated in varied locales, often in parallel and sometimes in direct competition for members. The success of the klan's mobilization efforts, in Mississippi and across the South, was also quite uneven, and adherents' orientation toward violence varied as well.

Even in areas in which the klan was highly active, its actions ran in parallel with the subtler efforts of business leaders who headed the Citizens' Councils, state agents who investigated civil rights action through the Mississippi State Sovereignty Commission, school board officials who had the power to expel students and fire teachers for civil rights advocacy, and so on—all of which exposed civil rights supporters to significant costs and risks. While this spectrum of segregationist resistance, and its associated complicities, has been documented, its existence poses a considerable challenge to tightly bounded examinations that view the KKK apart from the contours of this broader system of anti–civil rights enforcement.[3]

The goal of this essay is to add texture to existing accounts of the civil rights–era KKK in Mississippi, and thereby to move closer to an understanding of how its role differed both across communities and over time. By taking seriously how "the" Mississippi klan was in fact comprised of several distinct organizations—with highly uneven grassroots appeal, variable and often tenuous connections to other segregationist forces, and uncertainty about the tactical and ethical utility of violent action—the essay provides a more nuanced portrait of anti–civil rights efforts generally.[4] The overall approach here emphasizes breadth over exhaustive depth. The sections that follow outline the key dimensions along which klan mobilization varied, providing illustrations of, and in some cases systematic explanatory accounts for, these points of divergence. The conclusion considers the potential significance that this sort of textured account of the KKK in Mississippi holds for contemporary efforts to grapple with the legacy of anti–civil rights violence in the state.

The Rise of the KKK in Mississippi

For a number of years the KKK in Mississippi was distinctive mostly for its absence. While across much of the South various self-styled klan organizations took hold in response to the 1954 *Brown* school desegregation decision, it was not until 1963 that Mississippi saw any significant civil rights–era klan mobilization. That fall, an organizer for the Louisiana-based Original Knights of the Ku Klux Klan arrived in Natchez, recruiting approximately 300 Mississippians to his organization. Infighting soon resulted in the expulsion of Original Knights state officer Douglas Byrd, who promptly recruited two-thirds of the group's Mississippi membership into a new organization, the White Knights of the Ku Klux Klan.

The initial White Knights organizing meeting was held in Brookhaven in February 1964. Two months later Sam Holloway Bowers assumed leadership over the group. Born in 1924 in New Orleans, Bowers had spent four years in the U.S. Navy during World War II, and later attended both Tulane University and the University of Southern California. By the 1960s Bowers operated the Sambo Amusement Company, a vending machine operation in Laurel. He quickly transformed the White Knights into a militant and highly secretive organization dedicated to a brand of Christian patriotism that viewed the encroaching civil rights threat as a Jewish-Communist conspiracy against sovereign white Mississippians.[5]

White Knights membership grew rapidly, peaking in 1964 at an estimated 6,000 adherents spread over fifty-two chapters, known as klaverns. Bowers was clear that the group would use "force and violence when considered necessary," and within the highly secretive and tightly controlled organization he established four categories of "projects"—ranging from verbal threats to cross burnings, to beatings, to killings—that could be carried out with the approval of White Knights leadership. Throughout that summer the White Knights engaged in hundreds of acts of intimidation, including the burning of forty-four black churches.

But as Bowers's group was establishing its presence across much of the state, a rival klan organization was also making inroads in Mississippi. The United Klans of America (UKA) had first formed in Alabama in 1961, and since that time had become the preeminent KKK organization across much of the South. The group was headed by "Imperial Wizard" Robert Shelton, a wiry, clean-cut, and soft-spoken former Goodrich Tire salesman. A talented and tireless organizer, Shelton was continuously crisscrossing the region in support of the hundreds of klaverns affiliated with the UKA.

In early March 1964 Shelton's Alabama state leader, "Grand Dragon" Robert Creel, appeared at two UKA rallies in McComb. That summer Shelton himself spoke to an estimated 800 supporters at the McComb fairgrounds and then to a similarly large gathering in Natchez. In the fall Shelton and his newly appointed Mississippi Grand Dragon, the Natchez-based E. L. McDaniel, traveled around the state on a UKA recruiting campaign. Part or all of the membership in a number of White Knights klaverns shifted to the UKA, and in 1965 Shelton greeted more than 3,000 supporters at a rally in Natchez. By that point the UKA had organized seventy-six klaverns across

the state. The White Knights had managed to retain many of their units as well, though often only in a skeletal form. Figure 1 shows the locations of the White Knights and UKA klaverns active between 1964 and 1966.[6]

As the wholesale line-crossing between the White Knights and UKA illustrates, organizational boundaries among militant segregationists could be quite permeable and multivalent. Throughout this period, both the UKA and the Original Knights were active in Louisiana, and there was considerable communication and cooperation that crossed the state line into southwestern Mississippi, a klan hotbed. UKA Grand Dragon McDaniel spoke on several occasions at rallies in Louisiana, and Mississippi klansmen were involved in a number of acts of violence on the Louisiana side of the Mississippi River, including the murders of Ferriday shoe-shop owner Frank Morris and Vidalia motel employee Joseph "JoeEd" Edwards.

By late 1964 the elite underground "Silver Dollar Group"—so named because its members signaled affiliation by carrying a silver dollar minted in their respective birth years—attracted many of the most militant klansmen from the White Knights, the Original Knights, and the UKA alike. As an inverse variation on that theme, subgroups of klansmen at times referred to themselves as distinct sects within a particular KKK outfit, such as the Adams County–based "Cottonmouth Moccasin Gang," organized by a trio of White Knights. And Americans for the Preservation of the White Race (APWR), most active in Jackson and southwest Mississippi, blurred the lines between the KKK and the Citizens' Councils, largely by working at a grassroots level to pressure local businesspeople and other community leaders to maintain uncompromising support of segregation. According to federal investigators, typical APWR chapters "encompass[ed] all Klansmen in the area, plus a few non-Klansmen," often disgruntled Citizens' Council members. "You had a lot of people that belonged to the Citizens' Council that was members of the Klan," explained E. L. McDaniel. "A lot of Citizens' Council, a lot of them were members of the APWR, Americans for the Preservation of the White Race, and so on." Many of these adherents also belonged to one or more of the more mainstream local groups that emerged in most larger communities, promoting white supremacy under the guise of "constitutional government" or "religious integrity."[7]

KKK Mobilization: Competition and Organizing Dynamics

Mississippi's hard-line segregationist organizations appealed to adherents around the state to varying degrees, and for different reasons. Some areas boasted a full spectrum of white vigilante groups, while in other communities few or none were present. To understand why "reactive movements" like the KKK—that is, those that mobilize in response to a threat to the status quo—gain traction in some areas and not others, social scientists conventionally focus on the presence of interracial competition for political, social, and economic resources.[8]

It is clear that the UKA exploited such competition-based tensions in communities such as Natchez, where an influx of industry meant that the black workforce could vie for many semiskilled manufacturing jobs. Natchez mayor John J. Nosser acknowledged as much when questioned in 1965 by the U.S. Commission on Civil Rights about the kinds of jobs black workers held in his community. "We have got a lot of them working in these big industries right next to the white people," he responded, with apparent pride. "They get along fine all these years." This disingenuous claim of racial harmony was belied by the fact that two of Nosser's sons were at that time members of the White Knights, and the mayor himself was well aware of the prevalence of racially motivated violence in Natchez. In September 1964 stink bombs had been thrown into the two Jitney Jungle grocery stores that he owned, and shortly thereafter his house was bombed in response to an interview he granted to the *Chicago Daily News* that some in the community thought was overly critical of klan-style terrorism.[9]

In this charged climate, Natchez's industrial plants were considered "prime recruiting grounds" for the klan in 1964 and 1965. Federal investigators tried to convince the manager of Natchez's International Paper Company to fire known klan members, after discovering that nearly half of the area's 200 klansmen were employed there. At the time, interracial competition for jobs was mostly a potential rather than actual threat. Each of Natchez's three major industrial plants—Armstrong Tire and Rubber, Johns-Manville, and International Paper—adhered to segregated traditions, reserving most desirable jobs for whites, hosting segregated Christmas parties, and supplying separate white and black bathroom and cafeteria facilities. But still, as there existed virtually no other industry in southwestern Mississippi, many whites saw their economic position as tenuous, and increasing civil rights pressures locally and nationally contributed to an unstable racial climate in the factories.[10]

Some of the state's most brutal klan-perpetrated acts were tied to these workplace settings. George Metcalfe, who in 1965 was a fifty-three-year-old shipping clerk at Armstrong Tire and Rubber, was president of Natchez's National Association for the Advancement of Colored People (NAACP) branch and had long campaigned to desegregate the Armstrong plant and other Natchez institutions. His NAACP activity and willingness to host visiting Student Nonviolent Coordinating Committee (SNCC) workers had drawn vigilante ire in early 1965 in the form of a gunshot that shattered his front window. That summer he presented a desegregation petition to the local school board, and his name appeared prominently in a related story published on the front page of the *Natchez Democrat*. The newspaper's account included personal information about Metcalfe and other petitioners, though they had explicitly requested that signatories' identities not be disclosed given the acute threat of "reprisals and harassment." Two days later a bomb attached to Metcalfe's car engine exploded when he turned the ignition key in the Armstrong parking lot, throwing him completely out of the vehicle and leaving him with serious leg, arm, and eye injuries. Despite widespread suspicion that klan members employed by Armstrong were responsible, including a report made to Federal Bureau of Investigation (FBI) agents that Silver Dollar Group leader "Red" Glover had admitted planting the bomb, police arrested no one.[11]

A similarly tragic story unfolded two years later. Wharlest Jackson, a former NAACP treasurer and Metcalfe's good friend, left his shift at Armstrong Tire and Rubber at eight o'clock in the evening of February 27, 1967. He had normally ridden to and from work with Metcalfe, but a recent promotion meant that he worked days rather than his usual evening shift. His new position was as a chemical mixer, a job traditionally reserved for whites, and he had been selected for the promotion over two white men. His wife had begged him not to accept it, given the associated racial tensions, but his doing so allowed her, a Lupus sufferer, to leave her own job. On his way home from work, a bomb planted under his driver's seat detonated when he activated the car's turn signal. He was killed instantly, and again, no arrests were made.[12]

While the level of racial violence in southwestern Mississippi was unusually intense, the prevalence of the klan in Natchez mirrored the pattern around the South, with KKK organizations flourishing in communities where blacks and whites overlapped in the workplace. But in the least urbanized and industrialized state in the nation, the factory-floor conditions that incubated fears of racial competition were not widespread enough to account for the klan's appeal in fifty-three of Mississippi's eighty-two counties. Unlike in Natchez, in rural areas the entrenched racial division of labor often bound black workers to land owned by whites, which meant that African Americans were vulnerable to economic retribution. In many places the result was that the klan was suppressed in favor of the efficacious, and less distasteful, actions of landowners and business elites who often filled the Citizens' Councils membership rolls. As historian Annalieke Dirks has argued, where the white community had sufficient economic power, "it could choose to use a combination of economic threats and legalized repression and rely less on terrorist violence to subjugate the Black community."[13]

This dynamic helps to explain why the KKK had little presence in an otherwise highly racially repressive region like the cotton-farming Mississippi Delta. It also highlights the distinctiveness of Mississippi, where unlike other Deep South states or the Carolinas or Virginia, factors tied to racial competition and threat—that is, proportionally large black populations, high levels of labor market overlap, or even high levels of civil rights activism—fail to explain the patterning of klan mobilization. Instead, in Mississippi the predominant dynamic was tied to organizing and recruitment.

As the first KKK organization active statewide, the White Knights in 1964 built an infrastructure of core members and local resources that klan recruiters would draw upon for the remainder of the decade. The driving force behind the rapid growth of the White Knights was its charismatic leader, Sam Bowers. The importance of Bowers as an organizing force is strikingly apparent—even after accounting for key structural features of counties, the most significant predictor of klavern presence in Mississippi is a county's proximity to Bowers's home base in Laurel. Figure 2 again shows the locations of KKK units across the state, with shaded bands demonstrating the distance one would need to travel from Laurel to reach, respectively, one-third and two-thirds of the state's active klaverns. As the narrowness of those bands make clear, KKK organizing was driven by an infrastructure built by social networks centered on Bowers and his Laurel cohorts. E. L. McDaniel, a leader in the White Knights before his defection to the UKA, described the process:

Usually we had a contact. The way we did this is we organized [near our home] first. Then we organized in [the next county over] because there was somebody . . . that knew somebody . . . and we'd make a contact there. And we let them set the meeting up with prospects. . . . We wouldn't go into a town like Tupelo and just pick out somebody. They would have to know those individuals. And that thing just spread from county to county to county . . . they were passing the word from klavern to klavern, so-and-so up at Fayette wants to get a group of men together. And it just went like wildfire. We couldn't have done it if it hadn't of been that way, that quick, but

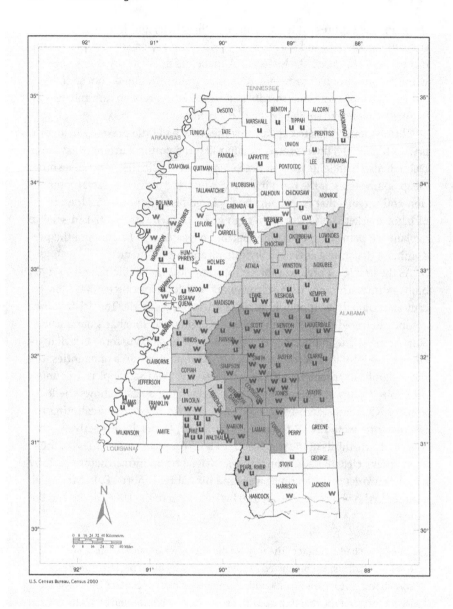

the people were ready for it. They were ready for something. They needed something to lead them.[14]

By the end of 1964 McDaniel had begun leading his recruits to the UKA, and many of the klaverns that had been organized initially by Bowers's White Knights had followed. Early on the UKA had established a large and active presence in McComb, and shortly after Natchez-area members of the White Knights traveled there to discuss shifting their allegiance. At times, such transitions were contentious, complicated by competing allegiances to Bowers versus McDaniel. When several White Knights klaverns gathered in Lauderdale County in February 1965 to discuss a move to the UKA, many adherents expressed dissatisfaction with Bowers's failure to provide financial support for klansmen implicated in the previous summer's killings in nearby Neshoba County. A majority voted to leave the White Knights, though a dissenting group maintained their loyalty to Bowers and stormed out of the meeting.

Such interorganizational debates were further enabled by McDaniel's intense dislike of Bowers, which fueled in part what federal investigators characterized as his "attempts to destroy" the White Knights. That personal conflict was likely rooted in McDaniel's contentious exit from the White Knights. Before his resignation, he had maintained an ongoing secret alliance with the UKA, helping to organize a Natchez unit for Shelton and winning a commendation "for outstanding work" at the UKA's national "klonvokation" meeting. Around the state, McDaniel trumpeted the UKA as "a strong national Klan that knows how to operate." After successfully recruiting White Knights officer Delmar Dennis to the group, he requested that Dennis provide names of disenchanted White Knights, who were then targeted in the UKA's membership drive (unbeknownst to either Bowers or McDaniel at the time, Dennis was also working as an FBI informant, and the bureau viewed this as a bit of effective counterintelligence). The resulting competition for allegiance among veteran members contributed to the pronounced overlap in the two klans' personnel profiles.[15]

McDaniel's reference to the UKA's "strength" was emblematic of the rhetorical wrangling over the sensitive issue of klan violence. Bowers had always been clear that his group would use violence "when considered necessary," and throughout the summer of 1964 the White Knights engaged in hundreds of acts of intimidation, including the burning and bombing of dozens of black churches and homes and the killing of three civil rights workers in Neshoba County. Over time, Bowers became increasingly vulnerable to criticism from his rank-and-file membership, especially over his alleged failures to provide adequate financial support to implicated klansmen. Shelton exploited this vulnerability directly by contacting UKA klaverns to raise money for White Knights defendants, while also publicly promoting the UKA's nonviolent approach during rallies and in media interviews. A typical rationale for a move to the UKA was offered by Adams County Sheriff Odell Anders (himself a suspected White Knights member) when he noted that many klavern members "were opposed to violence and therefore wanted to defect" from the White Knights.[16]

At the same time, however, certain UKA klaverns developed precisely the opposite appeal, attracting members who believed that the White Knights, with their elaborate system of authorizations for violent acts, was not sufficiently militant. In McComb, seventy miles east of Natchez, UKA members, operating under the guise of a secret sect dubbed the Wolf Pack, embarked on a brutal bombing campaign in the summer and fall of 1964. In a five-month period beginning in June, eight beatings, seven burnings, four shootings, and fifteen bombings were reported in the area. One accused klansman later admitted that Wolf Pack members chose their victims by drawing names from a hat.

In Natchez, the UKA's ostensibly nonviolent membership was suspected of carrying out the bombings that targeted the city's mayor. In a weak effort to explain this gap between nonviolent rhetoric and brutal action, McDaniel acknowledged that "there were some incidents happened that wasn't right— I'm sure that some Klansmen did some things that they shouldn't." While, unlike in the White Knights, bombings typically did not result from direct orders from top UKA leadership, it was clear that McDaniel also did little to prevent these campaigns. "I'm a strong believer in nonviolence," he maintained, "but I also believe in self-preservation."[17]

Meanwhile, in an effort to weather the legal and organizational fallout of their reign of violent terror throughout the summer of 1964, the White Knights temporarily and ambivalently retrenched. At a September state officers meeting in Meridian, the group's ambivalence veered toward self-contradiction. Bowers's Grand Dragon Julius Harper instructed members to avoid church burnings and other bombings, "as these were hurting the White Knights' expansion program." But klansmen should be ready to carry out violence under orders, he maintained, and have at the ready proper arms and explosives for these assigned missions. Bowers also continued to talk about elimination orders, maintaining that they be carried out "without malice, in complete silence, and in the manner of a Christian act." But in November, as the White Knights' mounting legal fees continued to create serious financial difficulties—one ledger showed the organization with over $18,000 in the bank but more than $23,000 in accumulated debts in late 1964—Bowers proclaimed a ninety-day moratorium on "4th degree projects" (that is, murders).[18]

But all of this back-and-forth over violence could not obscure a broader reality: both the UKA and White Knights were willing to undertake deadly violence to a degree unsurpassed by klan organizations anywhere else in the South. Debates over militance instead are best understood as delicate rhetorical strategies, where "strength" and "nonviolence" were trumpeted to appeal to particular constituencies. Similarly, it is clear that the commission of violence was not a product of a single organizational process—at different times, it was ordered by state leadership, proscribed by those same leaders, enacted autonomously (usually with active or tacit approval from leadership) by local units, or coalesced through grassroots plots engineered through parallel affiliations to informal collectives like the Silver Dollar Gang or Wolf Pack. The White Knights, as a strongly hierarchical organization, were prone to leadership-driven action, while the UKA more often provided a framework for autonomous activity.

Organizational Structures and Functions

As these spurious debates over violence demonstrate, the fluidity of membership across KKK outfits should not be taken as a signal that the groups were equivalent in their organization or orientation. While both obviously promoted an uncompromising, and often brutal, brand of white supremacy, members' experiences differed markedly. The White Knights was a highly secretive, top-down organization. New members took an oath of secrecy and were instructed never to admit their affiliation. While periodic missives from Bowers appeared in local papers or in the mimeographed sheets of the White Knights' own publication, the *Klan Ledger*, klaverns never held public meetings. For certain gatherings of Hinds County klaverns, members would be instructed to report to a public parking lot, where they would be led to the actual meeting site only after being recognized or providing a proper code. In 1965, under increasing pressures created by the presence of FBI informants and legal difficulties, White Knights state officers were reduced to communicating with members through coded numbers rather than names.

As Imperial Wizard, Bowers had "dictatorial powers" and authorized or vetoed most White Knights acts personally. While a dizzying array of officers under Bowers attended to the group's organizational, financial, spiritual, and investigative matters, decisions regarding White Knights "jobs" or "projects" filtered up to the top of the organization. Individual klavern leaders, known as "Exalted Cyclops," or ECs, were able to approve threats and whippings, but the so-called eliminations of klan enemies could only be authorized by state officers, and generally by Bowers himself. That sort of violence, or its threat, was central to the group's identity and reputation. New recruits were warned that they would be expected to carry out cross burnings, beatings, and possible eliminations. "It was an organization of action, no Boy Scout group," one member recalled being told. "We were here to do business."[19]

In contrast with the White Knights' underground apparatus, the UKA's appeal was rooted in the elevation of the KKK's public profile. "The United Klan was an open klan, more or less," explained McDaniel. "Mr. Shelton believed that this secrecy was not vital to the organization anymore, and he had come out in the open. All of the klansmen wanted to parade in their uniforms, their sheets or whatever you call them. And I said, 'Well, maybe this is what we need.'"[20] Indeed, the UKA organized public rallies, with members in robes and hoods, and based much of its appeal on carving out a civic space for the expression of klan values.

Shelton intended UKA rallies to be public spectacles. They generally were held on county fairgrounds, local airstrips, or other large fields. Typically they were well orchestrated, with arriving cars greeted by robed klansmen selling small rebel flags and handing out free literature, and directing drivers to a nearby parking area. Spectators bought food at a concession stand. Various pieces of UKA paraphernalia were for sale: copies of the organization's national newspaper, the *Fiery Cross*, for a quarter, and segregationist books such as *God Is the Author of Segregation* and *None Dare Call It Treason* for fifty cents each. Popular bumper stickers proclaimed "The Knights of the Ku Klux Klan is Watching You," "Be a Man—Join the Klan," and "You Have Been Visited by the Ku Klux Klan." Sometimes other items—TVs, toasters, motor oil, fertilizer, even used cars—were raffled off. Twenty different records, most featuring the UKA-affiliated string band Skeeter Bob and the Country Pals, were on sale for a dollar apiece.

Most spectators were dressed in overalls or other work clothes, though UKA members themselves typically donned traditional white robes and hoods. The rally itself began and ended with a prayer from a local preacher, and featured speeches by McDaniel and other klan officials. The nightly climax was the burning of a wooden cross covered in gasoline-doused burlap. The cross burning was a well-orchestrated ritual; robed klansmen would ceremoniously encircle the fiery cross, which could be anywhere from twenty to seventy feet high.[21]

These rallies were held nightly in North Carolina, where the UKA had its greatest organizing successes, though in Mississippi they occurred only a handful of times in 1964 and 1965. Beyond these large-scale events, the state's UKA members would attend weekly klavern meetings, and there were efforts to organize the wives of members into parallel women's groups. Shelton and McDaniel aspired to replicate North Carolina's more fully formed UKA organization, which additionally featured a number of other initiatives. Prior to Tar Heel State rallies, members in full robes would gather in the downtown business district of a nearby community for a "street walk," during which they would march down the main street. Full-fledged "Ladies Auxiliary Units" would mobilize women in a range of support tasks. Adherents could take part in UKA insurance plans. Klaverns also hosted regular social events, including turkey shoots, fish frys, and family lunches. In May 1965 a crowd estimated at 5,000 gathered in a plowed cornfield in eastern North Carolina to witness an official UKA wedding.[22]

While few parallel efforts were initiated in Mississippi, the UKA's public orientation lends insight into ways in which Shelton sought to build collective identity around klan affiliation. While Bowers's vision for the White Knights was narrowly centered on clandestine action and minimal group interaction in the name of a higher Christian mission, the UKA worked to construct a full-service klan community. The highly ritualized character of the UKA's meetings, activities, and organizational structure itself served to strengthen and reproduce social boundaries. Klan events, in effect, became vehicles for affirming solidarity to the klan world and rejecting the compromised character of other institutions.

Such functions had broad appeal in a state like North Carolina, where political elites rejected the "massive resistance" strategies advanced by other southern states in defiance of federal law. While the state pursued other, more "passive" means to preserve segregation, including an effort to amend the state constitution to provide local school boards with the authority to hold a public referendum to close public schools in the event of a desegregation order, it was clear that state policy would, in the end, follow the mandates of the 1964 Civil Rights Act. This orientation spurred the UKA's appeal in the Tar Heel State, as the klan served as one of the few outlets available to staunch segregationists. In communities where whites perceived their economic and political well-being as tied to the maintenance of racial separation, the UKA often filled a void, providing perhaps the only organized means for uncompromising resistance to federal policies. In Mississippi, white residents who feared the onslaught of federal reforms could count on a response from congressional representatives, school boards, police forces, civic elites, and so on that were solidly aligned against desegregation. Precisely because this context provided so many mainstream outlets for the maintenance of segregation, the solidarity-based appeals of klan institutions had much narrower resonance in Mississippi.[23]

John Dittmer explains the KKK's Mississippi revival as a product of "frustration, a gut feeling that the battle for white supremacy was being lost," in spite of the efforts of the Citizens' Council and political and economic elites. This argument importantly recognizes that the klan was but one of many white institutions determined to preserve and protect Mississippi's segregationist traditions, gaining strength from the perceived weakness of other, more "civil" white supremacist outlets. Bob Moses, like many other civil rights workers in Mississippi, viewed white institutions as self-consciously aligned to protect the racial status quo. "The full resources of the state will continue to be at the disposal of local authorities to fight civil rights gains," Moses argued. "The entire white population will continue to be the Klan."[24]

But while this conception of an aligned white supremacist field had visceral and strategic appeal to frequently besieged activists, it obscures the negotiations for resources and legitimacy that occurred across white supremacist organizations. In Yazoo City, in the corner of the Delta, Citizens' Council leaders spoke out against the klan. "Your Citizens' Council was formed to preserve separation of the races," their statement concluded, "and believes that it can best serve the county where it is the only organization operating in the field." As Dittmer notes, this klan opposition was often rhetorical—where the KKK was most active, law enforcement often directly supported its activities, and community leaders rarely were willing to engage in strenuous efforts to hinder its organization. But turning the issue on its head, to focus on why the klan was *unable* to make inroads in certain areas, in spite of ambitious recruiting campaigns, points to the important role played by interorganizational competition among white supremacist groups. Where a range of white constituencies aggressively moved to preserve segregation, creating the sense that local Citizens' Councils or sheriffs were getting the job done, the klan was often perceived to be redundant.[25]

This perspective poses a significant challenge to conceptions that fail to address how the KKK operated vis à vis other segregationist actors. The effectiveness of the state's segregationist apparatus varied across locales, and the appeal and function of vigilante actors within local white institutions differed as a consequence. Where the klan was active, its members maintained a diverse range of relationships with other white institutions. While klan members were frequently willing to engage in extralegal actions that others in the community would not, or could not, afford to actively support, partnerships within the white community were often considerably more complex than the traditional "compact" model outlined by Aldon Morris and others, in which "political elites relied on . . . the Ku Klux Klan to do the dirty work." To be sure, as more recent scholarship has demonstrated, the actions of klan adherents were intertwined with those of the Citizens' Council, the APWR, police officials, Mississippi State Sovereignty Commission investigators, and other institutional leaders, but equally important is the insight that the contours of these relationships varied significantly in different times and places.[26]

To take but one example, it is clear that police around the state had significantly differing orientations to local klaverns. In Clarksdale, in the heart of the Delta, mass civil rights action was largely suppressed by the vulnerability of black workers within the white-dominated, agrarian labor market. In such settings, as Charles Payne explains: "social distance between Blacks and whites was so great that no one ever needed to be reminded of it, rendering the Klan less necessary and lynchings less common." When NAACP and Council of Federated Organizations (COFO) efforts gained momentum, police confidently took matters into their own hands to harshly suppress threats to segregation, with Police Chief Ben Collins engineering a brutal campaign of police harassment. Over the course of a single two-week period in July 1964, at least fifteen complaints were lodged against Clarksdale police by civil rights activists. Several of those involved jailhouse beatings. Such accusations were compounded by the fact that Collins refused to seriously investigate segregationist violence committed daily by private citizens.[27]

In contrast, the best-known case of active police-KKK complicity was in Neshoba County, where Sheriff Lawrence Rainey and his deputy Cecil Price were both actively involved in the klan plot that led to the murders of three Freedom Summer workers in June 1964. They later appeared at UKA rallies in Meridian and Greenville. Rainey, in full uniform, received a thunderous ovation and even gave a brief speech. "I'm glad to be here and to see these fine people here," he told the thousand spectators gathered at Meridian's Suqualena racetrack. "I just thought I'd come down here and see what this was all about, and I can tell you I met some of the finest people anywhere in the Klan this afternoon and tonight."[28]

In Natchez, there was little hard evidence of police involvement in the area's many beatings and bombings, though klansmen enjoyed virtual impunity from police prosecution. After Jack Seale—a reputed member of the Silver Dollar Gang—was arrested for the bombing of a local jewelry store in December 1966, Sovereignty Commission investigator L. E. Cole Jr. arrived at the county jail to find Seale outside of his cell, "telling jokes" with Sheriff Odell Anders, Grand Dragon E. L. McDaniel, and two other UKA officers. Cole, for his part, seemed less troubled by this apparent miscarriage of justice than by the fact that several of the jokes "made light of the Sovereignty Commission and our work in front of these KKK officials." Natchez police chief J. T. Robinson later testified to federal investigators that he attended an "impressive" UKA rally at Liberty Ball Park. "I couldn't see anything that night that would make you think they were anything but upstanding people," he reasoned. Later, Robinson accepted an invitation to speak at a local APWR meeting, and insisted that membership in that organization would not be grounds for dismissal from the city police force.[29]

Even in communities like Philadelphia, Natchez, or McComb, where klan members exerted significant influence over anti–civil rights enforcement, their period of peak influence was quite narrow. Both the White Knights and the UKA were in serious decline by late 1965—less than two years after their initial mass mobilization. Continued violence perpetrated by the White Knights—including the 1966 killing of Forrest County NAACP leader Vernon Dahmer and a later bombing campaign targeting Jews in Jackson and Meridian—further eroded the klan's public appeal. Governor Paul Johnson referred to Dahmer's killers as "vicious and morally bankrupt criminals," and district attorneys and juries became less reluctant to indict klan adherents. Meanwhile, federal action—including an investigation by the House Un-American Activities Committee (HUAC) and a highly successful FBI campaign to infiltrate and neutralize the klan—sapped the KKK's resources. Organizational strife cut into membership as well; amid accusations of financial improprieties, Shelton expelled McDaniel and the state's other UKA officers in 1966 and began, with sharply diminishing returns, running the UKA's Mississippi Realm from his Alabama home base.[30]

By the close of 1968 both the White Knights and the UKA were shells of their former selves. Despite sporadic attempts by Shelton to revive his organization with early-1970s recruiting drives in McComb and elsewhere, the klan mainly made headlines in the courtroom. Bowers, along with seven other klansmen, served prison time after a 1967 trial for the Freedom Summer murders. Bowers also weathered four mistrials in the Dahmer killing before finally being convicted of murder and arson in 1998. He died in prison in 2006.

More recently, Edgar Ray Killen, a central player in the Freedom Summer murders conspiracy, was found guilty of manslaughter in 2005. Two years later, another former White Knights member, James Ford Seale (Jack's brother), was convicted of kidnapping and conspiracy in the 1964 murders of Charles Moore and Henry Dee, two young black men whom Seale and other klansmen had abducted, beaten, and dropped into the Mississippi River amid unfounded fears that "Black Muslims" had been stockpiling weapons around Natchez.

New investigations of civil rights "cold cases" can contribute to an understanding of the klan as embedded in diverse ways within local communities. Ongoing efforts to pursue a civil case against Franklin County for the Moore/Dee killings, charging that county officials were actively involved in the killings, and to form a statewide Truth and Reconciliation Commission to "bring to light racially motivated crimes and injustices committed in Mississippi between 1945 and 1975 . . . in order to shape an inclusive and equitable future," speak to the importance of understanding the ways in which KKK adherents at different times and places operated in parallel, or in partnership, or in opposition to other community institutions.[31] Only then will we possess a true contextualized understanding of the legacy of the state's civil rights–era KKK.

NOTES

1. While claims that klan adherents were responsible for much of the civil rights–related violence that shook Mississippi and other southern states throughout the 1960s are generally assumed rather than systematically demonstrated, it is true that the level of anti–civil rights violence committed in Mississippi counties correlates strongly with the presence of organized klan units (when proxied by David Colby's index of anti–civil rights violence and the census of KKK units by the U.S. House of Representatives, their correlation is significant at the 0.001 level [one-tailed test]). David Colby, "White Violence and the Civil Rights Movement," in *Blacks in Southern Politics*, ed. L. Moreland, R. Steed, and T. Baker (New York: Praeger 1987), 31–48; U.S. House of Representatives, Committee on Un-American Activities, *The Present Day Ku Klux Klan Movement, 90th Congress, First Session* (Washington, D.C.: Government Printing Office, 1967), 145–163.

2. For discussions of the "backlash thesis," see Michael J. Klarman, Brown v. Board of Education *and the Civil Rights Movement* (New York: Oxford University Press, 2007); and David M. Chalmers, *Backlash: How the Ku Klux Klan Helped the Civil Rights Movement* (Lanham, Md.: Rowman & Littlefield, 2003). The causal fidelity of

that argument has been critiqued in a number of studies, including Glenn Feldman, *Before Brown: Civil Rights and White Backlash in the Modern South* (Tuscaloosa: University of Alabama Press, 2004); and Aldon Morris, "Birmingham Confrontation Reconsidered: An Analysis of the Dynamics and Tactics of Mobilization," *American Sociological Review* 58 (1993): 621–636. I invoke it here not as a broad defense of its claims, but as an illustration of how klan action may have shaped civil rights outcomes.

3. For detailed examinations of the Mississippi State Sovereignty Commission, see Yasuhiro Katagiri, *The Mississippi State Sovereignty Commission: Civil Rights and States Rights* (Jackson: University Press of Mississippi, 2001); and Jennifer Irons, *Reconstituting Whiteness: The Mississippi State Sovereignty Commission* (Nashville, Tenn.: Vanderbilt University Press, 2010). Neil R. McMillen, *The Citizens' Council: Organized Resistance to the Second Reconstruction, 1954–64* (Urbana: University of Illinois Press, 1971), remains the seminal source on the Citizens' Councils. John Dittmer, *Local People: The Struggle for Civil Rights in Mississippi* (Urbana: University of Illinois Press, 1994), and Charles M. Payne, *I've Got the Light of Freedom: The Organizing Tradition and the Mississippi Freedom Struggle* (Berkeley: University of California Press, 1995), both provide a resonant sense of the scope of sanctions imposed by economic actors. My use of the terms "anti–civil rights violence" and "anti–civil rights enforcement" follows conceptualizations introduced, respectively, by Michael R. Belknap, *Federal Law and Southern Order: Racial Violence and Constitutional Conflict in the Post-Brown South* (Athens: University of Georgia Press, 1987), and David Cunningham, Daniel Kryder, and Geoff Ward, "Remedying Anti-Civil Rights Violence: Roles for Research in the Pursuit of Truth, Justice, and Reconciliation," paper presented at the Social Science History Association Annual Meeting, Long Beach, Calif., 2009.

4. Note that the usage of the capitalized "Klan" label itself reproduces this unitary conception. To reinforce the sense that the Mississippi KKK was in fact a heterogeneous set of organizations with distinct orientations to the civil rights struggle, I employ the lower-case "klan" throughout (though, perhaps hypocritically, retain the conventional uppercase acronym "KKK," as the lowercase alternative in this instance seems overly, and awkwardly, doctrinaire).

5. Joseph Crespino, *In Search of Another Country: Mississippi and the Conservative Counterrevolution* (Princeton, N.J.: Princeton University Press, 2007); U.S. House of Representatives, *Present Day Ku Klux Klan Movement*, 44–47; Memo from Appell to McNamara, April 22, 1965, HUAC investigative files, Box 15, Folder: United Klans—MS investigative memos, Center for Legislative Archives, National Archives, Washington, D.C. Note that the klan entered the state in a very limited way in 1957, when the incipient Independent Mississippi Klan established several chapters. Also, a number of klansmen in the Natchez area, near the Louisiana border, later claimed

that they were spurred to join the klan in 1962, after Governor Ross Barnett failed in his efforts to keep James Meredith from registering at the University of Mississippi. See Stanley Nelson, "Ex-Klansman Said Red Glover Admitted to Metcalfe Bombing," *Concordia (La.) Sentinel*, September 17, 2009. However, it is likely that most of this early mobilization occurred on the Louisiana side of the Mississippi River, and did not spill over into Natchez in any significant way until the following year. E. L. McDaniel claims to be the first Mississippian sworn into the Original Knights, though he does not provide a date. Edward L. McDaniel, interview by Orley B. Caudill, University of Southern Mississippi Center for Oral History and Cultural Heritage, 1977, 8.

6. David Cunningham, "Truth, Reconciliation, and the Ku Klux Klan," *Southern Cultures* 14, no. 3 (2008): 68–87; U.S. House of Representatives, *Present-Day Ku Klux Klan Movement*, 153–154, 163; Memo from Manuel to McNamara, May 18, 1965, Box 15, Folder: United Klans—Mississippi Investigative Memos, HUAC investigation files.

7. Crespino, *In Search of Another Country*, 110–111; Dittmer, *Local People*, 216; McDaniel interview, 10; Stanley Nelson, "Klansmen 'Took Great Pride' in Bombing Skills," *Concordia (La.) Sentinel*, January 22, 2009; "Retired FBI Agents Unsure Who Killed Morris, Edwards," *Concordia (La.) Sentinel*, November 5, 2009; Memo from Appell to McNamara, April 22, 1965, 12, Box 15, Folder: United Klans—MS investigative memos, HUAC investigative files. Jack E. Davis notes that in Natchez, local white supremacist organizations included the "Adams County Committee for Constitutional Government" and the "Adams County Committee for Racial Integrity." See Jack E. Davis, *Race against Time: Culture and Segregation in Natchez since 1930* (Baton Rouge: Louisiana State University Press, 2004), 180.

8. David Cunningham and Benjamin T. Phillips, "Contexts for Mobilization: Spatial Settings and Klan Presence in North Carolina, 1964–1966," *American Journal of Sociology* 113, no. 3 (2007): 781–814; Susan Olzak, *The Dynamics of Ethnic Competition and Conflict* (Palo Alto, Calif.: Stanford University Press, 1992); Nella Van Dyke and Sarah Soule, "Structural Social Change and the Mobilizing Effect of Threat: Explaining Levels of Patriot and Militia Organizing in the United States," *Social Problems* 49 no. 4 (2002): 497–520.

9. U.S. Commission on Civil Rights, *Hearings Held in Jackson, Miss., February 16–20, 1965*, Vol. 2, *Administration of Justice* (Washington, D.C.: U.S. Government Printing Office, 1965), 114; "A Discussion of Violence in Natchez, Mississippi, and Vicinity, in Date Order, Most of Which is Attributed to Klan Activities," Box 13, Folder: Klans—Mississippi Investigative Memos (2 of 2), HUAC investigative files; Davis, *Race against Time*, 172–173.

10. Davis, *Race against Time*, 132–136; Stanley Nelson, "FBI Interviewed Three IP Workers for December 1964 Murder of Frank Morris," *Concordia (La.) Sentinel*, November 26, 2008.

11. Davis, *Race against Time*; U.S. Commission on Civil Rights, *Hearings Held in*

Jackson, Miss., February 16–20, 1965, Vol. 2, *Administration of Justice,* 71, 107; "Desegregation Petition Filed," *Natchez Democrat,* August 20, 1965; "Natchez President NAACP Critically Hurt in Bombing," *Natchez Democrat,* August 28, 1965; Nelson, "Ex-Klansman Said Red Glover Admitted to Metcalfe Bombing." Remarkably, after exposing Metcalfe by naming him in their front-page article, the *Democrat's* editors responded to the bombing with outrage. Their page-one editorial, titled "We Condemn Lawlessness," expressed "shock" at the actions of the "hoodlums, renegades, and criminals" behind the bombing and advanced Natchez as a city of "peace, understanding, and culture." The following days belied that characterization, as the mayor and city council rejected a set of NAACP demands (including a call to publicly denounce the KKK), leading to a series of volatile street clashes, a citywide curfew, and the mobilization of 650 National Guardsmen to maintain order.

12. Davis, *Race against Time,* 201–202; Stanley Nelson, "Justice Eluded Exerlena Jackson-Vanison after 1967 Car Bomb of Husband," *Concordia (La.) Sentinel,* August 5, 2009.

13. Cunningham and Phillips, "Contexts for Mobilization"; U.S House of Representatives, *Present-Day Ku Klux Klan Movement*; Annelieke Dirks, "Between Threat and Reality: The National Association for the Advancement of Colored People and the Emergence of Armed Self-Defense in Clarksdale and Natchez, Mississippi, 1960–1965," *Journal for the Study of Radicalism* 1, no. 1 (2006): 80. For a similar argument about economic vulnerability and white vigilantism, see Lance Hill, *The Deacons for Defense: Armed Resistance and the Civil Rights Movement* (Chapel Hill: University of North Carolina Press, 2004).

14. McDaniel interview, 8. For an analysis demonstrating the primacy of competition dynamics in the patterning of klan units elsewhere in the South, see Cunningham and Phillips, "Contexts for Mobilization." Laurel, as "ground zero" on this map, possessed a workforce dynamic similar to Natchez. A significant number of Bowers's early recruits in that city were employed by the Masonite Corporation, which at the time was under pressure from federal authorities to provide equal employment opportunities for black workers. See Don Whitehead, *Attack on Terror: The FBI against the Ku Klux Klan in Mississippi* (New York: Funk and Wagnalls, 1970), 24. The relationship between klavern presence and distance from Laurel is significant at the .01 level (two-tailed test), and holds even when controlling for counties' key demographic and structural features (results available from author). The organizing diffusion effect would likely be even stronger if we accounted for Natchez as a second originating "node."

15. U.S. House of Representatives, *Present-Day Ku Klux Klan Movement,* 30–31; Whitehead, *Attack on Terror,* 221–222; Memos from Appell to McNamara, April 22, 1965, and May 27, 1965, Box 15, Folder: United Klans—MS investigative memos,

HUAC investigative files. Klavern defections, while more frequently characterized by a move from the White Knights to the UKA, also could go the other way. In late 1964, for instance, the leader of the UKA's Pricedale klavern, in Pike County, began making inquiries about a move to the White Knights. Memo from Appell to McNamara, April 22, 1965, 17, Box 15, Folder: United Klans—MS investigative memos, HUAC investigative files.

16. Whitehead, *Attack on Terror*, 221–222.

17. Crespino, *In Search of Another Country*, 113; Memos from Manuel to McNamara, May 18, 1965, and August 26, 1965, Box 15, Folder: United Klans—Mississippi investigative memos, 2, 5, 15, HUAC investigative files; "Klan Seeks Role as a Voting Bloc," *New York Times*, July 25, 1965; U.S. Commission on Civil Rights, *Hearings Held in Jackson, Miss., February 16–20, 1965*, Vol. 2, *Administration of Justice*, 449; "A Discussion of Violence in Natchez, Mississippi, and Vicinity, in Date Order, Most of Which is Attributed to Klan Activities," Box 13, Folder: Klans—Mississippi Investigative Memos (2 of 2), HUAC investigative files; Whitehead, *Attack on Terror*; McDaniel interview, 15. For a vivid and insightful account of the McComb bombing campaign, see Dittmer, *Local People*, 303–314.

18. Memo from Appell to McNamara, April 22, 1965, 13–14, Box 15, Folder: Klans—Mississippi Investigative Memos (2 of 2), HUAC investigative files.

19. Seth Cagin and Philip Dray, *We Are Not Afraid: The Story of Goodman, Schwerner, and Chaney and the Civil Rights Campaign for Mississippi* (New York: Scribner, 1988); Whitehead, *Attack on Terror*, 266; Delmar Dennis testimony transcript, *United States v. Price et al.*, http://www.law.umkc.edu/faculty/projects/ftrials/price&bowers/Dennis.html; Memo from Appell to McNamara, April 22, 1965, Box 15, Folder: United Klans—MS investigative memos, HUAC investigative files.

20. McDaniel interview, 11.

21. Stewart Alsop, "Portrait of a Klansman," *Saturday Evening Post*, April 9, 1966, 27; Peter B. Young, "Violence and the White Ghetto: A View from the Inside," 161, Box 1, Series 10, Federal Records—Eisenhower Commission [RG 283], Task Force I—Assassination, Lyndon B. Johnson Archives, Austin, Tex.; North Carolina State Bureau of Investigation Memo from Agent John B. Edwards to Director, May 24, 1967, Box 213, Folder: SHP & SBI reports, Gov. Moore General Correspondence 1967, North Carolina State Archives, Raleigh; North Carolina State Highway Patrol Memo from Sgt. A. H. Clark to Capt. T. B. Brown, May 3, 1964, Box 420, Folder: KKK, Gov. Sanford General Correspondence 1964, North Carolina State Archives. The discussion here draws largely on detailed accounts of UKA rallies in North Carolina, the state in which the UKA was most successful. The model described here, however, is typical of Shelton's UKA rallies across the South.

22. McDaniel interview, 13; Grady Jefferys, "Klan Stages Capital City Street Walk."

Raleigh (N.C.) News and Observer, June 27, 1965; John Justice, "Kluxers Gather to Burn Cross," *Greenville (N.C.) Daily Reflector*, October 18, 1965; U.S. House of Representatives, Committee on Un-American Activities, *Activities of Ku Klux Klan Organizations in the United States, Parts I–V, 89th Congress, First Session* (Washington, D.C.: Government Printing Office, 1966), 1756. Stanley Nelson notes that the UKA held a total of twelve Mississippi rallies in 1964 and 1965. See *Concordia (La.) Sentinel*, February 26, 1965.

23. For discussion of southern "passive resistance" strategies, including the "Pearsall Plan" backed by North Carolina governor Luther Hodges, see William H. Chafe, *Civilities and Civil Rights: Greensboro, North Carolina, and the Black Struggle for Freedom* (New York: Oxford University Press, 1980); Matthew D. Lassiter, *The Silent Majority: Suburban Politics in the Sunbelt South* (Princeton, N.J.: Princeton University Press, 2006); and Anders Walker, *The Ghost of Jim Crow: How Southern Moderates Used* Brown v. Board of Education *to Stall Civil Rights* (New York: Oxford University Press, 2009).

24. Dittmer, *Local People*, 217, Moses quoted on 198–199.

25. The Yazoo City Citizens' Council statement is quoted in ibid., 218. Crespino uses similar reasoning to explain the absence of KKK activity in the state prior to 1963, when he argues that "Mississippians had no need for the Klan" so long as the Councils were perceived to be effective. See Crespino, *In Search of Another Country*, 25.

26. Aldon D. Morris, *The Origins of the Civil Rights Movement: Black Communities Organizing for Change* (New York: Free Press, 1984), 257. For a similar articulation of this "traditional compact," see Payne, *I've Got the Light of Freedom*, 482; and Kenneth T. Andrews, *Freedom Is a Constant Struggle: The Mississippi Civil Rights Movement and Its Legacy* (Chicago: University of Chicago Press, 2004), 31. For an example of recent work that considers white resistance as an institutional field, see Andrews, *Freedom Is a Constant Struggle.* Andrews clearly demonstrates that in Jim Crow Mississippi, "state-sponsored resistance and private repression were intertwined."

27. Incidents against Clarksdale police are outlined by Françoise Hamlin, "'The Book Hasn't Closed, The Story Isn't Finished': Continuing Histories of the Civil Rights Movement" (Ph.D. diss., Yale University, 2004); Daniel Kryder, "Police Chief Ben C. Collins and Law Enforcement in Clarksdale, MS, 1961–1966," paper presented at the Southern Political Science Association Annual Meeting, New Orleans, 2009; and "Mississippi Summer Project—Running Summary of Incidents Transcript," http://anna.lib.usm.edu/~spcol/crda/zwerling/mz054.html. For more on Ben Collins's brutal reputation as a "mean policeman" who regularly "hurt people in the community," see Hamlin, "Book Hasn't Closed"; and Zoya Zeman, interview by John Rachal, University of Southern Mississippi Center for Oral History and Cultural Heritage, 1996, 25.

28. Rainey quoted in Whitehead, *Attack on Terror*, 231.

29. Investigation report by L. E. Cole Jr., December 6, 1966, Mississippi State Sovereignty Commission online file # 2-36-2-69-1-1-1. Robinson's testimony is in U.S. Commission on Civil Rights, *Hearings Held in Jackson, Miss., February 16–20, 1965*, Vol. 2, *Administration of Justice*, 154, 158; Payne, *I've Got the Light of Freedom*, 113–114.

30. Governor Johnson quoted in Whitehead, *Attack on Terror*, 237. For details on the HUAC KKK hearings, see U.S. House of Representatives, *Present-Day Ku Klux Klan Movement*. For a detailed account of Bowers's anti-Semitic bombing campaign, see Jack Nelson, *Terror in the Night: The Klan's Campaign against the Jews* (Oxford: University Press of Mississippi, 1996). For more on the FBI's intelligence and counterintelligence efforts against the KKK, see David Cunningham, *There's Something Happening Here: The New Left, the Klan, and FBI Counterintelligence* (Berkeley: University of California Press, 2004).

31. The incipient statewide Truth and Reconciliation Commission effort is being organized through the grassroots Mississippi Truth Project. See www.mississippitruth.org.

"It's Time for Black Men . . ."

The Deacons for Defense and the Mississippi Movement

Akinyele Umoja

The documentary film *Black Natchez* opens with an oath taken by an initiate of the paramilitary Deacons for Defense. Deacons member James Jackson repeated the beginning of the oath that Natchez activist John Fitzgerald administered to him. The oath began "I do solemnly swear that I will not reveal or invade any of these above secrets."[1] In the article "'We Will Shoot Back': The Natchez Model and Para-Military Organization in the Mississippi Freedom Movement," I argued that the organization of the Deacons for Defense increased the effectiveness of activists in the Mississippi freedom movement.[2] While blacks had employed armed resistance in the fight for freedom in Mississippi and the South since enslavement, paramilitary organization represented a significant transitional point in the Mississippi freedom movement. Mississippi activists were attracted to the paramilitary organizational model after the development of the Deacons for Defense in 1964 in Louisiana.

The Deacons for Defense was distinguished from previous armed resistance networks in the Mississippi civil rights movement because of its paramilitary organization. Paramilitary organizations have a specific chain of command and are composed of civilians, not professional military personnel. They are organized and operate similar to formal military or law enforcement groups. Unlike previous informal defense networks in the Mississippi civil rights movement, the Deacons for Defense was organized with a clear chain of command, and members viewed themselves as filling the vacuum left in the African American community by federal, state, and local law enforcement personnel who were either sympathetic or neutral to white supremacist violence.

This essay explores the role of the Deacons in the Mississippi civil rights movement. By distinguishing paramilitary organizations from previous forms of armed resistance in Mississippi and emphasizing the role the Deacons played in a significant consumer boycott, the essay contextualizes the political meaning and significance the Deacons had in the communities where the group was active.

Mississippi and the Tradition of Armed Resistance

Blacks quietly built institutions and organizations during the nadir period from the 1890s to the 1910s. The organizations and informal, clandestine networks blacks created in this period were effective assets for the activism that emerged in the 1950s. The organizing of groups like the Regional Council of Negro Leadership (RCNL) and the National Association for the Advancement of Colored People (NAACP) was supported by informal associations of armed blacks willing to provide self-defense. These same informal networks would provide assistance to Student Nonviolent Coordinating Committee (SNCC) and Congress of Racial Equality (CORE) workers who went to the state to organize voter registration efforts in the early 1960s. Some rural communities possessed a higher level of participation and efficacy in their defense networks. In particular, black majority communities with high percentages of black landowners provided relative security for mobile black activists. SNCC organizer MacArthur Cotton described these communities as "haven communities." Armed self-defense was essential for the survival of the Council of Federated Organizations (COFO) and its volunteers during Freedom Summer.

After Freedom Summer, SNCC and CORE activists considered an open embrace of armed self-defense. Several factors contributed to this change in position. First, the practice of indigenous Mississippi black activists influenced SNCC and CORE members. SNCC and CORE activists depended on local people for survival against the terror of white supremacists. As Bob Moses stated, "Local people carried the day" in terms of how weapons were to be used in the Mississippi freedom movement. The failure of the federal government, the Democratic Party, and the northern liberal coalition to support the challenge of the Mississippi Freedom Democratic Party (MFDP) in 1964 motivated several activists in a more autonomous direction. Armed self-defense represented an aspect of self-reliance. To protect themselves, those in the movement would rely on their own resources, rather than on an unreliable federal government.

The Deacons for Defense and Justice was one of the alternatives that presented itself to the Mississippi movement. First organized in Jonesboro, Louisiana, in July 1964, the Deacons received national attention because of the members' practice and open advocacy of armed self-defense. The Deacons publicly declared their existence and willingness to use their weapons in the cause of civil and human rights. The Deacons' public advocacy of armed resistance was a significant contrast to previous armed networks in the Deep South. The Deacons could also be distinguished from informal defense groups and patrols that protected African American communities and movement centers by their paramilitary structure, their identifiable chain of command, their laws, and in some cases their badges and uniforms.

The primary reason for the formation of the Deacons was the lack of police protection from Ku Klux Klan and other vigilante terrorists for movement activists and black communities in general. A prominent example was the formation of the original Deacons group in Jonesboro, Louisiana, after a reign of terror by the Klan in the summer of 1964. Local police initiated a campaign of harassment and intimidation in response to CORE voter registration activity. The United Klans of America klavern in Jonesboro also increased its activities in the spring of 1964. Voter registration workers were harassed by police and beaten in the streets of Jonesboro by white racist civilians in broad daylight, and mobs of young whites threatened the security of blacks in the evening. Klan cross burnings also were becoming commonplace in the small mill town. Any thought of receiving protection from local police was crushed on June 9, 1964, when a police car led a Klan caravan of twenty-five cars. The Klan caravan distributed leaflets demanding that blacks "stay in their place."[3]

The next evening a group of ten black World War II and Korean War veterans met to discuss how they could defend their community. Participants decided to form a paramilitary group to protect the voter registration workers in Jackson Parish and their community, particularly since the movement and the black community could not depend upon police protection. After deciding to form an organized armed response to the white supremacist reign of terror, their next move was to survey the black community to assess what weapons and ammunition were available to them. Originally called the Justice and Defense Group, by March 1965 the group was known and incorporated as a nonprofit organization under the name Deacons for Defense and Justice. By the time the Jonesboro Deacons were incorporated, the group had expanded from its original 10 members to somewhere between 45 and 150 members who regularly patrolled the black community.[4]

The Klan terrorism subsided after the patrols by the Deacons. The cross burnings, beatings, and other forms of abuse all decreased in the face of disciplined, armed black resistance, and CORE workers were able to conduct their voter registration drives in a qualitatively more secure environment. Members of the Deacons protected the CORE Freedom House at night, escorted CORE activists in and out of town, and provided personal security for leading CORE activists. The leadership of the Deacons warned police officials that armed blacks under a disciplined leadership would monitor police activity in the black community and that police brutality would not be tolerated. In fact, the Deacons constituted a parallel police force that represented the forces of the movement.[5]

The spokesperson and organizer of the Jonesboro Deacons was Earnest Thomas, often referred to as "Chilly Willy." Thomas, thirty-two years old when the Deacons were first organized, was a self-employed handyman by profession. He was responsible for organizing new chapters of the Deacons and traveled throughout the South and to northern cities like Chicago to recruit members and financial support for the work of the organization.[6]

One of the most important recruiting ventures Thomas made was his trip to Bogalusa, a town in southeast Louisiana. Bogalusa had "perhaps the highest percentage of active Klansmen of any city in the South."[7] Just as in Jonesboro, there was an acceleration of activity by the local Voters League with assistance from CORE, as members of the Bogalusa Voters League began to test segregated venues after the passage of the Civil Rights Act in the summer of 1964. In response to this offensive, the Klan and local police began to harass movement activists and members of the black community. Klan nightriders invaded and terrorized the black community in the evenings. The black community showed its willingness to respond to the proliferation of Klan terrorism.[8]

On February 21, 1965, Earnest Thomas was present at a meeting in Bogalusa in his capacity as spokesperson for the Deacons for Defense and Justice. The purpose of this meeting, which included the leadership of the Bogalusa Voters League and CORE, was to discuss the formation of the Deacons in Bogalusa. According to Federal Bureau of Investigation (FBI) surveillance reports, Thomas informed the Bogalusa activists what was necessary to form a chapter of the Deacons. He also discussed, based upon the Jonesboro experience, the type of weapons, ammunition, and logistical support necessary for this level of paramilitary organization. According to FBI reports, the Jonesboro Deacons' spokesperson revealed to the Bogalusa group that he had contacts in Chicago and Houston who could supply automatic weapons. Thomas also spoke of the use of paramilitary armed patrols to prevent law enforcement officers from arresting movement workers.[9] The day after the meeting with Thomas, the leaders of the Voters League met to discuss the merits of forming a chapter of the Deacons, and Bogalusa activists, including Hicks and Voters League president A. Z. Young decided to form a chapter.[10]

While Robert Hicks and A. Z. Young were considered the primary spokespersons for the Bogalusa Voters League, the public representative and leader of the Bogalusa Deacons was clearly Charles Sims. A veteran of the U.S. Army and World War II, Sims was an insurance agent by profession prior to his full-time commitment to activism in 1964. Sims had earned the reputation as a troublemaker in Bogalusa. He did not fit the stereotypical image of a southern movement leader. Having been arrested before his formal entrance into the movement for carrying a concealed weapon and assault, Sims was the prototypical "Bad Negro." Sims was not a minister or an idealistic young student but a bold-talking, gun-carrying "tough" who had a reputation for verbally and physically confronting local whites. Sims did not change his image as the leader of the Deacons. In fact, his image may have been an asset in the frontier climate in this Louisiana town, where civility was not a virtue in confronting the Klan.[11]

It was in Bogalusa that the Deacons received the most publicity and notoriety, as national media reported on the existence of an armed black military presence in the southern movement for the first time since Robert Williams was forced into exile in 1961. The *Wall Street Journal* and *New Times* magazine both ran features on the Deacons in 1965. Violent confrontations ensued between the Deacons and Klan forces in the spring and summer of 1965. On several occasions armed Deacons had to rescue CORE workers from white terrorist civilians. As in Jonesboro, armed patrols of the Deacons protected Bogalusa black neighborhoods in the evenings from invading nightriders. Personal security details were also assigned to Hicks and Young. Deacon Henry Austin was arrested for shooting and critically wounding a white male, Alton Crowe, who was physically attacking participants in a demonstration on July 8. Louisiana governor John McKeithen dispatched state troops to Bogalusa to prevent further violence and threatened to disarm Deacons and Klansmen alike. McKeithen also called for negotiations between the leaders of the Voters League and local officials. Movement leaders believed that without the presence of organized, armed blacks, the governor would not have intervened.[12]

The Deacons served as a model for blacks in Mississippi and throughout the South. The effectiveness of the paramilitary Deacons in Jonesboro and Bogalusa had gained the respect and admiration of movement activists and black people in the South and the United States in general. The lack of protection provided by the FBI and the Justice Department and the inaction and complicity of state and local police with white terrorists motivated many activists to reconsider the efficacy of nonviolence. The Deacons seemed to be the natural progression for many Mississippi black activists and supporters, and armed resistance would now become more overt and organized.

Deacons Enter the Mississippi Movement

The desire of the Louisiana Deacons to expand their organization carried them across the state border into Mississippi. Charles Sims and a contingent of Bogalusa Deacons came to speak at a meeting of the MFDP in Jackson in late August 1965. Sims and the Deacons were called to Jackson in response to turmoil sparked by the shooting of Rev. Donald Thompson on the evening of August 22, 1965. Thompson was a white Unitarian minister who had been active in the movement in Jackson and on the board of the local Head Start program. Dozens of angry black youth gathered in response to the shooting of Thompson and planned to retaliate. Elder activists pleaded and ultimately discouraged the youth from acting that evening.[13]

The shooting of Thompson motivated some participants in the Jackson movement to consider organizing a chapter of the Deacons. Sims was contacted and arrived with ten Louisiana Deacons at an MFDP meeting one week after the shooting of the Unitarian minister. Roy Byrd, another visible Bogalusa Deacon, also spoke at the rally. MFDP representatives from the city of Jackson and the rest of Hinds County, Madison County, and Forrest County were present at the rally. Sims and his Deacons delegation were well received by a predominantly black Mississippi audience. Reports of the size of the audience ranged from 175 to 300.[14]

Sims pledged that the Deacons would come to the state whenever needed. The organization's Bogalusa spokesperson argued that a Deacons chapter could have prevented the shooting of Donald Thompson. If the Deacons could not stop the shooting of human rights activists, he argued, they had the capacity to find the perpetrators. Sims declared that southern whites would not respect black people until "Negroes were ready to die for their families and for their beliefs." In a speech that received several standing ovations from his Mississippi audience, the Bogalusa leader challenged the audience, stating, "It is time for you men in Jackson to wake up and be men."[15]

Immediately after the MFDP meeting, the Bogalusa Deacons sent organizers to Greenville, Natchez, and the south-central Mississippi town of Columbia. Sims and Byrd offered to return to Jackson within months to form a chapter if financial support was raised for organizers. Ultimately no Deacons chapter was formed in Jackson. The Jackson MFDP was not unanimous about forming a paramilitary arm there. MFDP executive committee member Rev. Ed King stated that the organization was not taking a stand in support of the organization, but was providing the Deacons a forum. The Mississippi State Sovereignty Commission had informants at the August 29 Jackson rally and contacted the FBI for assistance in preventing the Deacons from establishing a chapter in the city. It is not known whether state and federal operatives in the Mississippi movements were critical in preventing the establishment of a Jackson group.[16]

Sims and Byrd were able to establish a Deacons presence in Marion, Forrest, and Jones counties in southern Mississippi. Blacks in Columbia, the seat of Marion County, complained to Deacons' field organizers about incidents of nightriders firebombing and shooting at the local Freedom House. Bogalusa Deacons Roy Burris and Henry Austin were dispatched to Columbia to organize a chapter of the Deacons. On October 7, 1965, a group of forty black residents attended a meeting organized by the local MFDP for the purpose of forming a Deacons chapter under the leadership of the Bogalusa Deacons. Most of the participants in the meetings were young African American males. According to historian Lance Hill, local white supremacists fell prey to Deacons' booby traps in the road that damaged their tires. The Klansmen never returned after falling into the Deacons' trap.[17]

Bogalusa Deacons also organized Deacons in Forrest County. The Forrest County Deacons were visible in the city of Hattiesburg after the murder of NAACP leader Vernon Dahmer. On January 10, 1966, Dahmer died after repelling Klan nightriders from neighboring Jones County with shotgun blasts. The Klan set Dahmer's rural home on fire, and the Forrest County activists grabbed his weapon and fired on the Klansmen as his wife, Ellie, and ten-year-old daughter Bettie escaped from the burning house to safety. Dahmer died days later in a local hospital due to burns in his respiratory tract.

Charles Sims and Roy Byrd led a contingent of Bogalusa Deacons to Hattiesburg for a demonstration on January 15, the day of Dahmer's funeral. On January 27 leaders presented Hattiesburg and Forrest County officials with a list of demands, including employment opportunities in the public sector, the desegregation of public facilities, and implementation of federal civil rights and voting legislation.[18] The Bogalusa Deacons returned to Hattiesburg to establish a chapter. In Hattiesburg, Deacons were known as "the police unit." Like Deacons groups in other southern towns, their basic responsibility was to protect movement leaders, activists, and the black community. The Boga-lusa Deacons were able to establish a chapter in neighboring Laurel through contacts made from their work in Hattiesburg. In Laurel, the Deacons sup-ported voter registration efforts and became the basis of the paramilitary organization of a local labor movement.[19]

The Meredith March and the Louisiana Deacons

One of the most publicized campaigns and massive efforts involving the Louisiana-based Deacons in Mississippi was their participation in the James Meredith "March against Fear and Intimidation." On June 6, 1966, movement activist James Meredith was shot one day after he initiated his March against Fear. Meredith's one-man march was a challenge to the intimidation blacks had endured from white supremacist terror for centuries. He said the march would "point out and challenge the all pervasive and overriding fear that dominates the day-to-day life of the Negro in the United States—and espe-cially in Mississippi." Meredith would travel from Memphis, Tennessee, 220 miles south to Jackson. Meredith's march was interrupted two miles south of the northern Mississippi town of Hernando as he lay wounded from birdshot fired from the shotgun of sniper Aubrey James Norvell.[20]

Leaders of the national civil rights movement converged in Memphis in response to the shooting. Allowing a sniper's bullet to bring Meredith's March against Fear to an end, they believed, would be interpreted as a sig-nificant defeat for civil rights forces. Martin Luther King Jr., representing the Southern Christian Leadership Conference (SCLC); Roy Wilkins of the NAACP; Whitney Young of the Urban League; Floyd McKissick of CORE; and Stokely Carmichael, Cleve Sellers, and Stanley Wise of SNCC all rushed to Memphis, where Meredith was hospitalized. Meredith had reluctantly agreed that the movement organizations should pick up the march from the point he was assaulted in De Soto County.

The national leadership of the NAACP, Urban League, SCLC, CORE, and SNCC met at Rev. James Lawson's Centenary Methodist Church in Mem-phis on June 9, three days after the shooting of Meredith. Wilkins and Young proposed continuing Meredith's march by including nationally known per-sonalities and liberal organizations. Their proposal sought collaboration with the administration of President Lyndon Johnson and an emphasis on draw-ing the attention of national media. The NAACP and Urban League lead-ers had been in consultation with the Johnson administration on legislative objectives. They argued the goal of the march should be to build support for a new civil rights bill that would guarantee federal protection for desegregation activists.[21]

Carmichael and McKissick wanted to issue a public statement critical of the Johnson administration for failing to protect movement activists, including Meredith. Carmichael presented a proposal emphasizing indigenous Mississippi participation to encourage black voter registration, black electoral campaigns, and promotion of local black leaders.[22] Carmichael also proposed that the Louisiana-based Deacons for Defense should participate in the march. Carmichael had worked with the Deacons in the effort to build an independent black political organization, the Lowndes County Freedom Organization, in the Alabama Black Belt. The Deacons requested to participate in the march after the shooting of Meredith. Deacons founder and national spokesperson Earnest "Chilly Willy" Thomas arrived in Memphis with a contingent of Chicago Deacons and planned to coordinate security with Louisiana and Mississippi chapters of the organization. According to one northern Black Nationalist publication, the Deacons "vowed to put trigger happy whites in the cemetery."[23]

CORE supported Carmichael's proposals to emphasize grassroots black participation and include the Deacons in the March. SNCC and CORE perspectives on development of local leadership and organization were similar. CORE had developed a relationship with the Deacons from the inception of the Louisiana-based paramilitary formation. King stood in the middle of this heated debate. He was sympathetic to the criticism of the Johnson administration and Carmichael's call for a locally based emphasis of the march, but he initially disagreed with including the Deacons in the march. He was ultimately convinced to allow their participation if the march maintained the banner of nonviolence. Sensing a loss of their positions, both Wilkins and Young abandoned the effort, left Memphis, and returned to New York.[24]

The Deacons said their goal was to "patrol the perimeters of the march and protect the campsites." Their role was to protect the marchers from Klan and other white supremacist civilian attacks.[25] Deacons' national organizer Earnest Thomas told *Jet* magazine, "Some of us will join the marchers. Others will go along as observers. If a white man starts shooting again, you'll know where to find him."[26]

The Deacons' role in a march sponsored by national civil rights movement organizations represented an important shift in the black freedom movement. While continuing to march under the banner of nonviolence, the public association and acknowledgment of the Deacons signified that the movement had entered a new period. SNCC, CORE, and the SCLC and their national leadership were relying upon organized black militants, not local, state, or federal government, to defend their organizations and the participants in this campaign.

The March against Fear became a venue for the debate between nonviolence and armed resistance. One white nonviolent protestor, Rev. Theodore Seamans, argued that "the movement is no place for guns." Seamans made his comments after he observed a .45 handgun in a vehicle driven by one of the Deacons. Responding to criticism from Seamans, Earnest Thomas retorted that it was dangerous to tell blacks not to fight back in such a violent and hostile situation. The debate between Seamans and Thomas sparked a vigorous exchange between nonviolent advocates and supporters of armed resistance. The debate caught the attention of media observers. CORE field secretary Bruce Baines intervened, "If you want to discuss violence and nonviolence, don't talk around the press. This march is too important." CORE chairman Floyd McKissick maintained a deceptive and conciliatory posture with the press concerning armed security. He told the press he was not aware of arms around the campsite and insisted telling all marchers, including the Deacons, "the march must remain nonviolent. . . . I don't believe in no damn war."[27]

A growing number of activists appreciated the presence of the Deacons. SNCC members openly praised the Deacons' security efforts and role in the movement. "Everyone realized that without them [the Deacons], our lives would have been much less secure," declared Cleve Sellers. Willie Ricks proclaimed to an audience in Belzoni, "We don't have enough Deacons." The Deacons gave some marchers a feeling of security and a confidence they could prevent white terrorism. SNCC executive committee member Jesse Harris sensed: "Along the march we had no problems because all the white folks, Klansman and everybody, they knew if they came in with a threat, if a church got bombed along the way, boom . . . the Deacons were going to find you."[28] All of the spokespersons, including Thomas, insisted the march was nonviolent. But while the Deacons leader acknowledged the march was nonviolent, he openly advocated armed self-defense. With a masculinist appeal, Thomas told a rally in Belzoni, "It's time for Black men to start taking care of their Black women and children."[29]

The mainstream media were obsessed with the Deacons and the significance of their presence. Unlike marches of the past, where blacks covertly secured their comrades, observers noticed "disciplined" black men communicating with "two-way" radios. Probably more troubling were the "bulges" detected "beneath the clothing" of young men patrolling the march. While often speaking in conciliatory terms, Deacons leader Thomas was frank to the press about the presence and purpose of the organization at the march. Thomas told the press the Deacons were guarding the campsite "with pistols, rifles, and shotguns. . . . But we don't take guns with us when the people are marching. . . . The march is nonviolent." The *Memphis Commercial Appeal* reported, "Appearance of the 'Deacons' in the Mississippi marching column marked a significant, and to many a frightening shift in tactics of Negroes who for 10 years had been lulled and led by the non-violent oratory of Dr. Martin Luther King, Jr."[30]

A common theme in national coverage of the March against Fear emphasized contradictions between King and those embracing armed resistance. Observers constructed a dichotomy pitting the nonviolent King against the "violent" Deacons and Black Power militants. On June 22 a *New York Times* article titled "Dr. King Scores 'Deacons'" stated that King publicly lashed out at the "Black Power" advocates, SNCC, and the Deacons.[31]

It is clear that consenting to allow the Deacons in the march did not mean that King had abandoned his allegiance to nonviolence. On the contrary, King was disturbed by the public advocacy of armed self-defense by the Deacons and also a growing number of young activists who had rejected nonviolence. Concerning the growing support of armed resistance, one black publication quoted him as saying, "I worried about this climate." King believed a violent confrontation during the march was potentially "impractical and disastrous." He not only supported nonviolence morally but believed it was tactically viable. King argued since black people were a minority, it was impossible to achieve a strategic victory against a hostile majority through armed resistance. While King was not opposed to self-defense in the face of racist or oppressive violence, he believed demonstrations utilizing nonviolence assisted activists in achieving a moral high ground to expose injustice rather than being perceived as an aggressive protagonist.[32] In spite of his concerns, King respected the Deacons and saw them as a viable part of the movement. King's associate Andrew Young said King "would never resort to violence, even in defense of his life, but he would not and could not demand that of others. . . . He saw the Deacons as a defensive presence not a retaliatory one."[33]

The presence of the Deacons and the debate around armed resistance during the march was a significant factor in the transition away from the perception of nonviolence as the primary tactic in the black freedom movement. The Deacons' bold rhetoric and armed profile would be replicated throughout the United States by militant Black Power formations.

The Natchez Movement and the Mississippi Deacons

Paramilitary organizations were forming in Natchez in August when Charles Sims and Louisiana Deacons organizers arrived in late August 1965. The Natchez movement would not form an extension of the Louisiana Deacons but instead formed its own indigenous Mississippi Deacons for Defense.

Natchez was a Klan stronghold. The Ku Klux Klan in Natchez, led by E. L. McDaniel, was among the most violent and organized in the state. The Natchez police chief J. T. Robinson was also a vocal advocate of white supremacy and had no problems using coercive force to uphold the system of segregation. Natchez mayor John Nosser called for racial tolerance but had no effective control over the Natchez police or Chief Robinson. Some local blacks also believed the Natchez police feared the Klan.[34]

An incident in the summer of 1965 hastened racial antagonism in Adams County. On August 27 NAACP leader George Metcalf was seriously injured after a bomb hidden beneath the hood of his car exploded after he turned on the ignition. Metcalf was fortunate enough to survive the blast but had to be hospitalized suffering from facial lacerations, a broken arm and leg, and other cuts and burns. The explosive completely demolished Metcalf's vehicle and damaged several other cars nearby. The explosion of Metcalf's vehicle occurred in the parking lot of the Armstrong Tire plant, where he had just finished a shift. Some local blacks believed his supervisors had collaborated with the perpetrators of the bombing since Metcalf was asked to work overtime the evening of the bombing. The attack on Metcalf occurred eight days after the NAACP submitted a petition on behalf of Metcalf and eleven other Natchez blacks to the school board to desegregate Natchez public schools on the basis of the *Brown* decision. Metcalf had also recently contacted the Adams County chancery clerk to seek compliance with federal voter registration legislation.[35]

The terrorist attack on Metcalf was a part of a series of attacks, including house bombings and church bombings, that had been initiated since the arrival of COFO in Adams County. COFO workers and black residents of Natchez were harassed and beaten by white vigilantes and hooded members of the Klan on several occasions between 1963 and 1965. On one Saturday evening in September 1964, two explosions jarred the home of Natchez mayor John Nosser and black contractor Willie Washington. Nosser, an American of Lebanese origin, believed his home was bombed because he attempted to serve as a "peacemaker" during the racial hostilities of Freedom Summer. Metcalf's home was also sprayed with gunfire from nightriders in January

1965. Leading up to the bombing of his car, the NAACP leader was the target of several acts of harassment and intimidation at his home and his place of employment.[36]

A small group of black men met secretly in Natchez to form a paramilitary organization weeks prior to the bomb attack on George Metcalf. As in Bogalusa and Jonesboro, the Natchez paramilitary group was formed due to the perception among local movement activists and supporters that they could not rely on the police for protection. Most of the men were workers who had grown up in Adams County and had known each other most of their lives. These men were also either members or supporters of the local NAACP. The Natchez paramilitary group began to protect Metcalf, his family members, and his home prior to the bombing.[37]

The activity and the size of the Natchez group accelerated after the attack on Metcalf. James Jackson, a barber and one of the leaders of the Natchez paramilitary group, publicly announced that a chapter of the Deacons for Defense and Justice was to form on August 28, one day after the bombing attack on Metcalf. The Natchez group had heard of the success of the Louisiana Deacons in neutralizing white terrorists in Bogalusa and Jonesboro. According to Bogalusa leader Robert Hicks, Charles Evers asked some of the Louisiana Deacons to come to Natchez and help establish the organization there. Charles Sims, the spokesperson for the Louisiana Deacons, arrived in Natchez to discuss the formation of the Deacons for Defense in Adams County the day following Jackson's announcement.[38]

According to Natchez activist James Stokes, the Natchez paramilitary group decided not to affiliate with the Louisiana Deacons. While Sims offered advice on how to set up a paramilitary organization, the Natchez group thought they had little to gain from a formal affiliation with the Deacons. Stokes remembered Sims pledging no significant material aid or reinforcements to the Natchez paramilitary group. According the Stokes, Sims primarily offered the Natchez group permission to use the name of the Deacons for Defense and Justice. Sims stated the Natchez group had to pay a percentage of their dues to the Louisiana-based group in order to identify themselves as Deacons. The Natchez group rejected Sims's offer and politely asked him to leave town.[39]

While the Natchez paramilitary group decided not to officially affiliate with the Louisiana Deacons, they had no problem using their name. To friend and foe, the Natchez group became known throughout the movement and the state as the Natchez Deacons for Defense and Justice. The Natchez group formed a foundation for the Mississippi Deacons for Defense and Justice and assisted other paramilitary affiliates across the state, particularly in south-west Mississippi. The Natchez Deacons, wearing overalls and white shirts, were visible on the streets of Natchez, providing security at marches and demonstrations by early October 1965, a little over a month after the attack on Metcalf.[40]

The Natchez Deacons were officially chartered in the state of Mississippi as the Sportsmen Club. On the surface the Sportsmen Club sounded like an apolitical hunting association, but conciliatory language in its charter revealed a broader purpose. While the Sportsmen Club's charter stated the organization was "non-violent," this hunting group pledged to "abide by the U.S. Constitution (including the Second Amendment, right to bear arms)" and to "protect property." The Sportsmen Club was authorized to function anywhere in Mississippi since it was a state-chartered entity. The Sportsmen Club charter was extended to other Mississippi Deacons groups in Wilkerson, Claiborne, and Copiah counties.[41]

Like the Deacons in Louisiana, the Natchez Deacons never revealed the size of their membership. This kept the Klan, police, and FBI confused about the actual size and capability of the group. Organized much like a secret society, the Deacons realized the less their enemies knew about them the better. James Young, who joined shortly after the attack on Metcalf, revealed that the actual size of the Natchez Deacons was about ten to twelve men. As in Jonesboro and Bogalusa, a few central leaders were identified to represent the Deacons to the public. James Stokes was appointed spokesman. James Jackson was the first president of the Natchez Deacons. James Young was selected secretary and was responsible for the development of the bylaws and the charter for the Deacons and the Sportsmen Club. According to Stokes "The strongest thing we had going for ourselves is that nobody knew, not even some of our members, how many men there were in the organization." Concealing the size of their organization served as a weapon for the Deacons to instill doubt and concern in white supremacists since they really did not know the capacity of the Natchez paramilitary group.[42]

Even movement folks outside the Deacons were not privy to the identities of the entire Deacons membership. SNCC activist Hollis Watkins remembered, "It was a situation where none of us knew all of them and in many cases that was the beauty of it. . . . In some cases they'd call and say 'we'll have two or three of the brothers at y'alls rally or at y'alls meeting.' . . . You don't know who they are, because you don't know all the people from the community."[43]

Since secrecy was essential for the Deacons' mission, it was important that the organization selectively recruited its members and that its membership did not reveal its secrets. Trust was an important factor for recruitment, so the initial group only recruited men they had grown up with and knew their background and character. "Everybody we had, we knew," said James Young. A Deacons recruit had to be sponsored by someone already in the group. Anyone with a history of abusing alcohol or a criminal past was not allowed to join. The Deacons did not want to have member who could be easily compromised by police coercion.[44]

A prospective member learned the seriousness of joining the Deacons before induction into the organization. The Deacons informed their recruits that revealing organizational secrets could result in death for the informant. A founding member by the name of "Otis" expressed his seriousness about protecting the integrity of the organization at the first meeting of the Natchez Deacons in late August 1965. On that occasion "Otis" stated, "Your tongue is the worst weapon against you. . . . I mean it from the heart, that I . . . swear before God, may he kill me now if I don't mean it, for something as important as this, I'd burn my brother. I'd blow his damn brains out . . . before I'd let one guy mess up a whole lot of guys."[45] In an interview, James Stokes also emphasized how serious the Deacons viewed internal security: "If he [a Deacon] leaked anything out, we let it be known, you better figure on dying." Stokes believed no member of the Deacons ever divulged information about the Deacons to local, state, or federal law enforcement personnel.[46] The Deacons' internal security methods were apparently effective and prevented the Mississippi State Sovereignty Commission, the FBI, local police, and the Klan from receiving an adequate assessment of the size and capability of the Deacons. A small group within the membership made all of the plans in order to maintain internal security. Individual members would know their assignments, but not the entire security plan. This also prevented information from leaking to the opposition.[47]

There was a proliferation of arms in the black community in Natchez in response to the white supremacist reign of terror, which heightened in Adams County around 1963. One unidentified source in the Natchez Deacons revealed that the organization possessed "hand grenades, machine guns, whatever we needed." According to this source, only one store in Natchez would sell ammunition to the Deacons. If white supremacists knew the Deacons had a limited supply of ammunition, the Deacons defense would be compromised. To counter this, the Natchez Deacons received ammunition from outside sources. According to the unidentified source, Fidel Castro's Cuba was one source for obtaining "all the guns and ammunition we needed."[48]

Mississippi law allowed civilians to openly carry loaded weapons in public. Citizens could also carry loaded firearms in their vehicles as long as they were not concealed. This allowed the Deacons to openly carry guns to protect demonstrations, mass meetings, and community institutions. According to James Stokes, "We [the Deacons] used to walk up and down these Mississippi streets with our guns in our holsters, day and night, and they were afraid to bother us."[49] The Deacons openly carried their weapons on marches and demonstrations to protect movement activists and supporters from attack. James Stokes described how the Deacons' security worked to prevent racist violence at a march. "They [white supremacists in a vehicle] would try to break through the line [of demonstrators]. . . . We would always have Deacons at the block intersection . . . and at the end of the block. . . . And if we saw a car coming, he would see us with our guns on and he wasn't about to come that way. This is how we protected people."[50] The Natchez Deacons and the Wilkerson County chapter of the Deacons for Defense combined to scatter a mob of white supremacists on September 4, 1967, in Centreville, a small town in Wilkerson County in southwest Mississippi. Twenty-five armed Deacons responded to prevent the demonstrators from harm after a member of the racist mob trained his weapon at participants in a demonstration for voting rights for blacks.[51] Deacon James Young described the situation that day: "These peckerwoods down there, they lined up at the junction of the 15 highway. . . . They was all bad and we pulled in there. The President of the Deacons got out and come up to them and said 'Ok, unblock that road.' . . . We pulled in there and started unloading all of this heavy artillery and they loaded up and left."[52] Also present that day was SNCC activist Hollis Watkins, who remembered the leader of the Deacons stating, "We represent the Deacons for Defense. If you come in here with that you're going to be in trouble." Hearing the name "Deacons for Defense," according to Watkins, was almost as effective in scattering the racist mob as the guns.[53] The armed presence and preparedness of the Deacons prevented the movement in Natchez and in southwest Mississippi from being terrorized and intimidated. White supremacist terrorists also were on alert that any foray into the black community or in the vicinity of movement activity was not without consequence.

As in Louisiana, Mississippi state officials opposed to the movement wanted to find means to disarm the Deacons. FBI documents from September 3, 1967, reveal that a proposal was forwarded by an unnamed source to the governor of Mississippi to make it illegal for members of the Deacons for Defense in the state to possess firearms. On September 4, 1967, the same day as the confrontation between the Deacons and the white mob in Centreville, three members of the Deacons were arrested for illegal possession of firearms. The State District Attorney for the Southwestern District of Mississippi gave the Mississippi State Highway Patrol the "authority to disarm all members of the Deacons for Defense and Justice." As in other southern states, Mississippi law made it illegal for anyone to transport rifles and shotguns in the cab of a car, instead requiring that rifles and shotguns be carried on a rack on the back of a vehicle.[54]

Even though state and local authorities challenged the Deacons' possession of firearms, being armed as an organized force served as an asset to the organization and the movement. The armed organized presence of the Deacons and their preparedness for combat, as well as the uncertainty on the part of whites of the Deacons' capabilities, provided the movement with a serious bartering chip. As Stokes stated, "White people had become so fearful. Anything we wanted they was always trying to offer you a deal. Come down and talk." The presence of the Deacons combined with effective boycotts to give Charles Evers and local leaders a position of strength from which to negotiate.[55]

To have an effective paramilitary operation, logistical support was necessary. The Deacons possessed walkie-talkies, citizens band radios, and vehicles that were equipped with radios to aid them in paramilitary functions. The Deacons developed codes to confuse enemy surveillance by the Klan and local police collaborating with white supremacists. The Natchez Deacons raised funds for communication equipment, vehicles, ammunition, and weapons through speaking engagements by their spokesperson James Stokes and financial contributions from civic groups in the North. In October 1965 Stokes participated in a fund-raising tour in California, speaking at San Mateo College and to civic groups and movement supporters.[56]

In the field visible members of the Deacons wore badges as identification and carried permits for their weapons. Law enforcement officers, particularly highway patrol and local police, were informed by Deacons' officials not to interfere with Deacons attempting to protect movement demonstrators from racist attackers. In some cases, the Deacons had negotiated with law enforcement officers to serve Deacons with traffic violations later, if they were speeding to come to the rescue of activists or members of the black community. James Young stated law enforcement officers were told, "If you see one of these men moving [to the defense of movement activists, supporters, or members of the Black community] . . . get his tag [license plate] and get out of the way."[57]

The Deacons became an essential ingredient in the Natchez and Mississippi movements. They provided the movements with an instrument to neutralize the violence of Klan and other white supremacist civilians. The potential of the Deacons for Defense and retaliatory violence also gave Evers and other leaders more potency in their negotiating position with the white power structure and allowed them to be more bold in their public statements. The Natchez movement was able to organize an effective consumer boycott. Their formula included the protection and visible security profile of the Deacons, rhetoric openly advocating armed resistance, and the use of enforcer squads to chastise blacks who attempted to shop in white-owned businesses in the Natchez commercial district. Evers's lieutenant, Rudy Shields, was the organizer of the enforcer efforts. This model of resistance would be replicated in other communities in southwest Mississippi and other parts of the state.

The Mississippi Deacons and the Natchez Boycott Paradigm

The formula developed in Natchez to combat the local white power structure to win concessions toward human and civil rights was utilized in other parts the state, particularly in southwest Mississippi communities. Other communities observing the success of the Natchez boycott began to organize boycotts using the model developed in Natchez. Evers and Shields were invited to provide leadership for boycotts in Jefferson, Claiborne, Wilkerson, and Forrest counties. The Natchez model had proven the necessity to utilize the threat of a coercive response to defeat external and internal enemies of the Mississippi freedom movement. When Evers and Shields became involved in boycott campaigns in Jefferson and Wilkerson counties—both of which were contiguous to Adams County—the Natchez Deacons became directly involved. Wilkerson County activists established their own chapter of the Deacons for Defense and Justice. While having their own chapter of the Mississippi Deacons for Defense and Justice, the Wilkerson Deacons received personnel and support from the Natchez Deacons and virtually came under their chain of command.[58]

Several communities established Deacons chapters that were more autonomous from the Natchez group than those in Claiborne and Copiah counties. When NAACP-led boycotts developed in Claiborne County and in the towns of Hazlehurst and Crystal Springs in Copiah County, these communities organized their own chapters of the Mississippi Deacons for Defense and Justice. In all of these communities, the Deacons and enforcer squads were organized as part of boycott campaigns to pressure the white power structure to concede to demands similar to those presented by black leaders in Natchez.

The Claiborne County Deacons for Defense and Justice was among the most visible paramilitary organizations in the state. The Deacons for Defense and the enforcer squads, now known as "Da Spirit," were organized in Claiborne County after the black community, under the leadership of Evers and the local NAACP, called for a boycott on April 1, 1966. The Deacons were organized after Rudy Shields arranged a meeting between James Stokes, state spokesman for the Mississippi Deacons for Defense and Justice based in Natchez, and local NAACP activists and supporters prior to the initiation of the boycott. After forming a chapter of the Deacons, Claiborne County activists officially resigned their membership in the NAACP.[59]

Friend and foe alike in Claiborne County called the local Deacons chapter "the Black Hats" because Claiborne Deacons wore black helmets while on duty during the evening and black straw hats in daytime hours. Khaki pants were also part of their uniform. The Black Hats first appeared in public on April 1, 1966, the day the boycott was initiated in Port Gibson. The Deacons came out to protect the NAACP picket of white merchants in downtown Port Gibson. Claiborne Deacons president George Walker remembered, "We [the Deacons] were in the street all day, because we didn't know what they [the white supremacists] were going to do." The Deacons also patrolled the African American community during the evening, specifically monitoring the activity of the local police, the Klan, and other white supremacist forces. The Claiborne Deacons for Defense and Justice were determined to prevent "another Neshoba County" from happening in their county.[60]

Rudy Shields, who served as the principal organizer of the boycott, received special attention from the Claiborne Deacons. Shields received an escort by armed Deacons when entering or leaving Claiborne County. Natchez Deacons took responsibility for Shields's security when the activist left Claiborne to travel south to Jefferson County. One evening in 1966 armed Deacons came to the aid of Shields in a confrontation with two police officers. The police were responding to an argument between Shields and a group of black supporters and a white merchant in downtown Port Gibson. Armed Deacons positioned themselves on a building above Shields and the merchant before the police arrived on the scene. When the two police officers arrived, arms drawn and threatening the boycott organizer and the other militants around him, George Walker remembered Shields responding, "I tell you what officer. . . . You got your weapon on me and you got your weapon on the rest of the people out here. . . . If you shoot me tonight, you gonna die too, 'cause if you don't believe it, there's guns on you too." According to Walker, upon hearing Shields's threats, the two white officers returned to their car and left the scene. Shields engaged in more bold agitation and confrontation with white merchants and police with the protection of armed Deacons.[61] The boycott of white-owned enterprises in Port Gibson lasted over three years, driving several white merchants out of business.

Rudy Shields left Claiborne County and worked with militant activists to organize boycotts in Ferriday, Louisiana (across the Mississippi River from Natchez), and in Hazlehurst and Crystal Springs in Copiah County during 1967. Shields established a paramilitary organization calling itself the Deacons for Defense in each of those communities as part of his strategy of organizing boycotts. Shields left southwest Mississippi in 1968 to organize a boycott in Humphreys County. He did not organize a Deacons group there, but, realizing that the white power structure feared the Deacons, he threatened on several occasions to bring the Deacons to the south Delta county. Along with his previous affiliation with the Deacons, Shields used his threats to involve Deacons in the consumer boycott and other activism to neutralize attacks by white supremacist civilians and police on movement leaders and the African American community. Shields later organized boycotts in Yazoo City (1969) and Aberdeen and West Point (1970) before returning to spark protests in Jackson (in the aftermath of the shooting deaths on Jackson State's campus) in 1971, and finally residing in Yazoo County, Mississippi, until he died in 1987. In Yazoo, Shields reorganized "Da Spirit" as a protective and enforcer squad not only to aid boycotts in the county but also as a permanent armed wing of the Yazoo County movement.[62]

Conclusion

The Louisiana Deacons and the homegrown Mississippi Deacons played a significant role in the Mississippi black freedom movement. The Deacons helped win significant concessions for blacks in communities such as Natchez, Port Gibson, Fayette, Woodville, Hattiesburg, Crystal Springs, and Hazlehurst, where the Deacons provided security for consumer boycotts and other movement efforts and often neutralized the violence of white supremacists. The Deacons were an essential component for the efficacy of the movement in these communities. The role they played in the 1966 Meredith March against Fear helped increase voter registration in the state and the overall sense of African American empowerment in the movement.

The shift to an emphasis on paramilitary organization represents an ideological shift in the southern movement. The rhetoric of nonviolence was challenged by militant voices that embraced armed resistance and openly challenged white supremacist forces. The language of reconciliation was being replaced with words of retaliation and the style of armed militancy. The tough speech of Earnest Thomas, Charles Sims, James Young, and Rudy Shields in some ways preceded or at least was parallel with that of Stokely Carmichael and H. Rap Brown in the Black Power stage of the movement. The profile of armed Deacons for Defense also served as a model for Black Power organizations like the Black Panther Party for Self-Defense.

The style of the Deacons also represented a greater emphasis on masculinity in the black freedom movement. By challenging black men to assume the role of protecting black women and children, Sims and Thomas were consistent with the masculinist appeal of their contemporary in the North, Malcolm X. Prior to 1964–1965 the nature of armed resistance and self-defense in the Mississippi Freedom Movement tended to be informal, compared to the character of the Deacons. Women like Ora Bryant, Annie Reeves, Laura McGhee, Unita Blackwell, and countless others regularly participated in the defense of their homes and communities. Women, though, rarely participated in patrols of the community. The original Jonesboro Deacons included four female members in its formation.[63] Subsequent Deacons groups were all male. The movement toward paramilitary organization further institutionalized the function of armed resistance as a male responsibility as it became more organized and specialized. The idea of defending the community became equated with manhood.

The Deacons helped change the style and emphasis of the Mississippi movement as it continued after 1964 until the late 1970s. Black activists continued the tradition of armed resistance and bold rhetoric in the black freedom movement in campaigns in West Point (1970), Okolona (1978), Holly Springs (1977), and Tupelo (1978). The Deacons established a legacy in Mississippi that was modeled in the Mississippi freedom movement for over a decade. The role and example of the Deacons were critical factors in the achievement of civil and human rights for African Americans in Mississippi and the South.

NOTES

Some parts of this essay were originally printed in Akinyele Umoja, "The Ballot and the Bullet: A Comparative Analysis of Armed Resistance in the Civil Rights Movement," *Journal of Black Studies* (March 1999). The sections are reprinted here with the permission of Sage Publications.

1. John Fitzgerald and James Jackson quoted in *Black Natchez* (videorecording), produced by Ed Pincus and David Neuman, Center for Social Documentary Films (1965).

2. Akinyele Umoja, "'We Will Shoot Back': The Natchez Model and Para-Military Organization in the Mississippi Freedom Movement," *Journal of Black Studies* 32, no. 3 (Fall 2002): 267–290.

3. Gwendolyn Hall, "Jonesboro: The Red River Valley Again" (unpublished manuscript), 1–4, Box 1, Folder 7, Gwendolyn Hall Papers, Amistad Research Center, Tulane University, New Orleans; Herman Porter, "An Interview with Deacon for Defense," *Militant* 29, no. 42 (November 22, 1965): 1.

4. Roy Reed, "The Deacons, Too, Ride by Night," *New York Times Magazine*, August 15, 1965, 10; Porter, "Interview with Deacon"; "Jonesboro 'Deacons' Offer Example for Rights Forces," *Militant* 29, no. 9 (March 1, 1965): 1; "Deacons for Defense and Justice Articles of Incorporation," Box 1, Folder 3, Gwendolyn Hall Papers.

5. "Jonesboro 'Deacons.'"

6. Porter, "Interview with Deacon"; Hall, "Jonesboro," 17.

7. "Bogalusa, Louisiana," Congress of Racial Equality (CORE) Papers, 1959–1976, microfilm; "The Bogalusa Negro Community," CORE Papers; "The Man in Middle," *Time*, July 23, 1965, 19.

8. Robert Hicks, interview by Robert Wright, August 10, 1969, Bogalusa, La., Civil Rights Documentation Project, Howard University, Washington, D.C.

9. "United States Government Memorandum, From: W. C. Sullivan, From: F. J. Baugardner, Subject: Deacons for Defense and Justice Information Concerning (Internal Security)," February 26, 1965.

10. Ibid.; "Bogalusa Incidents Addition," March 25, 1965, CORE Papers; Hicks interview.

11. For an example of Sims's attitude and demeanor, see interviews with him including "The Deacons . . . and Their Impact," *National Guardian*, September 4, 1965, 4–5; and "Charles Sims," in Howell Raines, *My Soul Is Rested: Movement Days in the Deep South Remembered* (New York: G. P. Putnam's Sons, 1977), 416–423.

12. "Man in the Middle," 19; "Deacons . . . and Their Impact," 4; Reed, "Ride by Night," 20; Roy Reed, "White Man Is Shot by Negro in Clash in Bogalusa," *New York Times*, July 9, 1965, 1.

13. "Jackson Mississippi" (August 24–25, 1965), Sovereignty Commission, Mississippi Department of Archives and History (MDAH), 2-161-0-2-1-1-1, http://mdah .state.ms.us/arrec/digital_archives/sovcom/result.php?   image=/data/sov_com mission/images/png/cd07/051486.png&otherstuff=2|161|0|2|1|1|1|50759|; "Serenity Home," http://transientandpermanent.wordpress.com/2008/06/09/rev-brooks-walkers-home-was-bombed-the-answer-to-todays-quiz/.

14. Roy Reed, "Deacons in Mississippi Visits, Implores Negroes to 'Wake Up,'" *New York Times*, August 30, 1965, 18, Pro Quest Historical Newspapers.

15. Ibid.

16. Ibid.

17. "Investigation of a report that the Freedom Democratic Party would have a meeting in Columbia, MS, on October 7 1965 for the purpose of organizing a chapter of the Deacons for Defense," Mississippi State Sovereignty Commission, MDAH, http://mdah.state.ms.us/arrec/digital_archives/sovcom/result.php?image=/data/sov_commission/images/png/cd01/006134.png&otherstuff=2|31|0|19|1|1|1|5976|; Lance Hill, *The Deacons for Defense: Armed Resistance in the Civil Rights Movement* (Chapel Hill: University of North Carolina Press, 2004), 212–213.

18. "Black Community Leader Killed in Klan Bombing, Hattiesburg, Mississippi," Vernon Dahmer File, University of Southern Mississippi Archives, Hattiesburg; W. F. Minor, "Rights Leader Buried in Mississippi," *New Orleans Times Picayune*, January 16, 1966, 2.

19. Mississippi State Sovereignty Commission investigative report by A. L (Andy) Hopkins, "Observation and Investigation in Hattiesburg, Forrest County, Mississippi, January 17 and 18," January 20, 1966, Governor Paul Johnson Papers, University of Southern Mississippi Archives; Sam Simmons, interview by author, July 25, 1994, Laurel, Miss.; Memorandum: From Lee Cole to E. Johnston, "Boycott in Hattiesburg, Mississippi," July 21, 1967, Sovereignty Commission, MDAH, 2-64-1-111-1-1-1, http://mdah.state.ms.us/arrec/digital_archives/sovcom/result.php?image=/data/sov_commission/images/png/cd04/026942.png&otherstuff=2|64|1|111|1|1|1|26439|.

20. "Mississippi Story," *New York Times*, June 12, 1966, 20, ProQuest Historical Newspapers; "Heat on Highway 51," *Time*, June 17, 1966, http://www.time.com/time/magazine/article/0,9171,899204,00.html. Norvell was apprehended and charged with assault with intent to commit murder. He pleaded guilty before trial and received a five-year sentence, of which he served eighteen months. Carolyn Kleiner Butler, "Down in Mississippi: The Shooting of Protester James Meredith 38 Years Ago, Seemingly Documented by a Rookie Photographer, Galvanized the Civil Rights Movement," *Smithsonian Magazine* (February 2005), http://www.smithsonianmag.com/history-archaeology/Down_In_Mississippi.html.

21. Roy Wilkins, with Tom Mathews, *Standing Fast: The Autobiography of Roy Wilkins* (New York: Viking Press, 1982), 315; Steve Lawson, *The Pursuit of Power: Southern Blacks and Electoral Politics 1965–1982* (New York: Columbia University Press, 1985), 51.

22. Lawson, *Pursuit of Power*, 51–52; Kwame Ture, with Ekwueme Michael Thelwell, *Ready for Revolution: The Life and Struggles of Stokely Carmichael [Kwame Ture]* (New York: Scribner, 2003), 496–497.

23. Ture, *Ready for Revolution*, 493, 497; Jesse Harris, interview by author, July 23, 2009, Jackson, Miss.; Hill, *Deacons for Defense*, 246; "Black Power," *Now: News of the Nation and the World* 2, no. 5 (Summer 1967): 5.

24. Ture, *Ready for Revolution*, 497–500; Henry Hampton and S. Fayer, *Voices of Freedom: An Oral History of the Civil Rights Movement from the 1950s through the 1980s* (New York: Bantam Books, 1990), 284–289; Cleveland Sellers, with Robert Terrell, *The River of No Return: The Autobiography of a Black Militant and the Life and Death of SNCC* (Jackson: University Press of Mississippi, 1990), 162–163; Harris interview.

25. Ture, *Ready for Revolution*, 502.

26. Chester Higgins, "Meredith Threat to Arm: Not Answer, Says Dr. King," *Jet*, June 23, 1966, 18.

27. Gene Roberts, "Marchers Upset by Negro Apathy," *New York Times*, June 14, 1966, ProQuest Historical Newspapers, 19; Lester Sobel, *Civil Rights 1960–66* (New York: Facts on File, 1966), 393.

28. Sellers, *River of No Return*, 166; Gene Roberts, "Marchers Stage Mississippi Rally," *New York Times*, June 18, 1966, 1; Harris interview.

29. Roberts, "Marchers Ranks Expand," 20.

30. James K. Cazalas, "Deacons Play Role at March," *Commercial Appeal*, June 26, 1966, Sovereignty Commission, MDAH, 11-11-0-20-1-1-1.

31. Martin Luther King Jr., *Where Do We Go From Here: Chaos or Community?* (New York: Harper and Row, 1968), 26–27, 55–59.

32. Higgins, "Meredith Threat," 18; King, *Where Do We Go*, 26–27, 55–59.

33. Andrew Young quoted in Ture, *Ready for Revolution*, 497.

34. "Cops, Race Strife Cut Tourist Trade in Natchez," *Muhammad Speaks*, September 25, 1964; James Young, interview by author, July 28, 1994, Natchez, Miss.

35. Jesse Bernard Williams, interview by author, July 24, 2009, Natchez, Miss.; "Natchez Mayor Offers Reward for Bomber," *Clarion-Ledger*, August 28, 1965, 1; Charles Horowitz, "Natchez, Mississippi-Six Weeks of Crisis," October 9, 1965, Freedom Information Center document, Freedom Information Service Archives (FISA), Jackson, Miss.; "Desegregation Petition Filed," *Natchez Democrat*, August 20, 1965, 1; Young interview; John Dittmer, *Local People: The Struggle for Civil Rights in Mississippi* (Urbana: University of Illinois Press, 1994), 354.

36. "Natchez Bombing Is Laid to Whites," *New York Times*, September 27, 1964; "Police Push Investigations of Blasts That Hit Natchez," *Clarion-Ledger/Jackson Daily News*, September 27, 1964, A1; "Two More Burned Out Churches Dedicated," *Clarion-Ledger*, March 22, 1965; "Statement of Events in Natchez, Miss.—November 1 and 2, 1963," Freedom Vote for Governor, FISA; "Leader Claims Five Slayings," *Jackson Daily News*, May 7, 1964.

37. James Stokes, interview by author, tape recording, August 1994, Natchez, Miss.; Transcript of film *Black Natchez* (1965).

38. Stokes interview; "Bombing Angers Natchez Negroes," *New York Times*, August 29, 1965, L51; Hicks interview.

39. Stokes interview; Young interview.

40. Horowitz, "Natchez," 6.

41. Ed Cole, interview by author, July 24, 1994, Jackson, Miss.; Stokes interview; Young interview.

42. Stokes interview; Young interview.

43. Hollis Watkins, interview by author, July 13, 1994, Jackson, Miss.

44. Stokes interview; Young interview.

45. *Black Natchez.*

46. Stokes interview.

47. Ibid.; Young interview.

48. Deacon Informant X, interview by author. This informant chose not to be identified in this study due to the sensitive nature of his comments. He was interviewed in the summer of 1964 in Natchez. He was active in the Deacons from its inception until its demise. Charles Evers also spoke of the Deacons possessing hand grenades in Charles Evers, with Grace Hansell, *Evers* (Fayette, Miss.: Charles Evers, 1976), 132.

49. Stokes interview.

50. Ibid.

51. "Marches Sponsored by National Association for the Advancement of Colored People at Woodville and Centreville, Mississippi, to Protest Election Results September 2, 4, 1967," 14, FBI Racial Matters, document, National Archives, Washington, D.C., September 6, 1967.

52. Young interview.

53. Watkins interview.

54. "Marches by NAACP," FBI Racial Matters, document, National Archives, Washington, D.C.; Stokes interview.

55. Stokes interview; Cole interview.

56. "Deacons for Defense and Justice, Inc.," FBI Racial Matters, report, March 28, 1966, 5–8.

57. Young interview.

58. Stokes interview; Lillie Brown, interview by author, July 29, 1994, Fayette, Miss.; Samuel Harden, interview by author, October 1994, Woodville, Miss.

59. George Walker, interview by author, September 29, 1994, Port Gibson, Miss.; Emilye Crosby, *A Little Taste of Freedom: The Black Freedom Struggle in Claiborne County, Mississippi* (Chapel Hill: University of North Carolina Press, 2005).

60. Walker interview.

61. Ibid.

62. Ibid.; Herman Leach, interview by author, 1994, Yazoo City, Miss.

63. "From: Frederick Brooks to: Oretha Castle—North Louisiana Director of CORE, Jackson Parish, Jonesboro, Louisiana," Box 3, Folder 14, Gwendolyn Hall Papers.

Robert Clark and
the Ascendancy to Black Power

The Case of the Mississippi Black State Legislators

Byron D'Andra Orey

> Let's see what you can do to deliver goods and services. . . . The thing I want
> to know is: are you going to feed my people? Are there going to be jobs and
> services and hospitals in my communities that are going to meet the needs of
> my people?
> —Andrew Young

The Voting Rights Act of 1965 arguably serves as the most important legislative victory for blacks, save for the Thirteenth, Fourteenth, and Fif-
teenth Amendments. Indeed, prior to the passage of the Voting Rights Act,
blacks in Mississippi had not been able to elect an African American to the
state legislature since 1896. The Voting Rights Act had an immediate impact
on the state of Mississippi, as the percentage of blacks registered to vote increased from 6.7 percent in 1964 to roughly 60 percent by 1967. Such an
increase posed a direct threat to white political hegemony, thereby leading
whites to stage a massive resistance to black political progress. Despite such
resistance, however, blacks were able to elect a black to the state legislature in
1967. Since then, blacks have seen their numbers increase exponentially, with
forty-nine blacks holding seats in the state legislature as of 2010.

While much of the scholarship on black state legislators has focused on
descriptive gains made by racial and ethnic minority groups, there has been
very little research addressing substantive representation. According to Hannah Pitkin, descriptive representation refers to the physical traits of an elected official (for example, race and gender). Substantive representation, on the
other hand, refers to whether the legislator introduces legislation on behalf of

his or her constituency.[1] Indeed, the above words of Andrew Young speak to the needs associated with progressive legislation on behalf of blacks in Mississippi. In addition to exploring whether the increase in black legislators has led to an increase in substantive representation, this essay also investigates the extent to which these legislators have acquired power in the state legislature. Political scientists have described power as occurring when one actor can convince another actor to behave in a way he or she normally would not behave. Given the racially polarized history of Mississippi, the question is whether blacks can persuade whites to help them achieve their progressive agenda. This essay makes use of the oral histories collection from the University of Southern Mississippi and Jackson State University's Oral History & Cultural Heritage collection.

In *Politics and Society in the South*, Earl Black and Merle Black conclude that despite the increase in black registered voters as a result of the Voting Rights Act, blacks remain "tangential" to the political process in the South because there are very few jurisdictions where blacks make up a majority of registered voters.[2] In addressing this issue, Frank Parker poses the question: "Do Mississippi's black voters remain tangential, or do they wield real political power now?"[3] In answering this question, the research here builds on my previous work on Mississippi black state legislators. In a 2000 article in the *Journal of Black Studies*, I examined the substantive nature of bills introduced by black state legislators, and the passage rates of these bills. The bills most frequently introduced by African Americans during the 1987 session were education bills, followed by suffrage bills and bills dealing with the legal system and health care. While the education, health care, and legal system bills are fairly obvious as fitting within the progressive category, the suffrage category is not so simple. Suffrage bills in Mississippi are those bills that are introduced by a legislator for the purpose of restoring voting rights to an ex-felon. In other words, if a citizen is convicted of a felony, one of the means for restoring his or her rights is by placing a request to his or her state legislator, whereby the legislator would introduce a bill to have the citizen's rights restored.[4] Admittedly, as an empiricist I failed to investigate the importance of these bills when first researching this topic. In other words, I simply reported the high frequency of suffrage bills without explaining why these bills were deemed to be substantive for the black community. Such an omission points to one of the weaknesses of conducting systematic analyses without investigating the background of the bill. Hence, one of the purposes of this essay is to provide anecdotes from members of the Mississippi Legislative Black Caucus documenting their experiences in providing substantive representation for blacks. Because the increase in black state legislators occurred over time, and given the fact that there were certain interventions (for example, laws and court decisions) put in place to assist in the election of blacks to the state legislature, this essay proceeds with a discussion of the events that served as the impetus behind the progressive changes that have occurred in the legislature.

Following the passage of the Voting Rights Act in 1965, the increase in black registered voters in the state of Mississippi posed a direct threat to white political dominance. As a result, white legislators staged a massive resistance to the political participation, and, by extension, the political incorporation of blacks by diluting the black vote.[5] One successful strategy adopted in combating black political empowerment was the creation of multimember districts. This approach proved to be extremely successful in preventing black voters from electing the candidates of their choice. However, in one instance, the resistant forces were unable to prevent the election of a black state legislator. In 1967 Robert Clark, an African American schoolteacher, defied all odds when he defeated a white incumbent, J. P. Love. Clark's victory allowed him to become the first black to be elected to the Mississippi state legislature since the Reconstruction era.

Clark's election is particularly noteworthy given that he ran as an independent under the Mississippi Freedom Democratic Party (MFDP), led by Fannie Lou Hamer. The MFDP, a product of the Student Nonviolent Coordinating Committee (SNCC), was organized in response to the state Democratic Party's exclusion of blacks from participating in any party activities. Despite the cohesive efforts on the part of whites in diluting the black vote, blacks failed to unify in their efforts to combat such resistance. During preparation for the 1967 elections, the MFDP collided with the National Association for the Advancement of Colored People (NAACP) over which strategies should be adopted to run black candidates for office. The NAACP's strategy was to force its way into the Democratic Party by running candidates under the party's label, while the MFDP decided to run candidates as independents. In all, thirty-two black candidates in eight counties followed the strategy of the MFDP and ran as independents. All of the candidates, with the exception of one, ran in counties located in the Mississippi Delta, the region housing the state's largest black population. The most intense effort by the MFDP occurred in majority-black Holmes County, where a slate of eleven candidates vied for political office.[6] Robert Clark emerged as the lone victor among candidates vying for state legislative seats.

Like many blacks, Robert Clark was inspired to run for the House of Representatives because of the failure of the political system in dealing with issues that confronted the black community. In Clark's case, he sought out support from the school board to create an adult literacy program in Holmes County. His rationale was rooted in the logic that educated parents would be better able to help their children with their homework. He met with the school board, which responded in what he took to be a nonsupportive way, informing him, "when the superintendent asks for an adult education program, we will have one."[7] In short, the board ignored Clark's plea. In response, Clark immediately announced his candidacy for superintendent. However, legislators from his district proposed and passed legislation making the superintendent position an appointed position. Hence, knowing that he would not be appointed, he decided to run for a seat in the state legislature and emerged victorious. Prior to being seated in the legislature, rumors had surfaced suggesting that Clark's opponent, Love, had attempted to persuade his former colleagues not to seat him. As a result, Clark was escorted into the chambers by attorney Marion Wright (now Wright Edelman). According to Clark, members of the legislature informed Love that "the people of Holmes County had spoken" and that Clark would be seated. While walking on the legislative floor, Clark recalls vividly seeing an

> elderly white gentleman, weighed about 240, and he stood about six four or five. And he came down the aisle, running towards me at a half-trot, and I didn't know what to expect. And just before I [attempted to drop] my shoulder on him, being a football coach, and him being that big, and I didn't weigh but 160 then. Just before I dropped that shoulder on him, he stuck his hand out and said, "I am Marvin Henley and I'm from Philadelphia, Mississippi." And when he said that, you know, right after the three civil rights [workers] incident in Philadelphia, I said to myself, "God in heaven knows, I'm glad I didn't know that you was from Philadelphia, because if I had, the way you was coming toward me, I would have attacked you first!" (laughter). But he stuck his hand out, and said, "I'm Marvin Henley. I'm from Philadelphia, Mississippi." And he says, "I want to welcome you to this house, and I look forward to working with you." And me and him developed a good friendship.[8]

In his bid for the state legislature, Clark campaigned on the platform of health care, justice under the law, and education. During his first year in the legislature, Clark assumed that his bills would not get out of committee. As a result, he attempted to impact legislation by offering amendments to proposed bills. However, that process was equally ineffective. Clark notes:

I found it very difficult to get recognized on the floor of the House. When I would stand, the speaker at the time would look over me to a certain extent. Then, somebody would get up and make a motion, move the previous question. Then, when I could get the floor, they would go to walking and talking and laughing, you know, and just ignoring me, just like I don't exist. And one of the things that I began to do. I knew how much time I had, and I would start to winding down, like I'm [getting ready] to stop, and they would come running back out of the cloak rooms and etc., but no sooner would they come back to the floor, I would start off again, just to harass them. But finding it very difficult to get to the floor of the House, one afternoon, my first year here, it was a gloomy afternoon in January. And I just got fed up with it. And I got up, and I couldn't get recognized to get the floor of the House. And I got everything in my desk drawer, and I cleaned it out, and started out. Bill Minor . . . was working for the *New Orleans Times Picayune*, and Butch Lambert from Lee County. Butch and I had developed somewhat of a friendship because I was an official before I came here, and Butch Lambert was an official. And we refer to each other as "Coach." So, Butch and Bill came out, and attempted to stop me, and I kept on walking, heading back towards my car. Then they got around me and surrounded me, and Bill Minor told me, Well, they are up there laughing, now. You've done exactly what they want you to do. And when Bill said that (laughter) I turned around, and when they knew anything, I was walking back in.[9]

Clark not only walked back into the House chambers, but he remained there for thirty-five years, retiring in 2003. It is not surprising that one of the primary interests of Clark, a former educator, was in the area of education reform. From his first day in the state legislature, Clark pushed for education reform. He was defeated at every turn. During his first year in the legislature, he recalls how the chairman of the Education Committee waited until he left to attend the funeral of Martin Luther King Jr. to kill his bill on education reform.

After a few years of experience in the legislature, Clark had learned a few strategies to persuade members to support his initiatives. However, other legislators were equally strategic. On several occasions when he had lined up support for his education reform bill, some members of the Education Committee would leave the room, resulting in the absence of a quorum. Clark responded with yet another strategy. This time he devised a plan to have some members leave the room and hide out in the cloakroom. Once the other members who were in opposition of the bill walked out, he found all of those in support of the bill and forced the bill out of the committee. While the bill did get out of the committee, it was killed by members of the Rules Committee, as they pushed the bill back to the end of the legislative calendar.

The Power of Committee Chairs

In 1976 Clark was appointed to serve as the vice chairman of the Education Committee in the House. Shortly after this appointment, the chair of the committee resigned to take an appointment with President Carter's administration. While it seemed a sure bet that Clark would move into the chairmanship, his chances were put at risk following a "self-help" speech made at an NAACP convention in Vicksburg. During that speech, Clark told listeners that the days of "handouts are over. Gifts are over. You've got to do it yourself. You've got to use what you have to do it for yourself." The next day the headline in the Vicksburg newspaper read, "Potential Education Committee Chairman Gives Black Power Speech to the NAACP Convention." This led to a letter-writing campaign to the Speaker of the House from members of the Speaker's district. A few days later the Speaker summoned Clark to his office. As Clark took his seat, he noticed all of the letters bashing his comments scattered across the Speaker's desk. So the Speaker said, "You see all these clippings?" In recollecting the incident, Clark said that he thought that the Speaker was about to say, "No way I can appoint you." To his surprise, however, the Speaker said, "There's not a vacancy, yet. But if there is a vacancy, I will appoint you."[10]

Clark eventually was appointed chair of the Education Committee. Despite having the influence to move his education bill out of committee, the bill continued to be pushed to the back of the calendar by the Rules Committee. Since the Speaker appointed the members of the Rules Committee, Clark rounded up his vice chair and another colleague and scheduled a meeting with the Speaker. Clark informed the Speaker that he would make a motion to have the bill moved from the "heel of the calendar to the top of the calendar." The Speaker responded by asking him not to do that. His justification was that "some of the boys can't stand the heat." Clark responded, "Mr. Speaker, first of all, there ain't supposed to be no boys on the floor of that House." He continued by stating, "But, if it is, they ought to be able to stand the heat or get out of the kitchen." The Speaker responded, "Well, I'm not going to recognize you." Clark then reached out his hand and shook the Speaker's hand, and said, "Well, Mr. Speaker, I'm sure going to make the motion, and I hope we'll still be friends." During the next session, Clark stuck to his word. He rose to his feet, and the Speaker asked, "What does the gentle-man from Holmes wish to seek to be recognized for?" Clark responded by asking for a motion. After motioning to move the bill up on the calendar, the Speaker abruptly rapped his gavel. He then responded, "You're not recog-nized!" Clark's vice chair stood, went through the same process as Clark, and the Speaker again indicated that he, too, was not recognized. At that time, one of the Speaker's supporters rose and motioned for the House to adjourn. During the vote, the ayes responded with a very small number, thus resulting in a very weak "Aye." The no voters responded in a resounding "No!" Despite the vote, the Speaker rapped his gavel and said, "House adjourned." In Clark's opinion, this dictatorial behavior was the beginning of the Speaker's demise.[11]

In 1982, working closely with Governor William Winter, Clark revisited his education bill by introducing the Education Reform Act. This bill in-cluded, among other items, provisions related to early childhood education, compulsory school attendance, and teachers' assistance. Two distinct bills passed in the House and Senate, thereby calling for the bills to be recon-ciled in the Conference Committee. Clark's colleagues, consisting of three members from the House and three members from the Senate, nominated and elected Clark to serve as the chair of the Conference Committee. Af-ter vehemently opposing any type of provision that would raise taxes, Clark eventually, through the advice of the Speaker (who ironically was against the bill) and governor, compromised to include an increase in the sales tax. Clark summarizes his decision as follows:

> I used my wisdom to understand that these little, poor children that I'd been fighting for years, and I had fought for many of their parents to get the same opportunity, but did not, and that if I did not vote for some sales taxes, who would be hurt the most? Would it be the people I wanted to help or the people they wanted to help? And I realized the situation that I was in. So, fi-nally, late one night, I decided to go ahead and put some sales tax in the bill. We limited the sales taxes, and when I went out of the room and attempted to get to the hall, a white senator from the Gulf Coast came up in my face, and called me a white-loving [nigger] S.O.B. Because I went for some sales taxes. And when he said that, I jumped at him, but I'm glad that the crowd was there and kept me from catching him because as fast as he was mov-ing, I don't know if I would have caught him or not. But I am proud that I did that, and I did the right thing because it was the poor people that was hurting, and the white people that was in business. They wasn't hurting right then, but they were going to hurt, if they don't get an educated populace.

The bill ultimately passed out of the Conference Committee and was signed into law by Governor Winter, marking a successful move on the part of Clark.[12]

Power in Numbers

Robert Clark served as the lone black legislator until 1976. In 1971 the Justice Department, under Section 5 of the Voting Rights Act, rejected Mississippi's reapportionment plan for the state legislature on the grounds that it possessed a "discriminatory purpose."[13] Following the orders of the district court, the previously submitted legislative plan was accepted, provisionally, after state legislators managed to create single-member districts in heavily black-populated Hinds County. The newly created districts in Hinds County, in addition to Clark's district, included three districts where the black population ranged from 70 to 91 percent. As a result, Clark was joined by three additional black legislators in the House. The three newly elected blacks, all from the state capital of Jackson, included Doug Anderson, a college professor; Horace Buckley, an assistant school principal; and Fred Banks, a civil rights attorney.[14]

Fred Banks returned to the state of Mississippi after earning a law degree at Howard University. Upon his return to the state, he immediately began working for the NAACP Legal Defense Fund. During that time he focused his energies primarily in the area of school desegregation. Once elected to the House, he simply continued addressing many of the same issues that he focused on with the NAACP Legal Defense Fund. He states,

> I campaigned on the theory that government ought to be an equal opportunity employer. And that my constituents could name more people who worked for Cook County, Illinois, than worked for Hinds County, Mississippi. And they could name more people who worked for the city of Detroit than for the city of Jackson. And that simply was not equal opportunity employment in the state or the city or the county.[15]

Banks's first order of business in the state legislature was to begin a letter-writing campaign surveying the number of blacks employed in state government agencies. In doing so, he requested that the agencies provide a list of the number of blacks who were employed by their agency. For example, he recalls the first response that he received, coming from the secretary of state's office. All fifty-seven of the employees in that office were white. Over time, the state increased the number of blacks working in state-funded agencies. Banks attributes two factors in influencing such hires. First, the increase in registered black voters put more pressure on white legislators at the state and local levels to eliminate the overt patterns of discrimination. Second, the threat of lawsuits had a strong impact on desegregation. Banks states, "We had to sue the fire department . . . in '72 . . . and it was settled in '74, to get the . . . first black firefighter in the city of Jackson, in 1974. In 1972 the highway patrol wouldn't even accept applications from black folks to join the highway patrol. They had to be sued to get the first black highway patrolman."[16]

Like Banks, Doug Anderson fought for equality on behalf of his constituents. One of his most memorable bills was the Emma Marshall Bill, which was inspired by a complaint made by one of Anderson's neighbors, the namesake of the bill. Marshall, an elderly woman, had received a balloon note on her mortgage. According to Anderson, Marshall had never been late with a payment, but was served a notice that the remainder of her mortgage was due in full.[17] Using his position as a state legislator, with high name recognition, Anderson initiated a fund-raising campaign on behalf of his constituent. He used Frank Bluntson's talk show, *Straight Talk*, to broadcast his campaign. As a result, he was able to raise more than $10,000—more than enough funds to pay the amount due on the house.

Representative Horace Buckley also attempted to increase equity, focusing on state contracts for small businesses. During his first term in the legislature he introduced a 10 percent set-aside bill for minority hiring. Although it passed each body of the legislature, it stalled in the Conference Committee.

In 1978 blacks witnessed a major breakthrough, as the state was forced by a court order to change its legislative election scheme from multimember districts to single-member districts. This decision was a direct function of a Section 5 objection by the Department of Justice. Section 5 of the Voting Rights Act provides a preclearance clause that allows the federal government to reject any punitive electoral policies (that is, those deemed to be dilutive or retrogressive) adopted by states and jurisdictions protected under section 5 coverage. The litigation was initially filed as *Connor v. Johnson* in October 1965 by the MFDP and served as one of the longest-running legislative reapportionment cases in the history of American jurisprudence. After the change from multimember districts to single-member districts, African American voters increased the number of black state legislators from four to seventeen, almost literally overnight.

Among the first to be elected in the newly created single-member-districting structure, due to a special election, was a young attorney from Canton, Mississippi, Edward Blackmon. Blackmon, who had run unsuccessfully in 1975, ran for an open seat that was vacated by the incumbent who resigned to take a chancery judge position. During his first term in office, Blackmon decided to challenge the most powerful person in the Mississippi state legislature, Speaker of the House C. B. "Buddie" Newman.

A brief digression is necessary to provide some background on the power possessed by Newman, as Speaker of the House. Prior to 1987 the Speaker of the House in Mississippi could be elected for an unlimited number of terms. Additionally, through his power to appoint members to important committees and as committee chairs, the Speaker was capable of forming a loyal group of followers who could control the legislative process, at least on the House side. Buddie Newman was known for appointing members from the Mississippi Delta to such positions. Prior to the changes, the Speaker had the power to appoint members to the Rules Committee, which had the responsibility of setting the House calendar. Hence, if the committee wanted to ignore a bill, committee members could simply move it to the back of the calendar, as they had done with Clark's education reform bill. Like many newly elected members who were ushered in under the newly created single-member district structure, some legislators received assignments to committees that were of little significance. As one member who led the charge in attempting to change the rules related to the powers of the Speaker states, his assignment was so insignificant that the committee never met.[18]

As a newly elected member in 1979, Blackmon recalls how he appealed

> the Speaker's decision to the floor of the House, and ask[ed] for a vote. And he immediately went to counsel with his lieutenants, and I heard him say from the podium, "Can he do that?" I saw the heads go up and down as he began to read, and he said, "Okay, the gentleman's proper motion," and put it to a vote. I got five votes. I got about 116 against me. [Laughter] But still, the statement was made. The five votes were the five blacks that were in the House, my vote and the four others at that time.[19]

Blackmon's courage to stand up to Newman was representative of the outsiders who were elected from the newly created single-member districts. Following the increase in the number of blacks elected to the House, in tandem with an increase in the election of a few progressive white legislators, a solid bloc had been forged. Determined to challenge the power of the Speaker, this group became known at the "House 26." According to Blackmon, upon their first efforts to challenge the Speaker, they were penalized by being placed on the worst committee in the House, the Agriculture Committee. Having nothing to lose, the "House 26" went after the Speaker, constantly challenging his authority and exposing his failure to appoint blacks to substantive committees. Blackmon recalls one press conference called by members of the Legislative Black Caucus "at which we had a computer printout that was from here to that wall, really. It was rolled up, and it was about 10,000 or more Conference Committee appointments made by the Speaker, and of that 10,000, only one black had ever been appointed to a Conference Committee." Ultimately, the "House 26" mobilized into a majority, which eventually led to the demise of Newman. According to Blackmon, "In the last year of his term, there was a rebellion, and out of that rebellion, we had a rules fight, and we diluted his power, created a Speaker Pro Tem position to further dilute his power."[20] Additionally, House Rule Number 11 allowed for members of the Rules Committee to be elected by the members, restructured the Appropriations and Ways and Means Committees so that members from each of the congressional districts were included based on seniority, placed a term limit on the Speaker's position and the newly created Speaker Pro Tempore's position, and prohibited any member from serving as chair or vice chair of more than one committee.[21]

As a result of the rules changes, longtime Speaker Buddie Newman resigned as the Speaker. As Parker notes, "On March 26, 1987, Speaker C. B. 'Buddie' Newman of the Mississippi House of Representatives announced that he was stepping down as Speaker, a position he had held since 1976."[22] Parker attributes Newman's downfall to a "successful revolt against the House leadership spearheaded by a 'New South generation' of young white legislators together with the members of the House Black Caucus who succeeded in enacting a change in the House rules at the beginning of the 1987 session that diminished the Speaker's power."[23]

As a result of the successful "overthrow" of the Speaker, and the support of the incoming Speaker, Tim Floyd, many of the key players were rewarded with key leadership roles in the House. For example, African Americans increased the number of chairmanships in the House from zero in 1987 to five in 1988. To be sure, blacks had held chairmanships before, but the five appointed in 1988 was the largest number ever appointed. Similarly, blacks were placed on important committees. Among those receiving such appointments was none other than Blackmon, who was appointed to the Apportionment Committee. This appointment proved to be one of the most important events leading to the increase in descriptive representation among blacks in the state legislature.

In recalling his first meeting on the Reapportionment Committee, Blackmon reveals how he made a motion to hire black lawyers and black staff in direct proportion to that of whites. He also motioned to have the committee develop criteria for the redistricting process. Knowing that he would ultimately lose on each of these motions, Blackmon, being a polished lawyer, had something else up his sleeve. His strategy was to document each of his attempts to create equity and fairness on the committee, so as to create a paper trail for the Justice Department. While the committee only possessed a handful of black members, the committee members were well aware of the stringent requirements of the Voting Rights Act and that their actions could not simply be "business as usual." So the committee compromised with Blackmon by hiring an African American lawyer to assist in the process. They chose someone they thought was fairly "safe" in Reuben Anderson, a former circuit court justice and supreme court justice. According to Blackmon, the committee did not recognize that Anderson had worked on many of the same progressive issues during his early years of practicing law.

Once the committee began to draft the redistricting plan, Blackmon worked alone in drafting his own plan, due to his discomfort about what might emerge from the committee. In the end, Blackmon's plan received support from the Black Caucus and a sizable number of whites in the legislature, but it eventually failed by a few votes. Because Blackmon served as the chief architect of the plan, the plan became known as the Black Caucus Plan. Despite the success of the committee's plan, because the plan failed to maximize the number of majority black districts, and because of the paper trail submitted by Blackmon and others, it failed to receive preclearance by the Department of Justice. For example, the record indicates that some committee members had privately referred to the Black Caucus Plan as the "nigger plan." It was also revealed that some officials made references such that if this plan "gets passed, we're either going to have to move to Arizona or learn to eat watermelon."[24] This forced the state legislature back to the drawing board, and ultimately eleven plans were submitted.

Because of the language supporters of the rejected plan used to describe the Black Caucus Plan, those supporting what was known as the Ford Plan, in reference to Speaker of the House Tim Ford, were considered to be racial conservatives. With this in mind, the next chain of events caught all members of the state legislature, particularly those who had supported the Black Caucus Plan, totally off guard. In a strange twist of events, Blackmon made a last minute decision to compromise with the Speaker, whereby the Ford and Black Caucus plans were compromised so as to increase the opportunity for the Speaker to maintain his control as Speaker of the House at the same time satisfying the Department of Justice. Blackmon's unapologetic rationale was that "you've got to decide which set of good ol' boys you're going to line up behind."[25] In other words, Blackmon's primary concern was to maximize the number of black districts that could be created. When asked whether the creation of so many majority black districts might work to "bleach" surrounding districts (that is, increase the white population), thereby resulting in more conservative and possibly Republican districts, Blackmon responded:

> I don't know whether it's true elsewhere, but it's not true here. . . . Drawing your lines, and whatever. That's never been the case here in this state, because we don't know the difference between a Republican and a Democrat, conservative or liberal, when it comes to issues that really matter to black folk, when it comes to that time in the legislative process. If it's purely a black issue, you can bet that, save for a few, whether they call themselves moderate, whether they call themselves Democrat or Republican, it comes down to black-white issue, and that's unfortunate.[26]

However, not all legislators saw this issue as a black/white dichotomy as Blackmon framed it. In fact, some white progressives felt betrayed by Blackmon. For example, Wheeler states that the compromise "eliminated 15 of the 38 progressive white" districts.[27] Another white legislator, Ayres Haxton, notes, "You end up with radicalized White districts and radicalized Black districts, in which the White representatives don't have to take into consideration the needs and wants of the Black people in the state, and Black people don't have to take into consideration the needs and wants of the Whites because they represent such a small number of them that they don't have to cater to their interests to get elected."[28] The criticism was not limited to white legislators. Indeed, one black legislator was vehemently opposed to Blackmon's compromise. According to Barney Schoby, Blackmon had abandoned an alliance of progressive whites to side with a group that included racial conservatives. Schoby later indicated that the compromise resulted in some white backlash toward the Black Caucus. He states, "There is an effort to send a message to us, and to black Mississippians, that no matter what your numbers are in the legislature, we're going to still control things. . . . We no longer have the clout that we once had with those progressive whites because they feel that they were betrayed [in the redistricting process], and in general they were."[29]

The compromise produced several factions in the House, as former Ford supporters were unsupportive of the substantial number of majority black districts created, and many of the members of the Black Caucus simply could not support a group they deemed to be racially conservative. As a result, the vote for the Speaker of the House did not possess many of the likely blocs that had been created over the years. For example, the original "House 26" were split. Of the nineteen remaining members, ten supported Ford's opponent, Ed Perry, and nine supported Ford. Among blacks, nine voted for Ford, and eleven voted for Perry. Despite the split, it appears that blacks as a whole were successful in increasing their political power in the state legislature. The number of black legislators increased from twenty-two to forty. Ford also chose Robert Clark to serve alongside him as the Speaker Pro Tempore.

The Making of a Black Female Legislator

Primarily because of the segregated South and massive resistance to black political empowerment in Mississippi, white women entered the state legislature much earlier than blacks. Almost immediately following the passage of the Nineteenth Amendment, which granted women the right to vote, two white women were elected to the Mississippi state legislature. In the first election following the passage of the Nineteenth Amendment, Nellie Nugent Somerville was elected to the House and Belle Kearney was elected to the Senate.[30] Each of these women had worked hard in successfully campaigning for women's suffrage. The ability of white women to be elected to political office points to the importance of the intersection of race and gender in American politics. Following the election of the first woman to the state legislature, it would take over sixty years before an African American woman could achieve this feat.

In 1985 Representative Fred Banks was appointed to fill an open seat on the circuit court when Reuben Anderson vacated the position to become the first black to be appointed to the Mississippi Supreme Court. In an open seat election, Alyce Griffin Clarke, a nutrition coordinator with the Jackson Hinds Comprehensive Health Center, became the first African American woman to be elected to the state legislature. Gender obviously played a role in the treatment of Representative Clarke during her early years in office. She recalls how Representative Edward Blackmon gave up his end seat "so that those boys won't have to step over you when they are coming in and out." She also recollects how the Speaker appointed her as the secretary of ethics, a position that, unbeknownst to her, was an important position. Clarke, upset over being appointed as a "secretary," barged into the Speaker's office stating very boldly, "I thank you very much, but I don't think I want to be a secretary." After she was informed by the Speaker of the importance of this position, she humbly apologized and accepted the Speaker's appointment. Clarke also notes how she was taken aback when she learned that she was facing discrimination not just as a black and not just as a woman but as a black woman. According to Clarke, a white female had just been elected to the House, and immediately after her swearing-in ceremony, she was notified that she had not received her key to the restroom. Upon hearing that there was a key to the ladies' restroom, located on the second floor, Clarke became visibly upset, asking, "What key?" She then asked her white female colleagues whether they had received a key. After they acknowledged that they had indeed received a key, Clarke stormed out of the legislative chambers. Eventually, Clarke was offered an apology and a key, and she accepted both. In addition, Clarke's double identity as a black woman also informed how she cast her votes in the state legislature and how she proposed bills. For example, she introduced bills that focused on funding halfway houses for women who were pregnant and who were using drugs. They were afforded the opportunity to live in the house until they found a job. She also successfully worked to create drug courts. These courts were created for the purpose of sending individuals to treatment rather than prison. As a result of her efforts, she is known as the "Godmother of the Drug Court."[31]

Two years following the election of Clarke, the state legislature saw its second African American woman elected in Alice Hardin, a schoolteacher from Jackson. The election of Hardin was monumental, as she became one of the first African American women in the South to be elected to a state senate. By 2001 five black females were elected to the state legislature, thereby surpassing the number of white females. As of 2008 twelve black women had been elected to the House of Representatives, compared to only five whites. On the Senate side, however, white women outnumbered black women three to one.

Black "Women" Power

The importance of black women in the state legislature became clear during the 2008 Speaker's race. The incumbent Speaker, Democrat Billy McCoy, faced strong opposition from a fellow Democrat, Jeff Smith. Smith, who admitted to having supported McCoy for Speaker in 2004, decided to challenge his Democratic colleague, citing McCoy's movement toward more liberal positions during his tenure as Speaker. In contrast to McCoy, Smith was a clearly conservative Democrat who was the preferred choice of House Republicans. With Republicans and conservative Democrats siding with Smith, black legislators were positioned to play a major role in deciding the contest. In the end, all but two black legislators voted for McCoy. Despite their support, McCoy was not immediately elected as Speaker. The decision would rest in the hands of one black woman.

The presence of the Legislative Black Caucus was felt in many ways. First, both of the candidates for the Speaker position chose members from the Legislative Black Caucus to serve as proxy candidates for a temporary Speaker. (The temporary Speaker presides over the election of the Speaker and can offer a tie-breaking vote. The result of the interim election is often an indicator of the Speaker vote, and often serves as a test vote to gauge the temperament of the preferences of House members.) McCoy chose Ed Blackmon, and Smith chose Robert Johnson. The decision by each of the candidates to choose an African American speaks to the power that blacks had acquired in the state legislature. Blackmon describes the process: "Each candidate for Speaker will have somebody running for temporary Speaker, that's a signal to how the vote will go with the Speaker, because if you're a shadow Speaker, the temporary Speaker serves one day, the temporary Speaker opens the House up for the election of Speaker and conducts that election. After that, your role as temporary Speaker is over with."[32]

Blackmon continues by noting that two blacks were chosen as proxy candidates because each of the candidates needed black votes to win. This is a perfect case pointing to the power of blacks in the state legislature. Given McCoy's moderate stance in the legislature, it is not surprising that Blackmon served as his proxy candidate. However, Johnson's support of Smith is not so simple, and needs a brief explanation.

At first glance it may be somewhat confusing as to how Johnson could support Smith, given their ideological differences. Indeed, Johnson states, "McCoy and I are closer philosophically, a whole lot closer than the gentleman I did support." However, according to Johnson, his move to support Smith was based on the potential acquisition of power for blacks. In an interview with Johnson, he indicates that by supporting Smith, Smith promised him that he would name "a black chairman of Transportation, a black chairman of Reapportionment and Elections, and [appoint] a black Speaker Pro Tem in the House of Representatives." Johnson says his strategy was simple, "If you have majority number of African Americans on those committees chaired by the people on those committees, you can leverage with other people. I don't care how conservative or right-winged they are, if I control Transportation, the dollars and where the highway is going to go—how that money's going to be spent, if I control Public Health or if I have control how districts are going to be drawn where people are going to get elected . . . then . . . people have to come through me." According to Johnson, given their similar political philosophies, he originally supported McCoy after McCoy had contacted him personally. However, Smith adhered to granting him three out of five demands on key committees, whereas McCoy's response was simply "those are the things that I cannot do."[33]

With the stage now set for Johnson to represent Smith and Blackmon to represent McCoy, the process began with Percy Watson nominating Blackmon, while Willie Bailey spoke on Blackmon's behalf during the seconding process. However, the most powerful move during the process came from an African American woman, Representative Linda Coleman. Initially, Coleman sided with another Legislative Black Caucus member, Chuck Espy, to support Johnson, the proxy candidate for Smith. This created a deadlock, at 61-61. After two ballots, however, Coleman switched her vote from the conservative candidate, Smith, and voted for the more progressive candidate, McCoy, thereby casting the deciding vote to elect McCoy as the Speaker of the House. This was a monumental occasion, illustrating the power possessed by the Black Caucus and black female legislators. According to Blackmon, he had a talk with Coleman the night prior to the vote. He felt comfortable approaching her because they had been seatmates in the legislature for sixteen years. Despite that talk, however, Coleman initially sided with Johnson in voting for Smith on the first two votes. However, Coleman changed her vote on the third vote, and supported McCoy.[34]

As a result of the overwhelming support by the Legislative Black Caucus, blacks were rewarded with a record number of forty chairmanships and vice chairmanships. One anecdote that epitomizes the importance of committee chairs involves the 2004 decision to create a tourism tax to build the Jackson Convention Center in predominantly black Jackson. The bill was referred to the Local and Private Committee in the House. According to the chair of that committee, Representative Willie Perkins (an African American), the bill had little chance of getting out of his committee due to ideological bloc-voting. The committee consisted of three Democrats, three Republicans, and one Democrat who voted with the Republicans. As a result, the Republicans had the majority, and given that it was a Democratic-sponsored bill, it was virtually dead upon arrival. Moreover, it was tradition that when bills were introduced pertaining to a specific local jurisdiction, the entire delegation from that area had to support the bill in order for it to move forward. In this case, the white legislators from the Jackson area opposed the bill, and the black legislators supported it. As chair of the committee, however, Perkins decided to ignore this tradition and brought the bill out of the committee for a vote. Despite the legislator's crafty move, the chair of the Local and Private Committee on the Senate side, Senator Ralph Doxey (a white), indicated that the bill would not see daylight once it arrived on his desk. As expected, he kept his promise. Once the bill was killed on the Senate side, the power of the black legislators went to work. Senator Doxey introduced a bond bill to help his district in Marshall County. Once the bill reached the Ways and Means Committee, the committee's chair, Percy Watson, an African American, assured that the bill would not see the light of day. After hearing that his bill had been killed, Doxey asked what was going on. He was informed that if he wanted his bill passed, he would need to revisit his position on the tourism tax. He immediately changed his mind; arrangements were made to resubmit the bill, and ultimately the legislature passed the tourism bill.

Conclusion

The MFDP successfully set the tone for black political empowerment at the state level with the election of Robert Clark. Clark's case proves to be an excellent account of how descriptive representation translates into substantive representation and, by extension, political power. As an educator he worked hard to improve the education of his mainly black constituents once he moved up the ranks in the state legislature. As a committee chair, he was able to leverage power by influencing his white colleagues that his legislation was beneficial not only to blacks but to the state as a whole. In addition to the persistence of the MFDP, activists also successfully made use of the Voting Rights Act to increase the number of black elected officials. Although only three additional blacks were ushered into the legislature in 1976, the Voting Rights Act proved to be the necessary tool in creating a critical mass of black legislators. Indeed, the *Connor v. Johnson* case, by striking down the use of multimember districts in the state legislature, single-handedly transformed the state legislature, resulting in an immediate change in the number of black legislators from four to seventeen.

The increase in the number of black legislators also increased the power wielded by blacks in the legislature. For example, blacks worked with progressive whites to overthrow longtime Speaker of the House Buddie Newman. Following the overthrow of Newman, Representative Edward Blackmon teamed with an unlikely alliance of racially conservative legislators to introduce a redistricting plan that ultimately increased the number of black legislators from twenty-two to forty. This is a clear case of descriptive representation translating into substantive representation.

To be sure, there has been a huge increase in the number of black state legislators since the election of Clark in 1967. Women, however, have failed to make such gains. Despite such small numbers, however, black women have played major roles in the legislative process. One of the most notable moves occurred in 2008 when Linda Coleman cast the deciding vote to elect Billy McCoy to be the Speaker of the House. Coleman's vote proved to be worth forty chairmanships or vice-chairmanships, further placing African Americans in powerful positions in the state legislature.

NOTES

1. Hannah Pitkin, *The Concept of Representation* (Berkeley: University of California Press, 1967).

2. Earl Black and Merle Black, *Politics and Society in the South* (Cambridge, Mass.: Harvard University Press, 1987).

3. Frank R. Parker, *Black Votes Count* (Chapel Hill: University of North Carolina Press, 1990).

4. Byron D'Andra Orey, "Black Legislative Politics in Mississippi," *Journal of Black Studies* 30, no. 6 (2000): 791–814.

5. Parker, *Black Votes Count.*

6. Orey, "Black Legislative Politics."

7. Robert Clark, interview by Harriet Tanzman, February 11, 2000, Civil Rights Documentation Project, University of Southern Mississippi (USM), Hattiesburg.

8. Ibid.

9. Ibid.

10. Ibid.

11. Ibid.

12. Ibid.

13. Mary D. Coleman, *Legislators, Law and Public Policy: Political Change in Mississippi and the South* (Westport, Conn.: Greenwood Press, 1993), 70.

14. Ibid.; Orey, "Black Legislative Politics."

15. Fred Banks, interview by Charles Bolton, March 5, 1998, Civil Rights Documentation Project, USM.

16. Ibid.

17. Douglas Anderson, interview by author, January 15, 2009, interview housed in the Political Science Department, Jackson State University.

18. Ally Mack, "The Mississippi Legislature," in *Politics in Mississippi*, ed. Joseph B. Parker, 2nd ed. (Salem, Wis.: Sheffield, 2001), 44.

19. Edward Blackmon, interview by author, June 26, 2009, interview housed in the Political Science Department, Jackson State University.

20. Ibid.

21. Mack, "Mississippi Legislature."

22. Parker, *Black Votes Count*, 130.

23. Ibid., 131.

24. Jere Nash and Andy Taggart, *Mississippi Politics: The Struggle for Power, 1976–2006* (Jackson: University Press of Mississippi, 2006), 238–239.

25. Ibid., 239.

26. Blackmon interview.

27. Nash and Taggart, *Mississippi Politics*, 239.

28. Orey, "Black Legislative Politics," 809–810.

29. Ibid., 809.

30. Kate Greene, "Women in Mississippi Politics: Past and Present," in Parker, *Politics in Mississippi*, 343–361.

31. Alyce Clarke, interview by Kimberly Cosby, November 13, 1995, USM.

32. Blackmon interview.

33. Robert Johnson, interview by author, February 5, 2009, interview housed in the Political Science Department, Jackson State University.

34. Blackmon interview.

"The Movement Is in You"

The Sunflower County Freedom Project and the Lessons of
the Civil Rights Past

Chris Myers Asch

As a fifth-grade public school teacher in Sunflower, Mississippi, in the
mid-1990s, I discovered to my delight that our school library had a complete set of *Eyes on the Prize*, the extraordinary Blackside documentary about
the civil rights movement. I had planned to incorporate civil rights history
into my state-mandated American history class, and I thought excerpts from
Eyes on the Prize would be a wonderful addition to my lessons. As I went to
check the videotapes out, I noticed that they had never been used in nearly a
decade since they had been purchased. Surprised and intrigued, I asked the
school principal about why they had not been used. "You are going to use
those with your students?" she asked, concerned. The principal—a tall, black
Mississippian who had been a teenager in the 1960s—issued a stern warning
to me, her naive white novice from the North. "You have to be careful because those tapes teach hate! You'll teach your students to hate white people."

Though it stunned me at the time, the principal's response is emblematic
of how many Mississippians of both races, particularly those in positions of
leadership, have viewed civil rights history: as a controversial and combus-
tible subject best left buried and unexamined. Many well-meaning people
who lived through the tumultuous civil rights years fear the passions of that
era and worry that teaching about the movement could "open old wounds."
Mississippi has made significant progress since the civil rights era—racial
violence is essentially a thing of the past, civility rules interracial interactions,
and the state has taken steps to prosecute civil rights crimes and honor civil
rights leaders. Yet two generations after the first sit-ins, much of Mississippi
life, particularly in the Delta, remains resiliently separate and unequal. Many

people harbor concerns that students, particularly young black students, who learn about the freedom struggles of the twentieth century may very well look around at the circumstances of their lives and wonder why more progress has not yet been made.

Teaching about the civil rights movement in early twenty-first-century Mississippi requires an appetite for controversy and criticism. The wounds of the civil rights era are indeed still fresh. Throughout the state, the leaders of massive resistance and their descendants remain important members of the community, and their presence is felt from the Ross Barnett Reservoir in Jackson to the James O. Eastland Law Library at the University of Mississippi. They mistrust efforts to confront the state's tortured racial past and prefer that, as the state's motto in the 1990s urged, "only positive Mississippi is spoken here." On the other hand, movement veterans and their allies in academia stand guard against watered-down, "feel-good" civil rights history that simply tries not to hurt anyone's feelings. They object to cosmetic changes that pay tribute to (and capitalize on) the civil rights past without addressing the deeper social, economic, and political reforms that the movement sought to achieve. In the face of such controversy and potential criticism, many teachers and schools tread very lightly or avoid the subject altogether.

One group that has embraced civil rights history as an educational tool is the Sunflower County Freedom Project. Recognizing that the battle to define the "lessons" of Mississippi's civil rights past takes place not only in public history debates, scholarly works, and academic conferences but also in classrooms across the state, the Freedom Project has worked for more than ten years to show how movement history can build academic skills, inspire social action, and develop youth leadership. To avoid teaching "hate," the Freedom Project takes care not to paint a facile "white = bad, black = good" equation; to avoid regurgitating the "Rosa-and-King-have-a-dream" pabulum often dished up during Black History Month, it broadens the menu to include the masses of local people who pushed policy makers to make needed changes; to avoid instilling students with a debilitating cynicism about a lack of progress, its overarching message is a positive one that emphasizes opportunity over oppression, diligence over discrimination, self-discipline over self-pity. The story of the Freedom Project offers one look at how young people growing up in Mississippi can understand the lessons of the movement. As a cofounder of the organization, I can claim no objectivity, but I do have insight into the ideas and actions that drove the founding of the organization and continue to animate it to this day.

Education Is the Seed of Freedom

I decided to ignore the principal's warning and proceeded to use the *Eyes on the Prize* series in a lengthy unit on the local and national civil rights struggle. My elementary school, after all, was located in the middle of Sunflower County, which was not simply a bystander during the movement, and the history we were learning was not an abstraction to the parents and grandparents of my students. Home to both Fannie Lou Hamer and James Eastland, Sunflower County sat at the epicenter of the Mississippi movement. Yet to my surprise and dismay, my students knew as little about the movement as they did about the American Revolution or the Civil War. Though they were unfamiliar with the history, my students' response to the material was almost uniformly positive—they were engaged in the lessons and motivated to learn more. I found that the themes and language of the movement helped underscore my larger classroom character themes of courage, perseverance, and self-discipline. Long after we had finished the unit, my students and I referred back to the personal examples and the lessons of the movement.

My experience with teaching civil rights in my elementary school classroom helped inspire me to join with three Teach for America friends of mine—Gregg Costa, Shawn Raymond, and Kevin Schaaf—to create the nonprofit Sunflower County Freedom Project in 1998. Having each taught at least two years in the local public schools, we were distressed not simply by the low student achievement levels and graduation rates, but more fundamentally with the sense of complacency and the low expectations that too many adults in the education system seemed to have for children in the area. Like many of the parents we knew, we thought that the public school system shortchanged children, depriving them of opportunities that most Americans took for granted. Funding cuts and state mandates, for example, had eliminated "frills" such as art, music, physical education, and most extracurricular activities from the school in which I taught. The problems extended far beyond the schools. The area suffered from rampant teen crime, a teenage pregnancy rate 30 percent higher than the state average, and a graduation rate that hovered around 60 percent. Even students who managed to graduate from high school generally were unprepared to enter college—the average ACT score for county students was a 15 out of 36, equivalent to less than 700 out of 1,600 on the Scholastic Aptitude Test.[1]

The founders of the Freedom Project were driven by a sense that the educational situation in Sunflower County was in many ways as bleak as it had been a generation earlier. Sunflower County sits deep in the heart of the Mississippi Delta, the vast alluvial plain that stretches between the Mississippi and Yazoo Rivers in the northwest section of the state. Home to vast cotton plantations of regional lore, as well as catfish ponds and processing plants that represent the area's "new economy," Sunflower County epitomized the Delta's extremes of wealth and power. The county's bright name belied the dull, disillusioning reality of poverty, discrimination, and despair that many of its citizens endured.

Despite the important legal and political advances of the civil rights movement, economic and educational inequities remained entrenched in the area. The movement destroyed official school segregation, but de facto segregation proved just as strong. White resistance had prevented desegregation for more than fifteen years after the U.S. Supreme Court's *Brown* decision in 1954. When the courts finally mandated that the schools integrate in 1970, almost overnight the public school system became the new black school system as whites ensconced their children in newly built private academies. Sunflower County became home to three such academies. White taxpayer support for the public system waned, and the schools suffered from inadequate funding and indifferent leadership. As the information revolution took hold, parents could see their children falling behind, as isolated and powerless in the new economy as illiterate sharecroppers had been forty years earlier or landless freed slaves were after the Civil War. Back then, one needed land to make "freedom" real; in this age, we believed, young people needed a challenging, achievement-oriented education that would prepare them for college.[2]

Despite all the disadvantages of growing up with limited educational opportunities, Sunflower County kids remained resilient. One student in Shawn Raymond's class, Charles Surney, was particularly inspirational. A young man from Fannie Lou Hamer's hometown of Ruleville, Charles had wallowed in the county's special education program up until the tenth grade, dismissed as a nonreader unable to function as a regular student. Given such expectations, he indeed failed to make academic progress—as a tenth grader, he still did not know how to read. But under Raymond's guidance, he learned to read and then enrolled in a model school in Massachusetts, where he excelled as a champion wrestler, star chess player, and ultimately a college-bound valedictorian. Charles's story both inspired and frustrated those of us who founded the Freedom Project. Why should Sunflower County children be forced to leave in order to have a chance to succeed? Why not offer model educational opportunities in Sunflower County itself?

So we decided to do something—though we were not sure exactly what to do. In the summer of 1998, we contacted a number of parents and community members whom we knew, and we called a series of town meetings to discuss what could be done to inspire young people to excel in school and get on the college track. Two key local people who got involved early on were Charles McLaurin and Mildred Downey. A Jackson native and former Student Nonviolent Coordinating Committee (SNCC) field secretary who decided to pursue his political ambitions in Sunflower County after the height of the movement, McLaurin was approaching sixty years old and had grandchildren in the public school system. Downey had been born and raised in Sunflower County—her father, a Chinese immigrant, and her mother, an African American whose family had owned land since the 1890s, had run the local grocery—but she had left for school and only returned after retiring in the 1990s. It was Downey's son Les, a Yale graduate who ran the family farm outside of town, who articulated the organization's first slogan—"Education is the seed of freedom"—that developed into the organization's name: Sunflower County Freedom Project.

As the name implied, from the beginning the founders of the Freedom Project took inspiration from the civil rights movement, and particularly the Freedom Schools established in Sunflower County and throughout Mississippi by SNCC in 1964. The problems young people faced were different than a generation earlier, but we believed that the Freedom Schools' model of intensive, relevant, and experiential education was the key to breaking through the despair and low expectations that entrapped young people.

The original Freedom Schools were part of a larger movement to crack open Mississippi's "Closed Society." As sit-ins, Freedom Rides, and other protests began to create change across the South in the early 1960s, Mississippi remained deeply committed to white supremacy. It was, as SNCC field secretary Bob Moses observed, "the middle of the iceberg." To bring national attention to the horrors of Mississippi segregation, SNCC brought thousands of college students from around the country to the state in the summer of 1964. During Freedom Summer (white authorities called it an "invasion"), these college students worked to register black Mississippians to vote and established nearly fifty Freedom Schools throughout the state, including two in Sunflower County, one in Indianola, and one in Ruleville.[3]

SNCC activists established these schools because they believed in the power of education to transform communities. In the words of one SNCC report, "education—the facts to use and freedom to use them—is the basis of democracy." But black Mississippians were not offered that kind of education. At that time, the state spent an average of four times more money for white students than for blacks. In rural areas the situation was even worse—one rural district spent $191.17 per white student but only $1.26 per black student! Classroom sizes in black schools ranged as high as seventy pupils. Certain subjects, such as black history or race relations, were strictly off-limits, while courses such as foreign languages, art, and drama simply were not offered. Taken as a whole, the system worked to subordinate black students and prepare them for life in a segregated society.[4]

Freedom Schools offered something revolutionary, what historian Charles Payne calls "education for activism." Located in churches, community centers, or even outdoors, the schools offered courses aimed at getting black children to question the system of oppression that kept them poor and isolated. Students were not simply passive recipients of a teacher's unquestioned wisdom; they were encouraged to engage themselves in their learning. The curriculum emphasized the students' own experiences and history while also offering traditional subjects that would prepare them for a future of freedom. The main goal of education according to the Freedom School model was to get people to think for themselves so they could change their own lives. These schools were remarkable, if short-lived, grassroots attempts to empower local people with educational tools to take control of their lives.[5]

They were also extraordinarily controversial. In a state where former governor James Vardaman had declared that "education only spoils a good field hand," the idea of using education as a means of arming black Mississippians for a freedom struggle was frightening, both in the 1960s and at the end of the twentieth century. Not long after the founding of the Freedom Project, I met with the head of the AmSouth Foundation, a major philanthropic force that funded educational endeavors throughout the state. The Freedom Project had applied for a grant and been rejected, and I wanted to find out why. He told me plainly: "I tell you what our problem is. You all are doing great things with kids in Sunflower, but your name makes some folks uncomfortable." A white man in his sixties, he explained that the word "freedom" made him think of the 1960s, a time he thought we should all just forget. "It turns people off," he said, suggesting that we change our name to something less controversial, such as the "Sunflower Education Project."

Like my principal, this foundation executive believed that teaching about civil rights was dangerous and should be avoided, as if the work of the movement was complete and thus could be boxed up, put away, and forgotten. But the parents who joined with us to create the Freedom Project believed that the movement's mission had not been fully accomplished. Indeed, during our first meetings about creating the organization they rejected the name

"Freedom School" in favor of "Freedom Project" because the latter connoted a sense of ongoing change, evolution, and work to be done.

With input from parents and community members, we began to develop an academic program aimed at middle school students—because that was when most students seemed to fall off the college track—and the summer— because there was little for young people to do during the extended school vacation. We aimed both to motivate students and to give them the academic tools they needed to excel in school. The program began slowly, initially offering a five-week, full-day academic enrichment program to thirty middle school students in the summer of 1999. Held at nearby Mississippi Delta Community College, the first summer program succeeded well enough that the parents and grandparents on the organization's board of directors demanded that it be expanded for summer 2000.

The program's success inspired the Freedom Project's leaders to consider expanding into a year-round charter school. As successful as our summer program was, we knew it was only a stopgap measure. If we truly wanted to alter the educational trajectory of our students, then we had to offer year-round programs, and a charter school, we believed, would allow us to create the kind of achievement-oriented, high-intensity educational culture that would produce significant results in our students' lives. In the early twenty-first century, the charter school movement was sweeping the country, and successful models such as the Knowledge Is Power Program (KIPP) schools showed how energetic leaders could build effective schools for students in low-income areas. We knew the leaders of KIPP and other charter schools, and we believed that we could build a successful school in Sunflower County. Two factors undermined our effort, however. First, the state legislature refused to pass expansive charter school legislation that would allow for "start-up" charter schools such as what we envisioned. The state's restrictive law—ranked by the Center for Education Reform as the weakest in the nation—only allowed existing public schools to turn themselves into charter schools. Second, we lacked community support for a charter school. Though we had strong support for continuing the summer program and expanding it into a year-round effort, many parents refused to support the idea of creating a new school that would compete with other schools in the community.[6]

Faced with a lack of legislative and community support, the Freedom Project abandoned its charter school proposal and instead created a six-year, year-round fellowship program that remains the core of the organization's operations. Following students from seventh grade through high school, the fellowship aims to ensure that all Freedom Project students graduate from high school on time and enter college by providing academic enrichment and leadership development. Through the fellowship, Freedom Project students are expected not only to achieve academically but also to become recognized, respected young leaders whose efforts inspire positive changes in their schools and communities. Students and their families must sign a contract agreeing to make a "Commitment to LEAD" in which they commit to attending a six-week summer school cohosted by the University of Mississippi, weekly Saturday School at the LEAD Center (named for the organization's four principles—Love, Education, Action, Discipline) in Sunflower, and nightly study sessions throughout the school year. In addition to the intensive academic commitment, students also commit to participating in extracurricular programs, including drama, fitness training, and media production. In 2002 the organization hired three full-time staff members (including me) to run the program year-round and purchased two run-down city lots to rehabilitate into a student study center. The LEAD Center expanded in 2005 and now offers more than 7,000 square feet, including classrooms, a library, a computer lab, a theater, and a fitness space.[7]

The "Freedom" in the Project

Through its academic program, the Freedom Project celebrates the history of the civil rights movement in general and SNCC in particular. Influenced by three books—John Dittmer's *Local People*, Charles Payne's *I've Got the Light of Freedom*, and the Rural Organizing and Cultural Center's *Minds Stayed on Freedom*, all of which had been published not long before we launched the Freedom Project—we deliberately steered away from a top-down history focused on Martin Luther King Jr. and the national movement. Our students got a regular dose of the King-centered synopsis of the movement each February during Black History Month, and it seemed remote and almost irrelevant. We wanted them to hear the voices of local people who made the movement real, older people in their own communities and their own families who took risks and hastened revolutionary changes in Sunflower County and the rest of Mississippi. We wanted them to understand the obstacles that people in the movement faced and to recognize that the movement's success was not foreordained but required patient, often dangerous, usually tedious work. We wanted them to see that "history" is not made by far-off people in powerful places but by people just like them, in places just like Sunflower County.

Students are introduced to movement history during their first summer in the program. They read all of Anne Moody's searing autobiography, *Coming of Age in Mississippi*, which chronicles her childhood in southwest Mississippi and her transformation into a SNCC activist. They read excerpts from Constance Curry's *Silver Rights*, which tells the story of Mae Bertha Carter and how her children became the first black students in formerly all-white Sunflower County schools. (Curry learned of the Freedom Project after the first summer, and she donated more than three dozen copies of her book to the organization. The books are a bit dog-eared, but they are still in use today.) Students also have the opportunity to conduct oral history interviews with family members or community members involved in the movement. Originally developed by historian Steve Estes, then a graduate student in the Southern Oral History Program at the University of North Carolina, the oral history class offers a powerful way for students to connect the "movement" to the people and the places that they know and love. To culminate the summer, the students take a trip to visit key sites such as Selma, Montgomery, Birmingham, Atlanta, and Memphis. This kind of experiential learning helps make the history real to students, particularly when they get the chance to talk with movement veterans along the way.[8]

The first summer's activities lay the foundation for other civil rights learning experiences throughout the course of a student's Freedom Project career. During the original Freedom Summer, drama was an important vehicle for self-expression and the examination of contentious social issues. The Freedom Project continues this tradition through its Freedom Troupe, which performs a collection of five original plays about the Mississippi movement, including plays about Fannie Lou Hamer (*Five Feet Four Inches Forward*), Emmett Till (*A Boy Named Bobo*), the sit-in movement (*Something's Gotta Change*), voting (*The Fruits of Our Labor*), and school integration (*Thirty Years From Now*). The troupe conducts two tours each year, performing across the state and region and as far away as North Carolina, Washington, D.C., and New York City. In the process of practicing and performing, students become the resident experts on the history they are teaching their audiences. As with the civil rights tours, the plays make the history come alive and help students feel the power and complexity of the freedom struggle.

But the plays address more than simply historical questions. *Thirty Years From Now* focuses on the dicey topic of school integration (which for all intents and purposes has yet to happen in Sunflower County), and the troupe has performed in front of audiences that included not only sympathetic parents, teachers, and activists but also a significant number of wealthy community members whose children attend private schools and even helped establish the white academies that are the subject of the play. The plays also shine a critical light on other difficult subjects, such as the casual use of the word "nigger" among black youth and the current complacency surrounding black-on-black crime. The last scene of *A Boy Named Bobo*, for example, concludes with the narrator lamenting: *"Yes, the terror remains. But you know, terror is different now. Black boys are still being killed, more than ever; black mothers still weep for their murdered sons, more than ever; the killers of black men still run free, more than ever. But now the killers are black."* These plays generate controversy and discussion whenever and wherever they are performed, and out of those discussions comes a greater sense of the passions and tensions of the movement.

The Freedom Project also takes advantage of new technology that the original Freedom Schools could not imagine. Students in the media production program have developed an interactive web site that includes video-taped interviews, a movement map, and a narrative history of the struggle in Sunflower County, and they have produced a number of video documentaries that are now linked to the web site. One documentary, entitled *Sankofa*, tells the story of the movement in Sunflower County and applies the lessons learned to what young people can do (and are doing) in the area today. The effort required students to conduct primary and secondary research (including several oral history interviews), write concise and accurate text for the web page, and speak confidently to a variety of audiences, from local activists to conference-goers in Cleveland, Ohio. These kinds of creative experiences give students the opportunity to write their own histories of the movement and build important twenty-first-century media skills in the process.

Not "All Freedom, All the Time"

All of these movement-related activities—the reading, the oral history, the tours, the drama, the media production—are fundamental to the Freedom Project, but the knowledge of the history is just a beginning, a way to give kids a vocabulary of freedom and an appreciation of the movement's impact. We want students to know about the struggles that came before them not so that they can spout names and dates but so that they can be inspired to make changes in their own lives and communities today. We seek to extend the movement by building upon its successes and instilling students with a sense of responsibility to pursue the opportunities the movement opened for them. For the Freedom Project, the "lessons" of the civil rights past involve people taking action, as individuals and collectively, to change the world around them. Whenever Freedom Project students ask, "Where is the movement today?," we echo the words of former SNCC member Charles McLaurin: "The movement is in you."

Though the Freedom Project takes inspiration from the past, it does not attempt to re-create the original Freedom Schools, which arose in response to a specific set of circumstances, nor does it seek only to look backward at a bygone era. The context in which young people are growing up today differs significantly from the context of the original Freedom Schools. Today, there is no unified, discernible mass social movement that has captured the national imagination; without vivid enemies such as Bull Connor or James Eastland, there is less clarity about whom or what to fight; there are any number of worthy causes, from environmentalism to AIDS prevention, that demand attention. In such a context, it can be difficult to determine the best way to create positive social change.

Despite the lack of a mass movement on the scale of the civil rights movement, however, the Freedom Project does see itself as part of a larger struggle: the movement to transform education in this country. Along with national organizations such as Teach for America, charter school networks such as KIPP, and nonprofit efforts such as Bob Moses's Algebra Project, the Freedom Project aims to use education as a lever of social change, a means of leveling the playing field to give all children a real chance to achieve their version of success. During the civil rights era, de jure segregation mocked American ideals of freedom, democracy, and equal opportunity. Similarly, in the early twenty-first century, persistent inequalities in the education that young people receive undermine America's moral authority.

As part of this larger effort, the Freedom Project places academic achievement at the heart of its program. While some of its programming does indeed emphasize the movement, it is not "all freedom all the time." Instead, the core of the academic program is reading. Throughout the six years that students are in the program, they read novels from a book list designed both to expose them to some of the best literature in the English language and to get them to question the assumptions of their society and their lives. Not all of this literature is directly related to the black American experience; students read Sophocles, Shakespeare, Twain, Orwell, and other "dead white males" alongside Malcolm X and Lorraine Hansberry. In addition to reading, students study math and writing, as well as project-based classes such as public speaking and media production.

Like the original Freedom Schools, the Freedom Project offers an "oppositional" culture that runs counter to the students' educational experience.

While we are *for* using education to raise academic achievement and build students' critical thinking skills, we are *against* the same kind of educational culture that Charlie Cobb wrote about in his proposal for the Freedom Schools more than forty years ago. Cobb noted that much of education was characterized by "a complete absence of academic freedom," where "students are forced to live in an environment that is geared to squashing intellectual curiosity, and different thinking." As Cobb recognized, the segregated culture of Mississippi in the 1960s extended far beyond simply the school system and included everything from television to newspapers to politics, all of which sought to prepare young black students for a second-class life. Similarly, the Freedom Project challenges a larger culture that patronizes black children and encourages them to accept and even seek out limited achievement.[9]

But contemporary students' lived experience reveals that the nature of the culture against which they must struggle has changed markedly. It is no longer the Ku Klux Klan and the Citizens' Council that are killing black youth—it is the Gangsta Disciples and other gangs that have infiltrated black neighborhoods, even in rural Sunflower County. It is no longer just racist white school officials who seek to limit black academic success—black superintendents, principals, and teachers often run schools that tolerate, rationalize, and even promote low achievement among black students. It is no longer a segregated admissions policy that keeps black kids out of college—it is students' woeful underpreparation, which is itself a product both of poor public schools and a negative peer culture that glorifies anti-intellectualism and mocks academic achievement. Black students who push themselves academically often face a barrage of negative attacks on their motives, their abilities, and their racial sincerity—they are branded for "acting white." The fact that these charges come from fellow black students (and even adults) only makes the struggle more difficult because any challenge to them brings more charges of race betrayal.

In a world that consistently expects black students to do poorly, academic achievement *is* social action. If poor black children in Mississippi ever hope to wield power effectively, then they must be educationally equipped to do so, both in a narrow academic sense—they need to be able to comprehend what they read, write clearly and coherently, speak intelligently, and use math well—and in a broad psychological sense—they must be willing and able to think differently, challenge conventional wisdom, and make intelligent choices. Building those skills is long, often tedious work, akin to the slow, methodical organizing work that made the civil rights movement succeed over time. The Freedom Project emphasizes old-fashioned academic achievement because it provides a solid foundation on which a constructive life of community engagement, civic leadership, and responsible parenting can be built. Long-term social change requires capable citizens able not simply to advocate and "resist" but to create and build.

If the original Freedom Schools were "education for activism," in Payne's words, then the Freedom Project could be characterized as "education for citizenship." The goal is to develop young people into thoughtful, contributing citizens—people who vote, raise honorable children, voluntarily pick up litter in the streets, help out at the local library, coach Little League, look out for neighborhood kids as they would their own, and advocate social change. The Freedom Project aims to instill in students the solid values that rural Mississippi taught generations of young children—respect for elders, family, and community; perseverance in the face of adversity; faith in oneself, one's country, and one's creator. In the Freedom Project's daily work with students, teachers do not deny or dismiss the presence of societal barriers; instead they use those barriers as motivation.

The Movement Is in You

The Freedom Project is not without its critics. Due in part to its abortive effort to develop a charter school in 2001, the Freedom Project has struggled to win allies within the school system. Some local school officials see the program as a competitor and view its very existence as a challenge to the schools. One principal at a local middle school went so far as to ban Freedom Project personnel from campus to undermine its recruiting efforts. In response, the organization has relied more heavily on Teach for America teachers in the school system to recruit interested students, which has only fed the concern among critics that the Freedom Project is an "outside" organization founded and run by people who do not hail from Sunflower County. Some of this criticism has had racial undertones. In an organization that works almost exclusively with black children—in its first ten years, no white students and only one Latina joined the program—a white man served as executive director for its first seven years. That fact has generated skepticism and concern, particularly among activists that Freedom Project students have encountered on trips outside of the region. Other activists see the program as being insufficiently radical and argue that it thus fails to live up to the model of the original Freedom Schools. William Ayers of the University of Illinois at Chicago, for example, has attacked the Freedom Project for not doing enough to challenge "hidden structures of oppression" and insists that by focusing heavily on academic achievement the program may inadvertently be "blaming the victim."[10]

The Freedom Project also has faced internal challenges. It has struggled with attrition, particularly as students enter their high school years and become more involved in other activities. The number of students actively involved in the program has fluctuated between twenty and fifty, and the Freedom Project's leaders have sought to find a balance that will maintain the program's intensity and standards while not discouraging students from participating. As a community-based nonprofit organization, it also has had to weather periodic financial difficulties. The global economic crisis in fall 2008 triggered an organizational financial crunch, forcing the Freedom Project to lay off two of its three full-time staff members. It has since recovered financially, but the specter of financial trouble remains an ongoing concern.

Despite the criticism and challenges, the Freedom Project remains committed to its goal of using the 1960s freedom struggle to inspire young people to become capable and compassionate young leaders. It is a small but sustained effort to create a leadership base for lasting change in the Mississippi Delta. The original Freedom Schools were extraordinary, but they were also extraordinarily short-lived—a few schools managed to live on through the summer of 1965, but not beyond that. The Freedom Project remains strong more than ten years after its founding, and its graduates are in colleges across the country, including Berea College, the University of North Carolina, and the University of Mississippi.

One alumnus, Chris Perkins, graduated from Berea in May 2010 and was hired as the Freedom Project's director of student activities—the first alumnus to work full time for the organization. Perkins embodies the Freedom Project's mission: a young leader prepared to assume a positive leadership role in his community. A few years ago he was a shy, thirteen-year-old seventh grader reading *Coming of Age in Mississippi* and interviewing his grandmother about her experience during the civil rights era. Now he leads a new crop of youngsters along that same journey. The movement lives in on in Chris Perkins and the students of the Freedom Project.

NOTES

1. Chris Myers Asch, *The Senator and the Sharecropper: The Freedom Struggles of James O. Eastland and Fannie Lou Hamer* (New York: New Press, 2008), 295; Public Health Statistics, Mississippi State Department of Health, "Teenage Vital Statistics

Data, 1999," http.//msdh.ms.gov/msdhsite/_static/resources/1999.pdf; Mississippi Department of Education, Mississippi Report Card 1999–2000, http://orsap.mde .k12.ms.us:8080/MAARS/maarsMS_TestResultsProcessor.jsp?userSessionId=458& DistrictId=912&TestPanel=1.

2. Asch, *Senator and the Sharecropper*, 283; J. Todd Moye, *Let the People Decide: Black Freedom and White Resistance Movements in Sunflower County, Mississippi, 1945–1986* (Chapel Hill: University of North Carolina Press, 2004), 172–179.

3. Moye, *Let the People Decide*, 122–128; Asch, *Senator and the Sharecropper*, 198–220.

4. John Dittmer, *Local People: The Struggle for Civil Rights in Mississippi* (Urbana: University of Illinois Press, 1994), 258.

5. Charles Payne, *I've Got the Light of Freedom: The Organizing Struggle and the Mississippi Freedom Struggle* (Berkeley: University of California Press, 1996), 302; Daniel Perlstein, "Minds Stayed on Freedom: Politics and Pedagogy in the African-American Freedom Struggle," *Educational Research Journal* 39, no. 2 (Summer 2002): 252–255.

6. In the first decade of Mississippi's charter school law, only one school was approved. The law was up for reauthorization in 2009 but failed to win enough support. See http://www.charterschoolresearch.com/.

7. The Freedom Project purchased the land and buildings that became the LEAD Center from John Sydney Parker, who had been a notoriously racist deputy sheriff of Sunflower County during the civil rights era. Despite his personal objections to the program, economic realities pushed him to sell the property to the Freedom Project. As part of the sale, Parker agreed to sell the property at a price significantly below market value; the difference between the sale price and market value was then considered a donation to the nonprofit organization and hence would be tax deductible. As a result, Parker became and remains to this day the largest individual donor to the Freedom Project.

8. Ironically, although many civil rights trip organizers (including the Freedom Project) explicitly reject a history focused primarily on Martin Luther King, they nonetheless find themselves drawn to King-centric tours because the tourism structures follow King's life and achievements. Atlanta boasts a number of attractive King destinations, including his boyhood home, his Sweet Auburn neighborhood, the National Park Service's King Historic Site museum, Ebenezer Baptist Church, and the King Center and gravesite. In Montgomery, students can visit King's church, the state capitol to which he marched from Selma, and the Southern Poverty Law Center's beautiful memorial designed by Maya Lin. In Birmingham, site of one of King's major campaigns, the extraordinary Birmingham Civil Rights Institute, the Sixteenth Street Baptist Church, and Kelly Ingram Park all beckon the civil rights tourist. And Selma

has the incomparable Joanne Bland at the National Voting Rights Institute, as well as the landmark Edmund Pettus Bridge—crossing it, preferably in formation, is de rigueur for civil rights tours. Many of the key sites in the Mississippi movement—the Money grocery store where Emmett Till had his fateful run-in with a white woman, the Greenwood playground where Stokely Carmichael galvanized a crowd with shouts of "Black Power!," the earthen dam where the bodies of James Chaney, Andrew Goodman, and Michael Schwerner were found—are either in disrepair or are nondescript places barren of any visible connection to the movement.

9. Charles E. Cobb Jr., "Prospectus for a Summer Freedom School Program," in *Teach Freedom: Education for Liberation in the African-American Tradition*, ed. Charles M. Payne and Carol Sills Strickland (New York: Teachers College Press, 2008), 67.

10. William Ayers and Chris Myers Asch, "And Who Gets to Define 'Freedom'?" in Payne and Strickland, *Teach Freedom*, 139.

"Looking the Devil in the Eye"

Race Relations and the Civil Rights Movement in Claiborne
County History and Memory

Emilye Crosby

In my research on the black freedom struggle in Claiborne County, Mississippi, and its county seat of Port Gibson, I have found that there is remarkable consistency in the stories that blacks and whites tell.[1] But though the
details are similar, the meanings they attach to these stories are quite different. This is particularly important to understand and acknowledge because
in Claiborne County, as in most of the country, white power has traditionally
translated into white control over the way history and race are interpreted
and presented publicly. Even though African Americans used the civil rights
movement to successfully challenge disfranchisement and the most blatant
forms of raw violence and discourteous treatment, whites have remained
fairly successful at projecting their perspective as if it were fact and as if it
represented the entire community. Although African Americans actively
contest this white-dominated vision, whites' role in establishing the public
framework for understanding race and history makes this an uphill battle. It
is essential, then, to juxtapose the white-controlled public version with the
sometimes less visible (but no less vibrant) black version and explore their
intersections and contradictions. This is true for Port Gibson, but also for our
entire country, as talk of a postracial America obscures persistent patterns of
inequality and segregation.

Claiborne County is located in southwest Mississippi, about midway between Vicksburg and Natchez. In the 1960s about 80 percent of Claiborne
County's approximately 10,000 residents were African Americans, while
whites and blacks were almost evenly divided among Port Gibson's roughly
2,000 residents. In the years since the movement, Port Gibson's population
has grown slightly, even as the overall county population has declined. Blacks

remain a significant majority and now hold most of the elective offices in the county, along with an increasing number in Port Gibson. Despite this, whites have maintained considerable influence, largely through their continuing access to privilege and continued disproportionate control of wealth and resources. All of this impacts contemporary race relations, the ways blacks and whites view the past, and how those intersect.

In the 1990s a white woman told me, "I'm so sorry that you won't ever see it like it was, and that my children won't see it like it was. The comfortable feeling. Everybody taking care of everybody. You know. And no hate. I mean, race just wasn't a word. You know? I mean, it was a word. Then, either you said, 'Darkie' or 'Colored man,' you know, to designate. . . . It wasn't a dirty word. . . . It was just a wonderful, warm thing. You know?"[2] Her views are typical. The legacy of slavery and the low wages paid African Americans allowed most white families to employ black maids and laborers to do domestic and yard work, and whites' ideas about interracial friendship were often influenced by this close proximity. A white merchant remembered, "We had one man that was just a gardener and sort of a handy man around. And I think he just kinda belonged to my father. He was raised there and his sister was our nurse."[3] A white woman recalled, "I was raised by this colored woman with a daughter my age . . . and she breast fed me. I sat on one side and [her daughter] was on the other."[4] Another white woman described the black families who lived on her family's plantation as "friends as well as servants." These black "friends/servants" did the cooking, washing, and yard work, and nursed the children.[5]

Blacks sometimes had positive memories of interracial interactions. For example, Ezekiel Rankin, who was born in 1917, said that in the rural area where he grew up, "The atmosphere was good." Blacks and whites "played together. We swum together. We worked together in the fields. . . . So, where I grew up, folks were neighborly. It made no difference." He added that they would even "sit down, eat at the table sometime with them," but concludes, "We really didn't know things as they really were."[6] As Rankin suggests, while these relationships may have been positive, they did not eliminate the power imbalance.

From whites' perspective, good race relations meant a hierarchy with unchallenged white authority and control. Civil rights activists who worked in southwest Mississippi in the early 1960s explain that whites and blacks shared "an intimacy, an air of easy familiarity" as long as there was no threat of "Black political challenge."[7] A white Port Gibson lawyer who came of age in the 1960s has a similar recollection. "Now black people and white people have worked together, you know, side by side and hand in hand, for years. That was alright, but nothing whatsoever on the social level. . . . Black people and white people just didn't do these things together like go to schools, eat, you know, nothing on a social level for sure."[8]

Southern children had the almost universal experience of reaching an age where white supremacy intruded on any interracial friendships they might have. Marjorie Brandon was deeply affected by her father's experience with this on the Rodden plantation where he grew up. She explains,

> My father had been there for years. He grew up on that plantation and the [Rodden] boys . . . was right along with my Dad. He said after they got a certain age that they were told "Now look, you have to call this Mr. Percy and Mr. Willy, you can't just say Percy, Willy any more cause they getting up in age and you have to mister them."[9]

In fact, courtesy titles were a major issue during the civil rights movement because of their centrality in expressing white supremacy. James Devoual, who joined the movement as a teenager, explains that whites "always referred to your mom, your father, as boy, girl. There were never any titles used addressing elders."[10] According to Ruth Juanita Stewart, her family's white neighbors always referred to her parents by their first names, though her mother said "'yes ma'am' and 'no ma'am'" to the younger woman. Whenever her mother would send her children to help the neighbors, she would instruct them, "'Go to the back now. Don't go to the front. Go to the back and yell out for Mrs. Price.'" Explaining that "I really really hated doing that," Stewart expresses frustration that since she never learned the neighbor's first name, even in telling the story she still has to refer to her as "Mrs. Price."[11]

Whites' and blacks' different experiences with race and their different understandings of its meanings became more public with the emergence of a mass movement. In Claiborne County, the civil rights movement began in late 1965. Within months, hundreds of blacks were attending weekly mass meetings. By April 1966 more than 2,000 African Americans had registered to vote, giving them an electoral majority. And on April 1 the National Association for the Advancement of Colored People (NAACP) initiated a highly successful boycott against white merchants. Many whites, who had been convinced that blacks were satisfied with the racial status quo, were bewildered by these developments. The movement appeared to shatter interracial harmony and "friendship."[12]

Druggist M. M. McFatter observed that "we had [black] people, the white people would just swear by. For instance, Mr. Hudson, he swore that his main man, he ain't going with that, but he did."[13] A black woman illustrated this by describing a conversation she had with a white social worker:

> The welfare lady came up and sat on my porch one day and . . . say, "I don't see what the black people's fighting about." . . . Ya'll seems like ya'll happy. Every time we see you, you laughing, happy. Look like you happy all the time." I say, "Yes, I guess we laughing to keep from crying." That's right. I say, "I know I'm not happy." . . . She thought black people was satisfied the way things was. . . . She said colored people seemed to be happy like they was.[14]

Nathaniel (Nate) Jones offers another example. For years banker Eli Ellis had hunted on Jones's land and handled his farm loans. Jones describes how, when the movement began, Ellis called him into his office and said, "'I heard that you was teaching hate down there.' I said, 'Naw, I never done anything like that.' . . . He said, 'Well, we been good to you. We . . . been letting you have anything you want.' . . . I said, 'I paid my debt. I been just as good to you as you been to me. I don't teach any hate, but I want my rights, just like you want yours.'" As he was leaving, Jones remembers that Ellis told him, "I know you a pretty good person. I didn't think you'd be caught up in a mess like that." Jones replied, "Well, I am. I'm in it."[15]

Because they refused to accept that blacks had never been content with this system, whites repeatedly blamed the new militancy on outsiders. For example, white leader Jimmy Allen says,

> I remember the agitators coming in from outside. They used churches you know, which was a good place for [them] to get their attention. Some outside preacher would come in and make these talks and all. Of course, the fact that it was actually turning blacks against whites, we didn't appreciate it a whole lot. We had been getting along with them for years. There were some people who abused them, there's no doubt about it, but generally . . . there was enough respect back and forth where there wasn't any complications.[16]

A black resident puts a different twist on this, explaining, "We *seem* to have gotten along well together, but that's because we accepted where we were."[17]

For most blacks in Claiborne County, memories of the movement are positive, marked by excitement and feelings of unity. For example, Julius Warner recalls, "Everybody pitched in and worked together. You've never seen

people so organized and so sincere about working together with each other."
He describes the black community during that time as "very close knit," noting that even those who "set back and watched" and "didn't want to be seen
... were really in favor and we knew that."[18] Warner's assertion is borne out by
the rapid increase in NAACP memberships and black voter registration. The
NAACP went from a handful of members before December 1965 to more
than 1,300 adult members by mid-April 1966, with another 400 joining before the year ended. This was more than 40 percent of the county's black
residents over the age of twenty-one. The youth branch included another
500 members. Moreover, by mid-May more than two-thirds of the county's
eligible black population had registered to vote, up from fewer than 100 in
December 1965.[19]

The Port Gibson boycott, initiated on April 1, 1966, after whites refused to
meet black community demands, heightened racial tensions and differences.
During the period of the most intense activism, roughly from March 1966
through February 1967, the vast majority of African Americans enthusiastically supported the boycott. Activist Marjorie Brandon explains, "Everybody
stood for the boycott. It was very united." One participant testified that when
the boycott began, he "avoided all white merchants like the plague," and another said, "I wanted to stand with black people."[20]

Despite considerable black support and solidarity, most whites assumed
at the time—and many continue to believe today—that the boycott was initiated and driven by outsiders and that most blacks only observed the boycott
because of coercion or boycott enforcement. A merchant insisted that "the
locals here were not really doing anything. It was the outsiders that came in
here and organized the boycott."[21] Many years later, former sheriff Dan Mc-
Cay characterized black demands as "unreal" and "impossible."[22] However,
what whites like McCay saw as unreasonable and "impossible," blacks saw as
basic and fundamental. Activist James Devoual explains, "The issues for the
boycott were not major kinds of requests. 'Call us "Sir" and "Ma'am." Give us
the clerk jobs and cashiers.' Basic decent rights. That's all we were asking." He
continued,

> They didn't want to give us basic human respect. That's what the whole fight
> was about. . . . They hold on to those traditional values that you are second-
> class citizens, that white folk are right, that you're not equal, . . . that I don't
> care what you say, we ain't going to school with you, we ain't going to hang
> out with you and we ain't going to let you be a part of the decision making
> process.[23]

A white woman who was more sympathetic than most to the movement illustrates just how much difference there was in how blacks and whites viewed their interactions. She explains that she was taught to treat the African Americans who worked for her family with respect and instructed to say things like,

> "Please, when you have time, Mammy, could you fix us a piece of cake or some milk?" You didn't snap out. You never raised your voice, and you did not sass anybody. And we were made fun of [by other whites] for saying, "Aunt," and "Uncle." But the reason we did . . . it was a term of respect.[24]

Thus even as she and many other whites believed that by saying "Aunt" or "Uncle" they were being respectful to blacks, blacks were insisting, in the words of NAACP leader Charles Evers, that "if a person's old enough, [call them] Mr. or Mrs., not auntie, uncle, we not your auntie, uncle."[25] The same conflict is evident in a confrontation between activist Rudy Shields and a white storekeeper. When the merchant called Shields "boy," he reacted by telling her that "'he was . . . no damn boy, he was a God damn man.'"[26] The reaction of a white man who witnessed this exchange shows just how reluctant whites were to acknowledge the depth of black anger over this persistent disrespect. He testified, "She called him a boy. He told her he wasn't no damn boy; he was a God damn man. He used that expression for *no more* than calling him a boy."[27]

Guided by their unwillingness or inability to hear blacks when they articulated their grievances, whites clung to their certainty that the boycott was driven by outsiders and boycott enforcement. They refused to offer meaningful concessions or engage in good-faith negotiations. A merchant testified that when NAACP leader Charles Evers "asked what we had to offer, we offered nothing." Another merchant contended, "My husband and I weren't going to give in. . . . And none of the other stores around here wanted to give in either." Marjorie Brandon explained that merchants "would rather . . . go out of business, sacrifice their business than to kneel to change."[28]

Ironically, in their effort to undermine the boycott and entice customers, whites did engage in some interesting reversals. Albert Butler insists that even as Piggly Wiggly grocery store owner James Hudson grew increasingly angry about the boycott, he began treating his black employees more respectfully. Similarly, white alderman Jimmy Allen recalled that during the boycott, whites began to shop for their black maids. Though his emphasis was on blacks' desire to shop with white merchants and their fear of retaliation from blacks, the very idea of whites shopping for black servants suggests a major reversal. When three black women ignored picketers and went into McFatter's Drug Store in April 1966 to fill a prescription, McFatter seated the women and brought them cold drinks. At the time, white shopkeepers were removing stools and closing their businesses rather than desegregate and permit blacks to sit down and eat. Moreover, it was unthinkable for a white man to serve black women. McFatter's atypical behavior was clearly intended to reward these women for breaking the boycott. Ironically, he and other merchants could have ended the boycott entirely by offering all blacks a small measure of such courteous, respectful treatment.[29]

The handful of blacks who continued to patronize white stores, people like these three women, became targets of "boycott enforcement," including ostracism, name calling, destruction of property, and, on rare occasions, physical violence. One of the most contested issues related to the movement is the extent to which enforcement explained the boycott's success. This is complicated for several reasons. First, the boycott had two periods of intensity, and enforcement played a different role at different times. The second issue is defining enforcement. Is it picketing? Peer pressure? Intimidation? Violence? Violence against property? Violence against people? And finally, in 1969 white merchants filed suit against the NAACP and more than 100 local blacks asking for damages and a permanent injunction against the boycott. The resulting case, *Claiborne Hardware v. NAACP*, was not settled until 1982 when the U.S. Supreme Court overturned an earlier $1.25 million judgment against the movement activists. All of these events and issues make it challenging to sort out exactly what role enforcement or coercion played in the boycott.

But peer pressure and persuasion were certainly the most important enforcement tactics. NAACP president James Dorsey maintains that movement supporters would "try to talk to peoples and explain to them what we were trying to do, and what it would mean for them and for their childrens and grandchildrens, you know." According to Marjorie Brandon, this tactic worked so well that violators would be "standing out to themselves. [People would] say, 'You just go on over there, you [act] white, why don't you go on over there with the whites.'" When peer pressure did not work, Claiborne County enforcers sometimes took and destroyed groceries or packages. Occasionally they threw bricks or shot at homes or cars belonging to persistent boycott violators. Even more rarely, they beat people up.[30]

Leesco Guster offers an example of enforcement that was probably typical. When Priscilla Duck violated the boycott and defiantly told Guster that she would "spend her money anywhere she want to spend it," Guster "turned her name in," and it was announced at an NAACP meeting. Shortly afterward Duck's picture window was broken. A devoted churchgoer, Guster interrupts her story with a laugh, saying, "I'm not supposed to be saying all of that" and quickly clarifies, "I didn't do it, I just told it." But then she makes it clear that she fully supported the act of retaliation, saying, "I didn't have any mercy on anybody. I told on my own sister."[31] Like Guster, most blacks believed the movement's goals were important enough to justify these occasional coercive tactics.[32] Although ostracism and some occasional physical punishment appear to have been widely accepted in the black community, they do not seem to have been widely needed or used. The Hinds County judge who ruled that the boycott was an illegal conspiracy enforced by violence could identify no more than twelve acts of enforcement, only three of which involved physical violence. A black man who never stopped shopping with whites testified that boycott enforcement was not a big deal. "Someone, I don't remember who, once indirectly threatened me for continuing to trade with whites, but I attached no importance to it."[33]

In fact, some blacks probably used whites' perception of enforcement to obscure their reasons for boycotting, finding it easier to let whites believe that their new shopping patterns came from fear of retaliation rather than support for movement goals. Celia Anderson provides a useful illustration. A sharecropper, she was also a strong movement participant. She went to meetings, marched, registered to vote, and canvassed among her neighbors and friends. She was called Mama Celie because of her fierce protection of the younger activists, including her own children and grandchildren. James Miller explains that Mama Celie "almost demanded" that her children "be a part of the movement." Although she bought nothing new during the boycott, Anderson made regular payments to Barbara Ellis for previous purchases. She explains how she allowed Ellis to believe her observance of the boycott was due to fear of retaliation. "Miss Barbara [would] come to the door and get it. 'Celie come on in here. Come on in here.' I say, 'No, Miss Ellis. I ain't going to let them whup me, you know.' We'd have a big laugh and I'd pay her and she'd give me a receipt. Something I already owed her for. Paid her out." Despite her comments to Ellis, Anderson never considered breaking the boycott.[34]

A May 1969 law enforcement effort to catch several men using coercion also illustrates how some blacks hid their boycott support behind the threat of enforcement. An investigator had a white merchant send an employee to drop shirts off at a dry cleaners while he stood watch, hoping to catch other blacks threatening or attacking him. The employee never actually tried to go into the store and instead went out of his way to talk to movement activists on the street. Yet he told his employer that he was unable to drop shirts off to be cleaned because enforcers "wouldn't let him go in."[35] Unaware that he was being watched, this employee used the excuse of coercion to justify his observance of the boycott.

Ultimately, most blacks insist that the boycott succeeded because of widespread support, not because of violent enforcement. Leesco Guster contends that "everybody was just together," while Marjorie Brandon concluded that it "really wasn't too much enforcement because people just didn't go in there. . . . Everybody believed in it and this is what everybody wanted. Ninety-nine percent of them felt like you know, if they getting our black dollar then they should have some black people in there working for them."[36] In contrast, most whites still believe that enforcement was the most crucial factor in the boycott's success. From whites' perspective, if race relations were good, enforcement was the only explanation that made sense. Moreover, once merchants filed suit, coercion was the key to their case.

Another important part of the difference in perception lies in white attitudes about public space and the kinds of behavior they found troubling in blacks. Whites were bothered by many of the changes that came with the movement, including things like the presence of black voter registration workers, demonstrators, picketers, and store watchers on the streets. Alderman and merchant Jimmy Allen described marches as "an irritation," and grocer Waddy Abraham criticized black participation in mass meetings.

> They'd carry on about what they gon' do, how the thing is going. You couldn't get down that street for the cars and the people. I'm talking about men, old folk. They . . . hardly could walk, they'd be there. Like a big family reunion. They want a good time, they go there. . . . And you know how they are, like to shout and carry on anyway.

Merchant James Hudson testified that he grew afraid to let his daughter walk down the streets because of his experiences of "having to push or go around a bunch of young blacks." He explained that blacks "would be walking two or three abreast or just crowding the sidewalk and you would have to get out in the street to go around them. They wouldn't let you by. Nothing like this had happened before the boycott was put on. After the boycott, it happened hundreds of times." Pharmacy owner Quitman H. McDaniel Jr.'s description of picketers conveys similar hostility. "They picketed up and down the entire business district, not just my store. They made noise; they would stomp, like storm troops."[37]

An encounter between movement activist Calvin Williams and several Port Gibson white men in April 1966 illustrates how whites believed they should control public space and how they struggled to hang on to that authority when it was challenged by the movement. Williams and several companions were walking down Main Street to investigate rumors of a movement-related confrontation when they encountered Police Chief L. L. Doyle standing with several other white men. Though Williams responded cooperatively to Doyle's request that the group disperse and even asked those with him to walk in twos, he was later arrested and charged with "disturbing the peace" and "blocking the public sidewalk and entrances to stores." NAACP president James Dorsey contends that whites arrested Williams because they "didn't want a lot of blacks to assemble together." In fact, the white men who believed Williams acted improperly failed to identify any unlawful behavior. Collectively, they testified that Williams and his companions had walked in a group down the street and stopped on a corner. None of them reported that Williams physically blocked the sidewalk or any store entrances. Chief Doyle, for example, justified Williams's arrest by testifying, "This group of Negroes were utilizing almost all of the sidewalk." Moreover, he and the other white men saw no irony in the fact that they too were standing in a group on a sidewalk corner. One of the things that appeared to bother Doyle most was that he believed Williams had violated an earlier agreement that blacks would not conduct any marches without explicit white permission. Like officials in a Louisiana town who conveyed ownership of the streets to merchants so they could arrest picketers for trespassing, Port Gibson white officials believed the streets belonged to them, and blacks could only use them with permission.[38]

In their court testimony in the *Claiborne Hardware* lawsuit, the merchants essentially interpreted constitutionally protected boycott activity as violent and criminal. Asked to give an example of how the defendants used violence to promote the boycott, one merchant testified, "There were people who I called guards in front of my store. . . . I don't distinguish pickets and guards." Although he testified that he did not "see anyone stop anyone by force," he insisted, "The defendants did something to me in that they quit buying from me." Similarly, Barbara Ellis testified, "I saw them stop any black customer who wanted to go into a white store. They would grab them and threaten them[,] . . . grabbed their purchases." When pressed, however, she backtracked. "I did not actually see any of the defendants stop customers and take goods away from them." Charles Dobbs testified that the actions of a picketer who "stood in front of my store a day or two and advised people that the store was under boycott" were "illegal because of the tone of voice used and her attitude." Another merchant conceded, "We sued the NAACP and 148 black people just because they didn't trade with us."[39]

Blacks and whites also had very different experiences with education— from the separate and unequal schools that dominated most of the twentieth century to the limited experiments with school integration starting in 1966 to the segregation that largely persists today. These differences are evident in black and white memories and help shape divergent contemporary perspectives. All of this is of considerable importance since the community's schools are most notable for their persistent segregation and declining quality, for blacks and whites.

Until September 1959, when white school officials opened Addison Junior and Senior High School for African Americans (and used buses to bring all of the black students to Port Gibson for nine months of school), the facilities, resources, transportation, and school terms for blacks and whites were vastly unequal. Addison was a direct response to the 1954 *Brown* decision and part of a statewide attempt to forestall integration by making a belated—and still somewhat incomplete—effort to equalize black and white education.[40] White and black memories of education before "equalization" reflect the persistent gap in school resources and opportunities. White students remember pleasant, comfortable schools with small, close-knit student bodies. For most, school was a positive experience, and memories of academic pursuits are often overshadowed by extracurricular activities. A 1941 graduate recalls beautiful grounds edged by roses and an environment that was "just about like a private girls school."[41] Mott Headley, who was elected to the county board of supervisors in 1965, remembers that he was primarily interested in football and girls and periodically tried to skip school by playing sick. He comments, "I didn't try real hard, but the ones that did, they got a good education and went on to big things."[42] For Ruth Willis, one of the best things about the small school size was the ease of participating in extracurricular activities: sports, band, student government, and a vast array of clubs and other projects.[43] Mary Ann Norton attended during the Depression and had trouble keeping up with her classes one year because she was several months late purchasing her schoolbooks. Her most vivid memories, however, were of basketball. Over the years, the team had to sew its own uniforms and raise money for expenses, but through student efforts and community generosity, they never did without.[44]

African American school memories are very different and begin with the effort just to attend. Before the 1940s the one-room, one-teacher schools that most blacks went to were organized around the rhythm of the cotton crop, operating on a split session totaling six months. Students went to school between the harvesting and planting of the cotton and again in the hot summer months after the cotton had been planted and chopped but was not ready for picking. Even when school was in session, work demands often kept black children out of school. Born in 1914, Nate Jones frequently relied on his sisters to bring home assignments, which he completed by lamplight after the day's work. Even with a three-mile walk each way, he looked forward to the snowy and rainy days that freed him from farm work so he could go to school. Despite these hardships and the requirement that he repeat a grade (because of the six-month sessions), Jones managed to stay in school long enough to graduate from the eighth grade (when he was sixteen).[45] J. L. Sayles's experience was more typical. Because of family labor demands and the difficulty of walking the seven miles to school in bad weather, Sayles never made it past the third grade. He recalls,

> We black folks, we didn't have anything. Just had to do the best we can, and back there I didn't even have a chance to go to school. My mother bought me a book, and that's the only thing that she ever bought. One book each and we was the ones to make a decision, what kind of book we wanted, speller, writing, mathematic.[46]

Because most black schools were poorly constructed with minimal facilities, teachers and students had to be resourceful. Students shared books, wrote their lessons in the dirt, and in the winter chopped wood for the woodstove. Parents and the larger community subsidized county education funds by supplying firewood, doing unpaid repair work, using church buildings for schools, providing transportation, and, when they could, supplementing teacher salaries.[47]

In a context of official neglect, where simply attending school and purchasing books required sacrifice, extracurricular activities, along with the gyms, auditoriums, libraries, and funds necessary to support them, were luxuries unavailable to most black schools and are similarly absent in the memories of African Americans. Unlike their white counterparts who compared classes to more pleasant childhood pursuits, for many blacks school was a respite from labor and a sought after opportunity. Their memories of hardship are tempered only by the parallel recollections of the dedication of teachers, the individual joy of learning, and the community commitment to education. A 1967 high school graduate and movement activist explains, "It was a general position of my parents and other parents of that generation, that once we got an education, we would be free. Everything would be hunky-dory."[48]

In fall 1966, less than a decade after the opening of Addison brought considerable improvement to black educational opportunities, forty-nine African American students enrolled in the formerly all-white Port Gibson High School, which housed grades one through twelve. As with equalization, this first small step toward desegregation was precipitated by outside events. The school board was seeking to retain federal school funding by complying with the 1964 Civil Rights Act requirement that school districts develop proactive desegregation plans. Although there is considerable evidence that Claiborne County blacks valued education, most made increasing resources for black schools a priority; there was little local push for integration. As a result, the first freedom of choice announcement in 1965 went largely unnoticed. When the second notice was published in spring 1966 in the midst of an energized mass movement, NAACP leaders encouraged students and their families to apply for transfers. Anecdotal evidence suggests about a hundred did, and the all-white school board reassigned forty-nine, five to the high school and forty-four to grades one through eight.[49] This number included all six of NAACP activist Marjorie Brandon's children: Ernest Kennedy (Ken), twelfth grade; Vivian, eleventh grade; Carl, eighth grade; Maxine, sixth grade; Dennis, fifth grade; and John, second grade. Like most who participated in freedom of choice, Brandon and her children saw integrating the white school both as movement work and an opportunity to access a better education. Even after the post-*Brown* equalization, the white school still had better facilities, smaller class sizes, and more advanced courses. (Despite these specific kinds of tangible differences, African Americans typically emphasize the high quality of most black teachers and insist that they were not rejecting the black schools.[50])

More than any other aspect of the civil rights movement, school desegregation felt to whites like an assault on their customs and way of life. In its earliest days, the boycott could be ignored by those who were not direct targets. (This was especially true since whites almost universally believed it would end quickly, never imagining that it would stay strong for ten months and then reemerge in response to subsequent racial conflict.) Similarly, although whites saw the implications of black voter registration as ominous, electoral change was still in the future. School desegregation was immediate and reached virtually every white family in the community. One white woman recalled that whites initially tried to ignore the civil rights movement. "If people had prejudices they kept them to themselves. They didn't openly discuss things. Now, when the integration started in the schools a lot of people did get real uptight and say, 'Well, my child's not going to that school anymore.'"[51] Although most white students stayed in the public schools, some prominent white civic leaders founded Claiborne Education Foundation (CEF), a private, segregationist alternative, which opened in September 1966 with seventy-three students and six teachers for grades one through eight.[52]

Many of the white students who stayed in the public schools expressed their hostility to integration by tormenting their new black classmates. African Americans were a distinct minority, and they faced a steady barrage of name-calling, spitballs, and harassment. In this context, the "friendliest" white students were those who simply ignored their black classmates; none of the black students reported making friends or having positive interactions with white students. White teachers also varied. Some were hostile, most made an attempt to be even-handed, and a number were friendly.[53] A few black students, exemplified by Ken Brandon, managed to excel despite the difficult context. Many more struggled, including Ken's younger brother Carl. Ken turned ignoring white students' harassment into a game, embraced the opportunity to take more advanced math classes, and graduated that year as one of the top students in his class.[54] In contrast, the eighth-grader Carl felt attacked and isolated, alone at his new school and cut off from his friends and community. At the end of the first year, twenty-one freedom of choice students were promoted and returned for a second year at Port Gibson High School. Another sixteen returned but had to repeat the same grade. Eleven left. Most of them, including Carl Brandon, were probably reluctant to face another year of loneliness and abuse.[55]

Anecdotal and statistical evidence suggests that the years of freedom of choice were years of gradual, almost imperceptible, adjustments and accommodations as the unrelenting isolation and harassment faced by the freedom of choice pioneers slowly began to fade. White students grew more accustomed to, if not accepting of, their African American classmates. In the third year (1968–1969), black students began to play sports and joined a few other extracurricular activities. The next year 169 African American students, 27 percent of the total student body, were enrolled in the formerly all-white schools. Two-thirds of them were returning for at least a second year, and twenty-five African American students, just over half of the initial group, were beginning their fourth year in the formerly all-white schools. Even based solely on familiarity and numbers, this final group of freedom of choice students had an experience that was quite different from that of the first isolated group of students.[56]

It would be a mistake, however, to simply describe the four-year period of freedom of choice as an ongoing evolution toward better race relations and effective school integration. Even though African American students were more comfortable, faced less torment, and had fewer academic setbacks, Port Gibson High School remained the white school and Addison the black school. Teaching staffs and bus routes were completely segregated, and the white superintendent and white-majority school board ran both school systems. The vast majority of African American students (more than 2,000) still went to all-black schools. Increasing numbers of white students left the public schools for private academies, and those black and white students who did share a school remained largely separate, maintaining distinct communities within one building.

This initial experiment with small-scale desegregation ended after the Supreme Court ruled in late 1969 that school districts could no longer operate dual white and black schools. Claiborne County officials began planning for one fully integrated school system, with desegregation of faculty, staff, and bus routes beginning in fall 1970. The school board predicted that if all students returned to the public schools, the black to white ratio would be about 80 to 20 percent: 406 to 82 at Richardson Elementary, 1,319 to 222 at Addison Junior High, and 661 to 145 at Port Gibson High School.[57] Although whites still controlled the school board and superintendent's office, this new plan meant that white students would be a distinct minority within classrooms, and many would be taught by black teachers in schools administered by black principals. Despite what appears to be a good faith effort by the superintendent and school board, when the county's schools opened in fall 1970, only 91 of the 2,504 public school students were white, less than 4 percent of the total and far fewer than the 449 projected earlier by the school board.[58]

Ruth Willis, a white student who stayed for her senior year, remembers being very afraid when the school year began. Despite her initial fears, she "never had any kind of what I'd call an incident." And ultimately, although she missed out on some of the fun she had anticipated—like playing basketball (because she could no longer make the team) and other extracurricular activities (because the white school and civic leaders did not support them in black schools or the public schools after "integration"), she had a largely successful year, graduating as valedictorian. She thought many of her new teachers were excellent and even spent time tutoring former classmates whose private school chemistry class was behind hers. Interestingly, even after four years of having black classmates through freedom of choice, one of her strongest memories is how different her world and perspective was from that of her classmates, now overwhelmingly black. "I can remember sitting in a class and saying, 'Okay, what music do ya'll listen to?' It was almost like I was talking to people from a different country instead of people in my same town. The cultures were so different."[59]

Few whites were as willing to give the black-majority schools a chance. Most white students and teachers left immediately for private academies in what one white parent (who was also a teacher) called "the mass leave."[60] CEF, the private school founded in 1966 for grades one through eight, expanded and relocated to Port Gibson, while Chamberlain Hunt Academy (CHA), a military boarding school with a longer history in the community, accepted white girls as day students for the first time.[61] Within a few years even the handful of white staff and students who had stayed in the public schools for the first year or two were gone, either retiring, graduating, or following their counterparts to the segregationist academies. Many blacks also believe that during the early 1970s white school officials found new ways to support white education by moving books, supplies, and furniture to the private academies.[62] Whites' abandonment of the public schools during this period essentially marked the end of any possibility of integrated public schools serving the whole community. From the mid-1970s to the present only a couple dozen whites have attended the public schools, and far fewer have stayed through graduation. Over time, the private academies softened their whites-only policies (in part to protect their tax deductible status), and since the late 1990s there have typically been a few African Americans at CEF and CHA.

By the 1990s at least some white leaders and parents began to see the community's racially divided black public and white private schools as problematic. The private academies drained family and community resources, and many parents were increasingly dissatisfied with the quality of instruction. For their part, many African Americans were also more and more unhappy with what they saw as the declining quality of public education. Some blacks blamed black elected officials, while others focused on what they saw as whites' active attempts to undermine public education and discredit black leaders. Many blacks were also angry at whites' persistent refusal to consider sending their children to black-majority and now black-run public schools, seeing this refusal as a barrier to any cooperative future. They saw this as an indication that whites would only accept integration and interracial cooperation on their terms.[63]

In this context, whites began to look back on freedom of choice with nostalgia and see it not only as viable, but ideal. White parent and teacher Carolyn Dobbs acknowledges that "hindsight is always so much better," but she still insists that the public schools and probably CHA (which predated "integration") "would be better off today if we all had been able to work it out." In her view, working things out would have meant maintaining freedom of choice. Looking back, she asserts, it "was working beautifully and it would have worked." She continues,

> That's something you can't recapture, just really prove, but . . . we were inte-grated in every way there at the school. The children were enjoying it. They were enjoying friendship. They were enjoying the football team and they were enjoying all the activities . . . and that's the way it should have been and I wish it could have stayed like that.

Ignoring whites' initial resistance and then grudging adaptation to freedom of choice, she explains, "I felt like . . . [integration] wasn't something that could just be crammed down your throat by the government and that's what happened when the freedom of choice was taken away. . . . That's when the mass exodus happened, and I still to this day think that was a big mistake."[64]

Other whites share her perspective, but it is one that is clouded by white privilege. For example, another former school employee says freedom of choice was "working nicely," but she overstates the black to white student ratio, suggesting it was an even fifty-fifty when the ratio was actually 73 percent white. Her belief that the school system was beginning to integrate teaching staffs is also faulty.[65] Moreover, even after black students began to partici-pate in more extracurricular activities, including sports and band, there were distinct limits. For example, the student council, yearbook staff, newspaper staff, class officers, and homecoming queens remained all white.[66] Of the many candid shots in the 1969–1970 yearbook, only two, wide angles of a classroom and a gym crowd, included African Americans. The yearbook also contains a picture identified as the class of 1970 taken in 1960. The African American seniors, who had been in the black school ten years earlier, were obviously absent from the picture, but there was neither an explanation nor another picture. As far as whites were concerned, larger numbers of black students and some black participation in school events did not change the fact that Port Gibson High School was still their school.

Calvin Williams Jr., who spent the 1968–1969 and 1969–1970 school years at Port Gibson High School, has vivid memories of how this white dominance and segregation played out. He explains, "There wasn't much exchange going on. You got the feeling there was some sort of enforced segregation on the part of the white students." This separation extended from classes to extra-curricular activities. For example, the chemistry teacher reassigned lab part-ners (initially determined alphabetically) to ensure that the students worked in segregated teams. Williams recalls being just as happy with this arrange-ment. "There was bad feeling among these people, and you'd rather be work-ing with someone you could trust anyway. Don't give me a lab partner that might try to blow me up or sabotage the experiment." In another instance, when Williams and a few other black students joined their white classmates at the National Guard Armory to work on a homecoming float, someone slashed their tires. White administrators made sure the black students got home and made arrangements to replace the tires. They did not, however, try to punish the perpetrators. Williams remembers, "It was like we're gonna fix it . . . but [there was] no measure of justice."[67] Overall, African Americans had mixed feelings about freedom of choice. It was never a primary focus, and most blacks continued to emphasize other work, including voter registra-tion, that they hoped would end white control over school resource alloca-tion and policy-making positions.

Given these limitations, it is tempting to argue that freedom of choice ac-complished little in terms of "true integration." This is probably true. Yet it is also important to acknowledge that freedom of choice did shift the center of debate and exchange, and with it the larger community's sense of what was possible. The unthinkable had happened. Even if they were not becoming close friends, white and black children were sharing classrooms and cafete-ria tables. Private school attendance was slowly growing, but the majority of Port Gibson's whites remained in nominally desegregated public schools. They seemed to decide that integration could be stomached as long as they remained the majority and in charge. In many ways, then, the story of school desegregation in Claiborne County is very much like the overall story of the local civil rights movement. African Americans worked steadily to challenge white supremacy—enrolling in the "white" school in increasing numbers, while persistently demanding full inclusion and trying to impact policy mak-ing. Whites accommodated some surface change, as little as possible, while working quietly to maintain control and minimize structural transforma-tions.

Whites who look back with nostalgia at freedom of choice and postu-late that it was the right way to achieve school integration disregard both the difficult and marginalized experiences of most African Americans who integrated the white school and the extent to which freedom of choice was irrelevant for the vast majority of blacks who remained in segregated (and still unequal) schools. In 1969, the final year of freedom of choice, for example, the 169 black participants were just over 25 percent of the population of the white schools, but were only about 7 percent of the approximately 2,400 black students attending school in Claiborne County. Moreover, whites who look back at the shift from freedom of choice to a unitary system as the cause of contemporary problems refuse to consider that the mistake, the critical moment, might not have been the Supreme Court's insistence that dual school systems were unconstitutional, but rather their decision to abandon the public schools entirely. From whites' perspective, it was fine for African American students to be an isolated minority, taught exclusively by white teachers, but they would not consider a variation of that for their own children, even when a white majority school board and superintendent still controlled the overall policies and there was nothing to suggest white students would encounter anything like the harassment aimed at the black pioneers. Thus those whites who look back to freedom of choice as an ideal and even talk of trying to replicate it through some form of magnet schools do not really see freedom of choice in terms of integration so much as a way of maintaining majority-white, white-controlled public schools.

From the vantage point of the twenty-first century, whites' refusal to give genuinely integrated schools a chance appears to be a real lost opportunity. Even with the limitations of freedom of choice for African Americans, the gradual lessening of hostility and slow shift toward acceptance by whites illustrate that there was at least some chance of change in race relations and expectations. At the very least, white students experienced sharing classrooms and even some activities with black students. This evolution, taken together with Ruth Willis's memories of good teachers and genuine exchange in the first year of a unitary system, offers a glimpse of what might have been possible had whites stayed in the public schools and added their talent and resources to those of the black community to work toward positive education for all the community's children. Instead, by leaving en masse and focusing their wealth and skills on creating a private alternative and, in some instances, actively undermining the public schools, white actions almost ensured a gulf that many still see as insurmountable today, even as racial attitudes and surface-level interactions have evolved.

Although school desegregation had the potential for generating long-lasting changes in the community's race relations, whites' refusal to invest in any serious attempt at full-fledged integration turned it into one more area of resistance and hostility. Given whites' refusal to work toward a cooperative interracial future, the movement's role in recasting the relationships between blacks and whites came primarily through African Americans' expressions of power. In this context, the boycott was particularly important in giving voice to blacks' insistence on dignified treatment and a say in community life. As the white merchants' *Claiborne Hardware* testimony illustrates, the boycott contributed to challenges over whites' entrenched authority over public space and black behavior. It also asserted blacks' refusal to be excluded from community decision making and provided blacks with a weapon for attacking a seemingly invulnerable white community. With the onset of the boycott, white merchants suddenly experienced a new reality. Instead of being in a position to offer or withhold credit and other favors, they were soliciting black customers and had to be careful not to insult or anger them.

Activist Unita Blackwell observed that the boycott was psychologically devastating to the white community and explains that they had "conned" themselves into thinking that they had their own self-contained economy and instead found out that they were dependent "on a bunch of 'niggers.' That's what they said. . . . They was so . . . in denial until they didn't realize that their economy was the so-called 'niggers.' Their whole livelihood was the so-called 'niggers.'"[68] Shortly before the boycott began, Nate Jones paid off all of his outstanding bills with white merchants. One of the debts was to Michael Ellis for a "blue serge suit," and Jones recalls that "I went and paid the $75 that I owed. It hurt that man. It hurt that fellow so bad to see me go. I had been one of his customers for years."[69] Michael Ellis's relationship with Jimmy Ellis also changed. Before the movement, Jimmy Ellis remembers that the black Ellises and white Ellises had a good relationship because "we wore the same last name." Michael Ellis gave Jimmy Ellis school clothes and "used to say that we were all related, part of the same family. Cut off the same family tree." Once the high school–age Jimmy Ellis became active in the movement, however, he remembers that Michael Ellis "told me to get out of the store and don't ever come back and what he said about family, that's a lie. You nothing but a no good nigger like the rest of them."[70]

During the early days of the boycott, the NAACP asked blacks who worked in white homes to quit their jobs. According to a white woman who was somewhat sympathetic to the movement, her maid told her that the NAACP "wanted to show us what it was like not to have any contacts of help and friendship from the black community." She remembers that "all of a sudden, all over town," whites felt a "loss" and a "great shock." Saying that she and her maid "loved each other," she insists that she "wasn't really hurt," and "it wasn't such a blow to me" because "I wasn't totally dependent on it." She explains that her children were mostly grown, and "I knew how to do all the work. I'd washed and ironed and done to take care of my own children."[71] Moreover, she remains convinced that her maid would not have quit if she had really needed her. These comments illustrate the dual nature of the loss white women experienced—of labor, and of their sense of emotional connection to the black women who worked for them.

The boycott also became a tool for punishing whites individually and collectively. When a Ford dealer refused to let a black customer use the restroom, picketers were outside his business within hours. In a similar incident Meyer-Marx owner Pete Jordan, who had also been exempt from the boycott because he employed a black clerk, cursed a black customer. In response, the movement "decided they would close that [store] down."[72] More significant, in 1969, when a white police officer killed an unarmed black man, Roosevelt "Dusty" Jackson, the black community responded with a renewed boycott. At a mass meeting the Monday after the shooting, NAACP leader Charles Evers told the crowd, "There comes a time when you really don't know what to do, but you know you got to do something. . . . We've been pushed to the hilt and there ain't nowhere to go." Locked out of city government and spurned by white leaders, blacks could do little to productively influence policy or decision making. About all they could do was articulate their outrage and punish white merchants—because they were the most vulnerable representatives of the white community.[73]

The boycott did not end the continuing disparity in resources and power, and in many ways whites' unrelenting defiance did much to slam the door shut on any possibility for serious cooperative efforts to create a humane, inclusive, integrated community, something the community is still struggling to overcome. Yet even though whites were slow to respect blacks, acknowledge the legitimacy of their grievances, or consider meaningful power sharing, ultimately they had to recognize that blacks now wielded a source of power that could hurt them.

In 1982 the U.S. Supreme Court ruled on the suit filed by white merchants. After thirteen years of litigation, the justices issued a unanimous decision in favor of the local NAACP and black defendants. In doing so, they overturned a $1.25 million judgment by the Mississippi Supreme Court and affirmed the right of people to use economic boycotts for political ends. By the time the court handed down its decision, the surface issues driving the boycott had largely been settled. Blacks worked as clerks in most stores, and white merchants were far more careful to use courtesy titles with their African American customers.

In the 1990s pharmacist Quitman H. McDaniel explained that he had participated in the lawsuit because the attorneys "led us to believe that they would be able to" stop the boycott, and "I wanted the boycotting stopped." In retrospect, however, McDaniel realizes, "They *couldn't* do it. There was no way in the *world* they could do it, [to] *make* people do things." This was an important lesson for whites to learn, that they could not control African Americans; it was undoubtedly one of the key changes brought by the movement. NAACP president James Dorsey recalls that when the boycott first began, whites thought Evers would leave and "things would be back to normal." They were mistaken, however, and, as Dorsey says, "things were never the same . . . after that."[74]

Although blacks and whites in Claiborne County share a past, they do not share an understanding of that past. Many whites' views of the community's history remain strongly influenced by their antipathy to the civil rights movement and their certainty that any discussion of it simply exacerbates current racial tensions by dwelling on a negative period of the past. Here, they are undoubtedly influenced by their overriding perception of the movement as a period of loss and betrayal. For many whites, especially those of the leadership class, life in Claiborne County before the movement was centered around their needs; the movement did, in some ways, shatter that world of privilege and replace it with conflict, uncertainty, and declining authority.

Locked in their own reality, few whites understand or acknowledge that the movement was a direct response to centuries of oppression, that for blacks it was a hopeful time, and that it was a necessary and partial corrective to the reality that the political, economic, and social structures of the community were arranged for the benefit of whites. Whites, then, fault African Americans for shattering their refuge in small, locally controlled, segregated public schools; intruding in politics; and, most significant, carrying out the boycott that they blame for destroying the downtown. The movement also called into question whites' deeply held beliefs about good race relations and interracial friendship, challenged their right to speak for the entire community, and introduced an element of insecurity into their sense of the world. So in many ways whites' view of the movement as a time of loss is accurate; however, what the vast majority of whites refuse to understand is that it was specifically their loss, not a widespread loss for the community. Furthermore, most of what whites lost, they never really had (like good interracial friendships) or never had a right to (like political control based on disfranchisement). Moreover, whites fail to concede that they still benefit, especially economically, from the enduring legacy of white supremacy.

By the 1990s some whites, mainly those involved in politics or business who needed to accommodate African Americans, had learned to publicly acknowledge that there were some racial problems in the era before the movement. However, they still typically refused to deal with specifics or concede the legitimacy of black grievances and tactics. Historian Wesley Hogan points out that during the movement, there was no action that black Mississippians could take that whites in authority would consider moderate.[75] That view has persisted so that even in retrospect, many whites insist that during the movement blacks were too impatient and used inappropriate tactics. Port Gibson whites' fixation on the boycott as vindictive, unnecessary, and the key factor in ruining the downtown is particularly telling, in that they adamantly refuse to concede that merchants and white officials could have easily ended the boycott by making minor concessions, doing things that they now consider routine—hiring blacks and addressing them with courtesy. Instead, whites persistently act as if they had no culpability. There is no meeting place between their acknowledgment that there were "some problems" and their bitterness toward the boycott. They insist that blacks should have negotiated, while conveniently overlooking white leaders' absolute refusal to negotiate.

Just as blacks challenged white control over the legal and political systems during the movement, they have also contested whites' right to interpret the community's history. One of the earliest and most substantive challenges came through the development and installation of "No Easy Journey," a permanent exhibition portraying the Claiborne County civil rights movement. At a time when most whites still refused to discuss the movement and commonly referred to it as "that old mess," Mississippi Cultural Crossroads (a cultural arts organization strongly identified with the black community) initiated the project and generated the funding. The black majority board of supervisors was an important source of local support, and the exhibit, which opened in December 1994, was also housed in the newly completed William "Matt" Ross Administration building, home to the supervisors and named in honor of the county's first twentieth-century black member of that governing body. There was considerable community involvement in the exhibit planning process and the opening events, which included a play, *What It Is This Freedom?* (based on local oral histories and performed by local residents) and a day-long forum featuring movement participants and opponents, historians, and current community leaders.

The work leading up to the exhibit opening facilitated some of the first meaningful conversations between whites and blacks who took markedly different positions during the movement. The community advisory board was integrated, and though some whites failed to attend meetings or engage in any substantive way, a few made important contributions. During one noteworthy discussion about locating material objects, Dan McCay, the white sheriff during the movement, wondered aloud about a minutes book he had confiscated from a black self-defense group known as the Deacons. George Henry Walker, a longtime movement leader and former member of the Deacons, responded with his own memories of that encounter, and the two men shared a laugh as they reminisced.[76]

McCay was also one of two whites on an integrated panel titled "Participant Memories," where he discussed his opposition to the Ku Klux Klan and efforts to keep the group from organizing in the community. Ironically, the other white member of the panel was attorney Melvin McFatter, whose father, M. M. McFatter, had led the unsuccessful effort to organize a Klan chapter. The younger McFatter, who had also been active on the community advisory board for the exhibit, described the boycott era as a "mean and ugly time" and emphasized his family's tradition of independence to explain some of his father's actions. For example, despite M. M. McFatter's sympathy for the Klan, he eventually broke with other white merchants to hire a black clerk and end the boycott against his store. In keeping with that independent tradition, Melvin McFatter seems more willing than most whites to juxtapose his understanding of white fears and reluctance to change with a recognition that the movement was necessary and that premovement race relations were actually flawed. In particular, he described how he and his father responded to rumors that blacks were going to burn the downtown by spending the night in their drugstore, armed to the teeth. He noted that despite his youthful disappointment, he is now grateful that the night passed with no violence. Interestingly, although McFatter did nothing to welcome the black students who attended Port Gibson High School during his senior year, his lone black classmate, Ken Brandon, remembers him with some fondness as someone who did not engage in taunting and as the person who was willing to walk beside him at graduation; now the two men offer each other friendly greetings whenever Brandon returns to Claiborne County.[77]

The willingness of a few whites to engage with blacks in a relatively open and honest manner, even if only to accept that blacks and whites experienced these events differently, demonstrates the potential of a genuine examination of the community's history. Yet most whites ultimately maintained their position of animosity and refused to support the exhibit or participate in the opening events in any real way. Other than panelists, there was essentially no local white attendance at the forum. Even participants generally only came for their portion. Mayor James Beesley gave a welcome and left, while Joan

Beesley, his wife and a community leader herself, and Robert Gage IV, president of Port Gibson Bank, skipped the presentations by historians and participants, showing up only for their part in the final community roundtable, "Claiborne County: Where Are We Today?"

Beesley and Gage illustrate the ways most white leaders' claims to leadership are based on an interlocking combination of family connections, wealth, elective office, and political power. For example, Robert Gage is the fourth generation of Gages to lead the bank. His father, Robert (Bobby) Gage III, headed the Democratic Party Executive Committee for many years (including when the movement was most active) and was instrumental in initiating and funding the white merchants' lawsuit against the NAACP and local activists.[78] The black participants both achieved their leadership positions through African Americans' postmovement political power. Percy Thornton was a member of the board of supervisors, the county's governing board, while James Miller was the county administrator hired by that board. Both Miller and Thornton were movement activists as young people (Miller in Port Gibson), and both of them had been instrumental in supporting the exhibit. The comments offered by these white and black leaders reinforce how much difference there is in the ways blacks and whites understand the community's history and its ongoing relevance for addressing contemporary issues. In fact, blacks see many of the current problems as legacies of white supremacy, while whites are more likely to frame them as problems resulting from the movement or the advent of black political power.

James Miller opened the session by asserting that during the movement, African Americans were "right in our position. It was wrong for us to be locked out of this, which is America." He also insisted that "if we do not speak candidly, if we do not look the Devil in the eye and deal with our situation, I don't think we'll be able to move forward." Having asserted the legitimacy of the movement, he then directed most of his comments at black elected officials who, he insisted, had an obligation to live up to the "high moral ground" of the movement and "do the greatest good for the greatest number." Percy Thornton, one of those officials, agreed that the black community needed to confront internal problems, stop blaming others, and understand that the movement was not just about getting blacks elected. However, he also insisted that whites and blacks needed to work together. In particular, Thornton urged that the schools be integrated (meaning that whites return to the public schools) "for the betterment of our community," so that young people learn to "respect each other at an early age." He also argued that "white citizens of this community can't afford to sit back and say that the blacks are in charge, and let them run things, and complain from their houses. They must come out and take part in their community too."[79]

Joan Beesley followed and opened her remarks by insisting both that "it takes time to change" and that "we have come so far from where we were in the 1960s." Then, in what seemed almost like a caricature, she used her remarks to emphasize her personal friendships with blacks, both in the past and present, as if they were a substitute for a close examination of the community's persistent racial divisions. In particular, she talked about her "best friend Dorothy," a black child who moved into the house behind hers when they were both almost five. Beesley barely noted that many of the details of her story were of race-based inequalities—like the children's need to ask permission to sit on one another's porches and Dorothy's half-days at school and then quick promotion to second grade because the black schools were so severely overcrowded. Finally, although she never saw Dorothy (whose last name she does not know) between the time Dorothy left Claiborne County after her high school graduation and her death at a young age, Beesley asserted with certainty that if Dorothy were present, she would say that "memories are wonderful and we need them" but we should not use them to "hurt." In essence, Beesley utilized two of whites' long-standing strategies for evading a serious examination of race: she hid behind the facade of interracial "friendship" and tried to provide legitimacy for her views by articulating them through a black spokesperson (in this instance a dead woman she had known only as a child and had not seen since the 1950s). Beesley concluded by insinuating that the entire day's forum (which, except for her small part, she had not attended) and its reflections on the civil rights movement were hurtful and exacerbated racial divisions. Instead of dwelling on the past, she asserted that Claiborne countians needed to "put down burdens that make us hate each other."[80]

Robert Gage was the final speaker, and he opened by referring to the "important comments" made by the speakers at earlier panels (which he, too, had not heard). Then he spoke in vague generalities, but appeared to direct his comments almost entirely at the black community, complaining, for example, that too many school-age children were on the streets and not in school, saying, "If we can't educate them, train them, they can't get a job." He then asserted that much of this (meaning high unemployment and other community problems) is "color blind," insisted that the world was wide open for "the minority businessman who gets his act together," and argued that bank loans had created a tremendous "transfer of wealth into the black community." Then, like Beesley, he ended by speaking through the words of a black spokesperson, referencing copanelist Percy Thornton's earlier comments, that the black community needed to look at itself in the area of "values, education, and accountability." In the process, he implied that the onus for the community's future was entirely on the black community.[81]

Ultimately, both white panelists were evasive, emphasized past change and current racial harmony in the most general terms, and refused to examine or concede the white community's historic role in shaping Claiborne County's contemporary problems or its responsibility for acting with blacks to improve the future. In contrast, although Thornton, in particular, called on whites to take some responsibility for the community's future, especially by integrating the schools, both he and Miller emphasized that the black community must also be accountable and identified things that blacks needed to do for the overall community's well-being. Thus, while the black commentators framed the community's past and future in terms of both blacks and whites, the whites ignored the past and placed current responsibility solely at the feet of African Americans. Moreover, though Gage was quick to use Thornton's words to criticize blacks, he completely ignored Thornton's call for school integration. Both Gage and Beesley seemed more interested in emphasizing that the community had changed than in exploring how it could move forward.[82]

At the end of the program, an audience member pointed that out and asked the white panelists why, instead of focusing on "how far we have come," they would not ask "where we should be and work toward getting us there?"[83] Beesley responded by asserting, "I no longer speak in terms of black and white. . . . 'We' are 'we' to me and we have come forward." Repeating "and we have come forward" as a refrain throughout her comments, she stressed the integrated nature of the day's events as evidence. "Twenty years ago, we would not be here in an integrated meeting, would we have been?" Beesley's use of the day's "integrated" forum is particularly ironic since local white attendance was virtually nonexistent. Her own participation was limited, clearly more a nod to contemporary politics (her husband's reliance on black electoral support and emerging efforts to generate tourism) than a genuine effort to engage with the community's history or participate in a discussion with African Americans about the community's future. The fact that Beesley and most other white leaders refused to support or participate in establishing "No Easy Journey" and that she, acting out of political necessity, was among the few whites to attend any part of the activities highlights the limitations of her claims about contemporary racial harmony and friendship.

Beesley's comments also illustrate how whites view shifts in form, like using courtesy titles or attending integrated meetings, especially ones led by African Americans, as breakthroughs and indications of tremendous change. In some ways they are. Yet as Percy Thornton pointed out, they are no substitute for integrated schools or a shared commitment to the community as a whole. Being civil and sharing a platform do not address the ramifications of decades of white supremacy or the community's long-standing racial divisions. As former Mississippi governor William Winter observed while speaking at a 2003 memorial service for three civil rights workers killed in Philadelphia, Mississippi, "White folks think we've come further in race relations than black folks do. As far as we've come, we still have a lot left to do."[84]

In many ways, the divided perspectives and opinions of the white and African American communities in terms of "No Easy Journey" are not very different from the period that the exhibit commemorates. There are a few important distinctions, however. Unlike thirty years ago, blacks are no longer completely locked out of public or governmental spaces and were able to marshal the resources to install an exhibit that celebrates the movement. A handful of whites made a genuine commitment to support the work and engage in dialogue. Moreover, a couple of white leaders felt obligated to participate, even if only in nominal ways. This latter is at least partly related to white leaders' growing understanding that to be successful at economic development and promoting tourism, they need to project an image of interracial cooperation. Unfortunately, most whites translate this into an updated version of premovement "good relations," operating within a white-dominated vision and framework. Like Gage and Joan Beesley, they might serve on a committee or attend a meeting with blacks, but they seem unable or unwilling to actually look, in any realistic or complex way, at the community's history, especially in terms of race.

In fact, the dominant white perception of the community's racial history and of the civil rights movement seems most notable for how similar it is to that of the whites who actively fought against the movement. This perspective is very clear in *Cannonballs and Courage*, a book published in 2003 (almost a decade after "No Easy Journey" opened) with active white civic and political support. The publication was partially funded by the two white-owned banks (both of which were instrumental years earlier in encouraging and helping bankroll the merchants' lawsuit against the NAACP), and the author, Jane Ellis, had strong family ties to a number of white merchants. The almost 200-page book does recognize the presence of African Americans, concede that blacks experienced some injustice, and includes a chapter on the civil rights movement, all of which are a testament to the changes wrought by the movement. Despite that, whites are at the center of the story, and their perspective dominates. In fact, the author's white orientation leaps off the pages. For instance, she refers to African Americans as "Our Black people."[85]

Throughout *Cannonballs and Courage* virtually every discussion of blacks is framed in terms of whites, with an emphasis on interracial friendship and cooperation. In one case, after acknowledging that slavery was wrong, Ellis insists, however, "One must not forget that mixed with the basic evil of slavery were love, trust, and mutual protection between Black and White people." She also features a photograph of a woman identified only as "Mammy Mary," and in the accompanying caption claims that Mammy Mary "embodies the love that existed between many Black and White families," and she "stayed with the Shaifer family throughout the [Civil War] and afterwards, serving in place of a mother to the young Shaifer boys." Ellis justifies her use of the word "mammy," writing, "Now I know that today many of our Black citizens find the title 'Mammy' offensive, but please take a minute and listen. As it was originally used, 'Mammy' was a title of endearment. As has happened so often, someone later turned the title into a caricature—and that was wrong—but for Mammy Mary, the title was used with love."[86]

That this is a story told from whites' perspective is just as evident in Ellis's handling of the civil rights movement. Although she uses images from the "No Easy Journey" exhibit, her text does not reflect any engagement with the exhibit's historical content or interpretations. Ellis persistently portrays the boycott as one of the most dire problems the community has faced, opening her chapter on the movement by asserting, "We have survived fire, floods, yellow fever epidemics, wars, and boll weevils, but the civil rights boycott in the sixties almost killed us." In an emphasis and approach reminiscent of Beesley's, the author quickly asserts that "the purpose in remembering this chapter of our history is not to open old wounds." She also employs the recurring tactic of using an isolated black spokesperson to bolster white claims of good race relations and deflect any serious examination of persistent divisions. She never addresses how Claiborne County blacks experienced the race-based inequality that prompted the movement, but implies that during the movement, local whites and blacks were both victims of outsiders and contends there had to be a "better way to solve our problems" (without offering any sense of what that might have been). The book emphasizes that the boycott brought financial ruin to white merchants and the downtown, asserts that school integration caused "emotional distress" for black and white students, and features African Americans who did not support the boycott.[87]

Thus even those whites who proclaim their desire to work with blacks, who are interested in promoting the community's history, and who emphasize the need to move forward on racial reconciliation remain staunchly unwilling to acknowledge the movement's centrality and meaning for African Americans. They refuse to concede that it is a legitimate topic for commemorating or examine its implications for understanding race relations, past or current. I think that it is essential to look at the divergence between blacks' and whites' perspectives on race relations and the movement because coming to some shared understanding of the past is probably a key to developing a shared sense of the present and future.

At one level this story is particular to Port Gibson, Mississippi. But to some extent I believe it is all of our story. We all need to honestly confront our racial past *and* the ways that white supremacy still shapes our present. At a conference in Mississippi in the summer of 2004, a historian described how movement leader Fred Shuttlesworth responded to a discussion about the museum on the Underground Railroad and a desire by some to ensure that the message of the museum be "upbeat." Shuttlesworth said: "If you don't tell it like it was, it can never be as it ought to be."[88]

NOTES

1. The quote in the essay's title is adapted from comments by James Miller, "Time for a Change" forum, December 5, 1994, videotape, in author's possession and part of the collection of Mississippi Cultural Crossroads, Port Gibson, Mississippi. I would like to thank Kathleen Connelly, John Dittmer, Simona Hill, and Wesley Hogan for their helpful comments on this essay, and Ted Ownby for providing such a collegial and intellectually stimulating environment for considering Mississippi's civil rights movement history and its implications for our world today.

2. Jane Ellis interview, June 25, 1992. Unless otherwise noted, all interviews are by Emilye Crosby. Some interviews are in the author's possession. Some are also available at the University of Southern Mississippi, Hattiesburg, and at Mississippi Cultural Crossroads, Port Gibson.

3. Bill Lum interview, July 29, 1992.

4. Mary Lee Trimble, *i ain't lyin'* 2 (Winter 1982): 22; *Port Gibson Reveille*, August 27, 1998.

5. Elizabeth McLendon, *i ain't lyin'* 3 (Summer 1983): 11.

6. Ezekiel Rankin interview, May 14, 1992; Ezekiel Rankin interview, April 28, 1992.

7. Robert P. Moses and Charles E. Cobb Jr., *Radical Equations: Math Literacy and Civil Rights* (Boston: Beacon Press, 2001), 25.

8. Melvin McFatter interview, May 18, 1992.

9. Marjorie Brandon interview, May 4, 1992.

10. James Devoual interview, July 28, 1992.

11. Ruth Juanita Stewart interview, September 11, 1994.

12. Emilye Crosby, *A Little Taste of Freedom: The Black Freedom Struggle in Claiborne County, Mississippi* (Chapel Hill: University of North Carolina Press, 2005), 106–117, 148–168.

13. M. M. McFatter interview, June 15, 1992.

14. Anonymous #3 interview, April 29, 1992.

15. Nathaniel Jones interview, March 12, 1992; Nathaniel Jones interview, June 30, 1996.

16. Jimmy Allen interview, February 9, 1994.

17. Albert Butler interview, February 16, 1994.

18. Julius Warner interview, June 29, 1992.

19. Gloster Current to Roy Wilkins and John Morsell, April 20, 1966, "Time to Dig," August 8, 1966, NAACP Papers, Library of Congress; Thomas Watts file, in Clement E. Vose, ed., *Southern Civil Rights Litigation Records* (microfilm), reel 109 (New Haven, Conn.: Yale University Photographic Services, 1997).

20. Marjorie Brandon 1992 interview; Alex Warner, *Claiborne Hardware, et al. v. NAACP, et al.*, Mississippi Supreme Court storage, 881 (hereafter cited as CHT); Katie B. Wells, CHT, 362.

21. Lum interview; *Port Gibson Reveille*, April 7, 21, 28, May 19, 1966.

22. Dan McCay interview, May 19, 1992.

23. Devoual interview.

24. Mary Kathryn Davenport interview, April 11, 1992.

25. Charles Evers interview, August 5, 1992. See also James Beesley interview, February 15, 1992; and Frances Nelson interview, April 13, 1992.

26. *Shields v. Mississippi*, in Vose, *Southern Civil Rights Litigation Records*, reel 110.

27. John Thomas Clark testimony, *Shields v. Mississippi*, in Vose, *Southern Civil Rights Litigation Records*, reel 110 (emphasis added).

28. Murad Nasif, CHT, 1188; Rosalie Abraham interview, July 3, 1992; Lum interview. See also McCay interview; Charles Evers, CHT, 4680; Evers interview; Marjorie Brandon interview, July 23, 1996.

29. Albert Butler interview; Allen interview; Melvin McFatter FBI file, (HQ) 44-32887, in author's possession; see also Marjorie Brandon 1992 interview; Alberta Coleman, Jack Chatfield Notes, 34, in author's possession (hereafter cited as JCN).

30. James Dorsey interview, May 4–5, 1992; Marjorie Brandon 1992 interview. See also James Gray interview, July 1, 1992; Charles Evers, CHT, 403; Charles Evers, *Have No Fear: The Charles Ever Story* (New York: Wiley and Sons, 1997), 187; Laura Cullins, CHT, 1101–1014; Murriel Cullins, CHT, 1109; Willie Myles, CHT, 1078–1079; Jasper

Coleman, CHT, 1080; Leesco Guster interview, July 3, 1996; James Scott interview, June 22, 1992; George Walker, JCN, 13; Gladys Watson interview, February 4, 1994; James Bailey Jr., CHT, 328; Nathaniel Martin interview, June 23, 1992.

31. Guster interview.

32. Jimmy Ellis, CHT, 756; R. L. T. Smith, CHT, 1228; Albert Butler interview; J. L. Sayles interview, May 20, 1992; Annie Jones interview, March 19, 1992.

33. "Brief for Petitioners," *Claiborne Hardware et al. v. NAACP et al.*, 8, 28–29; Arthur Wyatt, CHT, 591–592. See also George Walker, JCN, 13; Dan McCay, CHT, 139; Jasper Coleman, CHT, 1081; Willie Myles, CHT, 1078–1079; Vera Smith, JCN, 32–33; Warner interview; Scott interview; FBI report, May 19, 1966, Racial Demonstration, Port Gibson, Miss., May 13, 1966, Racial Matters, in author's possession; James Dorsey, JCN, 57.

34. James Miller interview, February 2, 1994; Celia Anderson interview, April 14, 1992. As Anderson recounts her conversation with Ellis almost three decades after the events in question, the dialogue she uses reflects the race-based inequality in courtesy titles that was one of the issues driving the boycott.

35. Director to file, May 2, 1969, Sovereignty Commission Papers, McCain Archive, University of Southern Mississippi.

36. Guster interview; Marjorie Brandon 1992 interview. See also Charles Evers, CHT, 4685; Hystercine Rankin interview, May 13, 1992.

37. Allen interview; Waddy Abraham interview, July 12, 1992; James Hudson, CHT, 105; Quitman H. McDaniel Jr., CHT, 1163.

38. *Williams, Calvin, v. Port Gibson* file, in Vose, *Southern Civil Rights Litigation Records*, reel 109; James Dorsey interview, December 1994; Adam Fairclough, *Race & Democracy: The Civil Rights Struggle in Louisiana, 1915–1972* (Athens: University of Georgia Press, 1995), 326; Crosby, *Little Taste of Freedom*, 153–155.

39. Murad Nasif, CHT, 1188; Barbara B. Ellis, CHT, 144–145; Charles R. Dobbs, CHT, 1182; Shreve Guthrie Jr., CHT, 1199. See also William Hay, CHT, 1169.

40. Emilye Crosby, "Common Courtesy: The Civil Rights Movement in Claiborne County, Mississippi" (Ph.D. diss., Indiana University, 1995), 255–310, esp. 262–263.

41. Anonymous interview #1.

42. Mott Headley interview, July 28, 1992.

43. Ruth Willis interview, August 7, 1992.

44. Mary Ann Norton interview, May 21, 1992.

45. Nathan Jones, *i ain't lyin'* 3 (Summer 1983): 49.

46. Sayles interview.

47. Crosby, "Common Courtesy," 270–273.

48. Miller interview.

49. John Dittmer, *Local People: The Struggle for Civil Rights in Mississippi* (Urbana:

University of Illinois Press, 1994), 390; *Port Gibson Reveille*, November 11, 1965; Carl Brandon interview, April 30, 1992; James Dorsey interview, February 10, 1994; Calvin Williams Jr. interview, February 2, 1994; *Port Gibson Reveille*, September 1, 1966, puts the number at 30 in grades 1–6 and 16 in 7–12. I have used the slightly higher number, 49, pictured in the Port Gibson High Yearbook for 1966–1967. Oral histories consistently provide similar numbers.

50. Williams interview; Port Gibson High yearbook, 1967; Ernest Kennedy (Ken) Brandon interview, September 11, 1994; Marjorie Brandon 1992 interview.

51. Anonymous interview #2.

52. *Port Gibson Reveille*, August 18, 1966.

53. Carl Brandon interview; Ken Brandon interview; Anonymous interview #1; M. M. McFatter interview; Marjorie Brandon 1992 interview; Williams interview; Coach Hines testimony, Raymond Hynum School Board Hearing, October 15, 1966, Claiborne County Board of Education Minutes, Microfilm, Mississippi Department of Archives and History, Jackson.

54. Ken Brandon interview.

55. Carl Brandon interview; Port Gibson High yearbooks, 1967–1968, 1968–1969.

56. Port Gibson High yearbook, 1969–1970.

57. *Port Gibson Reveille*, May 7, 14, 1970.

58. *Port Gibson Reveille*, September 3, 10, 1970.

59. Willis interview.

60. Carolyn Dobbs, interview by Aron Irby, June 29, 1992.

61. *Port Gibson Reveille*, July 16, 30, August 13, 27, September 3, 10, 1970.

62. Dorsey 1992 interview; Nancy Larraine Hoffman interview, October 22, 1992.

63. For an example of these attitudes, see "Time for a Change" forum, December 5, 1994 (videotape).

64. Dobbs interview.

65. Norton interview.

66. Port Gibson High yearbooks, 1966–1967, 1967–1968, 1968–1969, 1969–1970.

67. Williams interview.

68. Unita Blackwell interview, July 17, 1996.

69. Nathaniel Jones 1996 interview.

70. Jimmy Ellis interview, August 6, 1996.

71. Davenport interview.

72. Quote by James Dorsey, Dorsey December 1994 interview. See also McCay interview; Robert Butler Jr. interview, February 10, 1994; Charles Evers, CHT, 401, 4725; Gray interview; August 27, 1966, Racial Matters/Claiborne County, MS, 157-JN-6101; M. M. McFatter interview; Erle Johnston to file, December 8, 1966, Paul B. Johnson

Papers, McCain Archive, University of Southern Mississippi; *Port Gibson Reveille*, April 11, 1968.

73. At the time, Jack Chatfield wrote, "The boycott has gone beyond being simply an instrument in the social struggle." Instead, he argued, "The boycott itself—not its strategic aim—is the symbol of the new departure." Jack Chatfield, "Port Gibson, Mississippi: A Profile of the Future?" *New South* 24 (Summer 1969): 55.

74. Quitman H. McDaniel Jr. interview, June 27, 1992; Dorsey 1992 interview.

75. Wesley Hogan, *Many Minds, One Heart: SNCC's Dream for a New America* (Chapel Hill: University of North Carolina Press, 2007), 58–59.

76. I was an adviser to the exhibition and witnessed this exchange during one of the planning meetings.

77. "Time for a Change" forum, December 5, 1994 (videotape); "No Easy Journey" brochure; Ken Brandon interview; M. M. McFatter interview.

78. Crosby, *Little Taste of Freedom*, 37–38, 229, 234–235.

79. "Time for a Change" forum, December 5, 1994 (videotape).

80. Ibid.

81. Ibid.

82. Ibid.

83. SNCC organizer Hollis Watkins asked the question. Ibid.

84. Chris Allen Baker, "Memorial Held for Slain Trio," *Neshoba Democrat*, June 25, 2003; "Time for a Change" forum.

85. Mary H. Ellis, *Cannonballs and Courage: The Story of Port Gibson* (Virginia Beach, Va.: Donning, 2003), 7, 9, 154–155.

86. Ibid., 62, 65, 67.

87. Ibid., 128, 131, 136, 140, 145, 163.

88. David Blight, "Unsettling Memories: Culture and Trauma in the Deep South" conference, June 15–21, 2004, Jackson State University; Blight's account of Shuttlesworth's comments can also be found online. David W. Blight, "If You Don't Tell It Like It Was, It Can Never Be As It Ought to Be," Keynote Talk at Yale University, New Haven, Conn., and American Slavery, 2002, http://www.yale.edu/glc/events/memory.htm.

Contributors

Chris Myers Asch teaches history at the University of the District of Columbia. He is the author of *The Senator and the Sharecropper: The Freedom Struggles of James O. Eastland and Fannie Lou Hamer.*

Emilye Crosby is professor of history and coordinator of black studies at SUNY Geneseo. She is author of *A Little Taste of Freedom: The Black Freedom Struggle in Claiborne County, Mississippi* and editor of *Civil Rights History from the Ground Up: Local Struggles, a National Movement.*

David Cunningham teaches sociology at Brandeis University. He is the author of *Klansville, U.S.A.: The Rise and Fall of the Civil Rights-Era Ku Klux Klan.*

Jelani Favors is assistant professor of history at Morgan State University. He is completing a manuscript entitled "Shelter in a Time of Storm: Black Colleges and the Long History of the Student Movement."

Françoise N. Hamlin is the Hans Rothfels Assistant Professor of History and Africana Studies at Brown University. She is the author of *Crossroads at Clarksdale: The Black Freedom Struggle in the Mississippi Delta after World War II.*

Wesley Hogan is professor of history at Virginia State University and author of *Many Minds, One Heart: SNCC's Dream for a New America.*

Robert Luckett is assistant professor of history and director of the Margaret Walker Center for the Study of the African-American Experience at Jackson State University. He is working on a book manuscript entitled "Yapping Dogs: The Dynamics of Massive Resistance."

Carter Dalton Lyon teaches and chairs the Department of History at St. Mary's Episcopal School in Memphis. His scholarship analyzes the church visits campaign in Jackson, Mississippi.

Byron D'Andra Orey is professor and chair in the Department of Political Science at Jackson State University. His scholarship analyzes race and politics in the recent South.

Ted Ownby is professor of history and southern studies and director of the Center for the Study of Southern Culture at the University of Mississippi.

Joseph T. Reiff is professor of religion and chair of the Religion Department at Emory and Henry College. He is author of a forthcoming work on the Born of Conviction statement.

Akinyele Umoja is associate professor and chair of the Department of African-American Studies at Georgia State University, where he teaches courses on the history of the civil rights and Black Power movements. He is the author of *We Will Shoot Back: Armed Resistance in the Mississippi Freedom Movement.*

Michael Vinson Williams is assistant professor of history and African American studies at Mississippi State University. He is the author of *Medgar Evers: Mississippi Martyr.*

Index

Aberdeen, Miss., 223

Abernethy, H. B., 125

Abraham, Waddy, 274

Adams, Emmie Schrader, 18

Adams, Victoria Gray, 12, 17, 19, 24–25, 26, 169

Adams County, Miss., 184, 190, 199, 215–16, 218

Addison Junior and Senior High School for African Americans (Port Gibson), 276, 278, 280

Agriculture, 11, 20, 22, 64, 70–71, 112, 277

Alabama State University, 97

Albright, Joseph, 79

Alcorn A&M College. *See* Alcorn State University

Alcorn State University, 63, 74, 97

Alexander, Firnist, 100

Alexander, Margaret Walker, 94, 100–103, 111, 116

Algebra Project. *See* Moses, Robert

Allen, Jimmy, 270–71, 274

Allen, Louis, 33

American Association of University Professors (AAUP), 132

American Baptist Home Mission Society (ABHMS), 120

American Civil Liberties Union (ACLU), 129

American Federation of Labor and Congress of Industrial Organizations (AFL-CIO), 130

American Legion, 72

American Revolution, 59, 252

Americans for the Preservation of the White Race (APWR), 184, 195–96

AmSouth Foundation, 255

Anders, Odell, 190, 196

Anderson, Celia, 273, 297

Anderson, Doug, 237–38

Anderson, Lisa Todd, 31

Anderson, Reuben, 241, 243

Armstrong, Thomas, 143

Asheville, N.C., 123

Ashford, H. T., 73

Ashmore, Sam, 159, 165, 169–71

Atlanta, Ga., 95, 127, 258, 264–65

Atlanta Journal, 127

Atlantic City, N.J., 31, 49, 51, 133

Austin, Henry, 208, 210

Ayers, William, 263

Bailey, Willie, 246

Baker, Elaine Delott, 22

Baker, Ella, 16, 26, 41, 42

Baker-Motley, Constance, 128

Bamsey, Al, 146

Banks, E. W., 79

Banks, Fred, 237–38, 243

CPSIA information can be obtained
at www.ICGtesting.com
Printed in the USA
FSHW011340160121
77664FS